D0849996

Across All Borders

International Information Flows and Applications

Collected Papers

Marta Dosa

The Scarecrow Press, Inc.
Lanham, Md., & London
1997

SCARECROW PRESS, INC.

Published in the United States of America
by Scarecrow Press, Inc.
4720 Boston Way
Lanham, Maryland 20706

4 Pleydell Gardens, Folkestone
Kent CT20 2DN, England

British Cataloguing-in-Publication Information Available

Library of Congress Cataloging-in-Publication Data

Dosa, Marta L.
    Across all borders : international information flows and
applications : collected papers / Marta Dosa.
        p.   cm.
    Includes bibliographical references and index.
    ISBN 0–8108–3198–8 (alk. paper)
    1. Information services—International Cooperation.
    2. International agencies—Information services. 3. Information
services—Developing countries.   I. Title.
Z674.4.D68 1997
025.5'23—dc20   96–21269
                                                            CIP

♾ ™The paper used in this publication meets the minimum requirements of American National Standard for Information Sciences—Per-
manence of Paper for Printed Library Materials, ANSI Z39.48–1984.
Manufactured in the United States of America.

Contents

Figures

Foreword

The value of the present book goes beyond encapsulating the written testimony of Marta Dosa's contribution to international information activities and research, making easily accessible papers published in a variety of sources over a twenty-year period. The main significance of this volume is that it builds a bridge between the literatures of developing countries (the South) and those of industrialized countries (the North), as they struggle to explicate and understand the relationship between economic, social, and cultural development and the applications of information in its infinite forms and variations.

The judicious arrangement of these papers offers a perspective on a lifelong experience of rare diversity. Thus, this collection is important also because it allows those who did not have the chance to work or study with Marta Dosa to get acquainted with a most prominent figure in the international information scene. It is certainly significant for what it contains, but perhaps even more so for what it reveals to those readers who can see beyond appearances.

International information activities are fraught with many contradictions, vicious constraints, and uncertain outcomes. In this area and in many areas of the broad information field, success has been scarce because people have been considered as only the elements of background conditions rather than the main generators, movers, and appliers of information.

People in information and communication flows, and in all levels of information infrastructures, are the indispensable pillars of the subtle construction that turns data into a house of knowledge. Marta Dosa's work is a splendid illustration of the centrality of people in information use.

Marta Dosa is among the few information scientists who consistently search for and follow a humanistic vision. She also offers an outstanding example that vision, talent and knowledge are not the only principal ingredients in a proactive and successful involvement in international information affairs. Another ingredient is essential. Latin Americans call it "corazón." And Marta Dosa's heart knows no limits.

Michel J. Menou
International Consultant in
Information Management and
Maitre de Conférences
Department of Information and
Communication
Université Michel de Montaigne
Bordeaux, France

Acknowledgments

I am indebted to my coauthors Ann P. Bishop, Jeffrey Katzer, and Anis Y. Yusoff for their creative collaboration, the strength of their perception and thought, and their generosity in agreeing to the use of our joint papers in this collection.

This volume came into existence through the support and encouragement of many people. I thank Michel J. Menou for writing the foreword when he was between continents. Clifford M. Bishop's editorial efforts to improve this work and his willingness to contribute the introduction earned my deepest gratitude.

Research assistance by Hamidah Kassim and Faizah Mohd. Zain has been greatly appreciated. Special thanks go to Hannah King for providing the essential key to the volume by her expert indexing. Without the genuine caring and competence that Joan M. Watkins brought to the production of this book, this process would have been impossible.

The papers in this volume originally appeared as follows:

"Information Transfer as Technical Assistance for Development," originally published in *Journal of the American Society for Information Science.* 36 (3) 1985, pp. 146–152.

"Data Collection by Development Projects as a National Information Resource," originally published in *Transfer of Scholarly Scientific and Technical Information between North and South America.* Ed. by V. Rosenberg and G. Whitney. Metuchen, NJ: Scarecrow Press, Inc., 1986, pp. 199–228.

"Information Transfer as Development Support," originally published at Syracuse University, Maxwell School of Citizenship and Public Affairs, Center for the Study of Citizenship. "Information Transfer as Development Assistance." Syracuse, NY: Syracuse University, 1988. (Occasional Paper Series).

"Information and Indigenous Technological Capacity in Developing Countries," with Anis Y. Yusoff, originally presented at the 47th International Federation for Information and Documentation Conference and Congress, Omiya, Saitama, Japan, October 2–9, 1994.

"Community Networking in Gerontology and Health: A Centralized and a Decentralized Model," substantially revised version of paper originally published in *Special Collections.* New York, NY: The Haworth Press, Inc., 1982, pp. 53–72.

"Human Resource Networks for Rural Development," originally published in *Proceedings of the International Conference on Education and*

Training for Agricultural Library and Information Work, Nairobi, Kenya, March 7–12, 1983. Nairobi, Kenya: National Academy for the Advancement of Arts and Sciences, 1984, pp. 173–189.

"Electronic Networking in Support of South-to-South Cooperation," with Jeffrey Katzer, originally published in *Journal of Education for Library and Information Science,* 32(1/2) 1991, pp. 84–96.

"Environmental Information Transfer," substantially revised version of paper originally published as "Environmental Information Systems" authored by the Advisory Group for Aerospace Research and Development in *How to Obtain Information in Different Fields of Science and Technology: A User's Guide.* Paris, France: North Atlantic Treaty Organization, 1974, pp. 85–103.

"The Consultant as Information Intermediary," originally published in *Proceedings of the 41st International Federation for Information and Documentation Conference and Congress, Hong Kong, 1982.* Amsterdam, Netherlands: North Holland, 1983, pp. 181–196. Reprinted with permission in *Information Services and Use.* 3(6), 1983, pp. 301–318. Republished with permission and with revisions in Parker, J.S. ed. *Information Consultants in Action.* London, UK: Mansell Publishing Ltd. 1986, pp. 197–219. Reprinted with permission in *Journal of Library and Information Science,* 11(1), 1986, pp. 15–36.

"Transfer and Adaptation of a Group Problem-Solving Model for Community Organizations," with Ann P. Bishop (first author), originally published in *Proceedings of the 52nd Annual Meeting of the American Society for Information Science,* Washington, DC, 1989. Medford, NJ: Learned Information, 1989, pp. 183–187.

"From Informal Gatekeeper to Information Counselor: Emergence of a New Professional Role," substantially revised version of a paper written with Mona Farid and Paul Vasarhelyi and published as "From Informal Gatekeeper to Information Counselor: Emergence of a New Professional Role," The Hague, Netherlands: International Federation for Information and Documentation, 1989.

"Thoughts on the Social Implications of Information Theory," originally presented at the 47th International Federation for Information and Documentation Conference and Congress, Omiya, Saitama, Japan, October 2–9, 1994.

"A Future Perspective on Information Policy Research Needs," originally presented at the Seminar of the Education and Training Committee, International Federation for Information and Documentation, Havana, Cuba, September 17–18, 1990.

"The Regional Professional Association: A Key to Global Cooperation," originally published in *Bulletin of the American Society for Information Science,* 16:4, 1990, pp. 24–25.

"New Challenges to the Information Professional," originally published in *FID Bulletin* (International Federation for Information and Documentation) 42(3), March 1992, pp. 51–56.

"Conceptual Issues in Environmental Information Education and Training," substantially revised version of paper originally published in *Pro-*

ceedings of the Seminar of the Education and Training Committee, International Federation for Information and Documentation. The Hague, Netherlands: FID, 1981, pp. 110–118.

"Informatics, Technology and Education," substantially revised version of paper originally published in *Proceedings of Conference on Informatics and Development.* Harare, Zimbabwe: Ministry of Finance, Economic Planning, and Development, 1986, pp. 128–142.

"The Management of Innovation as an Integrating Theme in the Curriculum for Industrial Information Officers," originally published in *Information Management Review* 2(4), 1987, pp. 60–70.

"Recruitment of International Students: Suggestions from Syracuse," originally published in *Journal of Education for Library and Information Science,* 34(2), 1993, pp. 99–112.

"Training the Trainers in Information Management: Overview and Recommendations," originally presented at the Seminar of the Education and Training Committee, International Federation for Information and Documentation, Madrid, Spain, October 21–24, 1992.

"The American Transnational Corporation in Developing Countries," excerpt from the report, "The American Transnational Corporation in Developing Countries," produced with support of a Visiting Scholarship at AT&T Bell Laboratories, March 1992–March 1993.

Introduction

Most of the papers selected for this volume originated in Marta Dosa's work with international development projects and in consultancies and conferences over the past twenty years, and first saw print in international sources not easily accessed or widely known in the United States. The earliest paper was published in 1974, the latest in 1994. Except where indicated, all appear here only slightly revised: a few new facts and background sources incorporated, the style adjusted, or a paragraph streamlined. For the most part the author chose to preserve intact the record of her original work. Key ideas thus may be profitably revisited as they first appeared in print. Examples include Dosa's conception of the problem-context of information seeking, as presented in "Environmental Information Transfer" (1974); her formulation of the meaning of "information need" as distinguished from "information requirement," to be found in "Information Transfer as Development Support" (1988); and the concept of Distance Technical Assistance set forth in "Electronic Networking in Support of South-to-South Cooperation" (1991). But these are examples merely, and might be readily multiplied. Dosa addresses a striking variety of topics in this volume, and enhances all with novel perspectives made possible only by the multidisciplinary cast of her thought.

Publication skirts monologue, and monologue, for Marta Dosa, exerts little appeal. Dialogue is at the heart of her ethics. It is no coincidence that the interpersonal and the informal are, together, the chosen locus of her influence within the information professions. Most of these papers mark occasions whose primary aim was discussion, the attempt at true interchange, the complex and always open-ended tussle with Otherness whose fairest issue is not merely to confirm, but to extend, community. It is not without significance that some of these papers are the products of collaboration. Her inclusion of them amply demonstrates the values they espouse.

Five of the six parts that organize the volume reflect areas in which Marta Dosa's teaching and research have been concentrated: the role of information in economically developing societies; information sharing through human resource networks; the application of information counseling to problem solving; information policies; and information education and training. Her understanding of, and experience in, developing countries led her to the work presented in the final part of the volume, concerning information flows between the American transnational corporation and its contacts in Africa, Asia, and Latin America.

Mixing disciplines, crossing borders, exemplifying tolerance and the

1

cooperative spirit—these urges and strategies have molded her work from the start. She has concerned herself for the length of her career with problems which are not apt to be solved without recourse to the combined insights of diverse disciplines or the blended sensitivities and expertise of diverse cultures. She has actively sought out those topics—environmental science, health care, gerontology—where disciplines intersect, and those issues—information policy, technology transfer, cooperation among professionals, aid to developing countries—where cultures potentially clash. The reader will be surprised, perhaps, by the predominance of international concerns even in part V of this volume on Education, Training and Professional Development, where discussion of more parochial or practical topics might well have been expected, were the author other than Dosa. Always, her thrust is toward a global orientation of information activities.

Her elected geography evinces both intellectual and physical reach. Interdisciplinarity has characterized her research. Aside from her position as professor emerita at the School of Information Studies, Syracuse University, Marta Dosa is an adjunct professor in the College of Environmental Science and Forestry of the State University of New York and a frequent consultant to international organizations. In scope her work reaches from local communities in central New York to rural development in India and Nigeria. Her international work on information science education and policies was carried out in Australia, Brazil, China, Ghana, India, Japan, Kenya, Malaysia, Mexico, Nigeria, and the countries of the former Yugoslavia, where she has served as consultant to governments and universities.

As is the case with many writers, the apparent multiplicity of the publications which emerged from the breadth of research, teaching, and consultancy in Dosa's career is in fact reducible to a set of steadfast ideas and values. Part I of this book, Information and National Development, represents at its most comprehensive the circle of concerns addressed throughout the volume. The technical and intercultural complexities of information transfer, of innovation diffusion, of translating the actions of the North (i.e. industrialized countries) into genuine and lasting benefits for the South (developing countries), are a few of the key issues. Dosa's observations on these matters track, over the years, the transformation of development thinking from its early overemphasis on large-scale industrialization to its later efforts to incorporate indigenous thought and intercultural partnerships in smaller projects of a more sustainable nature. Her own voice from the first has insisted upon cultural sensitivity and on the need to ensure that it is not only the Westernized elites and established powers of target countries who benefit from development aid. In those same years, the role of information in the development process underwent a gradual reconceptualization. Information transfer came to be recognized as itself an important form of development aid and not as a mere adjunct to monetary grants or equipment transfer and other initially more obvious forms of assistance.

Together the papers in part I lay out important details regarding the information environments of developing countries, and all proceed from a central conviction as to the importance to the international information community of the lessons to be learned from cooperative efforts undertaken in these countries. The principal themes are clear. Development efforts by the North must respect the cultural differences ineluctably encountered in the South. Indigenous participation and genuine partnership in development projects represent one way to improve the probability that results will be appropriate to the target culture and therefore more likely to endure. Efforts at development aid are best conducted in a spirit of mutual interchange, for mutual benefit; the arrogance of deaf largesse too often typical of past efforts is to be assiduously avoided. Information inevitably plays multiple roles and has multiple purposes in any development project. Marta Dosa is among the strongest advocates of the need to discover and make appropriate use of the wealth of indigenous information to be found in oral histories, local archives, surveys, demographic data, marketing studies, or reports produced by previous projects. Such use of existing material serves two purposes: it saves money, in obviating the need to duplicate information already available; and— in being in a sense discovered, rather than imposed, data—it helps to ensure that development efforts suit the needs and values of the culture. It is, Dosa insists, one task of the information professional to uncover such buried or obscure sources and to make them available to project participants in a timely fashion and a usable form. No less necessary is a familiarity with information policies and practices at the national and international levels.

Dosa assembles, in these essays, a welter of scholarship from other disciplines in the process of reconstructing our image of the information profession and the role it must play. Her sense of what the information professional should be is not apt to reinforce whatever complacency now exists in the field. Cooperation is perhaps the surest path we have in attempting to approximate the ideal she envisions.

Right now, as technophoria more and more firmly grips the planet, Marta Dosa's emphasis on human resource networking in part II may be of special interest. New creative possibilities for information exchange are certainly at hand, and Dosa shares the excitement. It is not in the least from a Luddite perspective that she would remind us that computer-assisted communication is recent, whereas human resource networking itself—the sharing of experience and knowledge for mutual support—is ancient. Particularly, then, in terms of the essential understanding of institutional and personal relationships that underlie all information flows, the papers in this section invite study for their relevance to the further development and use of electronic networks.

Part III, on Problem Solving and Information Counseling, collects a variety of papers whose common thread is the evolving nature of the information profession and the ongoing need for transformation. It is here that Marta Dosa most forcibly and fully proposes specific changes. To a much larger extent than is currently typical, the new information professional will need to function well in several disciplines in order to filter and interpret information for its intended beneficiaries; will need to advise on information policy constraints and opportunities as they arise in various national contexts; and will need to be knowledgeable about any number of complex global issues—transborder data flow, intellectual property law, the role of standards in technology transfer—and about how local cultural conditions are apt to bear on the success of particular projects.

The fullest treatment of the topic, in the paper entitled "From Informal Gatekeeper to Information Counselor: Emergence of a New Professional Role," draws on international literature from several disciplines. Dosa's discussion is richly suggestive, and her call for more extensive study cannot be reasonably ignored. There can be no doubt about the value to be derived from such study, with the explicit determination to extract a set of attitudes and practices for adoption by information professionals. The value of informal communication, of personal networking, of resource sharing among partners across disciplines and cultures, is among the stressed themes of the volume. The information counselor can at the very least be profitably sensitized to the existence of those often hidden informal pathways in any organization or community where information naturally flows.

The parts on Information Policies (IV) and on Education, Training, and Professional Development (V), carry into new territory the allied themes established in the previous sections. The final paper, "The American Transnational Corporation in Developing Countries," in a section of its own (VI), collects and intertwines in one major statement the chief thematic strands of all the foregoing. Some may be surprised by the encouragement given in several of these papers to self-interest—the self-interest of nations, corporations, and professions alike—in the context of international relations. But such surprises are merely proof that Marta Dosa's idealism is sufficiently earthbound, capacious and elastic to accommodate reality at its drabbest. Mutuality—mutual benefit, an acceptable apportioning—remains the standard by which the play of self-interest is to be judged. Clear-sighted as Dosa may be with regard to human motivations, the tether of all her thought is always ethical, her work constant in its insistence on the primacy of the ethical. Competition and self-interest are givens. Yet Dosa would have us recognize the possibilities available still, and in fact would have us celebrate our interdependence and with it the implied necessity of cooperation.

The scope of her thought has always been international and her impulse, always, to shrink the globe. Her refusal to deny community to any who may seek it arises naturally from her own experience, a personal history of displacement and relocation that, like so many others of the time, reads like a catalogue of loss. Dosa was yet among the lucky, to the extent that her own struggle won her renewal and the capacity for new discovery. She was born in Hungary, that most singular of contested countries, where even the language—a cousin only to Finnish and a precious few others in the Finno-Ugric subfamily of Uralic—stands opaquely aloof from the languages of its neighbors. Her early years coincided with the direct clash, in that small country, of two of the dominant political ideologies of the century, National Socialism and Communism, with their divergent, if similarly effective, approaches to the delivery of disaster. It was, for the better part of Dosa's formative years, a context well suited to the inculcation of mistrust of the ideological. Where communication is severely restricted, and where the control of information is in the hands of powers characterized by a paranoid brutality, the necessity of personal trust becomes paramount. One's community is defined by the set of those with whom communication is safe. For Dosa the lesson was indelible. Yet with her it led to an adamant openness, a need to extend trust and to earn its return from others. Establishing contexts where such trust may flourish, whether between academic disciplines or across political borders, has been the object common to all her efforts. Readers of these pages will be struck by the depth and spontaneity of her faith in the powers of mutual respect, tolerance, and talk, even as she concedes their complexity, their harrowing vulnerability to catastrophe. Openness to the Other may be a minimal and, historically speaking, rather luckless savior; but its pedigree is sound, and its proffered hopefulness persists even as, perhaps, hope itself diminishes. To read Dosa without attending to this ethical subtext is to miss her entirely.

While the papers in this volume convey an invincible belief in the global community wrought by professional communication and cooperation, Marta Dosa recognizes, as well as any of us, that the possible steps toward impossible fulfilment are matters of infinitesimal increments. She is nothing if not a realist, and knows well the human birthright of discouragement. Her book, *Libraries in the Political Scene* (Greenwood Press, 1970), studied the role of scholar librarians in Germany under National Socialism. Her years of refugee life in West Germany after the war introduced her to material privation and to the symbolic poverty of statelessness. Only, she insists, with her immigration to the United States did she encounter once again the possibility of discourse.

That experience of loss and liberation was to be a decisive motivation in her later conceptual shaping of the issues faced by international development efforts and in the conduct of information transfer. The diversity of her topics is thus something of an illusion. Seen right, these apparent fragments coalesce to form a clear enough map of her thought. Bringing together people from different disciplines and different cultures to work toward the solution of problems of mutual concern has always been uppermost among her professional aims, through the whole of a career in which the professional and the personal have exhibited an exemplary integrity.

Clifford M. Bishop
Visiting Scholar
University of Illinois
Graduate School of Library
and Information Science
at Urbana-Champaign
Urbana, Illinois
United States

Part I

Information and National Development

1

Information Transfer as Technical Assistance for Development

Introduction

Technical assistance is governed by political, economic, and social forces. It blends governmental, commercial, and voluntary action. Consultants, researchers, managers, professional practitioners, and advocates of the poor work side by side and often at cross purposes. Critics of the process are more vocal than its champions. Failures abound, yet technical assistance creates more opportunities for person-to-person professional collaboration than any other process. Informal communications are often more important than formal information systems. The main determinant of the effectiveness of information transfer to a developing country* is the ability of the intermediary—individual or organization—to blend the information process with the culture of the particular society or group.

Development and Information

These are elusive concepts that have been defined differently in different contexts. Formal organizations supporting technical and social improvement efforts in developing countries tend to identify development information with scientific and technical knowledge, socioeconomic data, or a management information system. The term development, however, implies not only a technological or societal process, but also an intensely personal involvement. As Ong (1980, p. 201) observes, in those parts of the developing world where an oral culture exists, "education consists in identification, participation, getting into the act, feeling affinity with a culture's heroes, 'getting with it'—not in analysis at all." In this milieu, the structured and standardized procedures of a project are hardly relevant to local participants.

Neelameghan (1980) suggests that progress is characterized by both

---

*The term "developing country" will be used with the understanding that a wide range of economic, social, and cultural differences exist among nations as well as among population groups within each country.

qualitative and quantitative improvements in individual and social life. Development results from the efforts of people to continuously improve their condition and living environment. Information systems, then, would have to include empirical and subjective approaches to the quality and values of life (King-Farlow and Shea 1976). Indeed, in developing countries urban and regional planning goals have often been described as goals of environmental management. Knowledge in this context means a fundamental understanding of the need to treat human problems in view of their relationships to nature, society, and technology. A narrow vision of a public policy issue (energy, health, housing) can lead to inadequate coordination of planning in different sectors. Conversely, planning for development goals on the basis of information that takes into account both the nurturing and threatening aspects of the environment may result in economic and technological choices that are relevant to the needs of people (Schaefer 1981).

A review of the interpretations of "information" in the literature of development science encounters several problems. Two attitudes dominate. Authors either overestimate the role of information technology and present it as a panacea to all project-related problems, or consider information too fuzzy to be taken seriously and thus underestimate its potential. No overall conceptual framework related to development could be identified that would accommodate the meanings of data, information, and knowledge and their relationship. Observations are pigeonholed into a great number of works and separated by the methodological preferences and the jargon of the authors' disciplines.

In this article, "technology transfer" is used as the synthesizing concept. Stewart (1979, p. v.) identifies three stages in a country's ability to use technology for development: ". . . the ability to make independent technological choices . . . minor innovations . . . and . . . the capacity to create new technology . . . " The transfer and, eventually, the domestic production of technology are essentially part of a learning process. Within the technical assistance activity, one might subdivide technology transfer into three interrelated processes that correspond to Stewart's three stages of national learning:

- hardware transfer (broadly interpreted as devices, equipment, parts, materials, entire information systems, things)
- information transfer (data, documentation, software, standards, specifications, licenses, service contracts, manuals, maintenance handbooks, guidelines of use)
- knowledge transfer (an understanding of the origins and potential impact of the technology or process; the competence to plan, manage and evaluate applications; skills and know-how; relevant policy issues; the ability to adapt and diffuse innovation).

This is the functional interpretation of information transfer as technical assistance.

Another meaning of technology transfer is information dissemination. A critical element in technical assistance, dissemination may be an effort to alert local people to the objectives of a project, new practices and their potential benefits, changes that might affect them, and ways they can get involved in the activity. Information dissemination may also be unrelated to specific projects, as in the case of extension services for farmers or small enterprises. A critical question is not how information is given but by whom. Success usually hinges on trust and two-way communication, whether an extension agent is visiting a farm in order to demonstrate energy saving techniques or to gather feedback for program evaluation. Maruyama (1974, p. 319) describes the concept of "criticality resonance" in crosscultural research as "the understanding of the danger of information giving in the cultural context." Without trust, local people in a technical aid project's target area might perceive a data collector or an extension agent as an intruder. This is the cultural interpretation of information transfer as technical assistance.

The Impact of Development Policies

Waves of political directions and scientific development theories shape the goals and strategies of the donor/recipient relationship in development programs. The ultimate aim is always twofold: to solve the problems of mass poverty in low income countries and to serve the foreign policy interests of a donor government or of the member states of an international organization. Thus technical assistance, with some remarkable exceptions, is both an idealistic undertaking of global dimensions and a volatile political tool. The balance between these forces is often precarious. Professional and personal values of development strategists and practitioners inevitably enter the process, and perhaps often save it from dangerous excesses or bureaucratic rigidity. This is an area where private entrepreneurial investment, governmental directives, international relations, and voluntary action combine into an ever fluctuating scene.

Information, in its multitude of forms, weaves its way through the maze of relationships. At times, in the form of a dominant economic theory, information guides decisions and policy directions, but most often information functions themselves are guided by forceful political trends. At the microlevel, the aims and modes of information transfer change according to the style of technical assistance management. Changes have been evident in the approach to social data collection for project reconnaissance and surveys, in attitudes toward indigenous knowledge, in the various uses of management information systems, and in extension services to local populations. In the final account, it is individual commitment and value orientation that make the difference.

Emphasis on Modernization

The use of information in the development process has been determined by several factors, primary among them being trends in development assistance policies. Changes in the direction of emphasis (from industrialization through democratization to indigenous technological production) always brought about shifts in the goals and methods of information dissemination.

Official foreign transfers began to supplement external private investment in poor countries after World War II. The United Nations system of specialized agencies and other international organizations provided forums for debate and declarations, consultation, policy advice, specialized research, and training programs. Economics and rural sociology supplied the dominant paradigms. Throughout the 1950s and 1960s, international assistance to low-income countries aimed at maximizing the economic growth rate in the hope that benefits would trickle down to the poor. The strategy, guided by the modernization theory in development economics, was expected to lead to improved social conditions and fair income distribution within each country (Morqwetz 1977). Large-scale projects were directed mainly at the building of physical infrastructures. Much information was embedded in and accompanied technology transfer in agriculture, engineering, health, and transportation (Spencer & Woroniak 1967). Technical information emerged as a prime requirement for strengthening a developing country's economic and industrial base. Scientific and technical documentation centers began to spread under international sponsorship.

New Directions

By the end of the 1960s, the modernization concept lost its wide appeal. Economic growth did not prove to be equivalent with social development. It failed to diminish the gap between the poor and economically advanced nations, as well as between the poor populations and the modern sector within the same country. Moreover, in many cases innovations aimed at rural development were not sustained by local populations beyond the life of technical assistance projects. Causes of failures were identified as insufficient benefits for the rural poor, unintended consequences, and inequitable distribution of economic gains by governments (Lele 1975, The World Bank 1981). With rapidly growing populations, the employment opportunities created by modernization were grossly inadequate. Leading economists in developing countries began documentation of the impact of transnational corporations on their regions. They spoke of the export of raw materials, and the return of manufactured goods, a pattern that left low-income nations without viable capability to build their own industrial infrastructure (Aboyade 1976). In the early 1970s, many complex factors led to three robust movements in development politics: the basic needs approach, the North-South dialogue, and proposals for a new International Economic Order and a new International Information Order.

Adopted, to varying degrees, by most donor agencies, the new thinking emphasized technical assistance to the rural poor, smaller projects, flexible planning, and the involvement of local participants in planning. New ways were sought to mobilize human resources and institutions at the village level (Streeten et al. 1981). The World Employment Conference, held under the auspices of the International Labor Organization in 1976, identified basic human needs as adequate food, shelter, and clothing; essential services such as safe drinking water, sanitation, public transport; health, education, and cultural facilities; and freely chosen employment (International Labor . . . 1976).

By amending the Foreign Assistance Act in 1973, the United States Congress mandated the reorientation of bilateral development assistance. The "New Directions" policy required that the Agency for International Development (AID) concentrate on the poorest populations and involve them in rural development efforts. The change resulted in smaller and more interdisciplinary projects with focus on the equitable distribution of benefits. The reorganization did not take place without ideological conflicts within the agency. Supporters of a sectoral policy (economics oriented, concentrating on the development of food supplies and productivity in aid-recipient countries) found it difficult to adopt the participatory strategy (multidisciplinary, bringing together economics, politics, and social sciences). The legislative guidance was broad and the years of policy clarification that ensued created widespread information gaps in spite of a flow of reports, documents, and special studies (United States 1981). By 1977, the agency adopted a policy that included both the sectoral and participatory approaches within the basic human needs philosophy. However, this direction, too, was to be overshadowed in the 1980s by the agency's renewed emphasis on the role of the private sector in fostering overall economic growth in developing countries.

Early in the basic needs era, researchers and practitioners in the field discovered that very little was known about the conditions of the poor.

The gathering of social intelligence and the conceptualization of measurements of need and change became an information priority (Hicks and Streeten 1979). This period gave rise to a series of works on social and quality-of-life indicators by international organizations.

With the new directions in technical aid projects came the need to involve local people in planning and implementation. Development specialists were searching for innovative media and methods for information dissemination in order to reach the grassroots and identify local initiatives (Perrett 1983). Studies on the diffusion of innovations during these years indicate a growing concern about the negative attitudes of local populations toward technical aid programs. Resentment against top-down planning by sponsor agencies and overly structured and inflexible projects grew among foreign consultants almost as rapidly as among their local counterparts. Recipients of extension services and participants in training programs often felt that the information they received was tainted by foreign ideas and cultural connotations (Hardiman and Midgley 1978).

New Hopes and New Adjustments

A new controversy emerged from studies of the international division of labor, and became a political force against the economically and technologically dependent status of developing countries at the Sixth Special Session of the United Nations General Assembly in 1974. The agenda of the "group of 77" denounced the existing world economic system as favoring the rich nations ("the Center") at the expense of "the Periphery." The agenda, formalizing the North-South Dialogue, focused on those international economic and political factors which influenced the fate of the developing economies (Independent Commission . . . 1980). The disparity between the industrialized North and the poverty-bound South was especially severe in the fields of scientific research and technological development, the very means to rapid improvements in the economic and social conditions in poor countries.

Proposals for a New International Information Order gave rise to numerous analyses of the international distribution of scientific and technological information, patterns of technology transfer, and the role of communication networks (International Commission . . . 1980). The United Nations Conference on Technical Cooperation Among Developing Countries (TCDC) urged mutual support towards reducing the brain drain and inappropriate technology. The United Nations Conference on Science and Technology for Development (UNCSTD) called for the improved availability of technological knowledge and the building of indigenous R & D capabilities. Technical assistance projects now faced new issues: What is "appropriate" information technology? Are international or regional approaches more effective for improving the information capabilities of low-income countries? How can these countries gain access to international communication networks, scientific and technological information resources, and analytical tools of assessing the social impact of information technologies? What type of technical assistance is needed for information infrastructure and manpower development? These and similar questions guided technical assistance projects for years to come. Many of these problems are still acute, but new information policymakers in developing countries are getting closer to solving them.

In recent years another shift in development policies became evident. Although the dependency concept and the debate on the New International Economic Order succeeded in focusing the attention of donor agencies and governments on problems, they have not clarified what development strategies should be initiated by individual countries. Recession, stagnant markets, high interest rates of borrowing, and severe balance-of-payment problems have hit home. Nevertheless, some developing countries have demonstrated that progress was within their reach. International trade, especially with Europe, was possible. The controversial theory of "adjustment" suggested that, as the example of the newly industrializing countries (NICs) showed, some developing nations could adjust to the existing global economic order, increase their efficiency and productivity, and begin to take care of their own social policies (Emmerij 1983).

In the 1980s, the issue of technology transfer became complicated by the rapid developments in microelectronics. For the first time, development planners became aware of information flows as commodity flows. Instead of a sideline of technical assistance for development, information became the very target of economic and trade negotiations.

Telematics and Technical Assistance

The literature reflecting Third World views indicates that most leaders believe the future of their economies depends on the rapid acquisition of technological knowledge. In order to share in the benefits of the international flow of information, a country needs capabilities in telematics (the field based on the convergence of computer and telecommunication technologies), in domestic R & D, and in technological production. Without the latter condition, imported technology cannot be absorbed and integrated with domestic inventiveness and creativity. This line of thinking embraced education, training and the development of an indigenous workforce as basic requirements of national growth.

Transborder Data Flow

Transborder data flows (TDFs)—movements across national boundaries of machine-readable data for processing, storage, and retrieval—represent a special opportunity for developing countries. However, Sauvant (1983) identified two interrelated problems. First, developing countries are the suppliers of data for TDFs. (This includes, for example, remote sensing data and data processed through the networks of transnational enterprises.) In most cases, developing nations perform simple processing functions while the more complex, electronically based work is carried out in the technologically advanced countries. Second, developing countries are buyers of information, such as images of earth resources and processed data, as well as of information equipment and software. Sauvant warned that because of this market structure, domestic demand and capability for R & D, production, service bureaus, and related activities in the Third World may be retarded.

In this environment, the role of technical assistance is rapidly changing. Newly industrialized countries are looking for markets rather than aid. They invest in the improvement of their education and research base for increased competitive status. Other countries, especially those needy in both income and natural resources, require assistance in order to meet the most elementary needs of their poor populations and to build managerial and research skills in enterprises and governments. Rural development is as burning an issue as before, but approaches to it now include microcomputers for specialized information analysis centers, and new communication media for extension services (Courrier 1981). National information systems in various sectors need assistance in building new skills to assure compatibility and quality control. Technical aid agencies are responding to these needs. Examples are the International Labor Organization's software package (ISIS), and the International Development Research Center's database management package (MINISIS).

Information Policies

The real challenge to technical assistance is the need for information about the potential social and human impact of new technologies. Issues concerning the information culture, such as intellectual property, contractual relationships, technology assessment and adaptation, security, privacy, research ethics, marketing of information, legal aspects of human resource networks, and information repackaging have become critical with growing information power. Speaking for developing countries, Rada (1981, p. 58) said: "We must learn how to harness current changes, while avoiding the undesirable effects of the technology." Technical assistance agencies need to support mechanisms (regional workshops and current awareness services) for the exchange of information in these areas. National information policies are a matter of internal interests and external relationships. By knowing more about potential problem areas, policymakers may be better prepared to approximate a balance in access to information and data resources.

International Sources of Aid to Information Services

Cooperative development assistance strategies are dictated by both national legislation in member countries and multilateral instruments. Participants at a recent international meeting observed that donor agencies are spending considerable amounts on information services and related activities without clearly identifying underlying objectives (International Development . . . 1984). Information processes have not been systematically integrated with the development effort of donor organizations. Practices of management range from internal information supply to staff only to funding cooperative information projects in developing countries. Over the last two decades, international donor organizations have established and supported (1) large-scale cooperative information systems, (2) small, highly specialized information analysis centers, (3) regional information centers, (4) specialized information clearinghouses with referral responsibilities, (5) data centers for scientific or statistical data, and (6) networks for the sharing of development information.

Many international organizations conduct research and education programs in information science and management. Their policies vary according to the organization's perception of the role of information in the development process. For example, the TermNet program of the International Information Center for Terminology aims at constructing a global theoretical basis for terminology; the World Bank is engaged in the evaluation of socioeconomic data sets in order to improve the reliability of planning, and the funding and harmonization of education programs for information scientists, librarians, and archivists has been one of the major commitments of UNESCO.

Nongovernmental Organizations (NGOs)

In recent years, international NGOs—including scientific and professional associations—have significantly increased their efforts to disseminate information and know-how applicable to the cultures of individual developing countries. They serve as a bridge between the large bureaucratic intergovernmental organizations and the small national NGOs in developing countries. In technical assistance projects, members of NGOs have the advantage of speaking the same professional language as their counterparts in the Third World. Through contract funding from intergovernmental organizations, NGOs engage in collaborative research, training programs, and consultation.

One of the most significant current trends in NGO activity is the growing emphasis on human resource networking. Networks can enable organizations and societies to cope with rapid social change. In developing countries, NGOs have found networks to be excellent mechanisms to interlink scientists and professionals in various disciplines and to disseminate information by small, inexpensive newsletters. The International Development Research Center is exploring computer conferencing for developing countries, which could further increase the effectiveness of human resource networks.

Private Voluntary Organizations (PVOs)

PVOs are able to provide the most direct and flexible approach to technical aid by their small-scale projects and informal communication modes. It is customary for staff members to live in host countries and work with local people. Projects are often adapted to newly discovered needs and experimentation is condoned. PVOs engage in information dissemination in rural areas, and some of them have begun to provide training in information processing and microcomputer use to local institutions. Several international agencies have recommended that regional data banks be set up collaboratively to support the work of small voluntary organizations in achieving close contacts and information exchange with indigenous groups. It is likely that in the future PVOs will accumulate the most significant experience on indigenous cultural information processes.

Transnational Corporations (TNCs)

Private enterprises which produce and market in more than one country are the main instruments of technology transfer, and thus occupy the focal point in a worldwide controversy. A voluminous literature is available on both aspects of the issue: Are TNCs the exploiters of the resources in low-income countries, or are they sources of economic improvements?

The first view is that technology obtained in developing societies from the industrialized world through TNCs is usually large-scale and capital-intensive. It provides neither new skills nor the opportunity to adjust it to local needs. Without the creation of new capabilities, no long-range benefits can be acquired by the transfer. A further question is whether by marketing their products in developing countries, TNCs are meeting real existing needs or introducing new tastes, styles and expectations often completely alien to the local culture. Such doubts and questions, characterizing a large part of the development science literature, cast the TNC in a negative role, and warn against its communication campaigns.

The second argument proposes that through their subsidiaries and affiliates TNCs are instrumental in introducing innovations, the adaptations of new technology, and the creation of employment in developing economies. They are praised also for providing managerial skills and technical information. In addition, foreign subsidiaries of TNCs have expanded into several developing countries and, through these "second generation" firms, are producing goods appropriate for indigenous use. The know-how gained in this process enhances the rise of domestic enterprises in developing countries. A corollary benefit is the judicious selection of foreign technology for importation, a highly information-intensive process (Baranson 1984). Several international organizations assist in such developments and make available economic analyses, financial studies, and other practical information to the Third World business communities.

Information for Technical Assistance Projects

Whether it focuses on agriculture, medical clinics, or energy resources, a technical assistance project acts as a conduit for information between the sponsor organization and the host country. The more effective the information base a project assembles in the course of its work, the more useful the intermediary role its staff will play. Development specialists warn that rigidly structured and unnecessarily complicated organizational processes do not contribute to understanding and communication between projects and local populations. The importance of the impact of two-way communications on indigenous people is emphasized: "Regional progress is either the development of thinking human beings who have learned to participate in decisions that affect their destiny—or it is really nothing" (Mickelwait et al. 1978, v. 2, p. 294).

Information activities supporting projects fall into four broad categories:

- management information systems
- data collection and analysis for surveys of local conditions
- internal and external records and reports
- information dissemination to and exchange with people in the project area.

Much has been written about the role of effective communication and social networks in the change process (Rogers 1983). The transfer of useful information, be it scientific, technical, or cultural, from the project staff and consultants to their local counterparts should be part of this process. To enhance this activity, projects need an information system which supports the internal work and external communications of the staff. There are certain factors that need to be considered:

- the relevance of the information output (content, forms, and channels) to the goals of the project as well as to the societal beliefs and norms of the external environment
- the political ideology of local people
- level of poverty in the rural communities
- relationships of local units to the central government
- local priorities in regard to social change
- openness to or mistrust of foreign influences
- the impression former development projects left in the communities
- existing communication links in the region (telephone and telex, transportation, use of radio, television, microcomputers, local press, markets)
- enterprises and their role in the local social structure
- traditional class relationships
- formal and nonformal education programs.

All of these factors have potential messages for the information system planner.

Conclusion

Many authors write about the global "revolution" brought about by informatics and telematics. But the revolution, if there ever was one, ended about the time when "satellite" and "microchip" became symbols of power to be attained in practically every society. We are already in the postrevolutionary period of adaptation, institutionalization and the distribution of benefits. It is now that the meaning of information development and information literacy must be clarified.

We should not forget that technical assistance is meant for people who do not have food for their families or skills to recognize and use opportunities. They live—physically and mentally—isolated from the exciting world of satellites and microelectronics. The gap that needs to be bridged is much wider today than it was at the beginning of the technical assistance era. However, the tools of technical assistance are also much more effective than ever before. The question now is: Do we information professionals—in developing and industrialized countries—have the philosophical compass to guide the use of technology before the technology begins to guide the development process?

References

Aboyade, O. (1976). *Issues in the Development of Tropical Africa.* Ibadan, Nigeria: Ibadan University Press.

Baranson, J. (1984). *North-South Technology Transfer: Financing and Institution Building.* Mt. Airy, MD: Lomond Publications, Inc.

Courrier, K., ed. (1981). *The Educational Use of Mass Media.* Washington, DC: The World Bank. (Staff Working Paper 491).

Emmerij, L. (1983). Our grave new world, trends in international development and security. *Development: Seeds of Change,* 1, 5–12.

Hardiman, M. & Midgley, J. (1978). Foreign consultants and development projects, the need for an alternative approach. *Journal of Administration Overseas,* 17, 232–244.

Hicks, N. & Streeten, P. (1979). Indicators of development: The Search for a basic needs yardstick. *World Development,* 7, 567–580.

Independent Commission on International Development Issues (Brandt Commission). (1980). *North-South: A Program for Survival.* Cambridge, MA: MIT Press.

International Commission for the Study of Communication Problems (MacBride Commission). (1980). *Many Voices, One World.* Paris, France: UNESCO and London, UK: Kogan Page Ltd.

International Development Research Center. (1984). *Specialized Information Analysis Centers in International Development, Report of a Meeting, Quebec, Canada, 1982.* Ottawa, Canada: IDRC.

International Labor Organization. (1976). *Employment, Growth and Basic Needs: A One-World Problem.* Geneva, Switzerland: ILO.

King-Farlow, J. & Shea, W.R. (1976). *Values and the Quality of Life.* New York, NY: Science History Publications.

Lele, U. (1975). *The Design of Rural Development, Lessons from Africa.* Baltimore, MD: The Johns Hopkins University Press.

Maruyama, M. (1974). Endogenous research vs. delusions of relevance and expertise among exogenous academics. *Human Organization,* 33(3), 318–322.

Mickelwait, D.R., et al. (1978). *Information for Decision Making in Rural Development.* Washington, DC: Development Alternatives, Inc. 2 vols.

Morqwetz, D. (1977). *Twenty-Five Years of Economic Development. 1950–1975.* Baltimore, MD: The Johns Hopkins University Press.

Neelameghan, A. (1980). Information systems for national development—The social relevance of information systems. *International Forum for Information and Documentation,* 5(4), 3–8.

Ong, W.J. (1980). Literacy and orality in our times. *Journal of Communication,* 30(1), 197–204.

Organization for Economic Cooperation and Development. (1979). *The Impact of the Newly Industrialized Countries on Production and Trade in Manufactures.* Paris, France: OECD.

Perrett, H. (1983). *Using Communication Support in Projects: The World Bank's Experience.* Washington, DC: The World Bank. (Staff Working Paper 551).

Rada, J.F. (1981). The Microelectronics revolution: Implications for the Third World. *Development Dialogue,* 2, 41–61.

Rogers, E.M. (1983). *Diffusion of Innovations.* 3rd ed. New York, NY: The Free Press.

Sauvant, K.P. (1983). Transborder data flows and the developing countries. *International Organization,* 37(2), 359–371.

Schaefer, M. (1981). *Intersectoral Coordination and Health in Environmental Management.* Geneva, Switzerland: World Health Organization (Public Health Papers No. 74).

Spencer, D.L. & Woroniak, A., eds. (1967). *The Transfer of Technology to Developing Countries.* New York, NY: Praeger.

Stewart, F. (1979). *International Technology Transfer: Issues and Policy Options.* Washington, DC: The World Bank.

Streeten, P., et al. (1981). *First Things First, Meeting Basic Human Needs in the Developing Countries.* New York, NY: Oxford University Press for the World Bank.

United States. Congress. House Committee on Government Operations. (1981). *AID's Administrative and Management Problems in Providing Foreign Economic Assistance. Hearings.* 97th Congress, First Session, October 6, 1981. Washington, DC: U.S. Government Printing Office.

The World Bank. (1981). *Poverty and Basic Needs.* Washington, DC: The World Bank.

2

Data Collection by Development Projects as a National Information Resource

Introduction

Recent decades of international development assistance have brought disillusionment, critical searching and reflection to those involved. Investment in building physical infrastructures and industrialization dependent on capital flow and technology from the North have not helped alleviate poverty. One specialist expressed the anxiety of many:

> . . . a quarter century of experience has placed some constraints on our thinking, in the form of facts on how the process has gone. Sometimes these facts are summarized by saying that development has been disappointingly slow: poverty still persists, and because of the rate of population increase, is numerically greater than it was at mid-century (Keyfitz 1982, pp. 669–670).

A joint study of the Dag Hammarskjold Foundation and the International Foundation for Development Alternatives, in concert with numerous other efforts at reassessment, warned that capital flows to developing countries "will bypass the nearly 800 million people living in absolute poverty. Most of these people live in the thirty-eight low-income countries which have little or no capacity to participate in the world's economy." This new realism led to the recognition that

> . . . development cannot be reduced to economic growth; it is indeed a human-centered process aiming, through structural transformation, at the satisfaction of human material and nonmaterial needs, built from within the society on the basis of self-reliance and in harmony with the environment (Dag Hammarskjold Foundation 1981, p. 9).

The trend indicated by such observations implies that assistance policies are increasingly concerned with improving social conditions. As this requires an understanding of human needs, the methods of assessing poverty and the developing of standards for satisfying basic needs have become serious problems for development managers (United Nations 1979). Although many social scientists argue against attempts to quantify poverty measures, one must recognize that a combination of quantified evidence with qualitative narration is the first step toward understanding the magnitude of a problem.

Extensive primary data collection efforts have been initiated where creative insight could have identified the existence of data files compiled by previous projects. This paper investigates the international development assistance project as a resource for demographic, social, economic and environmental data. A project normally accumulates data relevant to the population, conditions, and cultural activities in the area, but data files produced are seldom known and used beyond the project's staff and consultants. Three broad issues concern us regarding the potential inventorying and utilization of these files and related documents: (1) international development strategies as the policy framework of projects and their information functions; (2) the nature of project-related data, and barriers to their dissemination and wider application; and (3) the potential of national networks of project-generated data pools and their use for planning, policy making and research.

Development Assistance Projects

The financing of assistance projects is undertaken by a wide variety of national and international agencies. The widely used term "donor agency" is misleading; many provide loans, rather than donations. Yet the process is somewhat similar in either case. Project objectives are identified, and consultants selected by an international organization, a consulting team, a technology transfer agency, a national government, a particular ministry or a private institution in the "host" country. Project teams may serve on reconnaissance missions, feasibility studies, project planning, design and implementation, or they may be employed for specific tasks such as need assessment, monitoring project performance or evaluating the entire impact of a development program. Technical assistance may be targeted on economic and technological improvements, on health, social, educational or communication infrastructures, on urban, regional or rural development, or on attacking a specific problem, such as the lack of clean water supply.

A technical assistance project usually evolves a three-way communication pattern determined by the relationships among the project team, the local counterparts in the "host" country, and the donor agency. The attitudes of project management and technical advisors towards their local counterparts and the target population, as well as their understanding of the particular needs of the sociocultural environment, usually have a decisive impact on the outcome of development efforts.

Experience shows that knowledge-generating and informing activities are interwoven with almost all processes of planning, implementing and evaluating development projects, although there is usually no systematic effort to coordinate information flows. A literature review identified at least four broad categories of information processes:

(1) Management of Decision Support Information

Activities and products may include reconnaissance, feasibility and planning surveys, administrative data collection, policy analyses and reports, management information systems and occasionally a more advanced decision support system. Normally these activities are carried out by managers and information specialists, and products are used internally.

(2) Applied Scientific Investigation

Environmental assessments, agricultural studies, rural sociological studies, industrial applications of technological research and development, and the social and economic analyses of living conditions are in this category. This type of information is usually produced by consultants and technical advisors who might be either foreigners or indigenous researchers. Products are often shared with academic institutions and government agencies in the host country.

(3) Local and International Information Resource Use

Projects may secure access to international databases and statistical information systems, and use the online/CD-ROM search capability of the donor agency; in addition to building up its own documentation, a project may draw on information clearinghouses and libraries in the region or in the donor agency's home country. Products are utilized mainly internally by staff and consultants.

(4) Interpersonal and Organizational Networking

A project often develops formal and informal linkages with government agencies, provincial and local offices and institutions as well as with domestic nongovernmental organizations (farmers' associations, trade organizations, educational programs, etc.). Projects might hire consultants with backgrounds in education, rural sociology or communication science to carry out such information activities. Networks extending to developing countries are usually non-electronic, informal, and based on personal contacts.

This overview of project-related processes, although far from comprehensive, will serve as background for focusing the present paper on project-generated data resources. "Information" and "data" are elusive concepts, abundantly used but seldom defined in project management documentation; interpretation depends mainly on the professional or methodological context. Are data needed by engineers for constructing a dam, or by community organizers for starting an adult literacy program, by quantitative methodologists or by action researchers? For example, a report on designing rural projects explains that a reconnaissance survey provides a way of synthesizing data into information, drawing on the analytical skills of rural development specialists (Weisel and Mickelwait 1978).

Trends in Development Strategies

In the late 1970s, three forces affected the approach of international and national agencies to technical assistance for developing countries. First, changes in the world economy drove up inflation rates, thereby reducing investment and employment and encouraging trade protectionism. Developing countries faced, and still face, a decrease in capital flows as well as in technical assistance. Secondly, Third World economies, especially those dependent on the importing of oil, are carrying a growing burden of national debt and are becoming increasingly aware of their dependence on external capital. With the emphasis on political self-determination and sovereign rights to protect national cultures, the relationship between industrialized and aid-recipient countries is strained.

Thirdly, past experience with development assistance adds little to the trust people in low-income countries place in projects and foreign consultants. In some cases modernization interventions introduced in agriculture, health care, family lifestyles or public administration by technical aid projects have been abandoned after the departure of foreign advisors. Inequitable distribution of the benefits of development and the lack of the recipients' involvement in planning are among the reasons reported for this abandonment (Ingle 1979, Kilby 1982). Analysis of the relation between economic development and income inequality has found no evidence of the "trickle-down" process by which the poor were supposed to benefit from overall economic growth (Stack and Zimmerman 1982).

Although advances in science and technology are seen as means to rapid improvements in the socioeconomic conditions of Third World countries, the technological imbalance between these countries and the industrialized nations causes growing frustration. The Overseas Development Council (1979, pp. 92–93), describing the failed effort by developing nations to introduce a mandatory technology transfer code, estimates that 90 percent of innovations take place in and for the industrial countries with only 30 percent of the world population. Importing more technologies to low-income countries under development aid arrangements is hampered by insufficient indigenous scientific and technological capabilities, lack of skilled manpower for adapting technologies to local needs and conditions, and the refusal of some governments to enforce foreign patent rights (United States . . . 1982). On the other hand, many developing countries express bitterness and resentment over the small number of technologically advanced countries and transnational corporations that initiate and control so much of technological innovation (International Commission . . . 1980).

Changes introduced in development strategies in the mid-1970s, by domestic legislation and international policies, mandated aid to the poorest populations and more determined efforts by project management to mobilize local participation in the planning and implementation of projects. It was expected that such local involvement might motivate people to support, adapt and continue new agricultural, health, business and educational practices beyond the life of a project (Uphoff et al. 1979). One of the basic conditions for involving the potential beneficiaries is their capacity to make decisions on the selection of technology and to adjust foreign know-how to their own cultural and social needs. Today, developmentalists see the information process not only as a supportive technical service for project planning and management, but also as a way of communication to reach and interact with participants. For example, a research study of local social conditions conducted for a development project may become a vehicle for communication with local people (Bhatt 1978).

Data Gathering by Development Projects

The literature of rural development stresses the need for indicators that gauge the impact of social innovations and the involvement of local groups in projects. A survey by Cornell University's Rural Development Committee evaluated land reform measures in Nepal ten years after their introduction, collecting data on land tenure, agricultural production, economic income and political participation, including participants' views of local government expenditures and taxation (Uphoff and Esman 1974). Mexico's PIDER, an integrated rural development project, made identifying measures to evaluate its social impact one of its priorities. Researchers in developing countries are increasingly using social and socioeconomic criteria to measure disparities in the quality of life (Arief 1982, Oyebanji 1982). In fact, the entire "basic needs" movement, advocating international development aid for adequate food, shelter, clothing, essential services and freely chosen employment to the poor, rather than for overall national income growth which normally tends to favor the elites, struggles with problems of identifying uniform standards and measurements. Hicks and Streeten (1979, p. 577) are not the only skeptics when they write that "it has proven virtually impossible to translate every aspect of social progress into money values or some other readily accepted common denominator."

Researchers stress that only a two-way communication flow between developers and local participants can assure the effectiveness of information dissemination as a development tool. Probably the most positive change in recent intercultural communication activities has been the recognition that neither development planning nor the diffusion of innovations can be successfully imposed from the top down (Rogers 1978).

Interviews can explore the perceptions of local officials and groups of people regarding the changes which are needed and feasible, and whether results of social interventions can be assessed from the viewpoint of those whose lives and work have been affected, provided the interviewers are from the same background as the interviewees. The problem is that a project plan, created for a donor agency thousands of miles from the project site, frequently turns out to be overly complicated and inflexible. In such cases, it may be impossible to bridge the cultural and technological gap between the development planners and the would-be appliers. Another gap exists between the appliers and the project's target people. Cultural and psychological distance also separates a younger, urbanized and westernized generation and a more traditional and provincial society within the same country. Frequently imposed information gathering methods turn into barriers between project management and local population rather than into opportunities to interact.

Trust between research teams and their subjects is as indispensable for an effective project as is trust between information disseminators and recipients. Moreover, as Lele (1975) pointed out, researchers and disseminators, too, must work together. Only by an effective dialogue between research and extension service can the current rural development effort have a noticeable impact. Highly bureaucratized large-scale donor agencies find it much harder to mobilize local participation than small private voluntary organizations with their more flexible and informal approaches (Sauerwein 1979).

The Cultural Aspects of Technology Transfer

The exchange of information and data is an inseparable element of introducing new technology in the course of a development project. In the case of international technology transfer brokerage firms, information is often the only commodity that is supplied. In a policy review paper, Stewart (1979, p. 1) states that "at the heart of any form of economic activity from the least to the most sophisticated lies the technology or knowledge of how the activity is carried out." Weiss distinguishes between hardware innovation and social innovation, suggesting that "an intervention focused purely on technology—whether indigenous or foreign and whether new, adapted, or transferred—is likely to be doomed from the start. In such cases, the introduction of hardware should be accompanied by and integrated with a package of policy and institutional changes . . ." (Weiss 1979, p. 1083). Indeed, newly industrialized countries (NICs) which are building industrial and information infrastructures simultaneously, are importing, together with the hardware, computer process control systems and communication systems (Porat 1978).

These examples show the need to distinguish between hardware transfer, information transfer, and knowledge transfer. Knowledge transfer often strains the adaptive capacity of government officials in the technology recipient country. They have to deal with indigenous issues of economic and cultural factors that affect the integration of foreign innovations into the local society. The inventiveness and communication skills needed for understanding this indigenous process are often missing in bureaucracies (Heper 1974, p. 9). One of the adaptive tools of administrative practice occasionally used in state offices and regional development organizations is the conversion of administrative data into information for planning and program assessment. But the consistent creation of data collection programs to support policy making is costly, cumbersome and seldom seen as justified except at the national level.

Innovative technology has often been introduced without sufficiently integrating it with the country's overall development goals and indigenous culture. A series of studies by the World Bank concluded that the transfer of inappropriate technology has contributed to serious dislocations and sometimes increased the hardship of the poor (Weiss 1979). On occasion, foreign consultants have used similar warnings as justification for selling outdated equipment to development projects or for teaching oversimplified methods.

To safeguard against repeating past mistakes, adaptive field testing has been developed as a management tool, allowing for experimentation with new approaches without drastic consequences. Olson (1978) suggests consideration of the following issues before field testing a proposed innovation: the availability of capable or trainable data collectors; the size of budgets to pay personnel; the attitudes of host country officials toward a field testing program; and ethical concerns about experimentation, including questioning the moral justification of intervening in a foreign culture under the aegis of assistance.

Most factors that may influence the outcome of field testing are sociocultural. Instead of thinking of them as "barriers" or "problems" and expecting people to adjust to foreign project models, one should consider them "opportunities" of development, and adjust the models to the cultural environment. Sociocultural factors include:

- cultural heritage and the historical approach to communication (oral or written tradition, openness to, or mistrust of, foreign influences)
- societal values and beliefs, language(s) spoken or written
- political ideology and dynamics, geopolitical alliances
- the economic and social systems as they bear upon development priorities
- educational programs and their relation to development programs
- level of urbanization and bureaucratization
- existing informal communication links in the region and the country
- capability to work with, absorb and use information.

Some of these factors may have only an indirect effect, but never losing sight of them when testing a prototype project or method should help build flexibility, tolerance and adaptive capability into the final plan.

Project Management and Data Collection Efforts

Reviewing a typical project cycle followed by most donor agencies will identify the processes that generate as well as require information.

Identification:	Study of a problem and need, generation and selection of project and site
Preparation:	Examination of the technical, institutional, cultural, economic and financial aspects of the proposed project
Appraisal:	Review of the proposed project and preparation of the appraisal report
Negotiations:	Discussions with representatives of the borrowing country; preparation of the agreement, plan and budget documents
Implementation:	The borrower's responsibility for implementation and the preparation of progress reports

Evaluation: Review of staff reports; audit and field visits; evaluation research.

To demonstrate the viability of a project, management has to collect technical, institutional and economic data about the project site and about conditions in the host country. For example, the World Bank requires mainly investment-oriented economic data, while the Food and Agriculture Organization of the United Nations needs evidence of rural migration to urban centers. Other organizations prioritize data collection tasks according to their policy orientation. In the past far greater attention was given by development programs to economic and technical needs than to social problems (Oyebanji 1982), but the World Bank has indicated a new policy emphasis on human development in the fight against poverty (The World Bank 1980), and it has recognized that technological projects that damage the human environment are poor investments (The World Bank 1979).

Each phase within a project may be further analyzed for steps requiring managerial decisions and decision-support data. Weisel and Mickelwait (1978) suggest the following as critical decision categories:

1. specifying project objectives, including indicators of success
2. identifying project components
3. determining project management arrangements
4. specifying project resource commitments.

Overstructured and inflexible projects leave no room for on-site adjustments, which are often essential even during the implementation period. Dawson (1978) recommends surveys of local resources and analysis of local problems that need solutions in order to distinguish between short-term results and potential long-run improvements. Certain indispensable processes beyond implementation are often overlooked; Rondinelli (1978) emphasizes the following:

- post-evaluation
- diffusion and demonstration of results
- transfer of resources to operating agencies
- follow-up action (assistance of output users and identification of further investment opportunities)
- adaptation of technologies used in project implementation to other development activities
- training of personnel for new projects.

The data gathering and manipulation activities usually connected with these processes are seldom integrated into a system that would allow each action to draw on the resources and experience of the others.

Data Collection for Management Support

I have set out in this paper to discuss the characteristics and potential uses of data files generated by technical aid projects in developing countries. Unfortunately, one cannot expect to locate data files and hope that today's users will be able to benefit from them without problems or uncertainties. Data may be several years old, tabulated inadequately, and uneven in quality, but such data may still represent unique resources for a given geographical or cultural area. To better understand the characteristics and usefulness of any set of development data, one should ask who had collected them originally, where and for what purposes.

As systems advisor to a small farm production project in the Philippines, Smith (1974, p. 3) defined a management information system as "a modern development of a more familiar, but less glamorous process known as 'reporting' . . . " As development projects became more complex and elaborate, teams affiliated with different phases of a project, often working at different sites, constructed their own information bases, often with little or no coordination (Hageboeck et al. 1979, Stewart 1979). The information support received by project managers has been criticized for needless complexity, lack of selectively collected and evaluated data, and emphasis on efficiency rather than on effective decisions. A study of rural development projects in several countries showed management information systems producing much under-utilized data and failing to provide any feedback to the local people who had supplied the data (Mickelwait et al. 1978).

Occasionally a project will draw on government-university cooperation to produce an experimental computer modeling system to allow the project manager to analyze problems and study alternative ways to approach them. Such a system is appropriate for project decisions because it serves specific managerial needs, provides data evaluation selectively, and performs comparisons and projections. Data sets assembled for this kind of flexible information support are usually relevant to specific problem areas such as coastal management or the prediction and prevention of epidemics.

Adelman (1979) and his research team compared two large-scale computer modeling efforts—by the International Labor Organization and the World Bank—constructed for the analysis of policies on income distribution and employment in developing countries. Both projects attempted to identify a set of policies which would, in time, lead to the satisfaction of basic human needs for the majority of poor populations in the world. Where available, national economic accounts, social statistics, household expenditure surveys and national census records served as data sources. Data sets included information on prices, taxation, farm management and flow of funds. Using these resources for secondary analysis might present some problems due to the uneven quality of the data, but the advantages of discovering such resources tend to outweigh the hazards. Therefore, the World Bank undertook to identify existing data for the analysis of income and labor relations in several countries for the use of researchers and planners (Visaria 1979).

Research Studies and Problems of Measurement

The difficulty of assessing existing conditions and changes introduced to alleviate poverty is widely discussed in the literature of development science. Most projects find that it is unclear what kind of information should be collected, and by what means, to understand local needs, and whether the information should be purely factual or should include people's subjective perceptions. Data on rural working conditions, urban blight, or changes in family life styles are far more difficult to obtain than those on economic relationships.

Development specialists have described problems of social measurements in many different contexts (Hicks 1982, Hursch-Cesar and Roy 1980, Pearce-Batten 1980, Rush 1977). The issue of the construction and use of social and quality-of-life indicators is seen mainly as a function of methodology rather than that of conceptualization. Those trained in a specific technique may be reluctant to collaborate with researchers of other methodological backgrounds. Definitions are controversial (e.g. "absolute" and "relative" poverty lines, "basic needs," "equity") and surveys are difficult to design because interpretations of concepts change with situations. Even international standards of social statistics may fail when used in different cultural contexts. Methodologies designed for large-scale cross-national surveys are not readily adaptable to small local projects sponsored with modest funds. Technical skills for field research are often lacking, and the application of analytic techniques must include extensive training.

Cultural distance between researchers and indigenous populations may vitiate research. Gulhati (1977, p. 362) argues that

> while the quick, airborne missions of international staffs were very appropriate when the focus was on modern, organized, high technology segments of Third World societies, they may prove quite ineffective in the context of designing poverty redress schemes requiring long and patient study.

In considering reanalysis of research data and the reuse of reports, one must consider the impact of the researchers' background on the nature of the data in culturally different regions. Local researchers, most familiar with conditions, may be expected to produce the most credible results. Researchers working in the limiting resource environments of development projects deserve the credit for advances in data collection methods.

Access to Local Information Resources

Today many development projects are mandated by donor agency policies to direct their efforts at the poorest regions and to involve the local population in intervention choices. To implement these policies, assessment of local economic and social conditions by formal surveys or action research became necessary. The use of local records is another way to document grassroots developments. Consultants bent on introducing new disease control practices, water supply improvements or local public administration procedures need to find out about existing social customs and local resources. Data thus gathered might be the only available intelligence on the project's area. Statistical surveys include reconnaissance studies, "area frame sampling," population sampling, and farm record surveys. Mickelwait, Sweet and Morss (1978) describe several "information bases" that the analysts were able to locate and use, saving both time and funds. Mayfield (1977) reports on a study of financial administration of Egyptian villages. Face-to-face interviews with local officials were supplemented by the administrative records of the Organization for Reconstruction and Development of Egyptian Villages. A University of Wisconsin team (1979) related similar experience in Tunisia.

Although perhaps difficult to locate, data on local populations in developing countries are available, and are well worth seeking out. Woodward (1980, p. 260) argues that

> by far the most important type of information, both in volume and value to any one country, is the locally produced information, and it is also this type of information which poses the biggest problems in organization and utilization. It consists of resource inventories, consultancy reports, project reports, studies of all types and, very important, annual and other administrative reports.

Woodward insists that techniques and products introduced by assistance projects need local testing and evaluation dependent on feasibility studies, analyses and reports of local researchers which hardly ever appear in the open literature. Their portrayal of local conditions can be extremely useful to subsequent projects.

Local documents are often unique means of access to information on town and village institutions. For four decades, assistance projects have accumulated extensive experience with community development, producing a large number of records (Holdcroft 1978). Local organizations are interlinked by a variety of activities and modes of communication (Korten 1979, Uphoff and Esman 1974). Projects intent on mobilizing participation strive to recruit local leadership and acquire important social and technical information about the community by contacting such organizations.

A New Information Resource in Developing Countries

As we have seen, managerial, research and extension work related to technical aid projects is likely to produce unique information embedded in data files and unpublished reports. While donor agencies and national governments have invested considerable funding in creating these data pools, development specialists continually deplore the lack of data on local conditions. The present paper argues that these fugitive data resources, assuming that their location and terms of availability were widely known, could be used by a wide range of planners, policy makers and researchers.

One type of project-generated resource is the evaluation report, which typically documents not only flaws and problems in the development process, but also positive experiences with decision making information (Brinkerhoff 1979, Morss et al. 1976, Rush 1977, Sobhan 1976). For example, we may learn from evaluation reports that

- management information systems designed for local and provincial governments may contain in their databases information on structures, processes and intergovernmental relations;
- many systems collect and archive socioeconomic data useful for secondary analysis;
- information systems created for fairly recent projects probably include information in their databases about local participation and resources;
- since donor agencies and national governments are increasingly concerned with energy problems, relevant scientific and social data may be embedded in their project documentation;
- demographic, household, and health-related information for local areas will almost certainly be present in the data files of former projects.

Since both surveys and management information systems are said to be the least effective when handling data on such "soft" topics as the project participants' reaction to new agricultural practices or their preferences in the choice of health services, a constructive outcome of bringing these problems to the attention of project staff might be renewed efforts for improvement.

Networks of Small Data Pools: A Proposal

Unpublished information sources are often shared among peers through personal contact. A trend toward the systematic use of formerly informal contacts emerged in the late 1970s when organizations and interdisciplinary research groups began to construct databases of consultants, specialized programs and resource persons.

There are numerous reasons why information professionals in a developing country would want to initiate a pilot project for inventorying and linking data pools of local information. Development planners and consultants benefit from networks, but information professionals form the specialized corps with expertise to conduct need assessment, implementation and evaluation. Costs would be modest: no attempt should be made to remove data sets from their original locations; access will be through network referrals. The smaller the area covered, the more effective the referral service is likely to be.

Negotiations with government departments and institutions storing the data will be necessary. An inventory of resources will indicate not only location, content, scope, coverage dates, collection dates, storage medium, and related documentation, but also the terms of access. Questions of ownership, jurisdiction, primary users, possible confidentiality and service charges might arise. In fact, a pilot project to locate underused data might have the added benefit of identifying and raising some very timely policy issues.

The Need for Exploration

Despite the alleged shortage of data, the real problem is lack of access. International organizations occasionally evaluate large-scale databases, but there is no funding available to accord the same treatment to the smaller data files housed in various ministries and private institutions; nor is their integration into national or regional data centers a realistic option. Organizations tend to develop proprietary attitudes toward information they house, even if the information is hardly ever used by the few officials or academicians who know of its existence. Politics, dearth of financial resources, and logistics currently defy any attempt to evaluate and bring data resources together.

The choice for national information strategists is between the total neglect of such potentially useful resources, or inventorying them in their current imperfect state. Information professionals have always endeavored to organize information resources into a near perfect order before making them available to users, but this habit needs rethinking. Awareness of possible difficulties with project-generated data should help intermediaries and users to exercise critical thinking and caution, but it should not deter them from tapping the resource when hard-pressed for specific locally relevant information. An education and training program for information managers who would maintain and update the network of resources and contact persons and handle referrals would seem the most productive approach. As development planning continues to emphasize human capital, it would be ironic to ignore the potential of human resources in the utilization of unique data.

References

Adelman, I., et al. (1979). A comparison of two models for income distribution planning. *Journal of Policy Modeling,* 1, 37–82. (World Bank Reprint 81).

Arief, S. (1982). Regional disparities in Malaysia. *Social Indicators Research,* 11, 259–267.

Bhatt, V.V. (1978). Decision making in the public sector. *Economic and Political Weekly,* 13(21), 30–35. (World Bank Reprint 96).

Brinkerhoff, D.W. (1979). Inside public bureaucracy: Empowering managers to empower clients. *Rural Development Participation Review,* 1(1), 7–9.

Dag Hammarskjold Foundation. (1981). The gap in international resource transfers. (With the International Foundation for Development Alternatives). Parts 1–2. *Development dialogue,* 1, 5–27.

Dawson, A. (1978). Suggestions for an approach to rural development by foreign aid programmes. *International Labor Review,* 117, 391–404.

Gulhati, R. (1977). *A mandate on behalf of the poor? International agencies and the New World Order. The Round Table.* 268. (World Bank Reprint 93).

Hageboeck, M., et al. (1979). *Manager's Guide to Data Collection.* Washington, DC: Practical Concepts Inc.

Heper, M. (1974). "Training for potential bureaucratic elites of the transitional societies." In: Swerdlow, I.; Ingle, M., eds. *Public Administration Training for the Less Developed Countries: Maxwell School Conference Proceedings.* Syracuse, NY: Syracuse University, pp. 4–12.

Hicks, N. (1982). Sector priorities in meeting basic needs: some statistical evidence. *World Development,* 10(6), 489–499.

Hicks, N.L. & Streeten, P. (1979). Indicators of Development: The search for a basic needs yardstick. *World Development,* 7(6), 567–580. (World Bank Reprint 104).

Holdcroft, L.E. (1978). *The Rise and Fall of Community Development in Developing Countries, 1950–65: A Critical Analysis and an Annotated Bibliography.* East Lansing, MI: Department of Agricultural Economics, Michigan State University. (MSU Rural Development Paper, 2).

Hursch-Cesar, G. & Roy, P., eds. (1980). *Third World Surveys: Survey Research in Developing Countries.* New Delhi: Macmillan Company of India.

Ingle, M.D. (1979). *Implementing Development Programs: A State-of-the-Art Review.* Washington, DC: U.S. Agency for International Development.

International Commission for the Study of Communication Problems. (1980). *Many Voices, One World: Report by the Sean McBride Commission to UNESCO.* London, UK: Kogan Page.

Keyfitz, N. (1982). Development and the elimination of poverty. *Economic Development and Cultural Change,* 30(3), 649–670.

Kilby, P. (1982). Evaluating technical assistance. *World Development,* 30(3), 649–670.

Korten, D.C. (1979). *Community social organization in rural development.* (Resource paper given at A and P Agricultural and Resource Staff Seminar, Jakarta, Indonesia). Manila, Philippines: Ford Foundation.

Lele, U. (1975). *The Design of Rural Development; Lessons from Africa.* Baltimore, MD: Johns Hopkins University Press.

Mayfield, J.B. (1977). *The Budgetary System in the Arab Republic of Egypt: Its Role in Local Government Development.* Washington, DC: U.S. Agency for International Development. (Field report).

Mickelwait, D.R., Sweet, C.F., & Morss, E.R. (1978). *The "New Directions" Mandate: Studies in Project Design, Approval and Implementation.* Washington, DC: Development Alternatives, Inc.

Mickelwait, D.R., et al. (1978). *Information for Decision Making in Rural Development.* Washington, DC: Development Alternatives, Inc. 2 vols.

Morss E.R., et al. (1976). *Strategies for Small Farmer Development.* Washington, DC: Development Alternatives, Inc.

Olson, C.V. (1978). *Adaptive Field-Testing for Rural Development Practice.* Washington, DC: U.S. Agency for International Development.

Overseas Development Council. (1979). *The United States and World Development: Agenda, 1979.* New York, NY: Praeger.

Oyebanji, J.O. (1982). Quality of life in Kwara State, Nigeria: An exploratory geographical study. *Social Indicators Research,* 11, 301–317.

Pearce-Batten, A. (1980). New measures of development. *Development Digest,* 18(1), 75–94.

Porat, M.U. (1978). Global implications of the information society. *Journal of Communication,* 28(1), 70–80.

Ramam, P. (1978). Project implications in the context of a plan: The missing links. *International Development Review Focus,* 20(1), 5–7.

Rogers, E.M. (1978). The rise and fall of the dominant paradigm. *Journal of Communication,* 28(1), 64–69.

Rondinelli, D.A. (1978). Implementing development projects: The problem of management. *International Development Review Focus,* 20(1), 8–11.

Rush, W.H. (1977). *Application of Comprehensive Computerized Surveys in the Collection and Analysis of Farm Data in Developing Countries.* Washington, DC: American Technical Assistance Corporation.

Sauerwein, V.T. (1979). United Nations restructuring: New challenges to PVOs. *International Council of Voluntary Agencies News,* 83, 3–5.

Smith, K. (1974). *The MASAGENA 99 Management Information System.* Manila: U.S. Agency for International Development.

Sobhan, I. (1976). *The Planning and Implementation of Rural Development Projects: An Empirical Analysis.* Washington, DC: U.S. Agency for International Development.

Stack, S. & Zimmerman, D. (1982). The effect of world economy on income inequality: A reassessment. *The Sociological Quarterly,* 23(3), 345–358.

Stewart, F. (1979). *International Technology Transfer: Issues and Policy Options.* Washington, DC: The World Bank. (Staff Working Paper 344).

United Nations. Department of International Economic and Social Affairs. Statistical Office. (1979). *Improving Social Statistics in Developing Countries: Conceptual Framework and Methods.* New York, NY: United Nations. [Studies in Methods. Series F, 25].

United States. National Science Foundation. (1982). *The Five-Year Outlook on Science and Technology, 1981.* Washington, DC: U.S. Government Printing Office.

University of Wisconsin. Regional Planning and Area Development

Project. (1979). *Opportunities for Development: A Reconnaissance of Central Tunisia*. Madison, WI: University of Wisconsin.

Uphoff, N.T., et al. (1979). *Feasibility and Application of Rural Development Participation: A State-of-the-Art Paper*. Ithaca, NY: Cornell University, Rural Development Committee.

Uphoff, N.T. & Esman, M.J. (1974). *Local Organization for Rural Development Analysis of Asian Experience*. Ithaca, NY: Cornell University, Rural Development Committee.

Visaria, P. (1979). "Demographic factors and the distribution of income: some issues." In *Economic and Demographic Change, Issues for the 1980s: Proceedings of the Conference*. Liège, Belgium (n.p.).

Weisel, P.F. & Mickelwait, D.R. (1978). *Designing Rural Development Projects: An Approach*. Washington, DC: Development Alternatives, Inc.

Weiss, C., Jr. (1979). Mobilizing technology for developing countries. *Science,* (203), 1083–1089. (World Bank Reprint 95).

Woodward, A.M. (1980). Future information requirements of the Third World. *Journal of Information Science,* 1, 259–265.

The World Bank. (1979). *Environment and Development*. Washington, DC: The World Bank.

The World Bank. (1980). *World Development Report 1980*. Washington, DC: The World Bank.

3

Information Transfer as Development Support

Introduction

This paper is about a project, supported by the W.K. Kellogg Foundation and carried out in the School of Education at Syracuse University, that assists the work of adult educators in developing countries with a new mode of information dissemination and exchange. The assumption is that information transferred to and from developing countries by appropriate technological means not only expands the participants' connectedness with adult educators elsewhere and facilitates problem solving in the course of their practice or research, but also represents an asset to American adult educators with a global perspective.

Interdisciplinary inquiry always brings about a certain wonderment in the face of so many diverse and complex areas of research and professional experience. One is reminded that creativity has been defined as the "recognition of an underlying relationship between apparently diverse phenomena" (Gordon 1979, p. 18). Often it is the heterogeneity of our approaches and conflicting interpretations of concepts that helps us to see problems in new ways. Once a problem appears to us from a different angle or with a heightened intensity, it may give rise to the excitement of possibilities. This can happen either when we think about the problem or when nothing is further from us than thinking about it. This is the unfolding phase of a project, usually the easiest, happiest, and shortest phase. Soon new uncertainties and questions set in, but by this time the shared vision of possibilities and a better understanding of individual reactions usually enables team members to enter a prolonged phase of realistic discussion. We struggled to recognize the limitations of our project, to identify what we mean by "adult educators in developing countries," and to explore how information support may be offered to Third World colleagues without sounding presumptuous.

The quandary raised by the accelerating impact of computer and telecommunication technologies on international human communication is this: On the one hand, probably few people living completely isolated from information flows (electronic or nonelectronic) can use their human potential to the fullest; on the other, information in any form is not neutral but implicitly or explicitly value-laden, and on occasion can be more disruptive than useful. The very ease of communication and information diffusion has created a totally new set of relationships, problems and responsibilities. These realities confront all projects, even those created and managed with the most serious determination to remain nonpolitical.

The conceptual framework of this paper can be expressed by three questions:

- Can the transfer of timely and relevant information to adult educators, researchers and policymakers working in environments of technology scarcity serve as a form of development assistance?
- What problems are encountered by an information service that navigates between the hazard of supplying irrelevant and useless information and the hazard of cultural imperialism by information dissemination?
- Will the experience with a computer-assisted information counseling service to developing countries help us to learn enough about the nature of international information transfer to identify the need for policies and for further research?

This paper will unfold along the following themes: Information as a form of development assistance; problems encountered by information delivery to adult educators in developing countries; and the lessons learned from the information dissemination program are discussed. Two major paradigms of the Kellogg Project's assistance to adult educators in developing countries are described: The International Information Sharing Network (IISN) and personalized long-distance Information Counseling (IC). Main features include information service, continuous evaluation and learning, probing into the elusive nature of development information, and the identification of problems for future research. Reflections on the role of adult education in Third World societies and on the nature of international information flows are interwoven throughout the paper in order to detect the individual and societal issues that arise at the interface of these two concerns.

Why, one might ask, should we be concerned with these issues? The paper argues that information, be it in the form of data, narrative or image, is not a neutral agent but reflects the values and expectations of those who produce, select, manage, transmit and use it. In recent years not only personal interpretations of information but also the international exchange of scientific, technological and socioeconomic data have been politicized. We must ask if education, research and civic activity are ready to deal with these issues.

A section on "Awakening from Innocence" refers to the realization, experienced by many development and information practitioners, that the best intentions to remain apolitical in the design and implementation of information services cannot justify an abdication of responsibility for examining relevant policy issues. Main concerns include the equity of access, the technology gap, information overload vs. deprivation, and the inadvertent threat of cultural domination by the dissemination of knowledge.

In regard to questions posed at the outset, information transfer is recognized as development assistance under certain circumstances, some policy quandaries are identified, and implications for professional discussions and future research are reviewed.

Timeliness of the Research

The major practical goal of the Kellogg Project is to strengthen practice and research in adult education through the following activities:

- Development of a text and image handling information system for an archive consisting of records of professional organizations and of major figures in North American adult education, using recent advances in optical disk and laser technology
- Promotion of computer-assisted information exchange among adult educators in a large number of countries
- Cooperation with other academic units at Syracuse University, especially with the Center for the Study of Citizenship, to address critical issues in the relationship of adult learning and civic literacy.

The project (a) brings together adult educators, historians, and social, computer and information scientists for research; (b) coordinates a visiting scholar program; and (c) provides an international electronic network, AEDNET, offering an electronic journal and a course.

At the beginning, as the project proposal hovered between ideas and drafts, it became clear that its international orientation could not be realized without the conviction that in developing societies there is a great richness of creativity and professional experience along with an appalling weakness of the information technology infrastructure. International research projects limited to information dissemination without the recipients contributing their own knowledge to the discourse miss an important opportunity. By describing the role of the Kellogg Project's interactive International Information Sharing Network (IISN) and the service of Information Counseling (IC) that together span physical distance and cultural pluralism, we hope to contribute to the probing of such questions as posed at the beginning of this paper.

Information connectedness is the result of two intertwining processes:

(1) the provision of information by one individual (sometimes by counseling and other times by spontaneous and informal action), and (2) the
receipt, scrutiny, acceptance, application, and critique of the information
by another person. The recipient often responds by sending back new
ideas and insights. Information connectedness is a dynamic relationship
in which each party gives and gains something.

Why, then, are both development and information specialists skeptical
about the possibility of "connecting" over cultural and political distances? (Bannon, Barry and Hoist 1982, Bell 1986, Hattori 1986, Lucas
and Freedman 1983). Critics speak against either the futility of attempts
to identify information needs from a distance, or the possibility of inadvertently creating a dependency relationship with recipients. This means
that information (given or received) is considered either too powerless to
make any difference or too powerful to avoid domineering. Maybe the
explanation is that neither critics nor advocates of long-distance information transfer know enough about the process. At the Kellogg Project
we decided to create the service against all odds, because we wanted to
inform and be informed in order to help and learn at the same time. As
Scott-Stevens (1987, p. 171) suggested, "the most effective, and 'ideal'
transfer of knowledge is one in which both parties learn something . . . ."

Additional motivation came from the following assumptions:

- Organizations engaged in technical aid perceive adult education
  practice and research as significant resources for socioeconomic
  progress. The warning that "educational strategies must be part of
  an overall development strategy" can be heard throughout the development discourse (Simmons 1979, p. 1014).
- In spite of this view at the international level, adult educators in developing countries find it difficult to participate in societywide discussions, perhaps because they are not seen by policymakers as
  perpetrators of technological progress.
- This image is beginning to change in the modernizing industrial
  sectors where the value of lifelong education for managers and
  technologists has been discovered (Ajuogu 1981).
- Similarly, the traditional low profile of the information specialist is
  beginning to shift to that of a more visible actor as governments in
  many countries turn to the task of drafting telecommunication and
  information policies (Wesley-Tanaskovic 1985).
- Although the technological infrastructure of education, information and telecommunication remains weak in economically hard-
  pressed countries, awareness of its key role in the economy is on
  the rise. It is now widely understood that before nations can develop their own research and development sector, human resources
  must be strengthened.

- It is at the crossroads of these trends that innovation in adult education by the increased use of information seems to be within reach. What people desperately miss in many societies is the possibility to change conditions.

Even though a long-distance information counseling and networking service is but one small contribution to this new and yet very fragile hope in developing countries, its introduction seems almost astonishingly timely. A study of the service furthermore provides insights into the relationship of adult education and the communication of information.

We have to emphasize that information dissemination is only one dimension of this effort. The other, more significant, objective is to create a flow of information sharing with the active participation of adult educators in developing regions. Indigenous experience and knowledge in grassroots development and institutional change form an invaluable resource in each country that can be shared with colleagues in other regions. Through referrals among network participants and a newsletter, the project has the capability to support local creativity and initiative. Information isolation is a serious barrier to development communication. By alleviating isolation and promoting human linkages even in small, incremental steps, the International Information Sharing Network (IISN) acts as a conduit for increasing information exchange in which adult educators in developing countries play the dominant role.

Reflections on Information

The genesis of the words "information" and "inform" embodies an ominous symbolism. Almost all of the modern social connotations and anxieties of the information age were already present in the Latin "information"; it meant "image" as well as the process of "giving form or shape" to something. The verb "inform" denoted not only "to form or shape" but also "to instruct and to educate." There was here an implication of a conscious attempt to influence the thought process, to transform ideas, to change opinions. Today, even if we claim objectivity and neutrality in respect to the transmission of information content, if we had a way of testing, we might find few messages without at least some degree of motivation to form somebody's thinking. For example abstracts, excerpts, summaries, other forms of condensation, and analytic reports of a text represent conscious selection. Automated indexing is a step toward the impersonal treatment of information, but it is available only for certain professional tasks.

Conceptually, the interpretation of the meaning of information for social and personal life depends on the context of the research discipline where the discourse or the characteristics of information originates. As to the interpretation of a message in the course of its use, many scientists agree that raw and fragmentary data can be transformed into finished and usable information in the framework of a user's situation and need (Repo 1987, p. 4).

Beyond these basic relationships, characterizations of the nature of information fan out into a voluminous literature encompassing the research fields of several disciplines. The focus on information phenomena shifts from the process of informing in anthropology through the relationship between information and uncertainty in the corporate environment studied in management science, to the value of information in economics, and communication between source and receiver in communication science, just to name a few. Research in several interdisciplinary areas, particularly cognitive psychology, linguistics, diffusion of innovations, and knowledge utilization, is committed to explore the patterns of thinking, expressing, interacting, problem solving and applying information at the subjective level.

With the exception of the latter direction, most definitions underlying earlier theories of information retrieval and dissemination miss the fact that information and knowledge can be either objective or subjective. Information phenomena must be verifiable and measurable in order to be tested. Scientific information lends itself readily to this criterion, and forms the conceptual basis of much research underlying the design and evaluation of information retrieval systems and dissemination programs. But then, why are information systems meeting human communication needs with such questionable results? Why do outspoken critics of the performance of information retrieval abound? Are there idiosyncratic approaches to the ways people seek information that systems fail to anticipate? This dilemma, in both its technological and psychological aspects, has challenged many fine minds, and has led to investigations in a number of disciplines. Some researchers are questioning even the basic philosophical context of research: "Current thinking about computers and their impact on society has been shaped by a rationalistic tradition that needs to be reexamined and challenged as a source of understanding" (Winograd and Flores 1986, p. 16).

The act of information exchange with adult educators in developing countries is not only a scientific but also a political and cultural problem that brings questions of rationality into direct interplay with questions of cultural relevance. This circumstance alone is capable of creating an almost painful ambiguity in the project environment. As researchers of the legislative process observed: "The vocabulary of science is elaborate and specialized, but objective and factual; that of politics is more everyday, and is centered on value judgments" (United States . . . 1971, p. 5). Our project deals with ambiguity also at the international level, because the information that passes between adult educators in Kenya or India and the Kellogg Project is characterized not only by technical features but also by an intercultural relationship.

We cannot but accept that subjective and unpredictable factors influence the course of each information transaction. It does not suffice to deal with project activities at the level of systematic facts, no matter how carefully and objectively collected and organized. Information is activated by its use. In the course of its use and by its application, information can change its meaning. We recognize that the challenge of two kinds of information—the rational/technical and the intuitive/personal—that pass through the international network, is upon us.

The Learning Organization Approach

Geographic distance creates a precarious environment for the design of international programs of information delivery and dissemination. Three factors produce unorthodox circumstances: Information requirements and needs pertain to a faraway and literally unexplorable user situation, face-to-face interaction with information requestors is impossible, and what long-distance interaction exists may be hampered by the doubts and reservations of participants. While trust between users and transmitters is always a significant component of information delivery, it is especially critical in intercultural programs. A distant information project is an ongoing struggle to overcome these hurdles.

Information production, dissemination and application form a continuum. Caplan (1975) outlined its phases as *diffusion* (the dissemination of research findings), *utilization* (putting knowledge to work), and *application* (knowledge that has an effect on action). A crucial link, however, was missing from this model. We suggest that *the acceptance* of information is the basis of all further actions by the recipient: consideration of the message, selection of the content or parts of it, use, learning, integration with what is known, judging the information's relative value, and its application to a task or problem (Brindle and Dosa 1980, p. 3). Although it is possible for people to become aware of the content of a message without the conscious act of accepting it, the application of new knowledge can hardly be successful without its acceptance by the applier in cultural as well as intellectual terms.

The concepts of trust and information acceptance are not factors usually considered by the planners of dissemination systems. But for many users, the important question about information concerns not the process by which it was produced and transmitted, but the person who produced or transmitted it. The central role of trust and acceptance of information possibly account for the formation of tight cliques in most societies for talking over important matters. Maruyama (1988, pp. 67–68) alluded to this phenomenon by describing the practice of excluding foreigners from decision making groups in multicultural corporations. Scott-Stevens (1987) analyzed the expressions of trust and their impact on technical aid projects.

When we recognized that the feelers of a formal information need-assessment study might not reach below the surface of generalities, we adopted the model of the learning organization as the most viable approach to a situation where traditional ways of systematic planning held little promise. The learning organization is one in which the prevailing management style encourages frank discussion of the roots of problems and ways of improvements in everyday organizational life. The concept is well known in development and technical assistance studies. Sometimes criticized as too idealistic, the approach has nevertheless penetrated several community development projects. In an organization where learning is a conscious act, an atmosphere of openness encourages staff members to exchange their ideas, experiments, errors and renewed attempts to bring goals and actions into harmony (Korten 1981, p. 498). This corresponds to our vision of a project that continually learns from participants, information users, and its own accumulating experience.

Information for Social Integration

Adult educators are in the forefront of development activities in rural areas, congested urban centers, and poverty-stricken urban fringes. They are involved with provincial and central governments, and increasingly play a role in people's reach for independent existence through small and medium-size private enterprises. The privatization of public services, a growing trend in developing countries, needs the concerted efforts of nonformal adult education in creating programs for new work-related skills and practices (Nankani 1988). Training in financial management, organizational communication, and the coordination of diverse activities in business ventures is in great demand. The Organization for Economic Cooperation and Development (1988, p. 25) reports that not only formal enterprises, but also "the informal private sector plays a critical role in development and should be encouraged." Social integration strives to bring all ethnic, economic, cultural, and political factions of the population into society building.

Another trend, evident in the entire range of development experiences, is the growing technology orientation of societies. In markets and in government-subsidized projects, information and communication technologies create a situation in which the problems of weak coordination policies become painfully visible. Existing institutions are faced with technical and administrative changes which could not be anticipated and built into the education system (Martin 1983, Nettleford 1982).

The propelling forces of change are economic and technological necessities, cultural drives, and human needs. Although we cannot develop an adequate understanding of the environment of each participant in the international information sharing network, experience with development projects gave rise to a perspective on the broader institutional picture. It became clear that the introduction of innovations in education and information activities is related to, and in some countries integrated with, national development plans (United Nations Educational . . . 1986). The factors that affect economic and social development also determine the process and outcome of information transfer.

Cutting across all economic sectors, three main forces exercise a potent influence on crossnational communication. First, the same economic determinants that drive institution building and the acquisition of technology also motivate the acquisition of information. Concerns for more favorable trade relations and for the strengthening of indigenous inventions are interwoven with efforts for literacy programs, the growth of vocational education, and the establishment of national centers of productivity and technological information.

Second, the tension between domestic poverty and regional and international competitiveness is beginning to leave its mark on social life (Kranzberg 1985). The slowness of institutions to react to the need for change can be especially harmful in cases of information-based agencies such as regulatory bodies, policy making ministries and cultural councils. Scientific as well as political information is needed to forecast and prepare for change. The gap between the graduates of foreign universities and those educated at home, as well as the gap between the information affluent and the information deprived, hinder the evolution of modern information systems and services. However, such inequalities manifest themselves mainly in the formal hierarchies at the workplace. Creativity, evident in small, informal local projects, has not been held back even by the lack of funding and weak research infrastructures. As the realization grows that information is not merely a support to, but an organic part of research production and dissemination, people engaged in these activities are becoming more visible players in societies.

The third main force exerting a powerful influence on crossnational communication is the trend towards popular participation in development and societal planning. This trend poses a new challenge to adult education programs (United Nations 1987). There are more people aware of alternative ways to a better quality of life and of the value of cultural identity than ever before. These trends are producing an unprecedented need for the integration of education and information policies in all developing countries.

We can identify some of the institutional forces behind the transformation of Third World societies, but we cannot easily define policies of an international network towards these forces. If information transfer is not a neutral agent in intercultural work, how can a technical assistance project avoid involvement in the internal educational and information processes of its host country? As social integration progresses in a community, will information provided by the long-distance counseling service support the individual information user or the larger process of society building? In other words, is it for the individual adult educator or for the social environment that a cultural bias inadvertently attached to an information transmittal might represent a certain threat? The following observations on networking and information counseling may render some of these questions even more urgent.

Information Sharing Networks

Many groups and individuals fail to define and describe their kinds of network. At present there are probably as many assumptions about the nature of networks as there are people involved in them. For example, consider the difference between the following two descriptions, one referring to a centralized communication mode of individuals, the other speaking of networking as a social phenomenon, characteristic of our age. One suggests a technologically controllable process, the other implies a force that seems to be stronger than its technological structures and boundaries.

> A personal communication network is those interconnected individuals who are linked by patterned communication flows to a focal individual (Rogers and Kincaid 1981, p. 347).
> The network is the institution of our time: An open system, a dissipative structure so richly coherent that it is in constant flux, poised for reordering, capable of endless transformation (Ferguson 1980, p. 213).

Research carried out in several disciplines resulted in the now familiar concepts of kinship and social support networks, invisible colleges, learning networks, interpersonal communication networks, diffusion networks and interagency linkages. Messages vary from confidential dialogues to formal information dissemination to participants, and they can cover every possible subject. The transition from traditional modes of interaction to electronic networks and electronic mail is affecting all types of professional work.

Development and coordination of a centralized or semicentralized network require not only the usual administrative decisions but also the resolution of new policy issues. These are especially demanding when (1) networks are computerized, (2) electronic networks assume new roles and responsibilities for the coordination of information flows, (3) informal networks grow and either fragment or formalize, and (4) a network uses mixed media because some participants have access to electronic communication while others do not. Policy measures which can keep a network from deteriorating into chaos include the extent of coordination; eligibility to participate; equity of access; quality control; the credibility and validity of information shared; ownership of ideas, software or data; confidentiality; free or fee-based participation; language problems and, above all, the cultural and practical relevance of information to its recipients. The complexity of information laws and regulations grows in proportion to the technological sophistication of networks. Some forms of network applications—electronic mail, bulletin boards, conferencing—are way ahead of research on their social impact and concomitant policies.

Human resource networks may be created in three ways. The person-to-person (snowballing or chainlinking) approach starts with a few contacts and grows in an informal and unstructured way. The other method results from a systematic search for expertise through directories, registers and membership lists of associations. The third is a subscription-based service allowing members to transmit inquiries, receive answers, obtain electronic journals and newspapers, or to use electronic mail. The first approach results in a spontaneous, flexible and heterogeneous network that cuts across different professional roles, programs and geographic regions. The second, more comprehensive method, usually is limited to specialized audiences and subjects. The third, and fastest growing, model provides electronic shopping for information. Advances in electronic networking tend toward the interconnection of a very large number of different and unrelated networks. The Internet is the best known example.

The most difficult problem in information sharing is to achieve equity of access to information sources. Adult education programs in low-income countries have a critical need for training skills and teaching materials acceptable by local cultures. However, a vast gap exists in each country between large-scale information systems introduced by the government or foreign consultants on the one hand, and community educators and developers on the other. Human resource networking and information sharing within communities is a mode of learning that is more likely to gain the trust of local participants than the large-scale official infrastructures.

How was the paradigm of networking applied by our project? The International Information Sharing Network (IISN) has been developed:

- for the purpose of information dissemination and sharing in a semi-formalized mode (the information dissemination being coordinated by the information counselor, but information sharing among participants carried out either through formal or informal contacts), and
- using mixed media (nonelectronic and electronic depending on the participant's choice).

We opted for the person-to-person process. International directories tend to perpetuate hierarchies of the educated elites in developing countries. Extending contacts step by step has more of a chance to reach not only ministries and universities, but also rural extension programs and community groups.

Information Counseling

For some people, "information" has the connotation of opportunities and the ability to make choices. For others, information means a maze of chaotic messages, meaningless facts and impersonal organizations which, as the standard complaint runs, "never respond to human need." Adult education practitioners in developing countries, many of them part-time trainers and volunteers, work in extension services, evening classes or nonformal rural settings where neither staff time nor resources allow for institutional information gathering. Experience passes orally from person to person. This process is the very strength of informal communication, but it also misses some potentially useful resources. For example, planners, researchers and program administrators indicate that they often need demographic and socioeconomic data for their work. They soon find that internationally sponsored data collection efforts are likely to be modeled on large-scale prototype projects requiring special skills to adapt them to local settings. The alternative is primary data collection, an expensive and time consuming activity.

The process of "informing" seems to be the answer to such problems. Many kinds of "informing" take place in education programs, social service agencies, extension programs and libraries. Information counseling is a new approach that has been developed by drawing on the best features of several guidance models. It provides in-depth and personalized assistance in the acquisition, use and application of information and data. It is an interactive process by which the information counselor (IC) determines the optimal way to meet the information requirements and needs of an individual or organization, assists the user in evaluating and applying the obtained information, and assures follow-up in order to evaluate the effectiveness of assistance. Although information systems have become more user-friendly, the complexity of resources, products and networks necessitates more individualized advising in converting them into usable packages.

"Good" information is relative. It depends on the cultural relevance and acceptability of its source, the circumstances of its use, as well as its timing, form, quantity and level of technicality. Information counseling for adult educators in developing countries deals with some or all of the following types of sources:

- PRIMARY DATA, the raw materials of factual information appearing in the electronic databases and reports of international organizations and technical assistance programs, and the statistical compilations of governments and nongovernmental organizations
- ANALYZED AND EVALUATED DATA in development plans, compendia, summary project reports and scientific papers
- INTERPRETATIONS OF DATA and comments on their implications embedded in government reports, professional responses, published policy papers, editorials and commentaries: the opinion literature
- CURRENT EDUCATIONAL MATERIALS such as teaching tools, textbooks, software, syllabi, program descriptions, manuals, tests and tutorial sources in print, electronic, audio or visual form.
- HISTORICAL MATERIALS and records in manuscript collections, monographs, papers, lectures, and computerized files
- PERSONAL EXPERTISE in organizations, professional societies, educational institutions, communities and local programs.

In the context of development, information is the vehicle of technology and knowledge transfer to and from developing countries. There is abundant evidence that this process succeeds only if carried out multi-directionally. Information sharing links can lead network participants to the recognition of their own priorities; the assessment of new educational technology in terms of cultural fit; and motivation of local creativity by helping trainers and organizers to learn about the experiences of programs in other regions or countries.

Information Requirements and Needs

Informing cannot be effective without the information counselor's understanding of the nature of information requirements and needs of potential recipients. When people respond to questionnaires or interviews probing into their information needs, they can express an interest only in the kinds of data, expertise and resources of which they are aware. They feel that they can or must use such support for their work or everyday life, so they require it. These kinds of wishes and demands are *information requirements*. On the other hand, people might feel frustrated by carrying out a task or making a plan, because something in the way they picture these decisions is missing. They might have an *information need,* but they are not aware of it.

Formal information need assessment by questionnaires presents a problem even in a homogeneous social and psychological environment, let alone in an unfamiliar cultural setting at a considerable distance. Conceptual interpretation of questions might be different enough from those of the researcher to render responses less than useful. Information *requirements can be identified* and *needs can be approximated* only gradually, in the course of interaction and information counseling. There are alternative approaches to eliciting information requirements and developing a "feel" for unspecified information needs. Electronic mail is beginning to be used in a few of the more advanced economies, but in environments marked by technological scarcity oral communication and, in distant relationships, personal letters are still valued means of contact. For example, letters by the information counselor to network participants express interest in their work and encourage inquiries. Responses are likely to bring to the surface a variety of information requirements and a few hints at needs implied by the respondents' work environment and task-related problems. Letters and, where available, email messages are analyzed by the counselor, and categories of "requirements" and tentative "needs" are charted. The results are usually more revealing than data extracted from questionnaire responses.

Unspecified and unexpressed information needs may be approximated only as one would map a distant land based on hearsay and secondhand experience. For example, an analysis of working conditions, tasks, struggles and aspirations of adult educators, as described in country case studies, may elicit likely information needs. In the following examples, the information counselor can identify unexpressed needs. A discussion of the training of community development extension workers in ten East African countries reveals that "international sharing of experiences, skills, resources is encouraged through joint training at subregional and regional centres . . . " (Nturibi 1982, p. 113). From a summary of a survey of nonformal adult education at Commonwealth universities we learn that there is a need "to develop a human resource data bank which would include the names and institutions of those with considerable experience in nonformal education and development, both in developing and developed countries . . . " (Draper 1986, p. 73). In a third case, we are told that "what perhaps lies at the root of the crisis in educational sciences and educational research is their lack of relevance to the development of individuals and societies. New forms of interdisciplinarity are necessary to meet requirements . . . " (Gelpi 1985, p. 252). Examining the description of each of the above cases, the information counselor charts the map of assumed information needs.

In our project, evaluation of the information counseling service is being assisted by two kinds of data collection. Each query and its answer are analyzed for the nature of the requirement, implicit needs, and the mode of response. This "monitoring" information is stored in the system. The other wave of data collection inquires into the perceptions of users. Conceptually, the assessment is based on the approach used by some development assistance projects, a combination of ongoing monitoring and retrospective evaluation (Cernea 1979, pp. 15–29).

Figure 3.1 is a rudimentary outline of adult education roles, types of information requirements, information needs one can infer from these roles, and potential resources for information counseling.

Adult Education, Information and Development

In 1980, the International Council for Adult Education established a Commission of Inquiry into Adult Education and Poverty. The question was raised, "How far was a separate identification [of adult education] necessary to enhance the contribution of adult education, given that integration into other development strategies and programs appeared crucial?" (Duke 1986, p. 31). At the time similar questions were debated by several other professions. Each evidenced a grave concern about the unmitigated social ills in large areas of the world, but no profession was financially and administratively capable of introducing development assistance programs without the backing of international agencies and the collaboration of other professions. Moreover, professional organizations were questioning the very effectiveness of international aid. It was widely recognized that interventions introduced in developing countries have not brought the world closer to bridging the gap between the poor and the economically advanced countries.

In the early 1970s most funding agencies introduced a new policy almost simultaneously. The mandate stressed assistance to projects in the

Figure 3.1
Information Requirements and Referral Sources

Potential Users	Type of Information	Sources
Learners	Course outlines	National organiza-tions
Teachers	Workshop topics	
Trainers	Text of lectures	
Counselors	Teaching materials	
Advisors	(AV, computer software)	Regional organiza-tions
	Textbooks	
	Evaluation tools	
	Course catalogs	
	Human expertise	Professional associa-tions
Administrators	Management techniques	Intergovernmental agencies
Managers	Analytic tools	
Coordinators	Assessment methods	
Consultants	Evaluation methods	
	Funding sources	Nongovernmental organizations
	Experience sharing	
	Basic approaches	
	Marketing methods	Clearinghouses
Planners	Planning models	Networks
Policymakers	Policy statements	
Program sponsors	Reviews	
	Studies	
	Demographic data	Databases
	Socioeconomic data	
		Libraries
Researchers	Research reports	
Evaluators	Journal papers	
Historians	Conference papers	Archives
Higher educators	Historical sources	
Publishers	Archives/Records	
	Data for secondary analysis	Special collections
		Adult education programs
		Specialists' expertise

poorest countries, and to efforts which mobilized indigenous participa-tion in the development process. Development policy thus became a ma-jor guiding factor in planning for adult education, literacy and commu-nity development projects in the Third World. But by the mid-1980s major agencies all but abandoned the emphasis on basic needs in favor of assistance to private enterprises, the privatization of several government services, and strengthening the economic base of struggling countries. Still, the philosophy that had originally undergirded the basic needs policy remains a strong influence on the work of professional groups, including adult educators, in development programs.

Experience-based case studies as well as the theoretical literature of development science recognize our lack of empirical knowledge about the conditions of the poor and their capabilities to use education for improving their quality of life. Concerned with the need for data as the basis of economic improvements, Srinivasan (1977) proposed that characteristic conditions of the poor—especially low income and unemployment—could be measured by people's lack of access to information about social services and to opportunities in education, skill training, and preventative health care. He held that unless a society provided channels to and assistance in using coping skills, access to opportunities remained a haphazard matter favoring the educated elite who are better equipped to "find out" on their own. The provision of opportunity-information, asserted a development specialist, was one of the basic human needs (Pradervand 1980).

Awakening from Innocence

The community of information professionals harbors a heterogeneous breed representing microcosms of service, business, research, technology and policy orientation. These categories of context and value pull information professionals in numerous directions, and occasionally create either a conflict of commitments or successful boundary spanning within the professional life of an individual. Service orientation is more a state of mind than a career choice. It can be awakened but not taught. It is the least exclusive of the many microcosms of values; indeed, it is often combined with research or technological applications.

For nearly four decades, information specialists with an international and service orientation, representing skills ranging from statistical analysis through librarianship and from teaching to community organization have been working on projects in countries that have emerged from colonialism. The history of foreign consultancy in this field is long and colorful. In the past, one of the main moral rewards of service rendered to developing countries arose from the assumption that information transfer to the Third World is always beneficial to the recipients. The picture of the world in which information moved from knowledgeable consultants to information-starved recipients was relatively simple and comfortable. Most (albeit not all) information services created for developing countries were motivated by good will, implemented on the basis of a schematic and often inflexible design, and evaluated with the underlying conviction that, possible flaws in any particular service notwithstanding, the information surely did lots of good to its users.

The emergence of the basic needs policy with its insistence on the local participants' active involvement in project planning, design and evaluation, has quite roughly intruded on the idealism of information service providers. The rise of disturbing doubts about information—its validity, credibility, appropriateness and relevance to the users—has shaken the remaining innocence of well-intentioned service consultants. Advocates of the basic needs philosophy tried to turn rigid project designs into revisable and open-ended processes. A new corps of information and communication scientists in developing countries came forth with a diagnosis of cultural imperialism in the form of sophisticated information dissemination programs and effectively packaged messages. Through case studies and examples, management information systems were criticized for being centralized in ministries, the production of unnecessary data, overemphasis on technology, excessive complexity, lack of capability to identify problems in project implementation, and the failure to disseminate reports (Mickelwait et al. 1978, pp. 219–344).

Targets of the resentment of local leaders against planning and communication patterns introduced from the top down included not only central governments and foreign advisers, but also expatriate consultants. Recipients of rural information dissemination services often felt that they had received meaningless advice from irrelevant foreign cultures (Prajuli 1986). Participants at a high-level seminar in Mexico, jointly sponsored by the Aiijic Institute of International Education and the International Council for Educational Development, commented that "in communication as in education, the high-tech hardware, such as computers and satellites, is starved by lack of software, or content . . . " (Hechinger 1985, p. 70). Global trade relations as well as cooperation among information professionals were adversely affected by political and economic controversies over international data flows (Konoshima 1986). By the mid-1980s, the awakening of service-oriented information consultants was nearly complete.

Information as Development Assistance

Many factors contributed to the transformation of the information provider's enthusiasm into disillusionment. Questions were raised about services, research and policies. Who has access to the systems? What is the difference between barrier-free information service and service free of charge? Who collects the data, under whose sponsorship and for what purpose? Who owns the data in a locally produced database: the sponsor agency or its indigenous counterpart? What is society's responsibility for making information available, who are the information poor, and what is "equitable" access? How can service providers identify "appropriate" information for transfer? The implications of these probings for decisions faced by information professionals can be overwhelming, but identifying solutions for individual information-giving situations can make professional struggles worthwhile.

For purposes of this project, we defined development as positive changes permeating the entire fabric of society and the quality of human life. Such changes, including economic, technological, cultural, social and political dimensions, are only partially measurable either quantitatively or qualitatively. However, a growing volume of research is available on alternative measurements applicable to basic human needs, the quality of life, and the quality of the environment.

The problem with the above definition is that the term "positive" is relativistic and ambiguous. What is "positive?" From whose benchmark is it envisaged? If the top elite of a country rises to relative economic security, is this a positive change for the large masses of the population who are not sharing the benefits of development? Obviously advocates of "trickle down" theories will answer in the affirmative, while development practitioners who consider meeting the basic needs of the poor the measure of development, will respond negatively.

The term "positive change" may be interpreted only within the framework of the different assumptions used by each movement, each social group, and each individual. It is with this understanding that the expression "positive change" can become acceptable as part of the definition of development. People, policymakers as well as all those affected by policies, have to define development themselves before others define it for them (Kassam 1986, Krueger 1986).

This relativistic approach to the definition is used because of the absence of any cohesive, theoretically based, and generally accepted definition of the development process. Nor can we fall back upon a universal philosophical grounding for technical assistance for development. The moral argument has always been present in the history of development aid, but it has been applied mainly on an ad-hoc basis without a comprehensive ethical system. Riddell (1986, p. 25) argues that

> What is perhaps most surprising, given the prominence that aid has had in the development literature and the vigour with which aid advocates have appealed to morality in lobbying governments to increase aid allocations, is that there has been little or no attempt within that literature to provide a systematic and rigorous analysis of the ethics of aid.

As we lack a comprehensive, internationally accepted ethical system of development assistance and as we search in vain for a standard definition of development, the concept of "positive change" has to be interpreted by each sector of the economy and each field of professional practice. Against the background of the development environment, many adult educators and information professionals are rethinking and redefining their roles.

The adult education and literacy movements in Third World countries are in constant flux. Throughout the innumerable small- and large-scale efforts one can distinguish two main trends which sometimes seem to run on a collision course and at other times mingle and overlap. One strong thrust, propelled by academic educators and government planners, aims at professionalization, quantification in planning and assessment research, and the introduction of high technology. The other direction emphasizes indigenous community forces and cultural heritage. In terms of information provision, these trends represent two broad categories of needs and requirements. The need for technical and demographic data, models of systematic planning, analytic tools to be adapted to local management practice, psychological studies on learning, and standards of professional performance are evident from the literature. At the other end of the spectrum strong arguments are voiced for culturally relevant knowledge, social learning, participatory research, information on people's perceptions of the quality of life, and movements promoting self-learning and self-help.

The day-by-day human existence in rural areas, suggests Medlin (1983, p. 32), should form the basis for education planning. "What better place to start than by examining the contexts in which the consumers of knowledge must struggle for improving their often miserable existence?" Equality in the availability of education and training is a primary goal of planning (Lourie 1985, p. 250). Gelpi (1985, pp. 149–150) believes that "disparities existing in education [are] aggravated by the concentration of information processing facilities . . . and by living conditions." The strengthening of local capacity for applied research plays a dominant role in the aspirations of innovators (Hall 1981). Urevbu (1985) relates the need for scientific information to adult education policy, and Kidd (1981) points out existing problems in need of in-depth investigation.

Part of the information problem in developing countries is the lack of social intelligence concerning trends in technology transfer, indigenous technology development, and the social impact of these processes. The following are a few examples of the new thinking related to information technology in developing economies, implicitly arguing that the strengthening of the information base of a society represents assistance to overall development:

- As information and communication systems are introduced, they create a profound need for the clarification of their social impact and for the conceptualization of their application to development activities.
- The fundamentals of the development process are being reexamined to assure the relevance of training in information provision and use, and in the selection and management of computer and telecommunication technology.
- Interest in the cooperation of various disciplines is growing, and is being supported by information sharing, computer conferencing and electronic mail where the infrastructure is available. Counseling must raise awareness of the potentially adverse impact of these communication devices on information equality unless adult education and other professions help to spread their benefits.
- Governments and several professions are turning their attention to the economics of knowledge and the privatization of information production and programs. Transferring responsibility to private companies is a new trend, giving rise to new and as yet poorly understood information needs.
- A growing number of policymakers urge development of a core of indigenous social science researchers in communication and information technology, but researchers lack basic resources and contacts with their counterparts abroad.
- Interactive community learning processes, formerly overshadowed by large-scale modernization projects, are gaining importance even though they are still lacking access to information resources.

In the light of these transformations in trends and thinking, one of the most crucial questions is: If information transfer is a form of development assistance, how can the counseling service and the information sharing network deliver culturally and professionally valid information without imposing foreign values on adult educators in developing countries? A few specific examples may illuminate this quandary.

First, we should consider that the classification of adult education goals by the outcomes of programs encompasses the following: social integration (concerned with acculturation), social responsibility (concerned with citizenship), social change (concerned with transformation), and technical competence (concerned with skills) (Boshier 1985, p. 13). Perceptive as this classification is in the American context, it could not be adopted for an intercultural information project without considerable difficulties. Even if an information counselor made every effort to avoid personal judgments, information resources are full of cultural assumptions and interpretations of facts, events and situations. The ambiguity of the situation and an information provider's inability to vouch for the nature of information resources raise the question: Will information concerning social change provided to adult educators in developing countries be construed as assistance for achieving social change, or interference in local cultures?

Another example is provided by assistance projects which use manuals and training tools to teach the uses of communication technology. Competence in computer-aided instruction or database searching is an important goal in training, but success will be assured only by the trainer's familiarity with the technological infrastructure in the recipient country. One dimension of this understanding is the ability to assess technology in the cultural context. "Technology" includes software, hardware, specifications, criteria for selection, social skills in introduction and popularization, impact on learning, and training. Development specialists expect that information support for technology assessment will represent a competence of growing significance (Ghosh 1984, Srinivasan 1982).

The third example addresses rural areas in developing countries where the past of the culture survives in oral history and traditional forms of communication. In comparison, in urban centers historical tradition is concentrated in museums, archives and ethnic crafts whose value has recently been discovered by both scholarship and tourism. All approaches to the preservation of culture need a conceptual foundation and state-of-the-art methods, and thus they benefit from information sharing.

Until recently, national development plans placed little emphasis on the role of local cultural expressions and informal networks in social transformation. High priority was accorded to large-scale projects, and centrally managed mass media were the preferred channels for development-related messages. Today, it is believed that social and human resource development must embrace all spheres of human activity, including oral, pictorial, and written expressions of local tradition (Odak 1985, p. 9). Colletta (1977, p. 14) observes that "a bridge is needed between development agents and rural people to facilitate the transfer of information, skills and attitude-sets relevant to village development." This bridge is discovered in traditional media: folk songs, dances, theatre, tales, poems, proverbs, riddles, and puppet shows.

Cultural resource management is a new interdisciplinary field that is attracting attention in developing countries. Cultural resource planners see knowledge in any form—whether deposited in archives, accumulated in village records, or passed from generation to generation as oral heritage—as a national resource. Taylor (1984, p. 1) commented that "as archivists we should not see ourselves as working in isolation serving small esoteric 'publics' but as part of a cultural environment upon which humanity depends for survival." Another specialist noted "the emergence of a new phenomenon in many countries: the curiosity of the general public about archives and, more generally, historical documents" (Duchein 1983, p. 9).

Does information counseling to cultural resource managers and policy makers in a developing country represent interference in internal affairs? Let us assume that two leading adult educators in a country hold opposing views of the cultural heritage of ethnic groups in national development. One argues that indigenous customs raise obstacles to modernization, the other considers traditional folk media the most effective channel for introducing change (Colletta 1977, p. 14). Will information provided to each of these ideologically-oriented adult educators, supporting two opposing trends in development, represent an unethical act in information counseling?

The information counselor has several options:

- *Blind transfer*
  Provides information in support of each opposing objective—modernization and tradition—ignoring what some professionals call the possibility of irreconcilable conflict.
- *Mediated transfer*
  Supplies the requested information for each opposing objective, at the same time mediating in the conflict by also supplying unrequested reconciliatory information.
- *Opinion-based transfer*
  Provides information in support of one of the trends in the form of reports, journal articles, and editorials that express a strong opinion.
- *Research-based transfer*
  Researches the conflicting development policy issues in order to make a considered decision and counsel one, or both, of the information users.

Research on the modernization/tradition conflict must begin with indigenous authors. Dimri (1986, p. 2), writing about folk culture and oral tradition in the Garhwal Division of Uttar Pradesh, India, finds that "women are chained by their tradition, customs, superstitions. . . ." On the other hand, she blames modernization for the destruction of religious sites by the construction of roads, dams, and industrial plants. Such criticism is often interpreted by Western development planners as resistance to all forms of technological development by traditionalists. However, referring to rural populations, Dimri (1986, p. 3) suggests that familiarity with traditional media will help communication planners "to contact people for adopting innovations through their age-old methods of communication and also enrich modern methods of communication by a proper blend with folk culture and oral tradition . . . " In these reflections, the modernization/tradition issue appears to be a solution rather than a conflict.

The benefits of a partnership between development planning, cultural customs and the media are identified by numerous authors. Rosinha (1978) traces the role of pictorial communication techniques in Mexico, while Ojoade (1986) observes the political use of oral literature. Even the management and use of forests, which in many countries represent both the basic livelihood and spiritual beliefs of local people, are linked with social policy on tribal participation in development (Bandhu and Garg 1986). Other studies approach the linking of indigenous culture with the development process through a regional perspective (Anand and Quisumbing 1981). Even development specialists from industrialized countries are beginning to add their support to the modernization/ tradition partnership. Cherns (1986, p. 98) acknowledges that

> Recognition has grown among planners and theorists that culture is highly flexible and pliable, and what passed for irrational was more often than not highly rational given the circumstances, experience and knowledge of those concerned.

Epskamp (1984, p. 62) describes the evolution of popular theatre into an artistic form of expression that "reinforces ethnic and class consciousness." He believes that "if folk artists are persuaded of the value of the message, they will translate it into dramatic terms in a way that an outsider, however well intentioned, cannot hope to accomplish." Epskamp (1984, p. 44) quotes Freire on the non-neutral nature of information: "Although theatre is neutral as a technique, it can nevertheless serve purposes of oppression as well as of liberation. As soon as it is used to transmit direct information, knowledge or skills (e.g. within a social and education context) neutrality is out of the question."

The above examples demonstrate that without understanding the evolution of development issues, the information counselor might make false assumptions and undertake "blind" efforts for information transfer. Conversely, research and insight into a controversial issue may lead the information counselor to personal commitment to one or the other side of an issue. In this case, the information counselor becomes an advocate. Information advocacy is the practice of using information in order to further a personal or social cause, or argue on behalf of an individual, an organization or a social issue. Two major types of information advocacy are relevant to the integrity and effectiveness of information counseling.

- *Case advocacy*
  A concept well known in the service professions, advocacy of the case of a client in information counseling means acting on behalf

of information users by identifying and supporting their quest for relevant and timely information.
* *Cause advocacy*
  A concept known in politics, civic affairs, social movements, and development strategies, cause advocacy in information counseling means the use of information in support of an ideological, political or social issue.

While the commitment to case advocacy is imbedded in all norms and codes of conduct of the information professions, cause advocacy has been considered anathema. This attitude has its roots in an earlier age when the non-neutral nature of information was ignored. Today, the power of technology to expand human information processing capacity underscores the potential hazards to the equity and integrity of information applications. The information counselor can no longer feel complacent in the knowledge that the quality of counseling depends solely on the client's satisfaction with the service. The factors that affect the quality of service include the counselor's belief that the information provided can be justified as "truthful" and "valid."

Based on the above reflections, "information as development assistance" may be defined as the personalized, in-depth process of information counseling to an individual or organization with the intention to support a specific cause in development. "Blind" information transfer that ignores the potential ethical and political consequences of information delivery and advocates for the *case* of the user, whatever it might be, does not represent development assistance. *Cause* advocacy does, and it implies research into relevant issues, feedback from users, judicious decisions on the kind of information to be transferred, and the responsibility for the integrity of the entire process.

Conclusions and Implications for Adult Education

Adult education has always been considered an effective channel by social movements that seek to transmit their messages and bring about social transformation. In recent years, new configurations of information and data, empowered by new technology, have been used by change-oriented social institutions for the support of their goals. In societies engrossed in a struggle for development and political stability, the role of both adult education and information transfer has been intensified by the pressures of economic and social upheavals. The need for these agents of change is obvious. Public awareness of their potential impact is rapidly growing, but the fragility of the scientific and economic systems and the weakness of the technological infrastructures prevent their adequate utilization. The mutual strengthening of adult education programs and information services is an essential condition for further development.

This paper sought to identify links between adult education, information counseling policies, and development aid in order to explore and reinforce such links as can be discovered. Using the case of the International Information Sharing Network (IISN), three questions were raised at the outset: (1) Can information serve as a form of development assistance, (2) what are the inherent problems, and (3) will an information counseling service to adult educators in developing countries help us to identify research and policy needs? It has become clear during the course of the study that no conclusions can be complete and fixed in time, since adult education and information transfer interact in an atmosphere of constantly changing development needs.

In response to the study's questions we suggest that distance information counseling, indeed, is a form of development assistance through adult educators, provided that it supports not only their work performance, program development, and analytic capability, but also social and development policy issues. The problems encountered by the information counseling service include a wide range of technological, professional, and political issues. Furthermore, ethical issues have been identified due to the non-neutrality of information. If ignored, these problems can fester and undermine the constructive interactions of adult educators, information professionals and development practitioners; awareness of them can lead to deliberate choices and solutions.

The combination of research and service in this project helped us to learn about adult educators' information needs in developing countries, as well as about information policy issues such as partnership versus intellectual domination; information sharing versus interference; and cultural relevance versus the culture of technological superiority. These issues, with implications for the international interdependence of educators and information professionals, need further research and understanding.

Being well informed about ways of dealing with everyday problems of life and work is one of the basic human needs. Without the motivation and ability to use applicable knowledge and experience, neither individuals nor social groups can improve their productivity and quality of life. In developing countries, continuous learning is a matter of survival. Social conditions are affected by the harsh forces of nature, inadequate economies, and explosive politics. Yet these societies are immensely rich in human creativity, cultural resources and ingenious ways of community life. It is the joint task of adult education and information transfer to equip people with the ability and skills to minimize hardship and maximize opportunities.

The International Information Sharing Network (IISN) is an attempt to use a combination of information and research processes in order to support the work of adult educators in developing countries. We had to accept that many aspects of information sharing cannot be accurately described, tested and measured. In the human enterprise of an international network, we often exchange imperfect information. However, the impact of information transfer is not always determined by timeliness, objectivity, relevance and usefulness. Most often information sharing is a subjective process dependent on the intent of the participants, on plain good will, on professional and personal ethics, and on tolerance of each other's shortcomings. Dependence becomes interdependence. In an atmosphere of trust, the formality of information provision matters less than informal communication. This form of information support encourages interaction across cultural and political borders, and it is more likely to provide development assistance than formal information systems.

The concept of a "learning organization," adopted for the project, allows the team to inquire into information phenomena which are often the unexpected results of intercultural communication. The project studied attitudes towards new technology, modes of interaction among adult educators, and trends in program development. Instead of waiting for the "perfect" information to be disseminated, such experimentation can open the way to new research questions. How can a network break through the isolation of adult education workers in hardship areas and encourage them to share experience? How did the recipients of information use it—unchanged or synthesized, extracted or expanded, by themselves or in a team? What is cooperation, and how can it be achieved?

As we recognize the non-neutral characteristics of information transfer, the international network can begin to share information in a more honest atmosphere. There is no need to pretend that communications are value-free, and to camouflage human preferences and biases. Respect for a plurality of expectations and wants helps to avoid dogmatic approaches.

Providing a distance information counseling service to adult educators, the IISN is strengthening their capacity to prevail under difficult conditions and to innovate programs against all odds. We are cognizant of the relatively limited number of people we can reach through the network, the barriers to communication, and technical difficulties. But we are constantly reminded of the nature of problem-focused research that combines the search for the increased understanding of a problem with the perennial human quest for ways of improvement.

References

Ajuogu, M.O. (1981). Technology dynamics in lifelong education and development of managers in developing countries. *International Review of Administrative Sciences,* 47(1), 71–76.

Anand, R.P. & Quisumbing, P.V. (1981). *ASEAN Identity, Development and Culture.* Quezon City, Philippines: University of Philippines Law Centre.

Bandhu, D. & Garg, R.K. eds. (1986). *Social Forestry and Tribal Development.* New Delhi, India: Indian Environmental Society.

Bannon, L., Barry, U., & Hoist, O. eds. (1982). *Information Technology Impact on the Way of Life.* Dublin, Ireland: Tycooly International.

Bell, S. (1986). Information systems planning and operation in less developed countries, Part 1: Planning and operational concerns. *Journal of Information Science,* 12(5), 231–245.

Boshier, R.W. (1985). Training of trainers and adult educators, editorial introduction to special report. *Convergence,* 18(3–4), 3–22.

Brindle, E.A. & Dosa, M. (1980). "Impact of Information and Data Support for Practitioners Working with the Elderly." In *Gerontological Information Systems and Services* by M.L. Dosa, E.A. Brindle, G.M. Gee. Syracuse, NY: Syracuse University School of Information Studies, pp. 120–144.

Caplan, N., Morrison, A., & Stambaugh, R.J. (1975). *The Use of Social Science Knowledge in Policy Decisions at the National Level.* Ann Arbor, MI: University of Michigan, Institute for Social Research.

Cernea, M.M. (1979). *Measuring Project Impact: Monitoring and Evaluation in the PIDER Rural Development Project—Mexico.* Washington, DC: The World Bank. (Staff Working Paper No. 332).

Cherns, A. (1986). Contribution of social psychology to the nature and function of work and its relevance to societies of the Third World. *International Journal of Psychology,* 19, 97–111.

Colletta, N.J. (1977). Folk culture and development: Cultural genocide or cultural revitalization? *Convergence,* 10(2), 12–19.

Dimri, A. (1986). *A Study of Communication Behaviour, Folk Culture and Oral Traditions in Garhwal Division of Uttar Pradesh.* Pantnagar, India: G.B. Pant University of Agriculture and Technology. (MSc Thesis).

Draper, J.A. (1986). Universities and Nonformal Adult Education. *Convergence,* 19(3), 70–75.

Duchein, M. (1983). *Obstacles to the Access, Use and Transfer of Information from Archives: A RAMP Study.* Paris, France: United Nations Educational, Scientific and Cultural Organization.

Duke, C. (1986). Relationship between adult education and poverty. *Convergence,* 19(4), 1–16.

Epskamp. K. (1984). Going 'popular' with culture: Theatre as a small-scale medium in developing countries. *Development and Change,* (15), 43–64.

Ferguson, M. (1980). *The Aquarian Conspiracy, Personal and Social Transformation in the 1980s.* Los Angeles: J.P. Tarcher, Inc.

Freire, P. (1970). *Pedagogy of the Press.* New York, NY: Seabury Press. Quoted in Epskamp, K. Going 'popular' with culture: Theatre as a small-scale medium in developing countries. *Development and Change,* (15), 43–64.

Gelpi, E. (1985). Problems of educational research. *International Social Science Journal,* 87(2), 149–156.

Ghosh, P.K. ed. (1984). *Appropriate Technology in Third World Development.* Westport, CT: Greenwood Press.

Gordon, G. (1979). Problem solving creativity and cognitive style. *NSPI Journal* (National Society for Performance and Instruction), 18–21.

Hall, B.L. (1981). Participatory research, popular knowledge and power: A personal reflection. *Convergence,* 14(3), 6–19.

Hattori, T. (1986). Technology transfer and management systems. *The Developing Economies,* 24(4), 314–325.

Hechinger, F.M. (1985). New communication technology is called a failure in serving Third World education. *Development, Seeds of Change,* 1, 70.

International Commission for the Study of Communication Problems. (1980). *Many Voices, One World: Report by the Sean McBride Commission to UNESCO.* London, UK: Kogan Page.

Kassam, Y. (1986). Adult education, development and international aid: Some issues and trends. *Convergence,* 19(3), 1–11.

Kidd, J.R. (1981). Education research needs in adult education. *Convergence,* 14(2), 53–62.

Konoshima, S. (1986). "Information services and trade: Barriers, issues and prospects for transborder data flow." In *American Society for Information Science. Proceedings of the 49th Annual Meeting 1986.* White Plains, NY: Knowledge Industry Publications, pp. 143–149.

Korten, D.C. (1981). The Management of social transformation. *Public Administration Review,* 41(6), 609–618.

Kranzberg, M. (1985). "The Information age: Evolution or revolution?" In *National Academy of Engineering. Information Technologies and Social Transformation,* ed. by B.R. Guile. Washington, DC: National Academy Press, pp. 35–54.

Krueger, A.O. (1986). Aid in the development process. *The World Bank Research Observer,* 1(1), 57–78.

Lourie, S. (1985) Educational planning. *International Social Science Journal,* 37(2), 247–258.

Lucas, B.G. & Freedman, S. (1983). *Technology Choice and Change in Developing Countries.* Dublin, Ireland: Tycooly International.

Martin, D. (1983). Pedagogy and politics: Adult education in Latin America. *Convergence,* 36(3), 16–22.

Maruyama, M. (1988). The Inverse practice principle in multicultural management. *The Academy of Management Executive,* 11(1), 67–68.

Medlin, W.K. (1983). A model for planning rural education development: Synthesis of experiences in non-industrial societies. *Convergence,* 16(2), 30–41.

Mickelwait, D.R. et al. (1978). *Information for Decision Making in Rural Development.* Washington, DC: Development Alternatives, Inc. 2 vols.

Nankani, H. ed. (1988). *Techniques of Privatization of State-Owned Enterprises: Selected Country Case Studies.* Washington, DC: The World Bank. (WB Paper 2, v. 2).

Nettleford, R. (1982). Ideology and nation building: Implications for adult education, training and employment. *Convergence,* 15(1), 27–44.

Nturibi, D.N. (1982). Training of community development agents for popular participation. *Community Development Journal,* 17(2), 106–120.

Odak, O. (1985). Let the past serve the future. *UNESCO Courier,* 9–11.

Ojoade, J.O. (1986). Oral literature: A manipulative force in African politics. *International Folklore Review,* (4), 21–27.

Organization for Economic Cooperation and Development. (1988). *Development Co-Operation, Efforts and Policies of the Members of the Development Assistance Committee,* 1987. Paris, France: OECD.

Ossandon, C.J. (1986). Methodology for continuous self-evaluation: Notes from the Latin American experience. *Convergence,* 19(3), 13–19.

Ouane, A. (1986). The Experience of Mali in training literacy workers. *Convergence,* 19(1), 13–14.

Pradervand, P. (1980). Knowledge is power. *International Development Review,* 2(1), 55–58.

Prajuli, P. (1986). Grassroots movements, development discourse and popular education. *Convergence,* 19(2), 29–40.

Repo, A.J. (1987). "Economics of information." In *Annual Review of Information Science and Technology,* ed. by M.E. Williams, v. 22. Amsterdam, Netherlands: Elsevier Science Publishers, pp. 3–35.

Riddell, R.C. (1986). The Ethics of foreign aid. *Development Policy Review,* (4), 24–43.

Rogers, E.M. & Kincaid, D.L. (1981). *Communication Networks: Toward a New Paradigm for Research.* New York, NY: The Free Press.

Rosinha, R.C. (1978). Pictorial Techniques for Communicating Technical Information, an Experiment Among Mexican Small Farmers. Madison, WI: University of Wisconsin. (Ph.D. Dissertation).

Scott-Stevens, S. (1987). *Foreign Consultants and Counterparts, Problems in Technology Transfer.* Boulder, CO: Westview Press, 1987.

Simmons, J. (1979). Education for development reconsidered. *World Development,* (7), 1005–1016.

Srinivasan, M. ed. (1982). *Technology Assessment and Development.* New York, NY: Praeger.

Srinivasan, R.N. (1977). Development, poverty and basic human needs: Some issues. *Food Research Institute Studies,* 16(2), 11–28.

Streeten, P. et al. (1981). *First Things First: Meeting Basic Human Needs in the Developing Countries.* New York, NY: Oxford University Press.

Taylor, H.A. (1984). *Archival Services and the Concept of the User: A RAMP Study.* Paris, France: United Nations Educational, Scientific and Cultural Organization.

United Nations. (1987). *Popular Participation Policies as Methods for Advancing Social Integration.* New York, NY: UN.

United Nations Educational, Scientific and Cultural Organization. (1986). *Educational Planning in the Context of Current Development Problems.* Paris, France: UNESCO. 2 vols.

United States. Congressional Research Service. (1971). Technical Information for Congress. *Report to the Subcommittee on Science, Research and Development of the Committee on Science and Astronautics.* House of Representatives, 92nd Congress, 1st Session. Rev. ed. Washington, DC: U.S. Government Printing Office. (Committee Print).

Urevbu, A. (1985). Integrating science and technology into a policy of lifelong education in Nigeria. *International Journal of Lifelong Education,* 4(4), 319–325.

Varese, S. (1985). Cultural development in ethnic groups: Anthropological explorations in education. *International Social Science Journal,* 37(2), 201–216.

Wesley-Tanaskovic, I. (1985). *Guidelines on National Information Policy: Scope, Formulation and Implementation.* Paris, France: United Nations Educational, Scientific and Cultural Organization.

Winograd, T. & Flores, F. (1986). *Understanding Computers and Cognition.* Norwood, NJ: Ablex Publishing Corporation.

4

Information and Indigenous Technological Capacity in Developing Countries

Marta Dosa and Anis Y. Yusoff

Introduction

While the issue of international technology transfer (ITT) has produced a remarkably large volume of research and policy studies, the generation of indigenous technological capacity (ITC) within developing countries has received considerably less attention. This is understandable, given the political, historical, and conceptual differences between the two processes. Globally visible and politically prestigious, the concept of ITT—the transmission of knowledge, products, processes, skills and information from one society to another by means of trade, development assistance, or institutional and personal contacts—is attractive to policy makers and researchers alike. Technology transfer is often connected with foreign direct investment in industrial expansion, and thus has the support of politicians and industry leaders.

It has generally been assumed by researchers that technology transfer flows originate in the industrialized countries of the North. It has also been believed that with a small industrial base and struggling R&D programs, the low-income economies of the South find the cost of original technology development prohibitive. Therefore, the concept of indigenous technological capacity (ITC) is a more recent occurrence in the research literature than ITT. Difficult to demonstrate politically and economically, ITC has been described as a nation's capacity to prioritize selected technologies for domestic production, to create long-term technological policies, and to plan, implement and assess indigenous technology in the context of development plans (Shahidullah, 1992). ITC means to foster local creativity and initiative, strengthen local markets and small firms, and develop the skills, benefits and complexities of an information-based economy.

Closely related to the theme of ITC is the study of indigenous knowledge systems, a broad term encompassing a variety of cultural phenomena from oral communication traditions to organizational practices in rural development. Bardini (1992, p. 33) urges that "the development process should use indigenous technological knowledge and encourage indigenous participation by blending traditional and modern technologies." In a project using microcomputers to create a communication interface between local and imported knowledge, Bardini is proposing a framework that is different from the prototype of information diffusion used by earlier researchers; knowledge of foreign origin is adjusted to the local context rather than the other way around.

Every country is searching for information assets in order to monitor, identify, and use opportunities for innovation. Lall (1982, pp. 5–7) asserted that "even very poor countries may develop a comparative advantage in the sales of skills and know-how" that are pertinent to local expertise and are also potentially valuable for exporting. Governments are seeking to evolve from the modest beginnings of the last two decades the information infrastructures and policies that not only meet the needs of managers and policy makers, but are also capable of merging into the mainstream of natural economic development (Bowonder et al. 1993, Palvia et al. 1990, Technology Atlas Team 1987). Information systems supporting activities in different economic sectors and forming essential parts of a nation's indigenous technological capability are the most recent policy targets in developing countries. The attention of researchers and policy makers is turning from the earlier perception of information technology (IT) as the only dominant information-related element in economic development to the cultural and legal implications of information (Lu and Farrell 1990, Organization . . . 1991).

This paper reviews some of the trends and factors that are leading to the recognition that the domestic production of knowledge and information responsive to local needs are key elements in long-range ITC strategies. The objective of the paper is to identify a conceptual framework of information policy areas in this domain upon which future research may be built.

Examples of National and Regional Trends

Industrial modernization in developing countries, first embraced as a panacea to all economic and social woes and as a guarantee for access to markets, became suspect during the last two decades. National development policies blindly supporting foreign direct investment and consultants indiscriminately introducing foreign organizational models were criticized as barriers to culture-based social transformation (Singh 1990). Whenever transnational corporations exerted overly strong control, host governments began to promulgate national regulations in order to curb foreign economic dominance. However, training in technological skills, examples of innovations, and available jobs at the transnational firms continued to demonstrate the benefits of their presence. Thus, developing countries began to seek solutions to this problem by joint ventures, the strengthening of domestic enterprises, the privatization of several state-owned services, and efforts to establish indigenous R&D and technology production.

In most countries, national strategies, expected to guide decisions on information technology, are still embedded in general industrial policies. Some countries strive to take full advantage of technology imports, while others are revising their industrial policies to include support to indigenous technology creation. For example, Taiwan furthers its domestic R&D by procuring licensed equipment and software from leading foreign research institutes, and simultaneously maintaining a science-based industrial park to attract scholars (Lee 1992). The Malaysian government expects foreign corporations to provide training and advising programs, and urges Malaysian technicians and managers employed by transnationals to assist local skill and expertise development. Malaysian nationals who open their own business operations following a period of experience with a transnational firm receive governmental assistance (Lee 1991). Indigenous technological development in Thailand is benefiting from connections established between businesses and universities in order to channel academic research to enterprises as efficiently as possible (Swierczek and Nourie 1992). In India, the satellite-based National Informatics Centre Network (NICNET) not only provides information services to central and state governments, but also conducts R&D on software and hardware development (Arora et al. 1992).

Latin American and Caribbean countries have recognized that in order to obtain, adapt, and apply advanced technologies, a scientific base is needed. However, most countries in the region lack financial resources for R&D and information support, sufficient numbers of state-of-the-art equipment, and postgraduate science programs. Consequently, thorough investigation of the applications and costs of a few imported advanced technologies are emphasized (Del Campo 1989). Mexico's treatment of ITT displays an uneven course of early institutional efforts (such as the Law on Technology Transfer and the Law on the Use of Exploitation of Patents and Trademarks), overshadowed by continuous economic hardship and ineffective coordination between research and industry.

One problem in using research findings and policy models to maximum benefit is the traditional separation of public and private sector roles with respect to development. In response, Sharif (1992) recommends functions for both the government and the market in developing technological self-reliance. Having identified the most critical problems in evolving local capacity for technology and the ways a few developing countries manage to leapfrog some development phases, Sharif offers an agenda for the cooperation of government and industry as a major policy paradigm.

Most countries are promoting coordination and mutual support among different sectors in society. For example, Odhiambo (1992, pp. 121–125) proposes that Africa needs "partnerships" among its scientific communities, geopolitical leadership, and industrial/financial establishments. Onyango (1991, p. 33) describes Kenya's efforts toward more technological independence in a case study. Kenyan development specialists have recommended "an appropriate, consistent and transparent policy framework," more open communication links between industrial enterprises and academic research institutions, and more effective information systems.

The Impact of Transnational Corporations on ITC

Transnational corporations (TNCs) differ in the use of their technologies in host countries depending on the companies' global strategy, relationship to the host government, and attitudes toward local labor. TNCs contribute to indigenous technology creation by teaching production skills to the local workforce. Marton (1986) identifies several factors that determine corporate decisions and success in diffusing new technology in a host society:

- National policies of the transnational firm's home country
- The firm's own strategies and its understanding of the complex ITC process and its consequences
- Duration of the firm's operations in the host society and the extent of its rapport with government and population
- Presence of other foreign corporations
- Nature of products/services offered by the firm
- Local economic and social conditions (e.g. availability of facilities, quality of workforce, privatization activities)
- The legal and regulatory framework (e.g. local technology transfer laws, patent and trademark laws, labor laws, environment/health laws)
- The corporation's interest in commercializing and integrating its technology in the host society
- Intent of project planners, managers, and consultants.

The Impact of Local Firms on ITC

With increasing participation of researchers from the developing areas, recent studies have scrutinized technology transfer from the point of view of the recipients. Yin (1992, p. 17) asserts that many researchers in developing countries begin their work with the assumption that "multinational corporations, as the major vehicles for commercial transfer, were often blamed for selling inappropriate technologies to LDCs regardless of local conditions." Such charges are frequently leveled also at foreign consultants for introducing inappropriate information systems. In comparison, local information providers are familiar with user needs and service requirements.

"The literature leads us to expect [multinational enterprises] . . . to be relatively backward in local technology development" (Lall 1985, p. 118). The reason given is that most TNCs allocate relatively small funding to conduct R&D within developing countries, and that they are not familiar with the extent of contribution to innovation and national development by local firms.

The success of domestic firms, in spite of their weak financial basis, is explained by their closeness to indigenous needs, the availability of government incentives, joint venturing with firms in other developing countries, and access to locally relevant business information. In a study of the impact of local cultural factors on information systems development, Lu and Farrell (1990, pp. 290–294) find that in most developing countries the small, family-owned, informal and people-oriented business, with its neighborhood roots and direct information distribution, is the dominant form. Management and systems development practices which emphasize organizational learning are said to be effective. Local firms also have ways to acquire foreign technology through licensing, contacts with sellers, and international development aid projects. They are in a good position to absorb and adjust new processes and products because of their own information dissemination networks in their countries.

The Impact of Institutional Relations on ITC

"Until recently, rapid industrialization was considered to be the only acceptable and proven strategy for economic development" (Sharif 1992, p. 367). Industrial development based on imports and the creation of jobs by foreign direct investment is still dominant in the short-term plans of developing countries, but long-term perspectives on academic and business relations have become more people-oriented due to improvements in science and education. Not only the goals of development, but also the strategies to promote growth have changed (Bell and Pavitt 1993, Van Arkadie 1990). In the past, governments were expected to operate key industries, allocate credit, and ration foreign currency. Today the government's role in providing goods and services, including information services, has diminished in comparison with private enterprises.

Within organizations managerial, communication and information activities interrelate in complex and seemingly intangible ways. These interactions are strongly influenced by larger patterns of the development environment. Society-wide elements of indigenous technological capability, upon which the effectiveness and performance of all firms depend, are described by Marton (1986) and Yin (1992) as

- the extent to which new technology can be integrated into society
- local components and processes imbedded in the production of technology
- the country's competitive export capability
- the country's capacity for self-sustained development (based on quantitative as well as qualitative indicators)
- R&D infrastructure and funding
- availability of facilities, equipment and skills
- regulatory and other policy measures.

The process of assimilating imported technologies is critical to the evolution of indigenous technological capacity. Studies by the Technology Atlas Team (1987) are particularly relevant to information policy planning as they suggest better measurement methodologies for assessing technological development, and national policies for technology imports, exports, and the use of traditional technologies.

Information as Integral Part of ITC

In the development context, individual information acquisition means a process more personalized and empowering than what formal information systems can deliver. Lall (1982, p. 65) regards all progress in gaining efficiency through technology applications as a form of learning, and distinguishes between technical learning (doing and adapting), and nontechnical learning (organizing, managing, marketing, negotiating). New communication and information systems are expected to go beyond the acts of communicating and informing to giving assistance to users in culturally absorbing the information and applying it within their social systems (Hanson and Narula 1990). This concept of social technology is a rich blend of human and technical elements in information use and learning.

Other models include the Group Production Systems (GPS) in China, considered a successful domestic innovation. The use of GPS—the application of knowledge from several disciplines to a task—has extended from the machine industry to several other economic sectors (Jiang et al. 1992). Studying local firms, Lu and Farrell (1990) observe that cultural influences are dominant, affecting economic, legal, political and educational conditions which, in turn, affect organizations. The "cultural context also adds a new dimension to the model of individual information processing" (Lu and Farrell 1990, p. 291). Thus information flows—and indirectly information policies—are deeply rooted in local cultures, a relationship not always recognized by exogenous researchers.

The focus of current approaches to information production in developing countries is on system design based on indigenous needs, databases constructed from indigenous knowledge, and growing regional professional cooperation (Bardini 1992). Emerging information infrastructures attempt to cover a broader range of information activities than ever, encompassing technology assessment, business, trade, scientific data, social intelligence, and information dissemination to urban centers, the peripheries, and rural areas. These efforts, still in their formative stage, seem to be the most effective where they are integrated into national development plans.

A major concern of international and domestic policies has been the lack of tested methods to measure the impact of information provision on national development. A project of the International Development Research Centre (IDRC) made considerable progress in this direction by identifying the context of information indicators and preliminary methodologies for research on this problem (Menou 1993). Results of the IDRC project can also provide the beginnings of measuring the impact of information on indigenous technological capacity (ITC).

Indications of the Need for a Conceptual Framework

To strengthen its ability to reduce technological imports and increase domestic technological production, a country needs a consistent and flexible technology policy. This is impossible to attain without creating and supporting an applications-oriented research infrastructure. With the growing availability of data resources oriented toward problems in different sectors, the economic fabric of a nation will begin to change (Summers 1993). Information flows create greater interdependence of specialized labor and emerging markets (Kelkar et al. 1991). The scientific and cultural production of ideas through education, research, and cultural communication attracts increasing support by governments and private enterprises (Romer 1993). Once indigenous creativity and the resulting public use of ideas are recognized for their economic value to development, the nation, as in the case of newly industrialized countries (NICs), is on its way to becoming a multilayered information economy.

Researchers in numerous disciplines have come to recognize the importance of research on the interdependence of the national economy, information, and indigenous technological capacity (ITC). However, explorations remain pigeonholed in different specialized literatures, even though in policy models and practice the various dimensions of national development are converging. Examples of such dimensions include (a) the promotion of advanced telecommunications; (b) economic, scientific, and trade policy activities; (c) the recognition of indigenous cultural communications and knowledge; and (d) the thrust toward a modern research establishment. Brief observations on each of these aspects of national development follow.

Investment in *telecommunication infrastructures* creates opportunities for the interaction of computers and communication networks. Benefits to society have been described as the reduction of telecommunication service costs, the introduction of universally valid standards and protocols for interconnectivity, and the support of learning processes in the use of advanced software (Organization . . . 1991, p. 37). Moreover, the introduction of improved telecommunication services in a country which necessitates changes in many organizational processes will draw attention to the need for the judicious preparation for these changes. Failures of transplanted Western models of organizational restructuring to accommodate the use of new technology have not been uncommon (Golembiewski 1993, Jones and Blunt 1993).

Jussawalla (1993, p. 32) distinguishes between the technical aspects of telecommunication services and the meaning of transmitted messages: "It is the content—the information itself—that adds value to the technology and imparts productivity to various sectors of the economy." Information transfer is critically involved with *economic, scientific, and trade policy activities,* and new information systems linking these institutional processes are likely to reveal the complex relationships between research, technology, and international trade. To the extent that research in different disciplines gains insights into these relationships, the results can contribute to our understanding of how the rise of indigenous technological capability in a country will affect its institutional and human conditions (Besley and Case 1993, Bhalla and James 1991, Gathegi 1992).

Next to economic factors, it is *indigenous cultural communication* that, of all aspects of national development, has the strongest influence on ITC. Mundy (1993, p. 41) believes that "central to participation [in development activities] is the concept of indigenous knowledge, specific to a certain place or culture, developed by local people and passed down through the society over generations. Parallel to and interlocking with indigenous knowledge is a system of indigenous communications." Mundy identifies the different players in development communication as the scientist, the development agent, the facilitator, the conservationist, the political advocate, the capitalist, and the skeptic, each with a different view of indigenous knowledge. Using many kinds of communication media from local storytelling and festivals to formal instruction, these actors are seen as potential links between local knowledge, traditional skills, and development.

The current literature emphasizes the imperative of adjusting newly introduced foreign technology and management practices to indigenous cultural needs. In a discussion of the potential role of computer-based expert systems in local cultures, Schoenhoff (1993) observes that some indigenous activities such as work in rainforest laboratories and folk healing made a transition from their original form to partially modernized institutions. The author predicts that expert systems constructed with the participation of local specialists will be accepted and used in healing, farming, and other daily activities, while importing expert systems from industrialized countries will ignore cultural differences in the processes of reasoning. Golembiewski (1993), Jones and Blunt (1993), Lu and Farrell (1990) and Rahim (1993) describe the problem of imposing foreign organizational models on developing countries. The above examples offer information professionals the opportunity to reflect on indigenous communications flowing in both directions: from local cultural beginnings to modernized practices meeting present-day needs, and from foreign models to local settings where these models often fail.

The thrust toward a modern *research establishment* in a country is a consequence of the recognition, in both the governmental and private sectors, of the value of upgraded telecommunications, information systems supporting economic, scientific and trade policies, and the expressions of indigenous cultures. None of these essential components of development could flourish without the reinforcing role of R&D. Research into the institutions and incentives of science is as indispensable as research into the determinants of domestic technological growth. Developing countries are striving to establish modern science- and technology-based enterprises, which depend on adequate funding, facilities, theory building, the ability to share research results, and the up-to-date training of scientists and skilled specialists (Gathegi 1992, Romer 1993).

One significant strand of research into the characteristics of emerging R&D establishments is the investigation of the status of the scientist and scientific work. Who conducts research in the country? Are there opportunities for interdisciplinary cooperation? Are there avenues for university-industry relations? What are the indicators of the quality of scientific performance? Where are the sources of research ideas? Such questions are raised only in societies where the importance of indigenous scientific work for development has been recognized (Gaillard 1991, Lowenberg and Yu 1992, Marglin and Marglin 1990, Shahidullah 1991). Considering the political tension between technology importation and domestic production, one of the unexploited areas of R&D is technology blending, "the constructive integration of emerging technology with traditional low-income, small-scale sectors . . . " (Bhalla and James 1991, p. 479). It seems likely that research projects on this topic will be initiated within several different disciplines, although a concerted interdisciplinary effort might be a more appropriate and promising approach.

A Suggested Conceptual Framework

This paper describes a conceptual framework that attempts to bring together the different dimensions of development into the unifying dimension of INNOVATION, a concept and process common to all development activities (Figure 4.1). Change takes place in the course of all technical assistance projects designed to improve indigenous technology, and change is usually based on an innovation, no matter how small. The purpose of the conceptual framework is to make a small step toward future research.

Innovation is the introduction, implementation, and testing of something new—a view, an approach, a procedure, a product, a policy. The process may take place at several levels simultaneously. Both macroinnovation at the national level and microinnovation at the organizational or team level have been addressed by researchers. Empirical studies have shown that innovations in different settings and locations are determined by cultural factors in addition to the usual economic and social determinants (Bardini 1992, Marglin and Marglin 1990).

The relationship between innovation and information is significant to our framework. "Information technology can be described as technological and organizational innovations that exploit modern communications systems to coordinate activities" (Organization . . . 1991, p. 33). Innovation itself is an extremely information-intensive process, determined by a multitude of social constructs, rules, traditions, institutions, and relationships.

The conceptual framework represents information policy areas relating to innovation. We assume that the hypothetical innovation is taking place in the domain of domestic technology creation. The configuration of the innovation—the CREATIVE PROCESS, APPLICATIONS,

Figure 4.1
Information Policy Areas Relating to Innovation

The Creative ⟷ Process	Applications ⟷	Diffusion of ⟷ Innovation	Impact →
Research	Development	Marketing	Assessment
Information Policies	*Information Policies*	*Information Policies*	*Information Policies*
Research Funding	Knowledge Gap	Market Research	Technology Assessment
Grant Policies	Diffusion of Research	Market Techniques	Impact Statements
Contracts	Technology Transfer	Factors Affecting Diffusion	Use of Indicators
Psychology of Creative Process	Domestic ⎱ Foreign ⎰	Public Awareness	Social ⎫
Ownership		Mass Media	Health ⎬
Patent Process	Industrialized Countries	Public Interest	Environment ⎭
Trademarks	Developing Countries	Law	Data Banks
Secrecy		Consumerism	Modeling
Breach of Secrecy	Laws/Regulation Federal Agencies	Repackaging of Information	
Projection Techniques			

DIFFUSION OF INNOVATION, and IMPACT—is not constructed in our illustration with the usual arrows indicating a linear flow, because in reality these phases are sometimes overlapping, sometimes occurring with great time-gaps between them, and other times are moving around each other in circular fashion. The innovation process is erratic, unpredictable and in constant flux.

The four phases (also identified as RESEARCH, DEVELOPMENT, MARKETING and ASSESSMENT) have spawned information policies which, in turn, tend to influence the outcome of each phase. Policies and human activities incorporated in this framework are suggestive rather than exhaustive. Each policy area (e.g. research funding, grant policies, contracts) is a complex social and institutional arena. Some areas (e.g. the psychology of the creative process, the knowledge gap) are not policy aspects but human or societal phenomena indirectly affected by policies.

The success of each component and process in this conceptual framework of innovation depends on information flows among the players: researchers, policy makers, technologists, bureaucrats, consumers, and many others. Empirical research in the future may collect quantitative data and qualitative information about each phase, or select one phase for closer analysis.

Conclusion and Research Perspective

The review supporting this paper found that most of the research and policy analysis in the area of technology transfer to and by developing countries focuses on technology acquisition, adaptation and diffusion. Much less attention has been given to the factors and policies that affect the building of indigenous technological capacity (ITC) within the policy context of sustainable development. This paper identified a conceptual framework in which the facilitators and barriers of indigenous research and technology production may be investigated.

The main human sources of indigenous technological capability (ITC) are initiative, creativity, and the motivation to overcome economic and social barriers. Gargan (1993) suggests that all professions face three continuous tasks in order to succeed: theory generation, theory translation combined with advocacy and dissemination, and theory implementation and routinization. Accordingly the challenge to the information professions is three-fold:

- Professional values and concepts have to be tested in view of new development requirements.
- Even though research is costly and usually requires international organizational sponsorship, research agendas must be developed from modest beginnings by the information professions.
- Research and education/training in information science have to become partners, informing and reinforcing each other, if they are expected to become major routes to development.

Investigations of how information relates to indigenous technological capacity (ITC) will be best performed by a collaboration of several countries and organizations. Research on the impact of information on the development process is already under way, and information processes in different sectors (e.g. agriculture, energy, health care) are being studied. The present paper suggests opening a window on a related, but barely explored domain: criteria and measurements capable of exploring information as part of indigenous technological capacity.

References

Arora, J., Kaur, S.P., Chandra, H., & Bhatt, R.K. (1992). Computer communication networks and their use for information retrieval and dissemination: Basic tutorial and current scenario of networks in India. *Microcomputers for Information Management, 9*(4), 241–261.

Bardini, T. (1992). Linking indigenous knowledge systems and development: The Potential uses of microcomputers. *Knowledge and Policy: The International Journal of Knowledge Transfer and Utilization,* 5(1), 29–41.

Bell, M. & Pavitt, K. (1993). "Accumulating technological capability in developing countries." In *Proceedings of the World Bank Annual Conference on Development Economics 1992,* 257–281. Washington, DC: The World Bank.

Besley, T. & Case, A. (1993). Modeling technology adaptation in developing countries. *American Economic Review,* 83(2), 396–402.

Bhalla, A.S. & James, D.D. (1991). Integrating new technologies with traditional economic activities in developing countries: An evaluative look at "technology blending." *The Journal of Developing Areas,* 25, 477–495.

Bowonder, B., Miyqake, T., & Singh, T.M. (1993). Emerging trends in information technology: Implications for developing countries. *International Journal of Information Management,* 13, 183–204.

Del Campo, E.M. (1989). Technology and the world economy: The case of the American hemisphere. *Technological Forecasting and Social Change,* 35, 351–364.

Gaillard, J. (1991). *Scientists in the Third World.* Lexington, KY: Kentucky University Press.

Gargan, J.J. (1993). Specifying elements of professionalism and the process of professionalization. *International Journal of Public Administration,* 16(12), 1861–1884.

Gathegi, J.N. (1992). The State and society: Intervention in the creation of scientific information in developing countries. *Journal of the American Society for Information Science,* 43(4), 323–333.

Golembiewski, R.T. (1993). Organizational development in the Third World: Values, closeness of fit and culture-boundedness. *International Journal of Public Administration,* 16(11), 1667–1691.

Hanson, J. & Narula, U. (1990). *New Communication Technologies in Developing Countries.* Hillsdale, NJ: Lawrence Erlbaum Associates.

Jiang, W.B., Wang, Z.B., & Sun, H.F. (1992). Group technology application in China. *Technovation,* 12(8), 509–515.

Jones, M.L. & Blunt, P. (1993). Organizational development and change in Africa. *International Journal of Public Administration,* 16(11), 1735–1765.

Jussawalla, M. (1993). Adding value to information: A case study of the Asian NIEs. *Development,* 3, 32–35.

Kelkar, V.L. et al. (1991). India's information economy: Role, size and scope. *Economic and Political Weekly,* (26(37), 2153–2161.

Lall, S. (1982). *Developing Countries as Exporters of Technology, a First Look at the Indian Experience.* London: Macmillan Press.

Lall, S. (1985). *Multinationals, Technology, and Exports, Selected Papers*. New York, NY: St. Martin's Press.

Lee, G.B. (1991). Transnational corporations in Malaysia: Visible but unrevealing. *Regional Development Dialogue*, 12(1), 21–44.

Lee, P.Y. (1992). Taiwan telecommunications development. *Transnational Data and Communications Report*, 15(2), 23–27.

Lowenberg, A.D. & Yu, B.T. (1992). The Role of the intellectual in economic development: A constitutional perspective. *World Development*, 20(9), 1261–1277.

Lu, M-T. & Farrell, C. (1990). Information systems development in developing countries: An evaluation and recommendations. *International Journal of Information Management*, 10(4), 288–296.

Marglin, F.A. & Marglin, S.A. (1990). *Dominating Knowledge: Development, Culture, and Resistance*. Oxford: Clarendon Press.

Marton, K. (1986). *Multinationals, Technology, and Industrialization, Implications and Impact in Third World Countries*. Lexington, MA: D.C. Heath.

Menou, M.J. ed. (1993). *Measuring the Impact of Information on Development*. Ottawa: International Development Research Centre.

Mundy, P. (1993). Indigenous communication systems. *Development*, 3, 41–44.

Odhiambo, T.R. (1992). Designing a science-led future for Africa: A Suggested framework. *Technology in Society*, 14, 121–130.

Onyango, R.A.O. (1991). Indigenous technological capacity: Can social intelligence help? A Kenyan case study. *Social Intelligence*, 1(1), 25–42.

Organization for Economic Cooperation and Development. Development Centre. (1991). *The Diffusion of Advanced Telecommunications in Developing Countries*. Paris: OECD.

Palvia, P., Palvia, S., & Zigli, M. (1990). Models and requirements for using strategic information systems in developing nations. *International Journal of Information Management*, 10(2), 117–126.

Rahim, S.A. (1993). Communicative action in development. *Development*, 3, 36–40.

Romer, P.M. (1993). "Two strategies for economic development: Using ideas and producing ideas." In *Proceedings of the World Bank Annual Conference on Development Economics, 1992*, 63–115. Washington, DC: The World Bank.

Schoenhoff, D.M. (1993). *The Barefoot Expert: The Interface of Computerized Knowledge Systems and Indigenous Knowledge Systems*. Westport, CT: Greenwood Press.

Shahidullah, S.M. (1992). *Capacity-Building in Science and Technology in the Third World: Problems, Issues, and Strategies*. Boulder, CO: Westview Press.

Sharif, N. (1992). Technological dimensions of international cooperation and sustainable development. *Technological Forecasting and Social Change,* 42(4), 367–383.

Singh, M. (1990). "Development policy research: The task ahead." In *Proceedings of the World Bank Annual Conference on Development Economics, 1989,* 11–20. Washington, DC: The World Bank.

Summers, L.H. (1993). Recent lessons of development. *The World Bank Research Observer,* 8(2), 241–254.

Swierczek, F.W. & Nourie, C. (1992). Technology development in Thailand: A private sector view. *Technovation,* 12(3), 145–161.

Technology Atlas Team. (1987). A Framework for technology-based national planning, Pt. 1. *Technological Forecasting and Social Change,* 32(1), 5–18.

Van Arkadie, B. (1990). "The role of institutions in development." In *Proceedings of the World Bank Annual Conference on Development Economics, 1989.* 153–175. Washington, DC: The World Bank.

Yin, J.Z. (1992). Technological capabilities as determinants of the success of technology transfer projects. *Technology Forecasting and Social Change,* 42, 17–29.

Part II

Human Resource Networking

5

Community Networking
in Gerontology and Health:
A Centralized and a Decentralized Model

Introduction

Theodore Caplow observed that "a greatly improved society might be within our present grasp if projects of social improvement were undertaken in a more rational way . . . we already have most of the theoretical knowledge required . . ." (Caplow 1975, p. vii). In an attempt to cope with the widely perceived need to manage and use knowledge more efficiently, modern societies have produced an immense apparatus of information in all industrialized countries where new communication and information technologies are available. New information needs, created by demographic, social and economic trends, have been recognized by national legislation as well as by the information marketplace. In the United States, congressional statutes requiring the creation of information dissemination centers and clearinghouses are concerned with a wide range of issues from engineering standards through community mental health and consumer product safety to health care statistics.

Federal data relevant to the planning, management and evaluation of human services are available in more abundance than most professional practitioners recognize. The United States Office of Technology Assessment (1979, p. 3) identified the problems connected with these data collection programs as the fragmentation of policy issues covered by surveys; burden on institutions that have to report data; low-level and inefficient use; and the consumer's inability to collect data that cut across federal agency jurisdictions. Some of these information resources are dynamic and use intensive methods to make potential consumers aware of their availability, while others are tracked down by users only with great difficulty.

Such problems notwithstanding, information resources are being created with ever increasing momentum, and research in information science and a number of other disciplines is investigating ways to improve access and dissemination. At present, most of the remedies and enhancements are technology-based and aimed at scientific and professional users. Less emphasis is placed in the literature on information sharing in less technology-intensive areas, although community information flows have been recognized for years as vital strains in the economic development process. Bhattacharyya (1972) characterizes community development as the efforts of people to integrate their local activities, including new knowledge generation, into the life of the nation. "Community development" as a political movement declined by the end of the 1960s, but many regions in developing countries are continuing to organize their informing and publishing efforts around the revival of their cultural legacy using a variety of distribution channels, media and machines (Collier, Jr., and Buitron 1971).

While it is widely acknowledged that developing countries have been left behind by the unprecedented progress in international knowledge production, it is usually taken for granted that American communities share in the benefits of the information economy. However, researchers in several disciplines oppose this view, asserting that poverty, technology scarcity, and lack of opportunities to use practical knowledge are not alien to communities in the United States either (Bengston et al. 1977, Holland 1976, Kochen and Donohue 1976).

This paper is motivated by the belief that communities in very diverse cultural and social environments, in both the United States and abroad, need to participate in the search for more adequate and equitable information acquisition (Press and McKool 1972, The World Bank 1975). The two experimental information dissemination programs described in this paper have been developed in an American community, and could not be applied in other countries without extensive adjustments. But the American community, with its culturally diverse social fabric, forms a continuum with its international counterparts. Provided that information dissemination models are fitted to local circumstances, they can fill similar needs in communities everywhere.

The first question is, can information produced by governments be sifted and channeled to local communities in some relevant way? Consumers face two closely related problems. One is the need of the practicing professional and policy maker for information about client groups, documented cases, regulatory events, research-generated data, and available alternatives of service and outcome. The other is our inadequate understanding of the information requirements of consumer groups. We know the imperative of designing information systems that will enable human service providers and counselors to assist the choices people must make by providing the right kind of information. We must also find a way to reach individuals who do not seek services but who may, by having access to information, cope more effectively with their problems, enhance their lives, and enrich others. Social and health service concerns are interrelated, because our society tends to build helping systems for situations where illness, poverty and isolation have already taken their toll. We need information simultaneously for professional work and for everyday coping and enriching. The second question is, can the same information systems provide work-related as well as personal consumer information? We hope that the description of the two information dissemination projects in this paper will help to answer these questions.

Although there is no shortage of innovative technologies and services, many decisions are made in the absence of valid data. In his study of information utilities in human services, Holland (1976, p. 33) concluded that "in most organizations, the collection and use of information is basically an informal process and decision making is far from routine or rational." Policy making or advisory bodies whose decisions affect the public have no firmer foundation of knowledge:

> To design and plan for the delivery of services to older persons, society, the Congress, and the executive branch need information on their well-being, the factors that make a difference in their lives, and the impact of services on them. Currently, this information is spread piecemeal through Federal, State, local and private agencies. The result: Federal agencies have not evaluated the combined effect of these services, and in the absence of such information, assessing the impact of various laws on the lives of older people is difficult (United States General . . . 1979, p. ii).

There is substantial evidence in the research literature that, although in recent years an abundance of information has become available in our society, the quality, timeliness and relevance of information have not substantially improved. Weaver (1975, p. 94) found that "as technology continues to produce ever more sophisticated . . . procedures, equipment and support systems, the vulnerability of the administrator to misplaced and distorted data and communications increases . . ." In this sense, researchers and practitioners share a common concern: the need for better knowledge organization and access.

Trends that Heighten the Need for Networking

Recent changes in society created an upsurge in research, public policies and programs for older persons. The fields of social gerontology and health care, currently receiving public attention, are both the background and the field environment of the two projects in the focus of this paper. The prominent themes in the health care and human services literature are patients' rights to self-determination, the legal and religious implications of advanced medical technology, and the ethics of professional practice (Neugarten and Havighurst 1977). Gerontologists and health professionals have observed that the complex demands of society exceed the coping capacity of most individuals to help themselves in extremely stress-related situations, and create new challenges to the service professions (Golant and McCaslin 1979, Meyer 1976). The projects were prompted by the realization that a "buffer-zone" is needed between the coping ability of people and their dependence on social and health services, a zone of information provision to empower prevention and self-help as well as access to service delivery.

Societal trends affecting gerontology and related information services in the United States are charted as examples in the following.

CHANGES IN THE SOCIAL DOMAIN	CHANGES IN THE INFORMATION AND KNOWLEDGE DOMAIN
Increasing numbers of older persons in the population	Diversification of information needs; new problems of assessment (rural elderly, minorities, handicapped, etc.)
Researchers' differentiating characterization of the young-old and the old-old	Changing assumptions of how different groups of people seek and use information
More demands for health and social services as well as for preventive measures	New kinds of information products and fee-based services, resulting from alternative approaches to information handling and electronic resources
Mounting economic problems for people on fixed income and skyrocketing of health care costs	Scattering of problem-focused information across the literatures of various agencies, disciplines and professions
The proliferation of enterprises for home health care services as alternatives to institutions	
The need for adequate measurements for economic status, poverty threshold, health status and environmental influences	Growing information needs about services provided by the private sector
	Keener data orientation; requirements for social, health, environmental, quality-of-life, and poverty indicators
The need for scientific, socioeconomic and legal intelligence in the planning, management and evaluation of services	Increased demands for scientific, medical, legal and other specialized information by nonspecialists
Consumer participation and the need for information and data to support advocacy efforts	Concern about the utilization of knowledge for policy making, professional practice, and community action
The rise of cultural considerations in recognizing the needs of various groups in society in both developing and industrialized countries	Proliferation of large-scale information systems and problems of access at the community level
Increasing need for interdisciplinary work in research and program development and resulting communication needs	Calls for effective communication among researchers, practitioners, and interdisciplinary teams in service delivery

Recognition of life-span crises and stress situations and the role of support networks

Ethical, philosophical and legal problems created by advanced medical technology

More leisure time in retirement and decreasing economic means for leisure activities and mobility

Struggle against social stereotypes and resulting changes in media images.

Availability of information technologies for networking and the problem of assessing their use for various situations

Need for direct access to information resources by people as well as the need for intermediaries who synthesize, translate and repackage knowledge

Need to understand the economics of information and measures of productivity and effectiveness

Need for baseline data and the adverse impact of social stereotypes on data interpretation.

These issues are intended to generate dialogues between researchers and practitioners concerned with understanding the role of information in the lives of older people and in the work of gerontologists. There are questions to be explored and information dissemination practices to be tested and evaluated. Parallels between human service delivery and information delivery have often been observed. Both depend on rigorous need assessment and a combination of ethical, legal and psychological considerations. The quality of both activities is difficult to evaluate because of ambiguity of definitions and assumptions, and the inadequacy of current qualitative measurement techniques. Both areas are affected by a fluctuating combination of governmental regulations and market forces. These parallel characteristics have led to cooperation between human services and information systems in the developing and testing of experimental field projects.

Two research projects will be introduced below for discussion: a centralized information system designed to support community services to older persons, and a decentralized information sharing network used by health professionals. The projects were conducted at Syracuse University's School of Information Studies, funded by the U.S. Administration on Aging and the National Library of Medicine, respectively.

A Centralized Model:
The Gerontological Information Program (GRIP)

This prototype program was developed and tested as an information dissemination mechanism to create closer links between academic gerontologists and service providers. The program used a three-pronged approach, integrating (1) an information dissemination and support system, (2) research on information needs and uses, and (3) individualized training of graduate students of various disciplines in the utilization of information and data resources.

Established with the cooperation of the All-University Gerontology Center at Syracuse University, GRIP conducted an assessment of the information needs of 65 administrators and service providers in four types of organizations: geriatric centers/nursing homes; senior citizens' groups and centers; specific services; and umbrella or coordinating agencies. A semi-structured questionnaire was used in person-to-person interviews. Analysis of the data concentrated on topics that the respondents needed information about; types and sources of information they used; and the kinds of information support they would prefer. We found that current methods of accessing information were not successful for this population as indicated by the lack of solutions to problems or dissatisfaction with the solutions.

Based on the need assessment study, GRIP has developed an information support system answering queries from service providers. Examples of topics that were emphasized included regulations, legislation, small-area demographic data, minority needs, family relationships, and architectural barriers. In response, information was extracted from the sources and organized in individualized packages for the user. The results of all searches were evaluated and assembled in the form, length, depth, and detail most appropriate for the requestor. As a by-product of the system, GRIP has developed an internal database containing sources relevant to the planning, management and evaluation of community services to older adults.

The evaluation of the service addressed local service providers, and service providers elsewhere. During a nine-month period 43 local individuals who worked with the elderly used the GRIP information service. Thirty-four could be reached and asked for feedback by means of a self-administered questionnaire. Thirty-three responded—a rate of 97 percent. In addition, questionnaires were sent to 43 GRIP users, elsewhere, including individuals in the national and international gerontological community including scientists and practitioners in developing countries. Thirty-two responded, a return rate of 77 percent. Both groups were asked to indicate the kind of activity for which they used the information received from GRIP; the kinds of "benefits" the information provided by the GRIP service led to; and ways the information service affected job-related roles and reasons for its impact.

It was in the area of information sharing that GRIP proved to be especially useful to the human service agencies and practitioners. The information packages prepared for the requestors were often shared with co-workers and administrators (66.7 percent of the local respondents and

53.1 percent of the national and international respondents). This led us to believe that the information dissemination service stimulated communication among service providers.

In reference to our questions concerning the role of information dissemination and support service to human service providers, we found that

- practitioners in services did not have ready access to information and the kind of query answering service GRIP has offered;
- the GRIP prototype project provided a connecting link between information and referral services, management information systems and libraries by supplementing rather than duplicating their functions;
- this kind of information dissemination service can make a positive impact if there is trained staff to individualize the packaging of information in response to queries, and anticipate as well as assess needs;
- the joint training of graduate students from various disciplines was believed to build constructive researcher-practitioner relations for the future;
- the prototype information service was expected to be replicated by other organizations.

The investigation opened up a number of new research questions. What would be the optimum way of packaging the retrieved information for the user? How can "value" be conceptualized, and measurements developed either for human services or information services? What happens in "chains" of information acquisition when results are passed from one user to others? How can "failures" of support be measured by ascertaining problems that were not solved by the information and reasons for the lack of success? How can the service be maintained following the funding period? Such questions may be built into future projects replicating GRIP.

A Decentralized Model: The Health Information Sharing Project (HISP)

This four-year field research examined a new mode of improving the flow of health-related information and data in a community. The main objectives were experimental development and evaluation of a prototype decentralized information sharing network and empirical evaluation of HISP in terms of benefits to the participating organizations and individuals as well as its potential problems. The study examined informal information processes that link health professionals. Informal exchanges occurred not only at the work place, but also at parking lots, laboratories, the corridors of hospitals and cafeterias. HISP then (1) identified unpublished information resources (e.g., surveys, data collection efforts, policy analyses, training packages, research papers) produced by local health agencies that were presumed to be available through informal communication, (2) determined the location, forms and terms of access, (3) made this information available to health professionals and organizations, in the form of a computerized resource database and directory, (4) facilitated information exchange by the network of agency contacts (gatekeepers), (5) organized face-to-face group problem-solving sessions, and (6) probed into the informal interactions of health professionals.

We used a field experiment to examine information exchange patterns of participating agencies and people to obtain data on the effect of HISP in enhancing interagency contacts and to show whether an informal information sharing arrangement such as HISP had promise. In the first year, we carried out unstructured personal interviews with 284 staff members at 49 health agencies in Syracuse, N.Y. In the second year, a postmeasure was administered to the same individuals to establish to what extent, if any, the introduction of the HISP resource database, the network of contact persons, and the experience exchange sessions contributed quantitative and qualitative changes in the information sharing patterns.

We found that contact persons or gatekeepers were quite active not only within their agencies but also externally, forming links with health workers in other agencies in the community. The role of the gatekeeper was crucial to the diffusing of HISP throughout each agency. Methods of diffusion were identified. All those using the resource database (two thirds of the sample) said that HISP helped their information seeking. Three major factors contributed to positive attitudes toward HISP:

- Satisfaction with the overview of available information resources and contact persons
- Reliance on informal and personal contacts in information seeking or accidental discovery
- Assistance in avoiding duplication of services and programs.

The Syracuse community prototype was replicated in Binghamton, N.Y. and Albany, N.Y., to study the effects of the HISP network in three settings characterized by different social, economic and institutional structures. In the three communities, a total of 145 organizations participated. A field experiment evaluating the effects of HISP was conducted at each of the three sites. HISP developed thorough project documentation to allow replication.

New research questions identified by this project were: What type of agency might assume leadership for the future of HISP? Can a decentralized network sustain itself or does it need focal initiative and coordination? Can the network be utilized for purposes other than interagency information sharing? Can it be successfully merged with an information support service to participants? Are health professionals participating as agency representatives or individuals? These questions, together with the GRIP project, led us to inquire into the transferability of research models from one setting to another and the use of research findings as a consequence of transfer.

Research Utilization

During our field study we became keenly aware of the significance of practitioner-researcher communication. Without feedback and suggestions from health professionals for specific problems that merit further exploration, we could not have overcome occasional conceptual barriers as the project unfolded. This experience led us to focus on information dissemination and utilization in our own activities.

The ongoing transfer of research findings to practitioners and policy makers, also referred to as technology transfer, is an integral part of rendering knowledge useful. Interdisciplinary program-related experience is accumulating in the form of feasibility studies, program analyses and evaluation reports: a fugitive kind of literature. Legislative, regulatory and judicial information is becoming inseparable from effective program management. These resources are needed by decision makers, but they cannot be easily tapped because most of them are not included in accessible databases. Most difficult is to detect and acquire local and international information in any form. We realized that these two categories share several similarities: lack of commercial distribution and advertising, small stocks, and absence of listing in standard bibliographic formats.

Two general models of knowledge utilization might be distinguished in the research literature: (1) use of research targeting specific goals (the problem-solving model), and (2) the ongoing scanning and use of generalized research findings (the enlightenment model). The latter "provides the intellectual background of concepts, orientations and empirical generalizations that inform the professional activities of the user" (Weiss 1977, p. 544). Knowledge utilization is often conceptualized as a one-way process either from the researcher as information dissemination, or from the practitioner as information gathering. In either case, the process is characterized as practical. With similar emphasis on the value of experience, the philosopher Michel Philibert (1979, p. 391) insists that [in gerontology and in geriatrics], the progress is not from knowledge to know-how and thence to know-how-to-be, but only the other way around, from a quality of being to intervention and through intervention to knowledge.

Recent empirical studies of diffusion patterns address organizational behavior, the role of communication channels, and the innovation process (Nuehring 1978; Zaltman and Duncan 1977). Greer (1977) provides an analysis of diffusion studies concerning health care organizations, identifying three broad theoretical approaches: adoption of innovation by individuals; organizational attributes influencing the adoption process; and decision making in health institutions.

These studies argue convincingly that the social usefulness of research depends on the processes of disseminating findings by researchers and acquiring findings by professionals in the field. This is a demanding criterion of successful transfer even within the same country. What are the dimensions of using the nongeneralizable results of prototype projects such as the GRIP centralized information service and the HISP decentralized network in the social and cultural environment of another country?

Transfer of Projects to Developing Countries

An extensive international research literature deals with the migration of knowledge ("technology") from one culture to another. A developing country draws on research conducted both in other developing economies and in industrialized areas. A consensus seems to be emerging among researchers that the success of research migration or transfer depends on the applicability of the inquiry to the recipient culture, and on the skills of transmitters (e.g. consultants, project managers, trainers) and recipients in adjusting the original research findings to local needs. Such skills emanate from the recipients' environment, specifically from the combination of the indigenous R&D infrastructure and professional preparation for analytic and problem-solving capabilities. Therefore the status of research and professional training in developing countries needs to be understood.

There are numerous national and international organizations engaged in information science and communication research bearing upon social institutions in developing countries. Some are creating networks of investigators and consultants to facilitate the exchange of project experience and the dissemination of information. Indigenous research in information science is still not a widespread activity in developing countries. Researchers in these societies have few technological and institutional means to interact with and acquire new information directly from peers abroad.

Research is often discussed as either basic or applied. However, there is a third approach that has been neglected by the literature: problem-focused research. "In this area, the desire for knowledge is to a certain extent linked with the desire for action" (Bie 1970). Problem-focused research provides an appropriate framework for R&D in developing countries and facilitates the skills needed for problem analysis in the course of transferring and adapting research models. A problem, suggested Bartee (1973, p. 439), may be defined as "an unsatisfied need to change a perceived present situation to a perceived desired situation." The key concept here is perception, leading to an almost intuitive recognition of a problem. Problem analysis is a subjective and culturally determined process because it depends on assumptions about "how things are" and "how things should be." Ideally, the investigation of problems and the adaptation of foreign research models should be conducted by indigenous researchers.

In his study of professional development in the United States, Schein (1972, p. xi) suggested that "the values and needs of . . . students are . . . changing as they . . . advocate extending professional services to clients who have been historically underserved . . ." In recent years, the rate of change in American professional attitudes has quickened and became more controversial. Commercial advertisement of services, collective bargaining, fear of malpractice suits, and conflicting values within the same professional field became key issues abundantly discussed by gerontologists and health professionals through the GRIP and HISP networks. At the same time, low-income societies have been hindered in developing their professional workforce by the scarcity of educational opportunities, resource constraints, and the slow rate of change in postgraduate curricula. Even where educational innovation has been pioneered, problems of recruiting qualified teaching staff, establishing research programs, and producing training materials abound. We must ask, how relevant are the community networking models of GRIP and HISP to developing countries?

The answer, a positive and encouraging one, may lie in the nature of problem solving postulated by Bartee (1973). Researchers in both developing and industrialized countries may recognize and identify themselves with Bartee's components of the problem-solving process postulated as PERSONALIZATION (individual problem solving), COLLABORATION (data exchange and joint use), INSTITUTION-ALIZATION (problem-related decision making in organizations), SO-CIALIZATION (the introduction of change into society), and DIFFU-SION (the wide-ranging exchange of experience). In these concepts universal elements blend with culture-based elements. It is in this framework that the experience of community networks in culturally diverse environments can be shared and cooperation between experimental projects conducted in different countries can be achieved.

Questions we have posed at the beginning of our research may now be answered on the basis of our prototype project experience together with the analysis of the international literature, with at least a modest extent of certitude. First, we suggest that in any country, even those marked by technological scarcity, governmental and international information can be channeled to local users and adjusted to local needs by the establishment or enhancement of community networking relationships. Secondly, we believe that informal community networks can augment formal information systems created by technical aid projects by providing both work-related and personal coping information. These hypotheses and suggestions need to be tested in the grassroots environment of developing countries.

Conclusions

Community networking in support of information and experience sharing is a new exploration of the potential benefits and hazards of informal contacts for cooperation. Advances in technology can be expected to increase both benefits and hazards, but continued experimentation with field research projects will help to test the blend of technical, social and psychological elements in networking. The transfer of research models to other cultural environments needs extensive assessment, adaptation and repeated evaluation under the new conditions. Only active cooperation between high-technology and low-technology countries will permit testing of research models in diverse environments, and then foster knowledge about the international utilization of research.

To the extent that the literature of a number of disciplines addresses the need for sharing and using the findings of research in practical ways, we have some rudimentary understanding of this process.

The traditional view of knowledge utilization encompasses three phases: the dissemination of research findings; use by practitioners and policy makers; and application to the solving of practical problems. Our experience with the community networking projects suggests a few changes.

- We should differentiate between the concepts of knowledge utilization and information utilization. In the literature, "knowledge utilization" is most often restricted to the use of research findings. "Information utilization," on the other hand, is the use of any source that supports problem solving, decision making or updating one's view of the world.

- As part of the utilization process, the acceptance of information on the part of the user plays a major role and needs to be studied.
- Feedback from practitioners, especially the identification of problems that were not helped by the information, is as important as dissemination.

The role of intermediaries in research utilization needs more in-depth exploration (Figure 5.1). During the interaction between researcher, intermediary and practitioner, the flow of information is multidirectional. Researchers investigate phenomena and problems in different fields, but

Figure 5.1
The Role of Intermediaries in Research Utilization

RESEARCHER	INTERMEDIARY	PRACTITIONER
Identification of Problems	Identification of Problems	Identification of Problems
Research Production	Identification of Research	Seeking Research Information
Recommendations for Application		
Dissemination of Findings	→ Collection of Findings	
	Synthesis/Translation	
	Packaging	
	Dissemination	→ Acceptance and Consideration of Findings
	-For current awareness	Utilization
	-In response to queries	Application
	Monitoring Feedback	
	Synthesis of Feedback	← Feedback
Acceptance and Consideration of Feedback	← Dissemination of Feedback	Experience Production
	Collection of Recommendations for Research	Identification of New Problems
	Synthesis	← Recommendations for Research
	Packaging	
Seeking Experience Information		
Acceptance and Consideration of Recommendations for Research	← Dissemination	

they tend to underestimate the role of feedback and recommendations for research needs by practitioners. Intermediaries act as facilitators, organizers, and information interpreters. Such assistance may be provided at four levels: (1) referral to an information source (often a contact person), (2) retrieval of information and document delivery, (3) the content of information based on the analysis of the information source(s), and (4) evaluated and interpreted information for advocacy. Information intermediaries can enhance their effectiveness by accessing not only formal information systems but also human resource networks. Practitioners in different professions often feel that there is an unbridgeable distance between research and being "on the firing line." However, practitioners can be extremely helpful to researchers by offering feedback, the benefits of experience, and suggestions for future studies to intermediaries who assemble this information and disseminate it to researchers.

A community network can provide direct links between researchers and practitioners. Based on the GRIP and HISP projects we have raised several questions that merit future exploration. But the question that spans the topics of both communications in the community and the practical use of research findings will address *the role of the community network as intermediary*. Therein lies our hope that the findings of our prototype projects may someday be integrated with the findings in developing countries into a more comprehensive and valid intercultural learning experience.

References

Bartee, E.M. (1973). A holistic view of problem solving. *Management Science,* Pt. 1, 20(4), 439–448.

Bengston, V.L. et al. (1977). Relating academic research to community concerns: A case study in collaborative effort. *Journal of Social Issues,* 33(4), 75–92.

Bhattacharyya, S.N. (1972). *Community Development in Developing Countries.* Calcutta, India: Academic Publishers.

Bie, P. de. (1970). "Problem-focused research." In United Nations Educational, Scientific and Cultural Organization. *Main Trends of Research in the Social and Human Sciences. Part 1.* Paris, France: UNESCO.

Caplow, T. (1975). *Toward Social Hope.* New York, NY: Basic Books.

Collier, Jr., J. & Buitron, A. (1971). *The Awakening Valley.* Otavalo, Ecuador: Otavalenian Institute of Anthropology.

Golant, S.M. & McCaslin, R. (1979). A Functional classification of services for older people. *Journal of Gerontological Social Work,* 1(3), 187–209.

Greer, A.L. (1977). Advances in the study of diffusion of innovation in health care organizations. *Milbank Memorial Fund Quarterly,* 55, 505–532.

Holland, T.P. (1976). Information and decision making in human services. *Administration in Mental Health,* 26–35.

Kochen, M. & Donohue, J.C. eds. (1976). *Information for the Community.* Chicago, IL: American Library Association.

Meyer, C.H. (1976). *Social Work Practice: The Changing Landscape.* New York, NY: The Free Press.

Neugarten, B.L. & Havighurst, R.J. (1977). *Extending the Human Life Span: Social Policy and Social Ethics.* Washington, DC: National Science Foundation.

Nuehring, E.M. (1978). The Character of interorganizational task environments. *Administration Society,* 9(4). 425–447.

Philibert, M. (1979). "Philosophical approach to gerontology." In Hendricks, J. & Hendricks, C.D. *Dimensions of Aging: Readings,* 379–394. Cambridge, MA: Winthrop Publishers.

Press, I. & McKool Jr., M. (1972). Social structure and status of the aged: Toward some valid cross-cultural generalizations. *Aging and Human Development,* 3(4), 297–306.

Schein, E.H. (1972). *Professional Education: Some New Directions.* (With Kommers, D.W.). New York, NY: McGraw Hill.

United States General Accounting Office. (1979). *Conditions of Older People: National Information System Needed.* Washington, DC: Government Printing Office.

United States Office of Technology Assessment. (1979). *Selected Topics in Federal Health Statistics.* Washington, DC: Government Printing Office.

Weaver, J.L. (1975). *Conflict and Control in Health Care Administration.* Beverly Hills, CA: SAGE Publications.

Weiss, C.H. (1977). Research for policy's sake: The Enlightenment function of social research. *Policy Analysis,* 3, 531–545.

The World Bank. (1975). *The Assault on World Poverty: Problems of Rural Development, Education and Health.* Baltimore, MD: The Johns Hopkins University Press.

Zaltman, G. and Duncan, R. (1977). *Strategies for Planned Change.* New York, NY: Wiley.

6

Human Resource Networks
for Rural Development

Introduction

This paper suggests that the preparation of staff for information management in rural development needs intensive attention by project planners and managers. The products of rural development research incorporate data on social impact, and analytic tools for risk assessment, technology transfer, and the management of natural resources. This information can vastly improve our understanding of the relationships between economic and sociocultural factors that affect improvements in the rural areas of developing countries. Education and training programs are beginning to realize the importance of this knowledge. Networks linking practitioners, educators, and policy makers involved in rural development work in Africa without the benefits of a telecommunication infrastructure, and using traditional means, form the core of this paper.

A six-year field research project testing information sharing patterns of small local organizations in three different locations in the United States will be described. The findings of the research supported previous claims in the international literature that human resource networks, even if not yet computerized, are excellent mechanisms of information exchange. With the expanding use of electronic networking, already existing information sharing relationships will be greatly empowered. However, results of a prototype study conducted in the United States cannot be generalized for developing countries where economic, social and cultural conditions pose entirely different information requirements. This paper, therefore, will consider not only potential benefits, but also possible problems that might be expected when a project undertakes to implement a human resource network.

Local Participation in Rural Development

In the 1970s research found that local participants in development projects tended to resist innovations unless they were not only participants in name, but had the opportunity to contribute to planning decisions. Even though people were willing to temporarily use new practices, technologies and services, they were often reluctant to absorb these innovations into their local culture. This attitude toward change imposed from the top down has been known to include small innovations introduced by indigenous government officials and advisors as much as foreign project managers and consultants. As Jedlicka (1981, p. 259) reported, "farmers will resist [technology] transfer programs that do not solicit their involvement or are not designed according to their specific constraints and environmental knowledge."

Even in the case of a congenial relationship between exogenous advisors and local counterparts, the recipients of rural technical assistance programs often express the feeling that interventions and information leading to innovations are tainted by foreign ideas. Thus the recipients of aid are not always prepared to maintain the changes beyond the life of a project (Ahmed 1974). The real test of acceptance of a new service or technology by the local population is the willingness to assume the recurring costs for the ongoing maintenance of project results. Such observations are confirmed by empirical research on the diffusion patterns of innovation in rural development (Feder, Just and Zilberman 1982).

As the trend toward local involvement in development planning is growing, supportive local institutions, educational programs and information dissemination are increasingly seen by project management as assets. An agricultural development policy paper proposed that local institutions can "facilitate broad-based production growth by diffusing risk, conveying technical information, or facilitating communication between local people and government officials" (United States Agency . . . 1978, pp. 29–30). The purpose of formal and nonformal education and information dissemination is to assist farmers, small entrepreneurs, and local officials to increase their capacity for the evaluation and adaptation of new technology and practices. As Cusack (1981, p. 263) observed, "development projects usually fail, not because of constraints, but because these constraints were not taken into consideration when the project was designed, or were not adjusted to with flexibility during implementation." Local participation calls for unorthodox information activities that will provide support to small organizations, groups and individuals, and will assist them to become active information providers themselves.

Information and Development Decisions

This paper builds on the assumption that information used to measure the impact of change on the lives of people is central to the development process. In a rural development project information may play several roles. The following examples will provide a preliminary framework for the discussion of human resource networks.

1. *Data Collection and Analysis*

Data reflecting local social conditions and information representing the population's perceptions of development needs are collected to support project planning and implementation (Gehrmann 1978, Hyman 1981, Pearce-Batten 1980). But change cannot be measured from the point of view of project management only. In order to collect meaningful data from local leaders, officials and farmers through personal interviews, people must be included in the total communications process of the project rather than remain relegated to the passive role of "subjects." Before participants can be expected to answer questions of data collectors or otherwise *give* helpful information to project management, they should *receive* information about the project's expected implications for their daily life and work.

2. *Monitoring and Evaluation*

Various data generation and reporting methods are used to measure the effectiveness of development projects. Monitoring has been defined as the gathering and analysis of information on inputs, outputs, and other project-related data throughout the life of the project, while evaluation refers to the comparison of original plans with actual project impacts (Deboeck and Kinsey 1980, pp. 59–61). The major objective of monitoring and evaluation during the implementation phase of a project is to gain sufficient insights into interim successes and problems in order to revise the initial approach. Whenever innovations introduced by a project involve behavioral changes in people in the target area, original project designs will need flexibility and frequent adjustment (Cernea and Tepping 1977).

Much has been written in recent years about the role of management information systems and decision support systems in development. Sobhan (1976, pp. 19–20) offers a theoretical framework for rural development decision making by classifying factors that may help a project to succeed, and selecting indicators for measuring these factors. Among other variables, he describes such viable but difficult-to-define indices of project success as the "Agricultural Knowledge Index" and the "Self-Help Index," the latter designed to measure formal and informal group participation that complements other project activities. Mickelwait, Sweet and Morss (1978, pp. 58–68) provide case studies in ten countries to illustrate local decision making. The analysis of data from these projects is used to illustrate strategies of indigenous participation in project-related decisions. For example, one of the case studies describes local councils created in Ghana as the primary political/administrative entities of their districts to collaborate with development projects. In spite of the growing emphasis on including the perceptions of local people in data collection, the underutilization of information systems reporting the analysis of data is identified by Mickelwait, Sweet and Morss as a major problem in project evaluation.

3. Modeling and Forecasting

Several methods are used by researchers to create scenarios of possible consequences due to alternative paths of action. Global models of growth trends and projected changes in resources have been constructed since the early 1970s. The Model of International Relations in Agriculture (MOIRA) foresees a doubling of world food production between 1975 and 2000, and a 36 percent rise in per capita consumption. Nevertheless, "because of unequal distribution, the number of people subsisting on two-thirds or less of the biological protein requirement rises from 350 million in 1975 to 740 million in 2000" (United States Council . . . 1980, p. 44). The Council points out that when constructing its data base, the model had taken into account the effects of agricultural policies, but not the consequences of environmental degradation.

The above example underscores one of the flaws of modeling: results can be interpreted only with a full understanding of assumptions. Another problem is that large-scale modeling has little or no relevance to the immediate information needs of the rural poor unless an agricultural development project has specialists on its staff who can translate large-scale trends and projections into local conditions and needs. However, with steady improvements in simulation, modeling and forecasting techniques, these tools hold considerable promise for rural development planning as long as they are used with the local economic and cultural context in mind.

4. Information Dissemination

The dissemination of practical know-how to farmers, villagers, and rural organizations in the form of traditional extension services or the more recent Training and Visiting System (Benor and Harrison 1977), can help local people to assume more responsibility for development decisions. Information dissemination in support of a change brought about by intercultural technology transfer is essentially similar to what is termed the diffusion of innovations by several disciplines. Reviewing theoretical and empirical studies of the adoption of agricultural innovations, Feder, Just and Zilberman (1982) found a remarkable diversity and identified differences in research results stemming from different socio-economic environments.

The role of the process of "informing" is implied by Srinivasan (1977, p. 2) who suggests that some of the causes of poverty might be related to people's lack of access to opportunities. What we need to learn about a society is whether or not it provides a system that allows people to discover possibilities open to them. Srinivasan posits that unless a society provides organized channels, access to opportunities will remain a haphazard matter favoring the educated who are better equipped than others to "find out." The World Bank (1982, p. 39) reports that "farmers have access to an agricultural science that is a much greater source of innovation and a better catalyst of productivity growth than ever before. But this is true much more for some groups of farmers than for others." This observation suggests that information dissemination services may be evaluated by the examination of at least two factors: The extent of the equity of access to information for users, and the link between information and agricultural production—a major challenge.

5. *Information and Library Services*

In addition to internal information systems for management and communication links with people living in the area, the rural development project is concerned also with external information resources. In recent years the integration of public and commercial producers of information, specialized information centers, and statistical data banks into a national infrastructure has become an issue for central government planning. The in-country acquisition of information depends on the contacts a project develops with indigenous institutions. More importantly, a project can play a catalyst role by forming links among different organizations and rural institutions, and building people's capabilities to apply external information to their work and generate indigenous information based on local knowledge and skills.

The characteristics of information resources that rural development projects may use vary from country to country and, within each country, from one location to another. In many developing societies, funds from international organizations and national governments flow mainly to scientific and technological information centers rather than to rural areas. However, information systems in agriculture, energy, tropical medicine, human settlements and other sectors are beginning to play a visible role in support of rural development. Moreover, in several developing countries a trend toward the computerization of social, demographic and economic data files is evident. A landmark report on national statistical systems by the United Nations (1979, p. 7) emphasized "a practical program of establishing a permanent reporting structure, to create a mechanism for coordination, to develop a means for ongoing evaluation and to provide a capability to carry out surveys on a planned sample basis."

6. *Informal Information Channels*

Formal data collection, information retrieval, document acquisition, and extension activities have always been supplemented by informal communications. In rural development, informal channels represent effective links among small organizations and rural people. As the United States Agency for International Development began to implement its New Directions policy, it perceived "linkages and general conditions leading to effective local actions within rural development programs as one of the means of involving small farmers, entrepreneurs and local organizations" (Morss et al. 1976). Confirming its commitment to human resource development, the World Bank (1980, p. 37) stated that "human beings are the source of ideas, decisions and actions on investment, innovations and other opportunities." In the domain of social data, the United Nations (1979, p. 19) noted that "the limited body of statistics actually used for planning and administration is circulated somewhat more promptly by informal means within a project or ministry." The literature of rural sociology, anthropology, and development identifies the value of local inventories of indigenous cultural products and oral tradition. Social entertainment forms such as street theater, puppet shows or musical events are information resources, "because these forms are integrated into, and are integrators of, the life of the community" (Colletta 1977, p. 15). Thus, in the wake of new development strategies, informal social networks have been discovered as useful information carriers for development projects.

Information Resource Networks

In the information and computer sciences, a network denotes connections among systems, but in the rural development literature the term means information exchange relationships among individuals and organizations. A resource directory or database normally forms the basis of such interactions which might be (a) *informal* (individuals communicating with each other to acquire information), (b) *semiformal* (individuals either contacting each other or turning to a network focal point for referral), or (c) *formal* (all participants obtaining information through a focal point). We know very little about the nature of networking in rural development, but studies of informal networks (e.g. invisible colleges, expert groups) in industrialized countries have been extensive. Following two decades of research, a trend toward the systematic utilization of interpersonal communication patterns is emerging. Several organizations and institutions responsible for the dissemination of specialized information are developing databases of resource persons. These efforts represent the "formalization" of informal human resource networks. In the international development community, informal and unstructured ways of creating a network will reach a number of individuals. This gradual expansion of contacts is essentially a by-product of development projects, and requires minimal initial funding.

In the long run, however, the unstructured approach might not meet the objectives of networking for two reasons. First, it runs the risk of emphasizing obvious contacts (e.g. contacts in international organizations and sponsor countries) rather than the less visible institutions and potential consultants in developing countries. Second, this method might produce a network of academics and researchers without appropriate participation from the field, since researchers usually become aware of new opportunities to access information sooner than policy makers and practitioners who work under the pressure of deadlines. Lele (1975, p. 53) pointed out what many rural development specialists have come to believe, that "it is only when an effective two-way dialogue between research and extension is established that the current rural development effort will have a noticeable impact."

Information Equity

In spite of the growing interest in networking, human resource directories and databases will not be sufficient to ensure effective knowledge sharing. The ethical, political and administrative implications of even partially formalized communication links among a large number of people can produce unexpected problems. As long as the exchange of ideas and personal information sources takes place in the spirit of collaboration, most problems can be handled informally. But when questions about the ownership of information, liability for misuse, the credibility of data, or the confidentiality of records arise, human relationships become very complex and the balance between informality and lack of policy can turn precarious.

Undoubtedly, the most difficult problem in information sharing arrangements is to achieve information equity. Many institutions in low-income countries have a critical need for expertise and technical know-how, but participation in networks that had been initiated in industrial countries may be either technically impossible or exceedingly costly. In addition, differences in ease of access within each country call for serious consideration. Connection to international networks is restricted to one university and, occasionally, one additional institution in low-income countries. Document and book packages mailed from the United States to central ministries or academic institutions will hardly ever reach small provincial or local institutions. Since in every country an immense gap exists between large-scale information systems and the grassroots where people are in dire need of information, the *international* information sharing network should be linked to *local-level* networks that can serve as transmitters, interpreters, and cultural filters.

The joining of computer and telecommunication technologies offers exciting promise for network development. For example, the new International Centre for Genetic Engineering and Biotechnology (ICGEB) is a research and scientific training institution serving the needs of developing countries, and as "the hub of an international network of data exchange" (O'Sullivan 1983, p. 18). In order to share effectively the benefits of such a unique resource with rural development and agricultural projects, the international network must include participants who are committed to the dissemination of information to geographically dispersed areas and local networks. Connections between a specialized international network (e.g. Genetic Engineering and Biotechnology) and small rural networks (e.g. Agricultural Extension) need technology, personal contacts, and a policy framework. Because many developing countries lack the necessary telecommunication infrastructure, the policy framework of an international network needs to accommodate both traditional and electronic information sharing networks.

Before the policy framework is formulated, legal, social and ethical issues of the international network should be explored. Three questions should be tested and studied.

1. Are formalized interpersonal networks, coordinated by a focal point, more effective than semiformal networks that operate on the basis of direct contacts among the participants without a central referral center?
2. With some participants of the international network living in industrialized countries and others in low-income countries, what will be the impact on the equity of access to the information network when the "haves" use computers while the "have-nots" rely on traditional modes of communications?
3. How does an international network affect confidential or proprietary information?

Researchers and planners of rural development projects cannot turn their attention to social, cultural and legal issues too soon. In the meantime, international information sharing networks may want to keep as much informality and flexibility in their operations as possible in order to handle controversial issues before the policy framework is in place.

A Local Information Sharing Network

In a specialized international communication network participants share the same interest in a discipline, profession, or topical area. Information passes several national and cultural boundaries separating participants. A local communication network links individuals who share the same cultural background and may also have the same interest, for example, rural development.

The following observations are based on six years of research on local information sharing networks at Syracuse University. The field experiment used in the study identified preferred methods of information diffusion within health institutions in three communities; factors that influenced the attitudes of people toward information sharing; and the role of personal trust in the acceptance and use of a new information resource. Rural development studies, too, stress the importance of informal connectedness among organizations and individuals. Researchers report that in developing countries small rural organizations are linked by a variety of activities and modes of communication. Strengthening these relationships by organizational and technological but nonbureaucratic arrangements contributes to the self-development of people (Khan 1978, Korten 1979, Nash et al. 1976, Uphoff and Esman 1974). As noted before, we cannot assume that a process tested in North American communities will prove successful in a rural development project in another country without adjusting the prototype process to local needs and conditions. "Adaptive field testing" has been described as "experimentation conducted within the context of an ongoing development project, which aims at predicting with greater certainty the outcome of an intervention" (Olson 1978, p. 2).

With these considerations in mind, the involvement of indigenous participants in an information and experience sharing network can have many benefits. Initially, a mapping of local organizations and their experience in certain activities takes place. To alleviate natural suspicions and reluctance to reveal organizational matters, this process is kept at the informal level and is carried out with the cooperation of local leaders. The focus of the network is the community or a group of communities. Some of the following types of organizations are likely to have experience, skills and information resources that may be tapped by the network:

- State and district offices
- Local councils and boards
- Regional planning agencies
- Associations, cooperatives and farmers' clubs

- Educational and training facilities
- Agricultural and other research stations
- Extension services
- Religious and self-help groups, women's groups, youth organizations
- Clinics and health extension
- Land use and tenancy offices
- Offices of local services (water supply, irrigation, sewage disposal, etc.).

Each participating organization is invited to designate a "network contact," and villagers select additional contacts. Bringing together these individuals for face-to-face experience sharing meetings is useful to all participants. Weisel and Mickelwait (1978, pp. 54–55) describe a rural development project in a relatively poor country with a large subsistence agricultural sector. The team collected data by holding group meetings of farmers and leaders for the discussion of the following issues:

- The viability of local-level organizations
- Local ecological and demographic characteristics
- Adequacy of the social and economic infrastructure (e.g., health and educational facilities, roads, water)
- The links between central government ministries and local organizations; extent and adequacy of government staff, and funds available in the project areas.

The information thus gained was used by the project for planning and implementing improvements in organizational management and communications, the utilization of information about the project's environment, the ways local services are planned and staffed, and the relationship between government and local agencies.

The Cultural Relevance of Interpersonal Networks

How does human interaction for information gathering or exchange take place? Many rural communities cannot depend on telephone contacts between organizations and groups because of frequent breakdowns of the communication system.

The village or town meeting is still the customary decision-making forum, and personal encounters are mainly face-to-face, often at the market. Existing patterns of community life, that is, play a central role in diffusing information by development projects. They also offer established structures upon which to plan and start a local communication network. One problem is the network's occasional use by assistance agencies for promoting their own politics, or by local groups for building personal powerbases. To forestall this course of events, the network, jointly operated by local and exogenous project staff, should emphasize practical skill-related information, demonstrate the tangible benefits of cooperation, and be open to all groups and individuals in the community. Such conditions can never be imposed from the outside. The network, after all, is a product of the people in local organizations and groups. Unless an information sharing arrangement benefits each participant, the network easily deteriorates. If local participants and the staff of rural development projects are to be linked by communication channels that are not hierarchical and mandatory but informal and voluntary, each individual has to be motivated to use these channels as well as to contribute his own experience.

The characteristics of data needed and collected by rural development teams from farmers are more relevant to the economic and social aspects needed to understand the project's environment than to the technical details of the project's task. It takes skillfully coordinated interdisciplinary teams to meet this challenge. As a United Nations (1979, p. 9) study stated: "The approach to social welfare and development must necessarily be multisectoral and take into account the implications of a wide range of policies. Information on a variety of social and economic dimensions may be required for the formulation of policies for any single sector." Some of the data categories collected by Weisel and Mickelwait (1978) include:

Farm production
Farming practices used
Availability of land, equipment and other farm assets
Storage problems
System of land utilization
Adequacy of the agricultural support system (input supply, markets)
Infrastructure needs
Adequacy of extension
Availability and applicability of research results
Credit availability
Family decision making in agricultural activities; and
Pricing problems.

Except where confidential, such data can form a valuable pool in an information exchange program. In this context, "valuable" means that the data are useful because they reflect the needs and expectations of local farmers. Although caution should be exercised concerning the usefulness of the data for quantitative analytic purposes, this mode of information gathering can be well integrated with the meetings of the local farmers and can be used effectively for the qualitative assessment of the population's needs.

Benefits and Problems of Local Networks

The balancing of potential advantages and disadvantages of a new approach to information is a necessary ingredient in policy analysis. Who is going to gain? Who is likely to lose? The informal nature of information sharing networks should not suggest a lack of thoughtful consideration. There is a need to safeguard informality, encourage active participation, and deter misuse. The concept of the information sharing network is built on mutual support and shared experience. Although a technical aid project might contract out the initial planning of the experience-sharing meetings and the data survey, members of the community should develop the responsibility for organizing the meetings as a public activity and inventorying resource organizations.

Benefits of the network may be uncovered only in considerable time, following implementation, even four to five years. Evaluation may be supplemented by demographic data, as well as by analysis of the queries addressed to the network and the responses supplied. Benefits may include the following difficult-to-measure, intangible consequences:

- Developed from within the community, the information sharing network may be expected to enhance local initiative, pride and self-expression. It may also help participants to identify their own needs.
- A record of local experiences and accomplishments will be created; failures of past ventures may be examined as part of every human learning. Gradually, out of the experience sharing, there might emerge a feeling that failures can be overcome and accomplishments can be used as building blocks for future planning.
- Informal information sharing fosters trust in community resources. As people in organizations and groups begin to use practical everyday information through the network, this experience can gradually be extended to contacts with organizations at the district, state and national levels. Thus the isolation of some communities might be ameliorated.
- A multidirectional, informal communication pattern can be established between the community and the rural development project. This would assist the project staff in better understanding local conditions and participants. One can also conjecture that people living in the project area would come to understand the goals of rural development better through meetings, information processes and technical advice they would receive through the network.

The *problems* one anticipates when implementing a local information exchange network in a rural environment are numerous. One set of potential disappointments relates to the transfer of the network model from industrialized countries (Smith 1980). Another problematic issue concerns the credibility, usefulness and appropriateness of the information passed through the network.

- *Credibility*. The cultural gap between the expatriate staff of a technical aid project and the rural poor cannot always be bridged. Suspicions of urban and foreign bias prevail, and support for the project is not always forthcoming from the local communities because management failed to involve those who should be aided by the project (Kilby 1979, Westphal 1978).
- *Usefulness*. In many cases the design of the project's intervention into the traditional flow of rural life is of high technical quality, but management and consultants fail to realize that local people are not about to take a risk and adopt a technique or product alien to them. The same may be true for the information sharing network. People might confuse it with extension work, and see it as overly complex and burdensome. Only information truly practical for everyday life and cooperation with local opinion makers may alleviate such natural problems of the change experience.
- *Appropriateness*. The introduction of new technology in project areas is not always integrated with local development goals. After project subsidies end, the ongoing maintenance of the new technology becomes a recurrent item in the local public budget, resented by people in the entire area. In the struggle to meet recurrent costs, opportunities for experimentation, with a new approach to work, and creative adaptation to local needs may be lost. Abandoned projects are often more harmful than a lack of projects. A series of country and sector studies concluded that the transfer of inappropriate technology contributes to dislocations and increased economic hardship for the poor (Weiss 1979). In such cases the local information sharing network introduced by the project will be rejected along with other project products.

It has often been said that no rural development project can be so precisely designed and its impact so correctly predicted that the implementation will be entirely free of frustrations. In a human enterprise that tampers with people's lives, nothing can be as valuable as the open distribution of information. Although information sharing networks may experience several difficulties while taking off, their potential benefits outweigh their problems. When local people find it hard to identify with a development project's goals and activities, a local network may provide the human experience that forms the connecting link.

Implications for Education and Training

Deboeck and Kinsey (1980) analyzed the professional challenges and problems involved in managing information systems and services for rural development in Eastern Africa. One of the most demanding challenges in any practicing (and practical) profession is the need to understand the ever-changing needs of the client. Rural development research is an interdisciplinary enterprise. Information workers have to draw on numerous fields in order to sharpen their perceptions of the great variety of potential applications of information delivery. Research literature in rural development suggests several thoughts for educators and trainers.

First, education and training programs are natural vehicles for innovation. Program designers have accepted the responsibility for preparing information managers in rural development. Second, perspectives and skills are needed that are in accord with current trends in development policies. An international seminar might begin by exploring the techniques and uses of different kinds of human resource networks. This approach would yield a two-fold benefit: Emphasis on interpersonal communications, and development of an experimental pilot network by seminar participants for ongoing experience exchange following their return home. The seminar would offer modules in management areas which strengthen analytic and interpersonal skills, for example:

Analysis of user needs
Trends in rural development policies
Relationship of the researcher, the entrepreneur, the extension worker
    and the information manager
Cost-benefit analysis
Interpersonal communication and networking
Marketing of information services.

Although these areas represent essential perspectives and competencies, they are not sufficient by themselves; they need a harmonizing theme. Education has always depended on the integration of philosophical values, bold ideas and down-to-earth applications. The best educators know not only how to teach but also how to listen. By listening to the current needs of rural development, educators and trainers will learn to combine scientific and technological information with the intuitive understanding of rural culture and tradition. The first kind of knowledge may be captured by an international network of expertise. But it is the local information sharing network that will assure the cultural understanding of how to apply specialized knowledge to local needs.

References

Ahmed, A.G.M. (1974). *The Relevance of Indigenous Systems of Organization of Production to Rural Development: A Case from Sudan.* Khartoum, Sudan: National Council for Research.

Benor, D. & Harrison, J.Q. (1977). *Agricultural Extension, the Training and Visit System.* Washington, DC: The World Bank.

Cernea, M.M. & Tepping, B.J. (1977). *A System of Monitoring and Evaluating Agricultural Extension Projects.* Washington, DC: The World Bank. (Staff working paper 272).

Cohen, J.M. & Uphoff, N.T. (1976). *Rural Development Participation: Concepts for Measuring Participation for Project Design, Implementation and Evaluation.* Ithaca, NY: Cornell University Rural Development Committee.

Colletta, N.J. (1977). Folk culture and development: Cultural genocide or cultural revitalization? *Convergence, 10,* 12–19.

Cusack, D.F. (1981). The Transfer of computer-based technology in agroclimate information systems. *Interciencia, 6,* 261–267.

Dawson, A. (1978). Suggestions for an approach to rural development by foreign aid programmes. *International Labor Review, 117,* 391–404.

Deboeck, G. & Kinsey, B. (1980). *Managing Information for Rural Development: Lessons from Eastern Africa.* Washington, DC: The World Bank. (Staff working paper 379).

Feder, G., Just, R.E., & Zilberman, D. (1982). *Adoption of Agricultural Innovation in Developing Countries, a Survey.* Washington, DC: The World Bank. (Staff working paper 542).

Gehrmann, F. (1978). "Valid" empirical measurement of quality of life? *Social Indicators Research, 5,* 73–109.

Hyman, E. (1981). The Uses, validity, and reliability of perceived environmental quality indicators. *Social Indicators Research, 9,* 85–110.

Jedlicka, A.D. (1981). Technology transfer to subsistence farmers: Management process and behavioral technique. *Interciencia, 6,* 257–260.

Khan, A.H. (1978). *Ten Decades of Rural Development: Lessons from India.* East Lansing, MI: Michigan State University, Department of Agricultural Economics. (MSU Rural Development Paper 1).

Kilby, P. (1979). Evaluating technical assistance. *World Development, 7,* 309–323.

Korten, D.C. (1979). Community Social Organization in Rural Development. Resource paper given at A and P Agricultural and Resource Staff Seminar. (Unpublished). Yogyakarta, Indonesia and Manila, The Philippines: Ford Foundation.

Lele, U. (1975). *The Design of Rural Development, Lessons from Africa.* Baltimore, MD: The Johns Hopkins University Press.

Mickelwait, D.R., Sweet, C.F., & Morss, E.R. (1978). *The "New Directions" Mandate: Studies in Project Design, Approval and Implementation.* Washington, DC: Development Alternatives Inc.

Morss, E.R. et al. (1976). *Strategies for Small Farmer Development.* Washington, DC: Development Alternatives, Inc.

Nash, J. et al. (1976). *Popular Participation in Social Change.* The Hague: Mouton Publishers.

Olson, C.V. (1978). *Adaptive Field-Testing for Rural Development Projects.* Washington, DC: U.S. Agency for International Development.

O'Sullivan, D.A. (1983). Global Biotechnology Centre to Aid Developing Countries Planned. (January 10). *Chemical and Engineering News,* 18–19.

Pearce-Batten, A. (1980). New measures of development. *Development Digest,* 18(1), 75–94.

Smith, A. (1980). *The Geopolitics of Information: How Western Culture Dominates the World.* New York, NY: Oxford University Press.

Sobhan, I. (1976). *The Planning and Implementation of Rural Development Projects: An Empirical Analysis.* Washington, DC: U.S. Agency for International Development.

Srinivasan, T.N. (1977). *Poverty: Some measurement problems. International Statistical Institute, 41st Session, Proceedings.* New Delhi, India: ISI. (World Bank Reprint No. 77).

United Nations Department of International Economic and Social Affairs. (1979). *Improving Social Statistics in Developing Countries: Conceptual Framework and Methods.* New York, NY: UN.

United States Agency for International Development. (1978). *Agricultural Development Policy Paper.* Washington, DC: U.S. Agency for International Development.

United States Council on Environmental Quality. (1980). *The Global 2000 Report to the President. Summary Report.* V. 1. Washington, DC: CEQ.

Uphoff, N.T. & Esman, M.J. (1974). *Local Organization for Rural Development: Analysis of Asian Experience.* Ithaca, NY: Cornell University, Rural Development Committee.

Weisel, P.F. & Mickelwait, D.R. (1978). *Designing Rural Development Projects: An Approach.* Washington, DC: Development Alternatives, Inc.

Weiss, C., Jr. (1979). Mobilizing technology for developing countries. *Science,* 203, 1083–1089. (World Bank Reprint 95).

Westphal, L.E. (1978). Research on appropriate technology. *Industry and Development,* 2, 28–46. (World Bank Reprint 88).

The World Bank. (1980). *World Development Report 1980.* Washington, DC: The World Bank.

The World Bank. (1982). *World Development.* Washington, DC: The World Bank.

7

Electronic Networking in Support of South-to-South Cooperation

Marta Dosa and Jeffrey Katzer

Introduction*

Aware of the growing role of problem-solving information and data in development, several national governments and intergovernmental organizations have been investing in the information workforce in developing countries. As a result, a number of information studies programs in these countries have introduced innovations in curricula, technological applications and research orientation. At the same time, a growing number of governments organized high-level expert meetings to formulate the fundamentals of national information and telecommunication policies (Montviloff 1990).

"Information workforce" implies capabilities in the planning and implementing of databases and information systems, based on a combination of computer and telecommunication technologies, in the framework of national socioeconomic development goals. The cooperation of all sectors of the economy in sustainable development planning necessitates improved access to information. National needs for data resources fall into several broad categories: scientific research results; R&D data; multidisciplinary planning data; information for and about technology transfer, assessment, and forecasting; survey of manufacturing and service economies; social intelligence on the conditions of the poor; culturally appropriate information for dissemination to rural areas and urban centers; and information for various sectors (e.g. agriculture, energy production, environmental management, health care, housing).

Information studies are under pressure to train information managers who are capable of working with demographers and planners in order to create the data systems necessary for development planning. Systems designers and information intermediaries are needed to evaluate specialized information systems. Rural communicators must be trained for work with

*We gratefully acknowledge the support of Dr. Yves Courrier, Chief of Education and Training Section, General Information Programme, United Nations Educational, Scientific and Cultural Organization, in the feasibility study described in this paper.

isolated groups of farmers, cattle rangers, and tribes on the move. These needs represent the environment of information education in developing countries. Thus key information professionals trained in these programs must be knowledgeable not only about the technical aspects of the national information infrastructure, but also about the laws, regulations, international treaties and other policy instruments that affect the use of information in support of decisions across all population sectors.

Sauvant, an affiliate of the United Nations Centre for Transnational Corporations, asserts that data products and services play a major role in international trade. Technologically advanced countries with domestic data resources and processing capabilities are at a great advantage in trade transactions. Developing countries of the South, without sufficient skills for data generation and transfer, continue to exist in a dependency relationship with the North.

> It is not surprising that countries increasingly seek, first and foremost, to strengthen domestic data resources; second, to ensure access to those data services that cannot reasonably be developed locally; and third, to improve their physical and intellectual data infrastructure (informatics, telecommunications and skills) to place the country in the best position to use data resources (Sauvant 1986, p. 9).

As leading schools of information science in developing countries forge ahead to prepare professionals for functioning effectively in the new information-based economies, a major question in the minds of policy makers focuses on the sustainability of educational innovations. What happens to these pioneering schools when international funding for the revision of education programs expires? Do national development plans incorporate information policies? Do information policies lend the kind of support to information education programs that is commensurate with the importance of an up-to-date information workforce? How can scientific and technological innovations in information and telecommunication systems be sustained and continuously updated? These questions need resolutions to assure the long-range effectiveness of education.

The success or failure of information education programs can have a long-lasting impact on national information services and policies. Education programs, dealing with human beings in terms of preparation for real-life problems, are particularly sensitive to the uncertainties that often beset institutions in the aftermath of change. The process of institution building in any field harbors two latent problems which have been known to emerge after the initial momentum of innovation: potential crisis or potential stagnation. Either situation might be more severe if broad segments of the information creator, transmitter and user populations are not involved in national planning and the innovating education program is left in an intellectual vacuum. Sustainable development policies that emphasize human resources, leadership and vision represent a trend toward forestalling both crisis and quiescence in the change implementation process. Projects strive to balance investment in natural and physical resources (e.g. land, energy, industry, materials) and knowledge-based resources (e.g. learning, ideas, innovation, information, skills) which build human capital (Korten 1986, Perrett and Letham 1980, Scott-Stevens 1987, Vernon 1989). One of the main principles is the strengthening of indigenous inventiveness and creativity as the drivers of innovation (Redclift 1987).

The purpose of this paper is to describe the goals and research results of a feasibility study of an electronic network project carried out at Syracuse University on behalf of UNESCO in 1989. The ultimate objective of the proposed network was to strengthen South-to-South (developing country-to-developing country) cooperation in information science and management. The study proposed steps to be taken to increase the leadership capacity in developing countries in both public and private sector policy making for information systems and telecommunications. Specifically, the study examined the potentials and problems of an electronic network linking information science schools in developing countries (Dosa and Katzer 1990). In this paper as in the study, the term "developing country" is used with the understanding that the rich diversity of these countries cannot be subjected to generalizations.

Background

The provision of information has been recognized by development specialists as a major tool for decisions on national development priorities (Bell 1986, Howell 1988, Samarajiva 1989). The development of a modern telecommunication infrastructure and a domestic computer industry including software design, manufacturing and marketing, require both foreign aid and the acquisition of research and technical skills. Problems in this critical area of technology transfer have been identified by a number of specialists (Altbach 1987, Lucas and Freedman 1983, Stewart 1987). In satellite communications access to the geostationary orbit and the radio-frequency spectrum became the focus of intense controversy, because these resources may be depleted before equitable access to them can be achieved (Howell 1988, pp. 604–611).

The social impact of information technologies applied to development goals is still poorly understood. They affect the economy, labor relations, resource management, and sociopolitical movements. Technology is not neutral. On the one hand, it reflects economic structures, and on the other it influences cultural values (Shields and Servaes 1989). The use of information technology is dictated, to a great extent, by the services available to support it. Educators and communication specialists have become disillusioned by national priorities giving preference to technological imports at the expense of indigenous human resource development.

The cultural background, resource needs and management capabilities in countries which receive information technologies through technical assistance are often not taken into account by the international sponsoring agencies. New telecommunication and information systems are frequently implemented on an ad-hoc basis, leading to a lack of coordination among different projects, and thereby decreasing overall effectiveness. Probably one of the most overlooked problems of information infrastructures is the appeal of technology to politicians as a turnkey solution to all kinds of ills, resulting in a poorly planned patchwork of systems.

Such problems of information technology transfer, widely reflected by the international development experience, point to a two-fold requirement: (1) A new corps of information scientists and managers capable of dealing with the social and ethical as well as the technical aspects of technology, and (2) increased experience-exchange among educators and planners working in different developing countries. Meeting this requirement incrementally could lead to a more balanced and longer lasting South-to-South cooperation. It has been observed that developing countries have much to share in terms of technological processes and experience. Systems and methodologies obtained by countries from economies at similar levels of development have been found more relevant and useful than those imported from high-technology countries. it is encouraging that during the 1980s, the trend has been toward regional collaboration (Cooperation South 1988).

Information supply to developing countries may be seen as a form of technical assistance delivery. Many intergovernmental organizations, development banks and nongovernmental organizations support the production of computerized information systems, software, and telecommunication infrastructures in the developing economies either by technical aid or by lending. It is the premise of the feasibility study described in this paper that the supply of accurate, up-to-date and relevant information and data in support of education and research is a critical need that must be addressed by development aid planning.

In the past seven years at Syracuse University, a new approach has been introduced and tested: DISTANCE TECHNICAL ASSISTANCE (DTA). In various years, this international program which incorporates a clearinghouse and information dissemination for information educators, has been supported by the International Federation for Information and

Documentation (FID), the United Nations Educational, Scientific and Cultural Organization (UNESCO), and the United States government. In 1987, a major evaluation project found the DTA approach extremely effective. Through the DISTANCE TECHNICAL ASSISTANCE network, which uses nonelectronic media, information educators, researchers and policy makers in developing countries have the opportunity not only to receive information in response to their queries, but also to share their creative ideas, innovations and announcements of publications.

During 1989, UNESCO's General Information Programme (PGI) supported a feasibility study of a new electronic network planned to link schools of information studies in Brazil, the People's Republic of China, Ethiopia, Kenya, Malaysia, Mexico, Morocco, Nigeria, the Philippines and Venezuela. The concept of this network evolved over a period of several years during which numerous faculty members and administrators from developing countries participated in international seminars, workshops and conferences jointly organized by FID and UNESCO. The exchange of their experiences greatly stimulated the participants, but between meetings continuity was lost and isolation set in once more. The initiative for the electronic network, a technological upgrading of the existing DTA exchanges, partially came from these participants who also constitute the leadership for the pilot project proposed by the feasibility study. Conducted by Dosa and Katzer at Syracuse University, the study was aimed at a better understanding of how innovations in information science and management occur in the development environment, how implementation is managed after the introduction of the original curriculum change, and what are the expected effects of information sharing across political and cultural boundaries through an electronic network. The initial inclusion of the ten schools in the study was based on their own initiatives and UNESCO/PGI's experience in working with them. An important aspect of the inquiry was to identify the realistic costs of acquiring and maintaining the technology needed for networking by each participating school.

The inquiry raised the following questions: If information transfer is a form of development assistance, how can information studies programs in developing countries assist one another by networking? Research in development science found that innovations introduced by foreign intervention were often resented to the extent that their benefits were lost (Choi 1988, Ghosh 1984). The hypothesis is that by strengthening cooperation in information education and research in the developing regions, it may be possible to sustain the benefits of innovation.

Empirical data of the feasibility study demonstrated that an electronic network linking schools of information studies in different developing countries could be expected to provide an excellent opportunity for the participants to study issues of technology and information policy. Examples of issues include the financing of information resource sharing programs; obstacles presented by human and technical communication problems; the ethical aspects of information access and equity; and the value of information as scientific resource, entrepreneurial property, and public service.

Literature Review

In support of the feasibility study, an extensive literature analysis was conducted. The following trends emerged from the review:

- In past years information scientists in developing countries found it difficult to participate in policy discussions because they were not seen by policy makers as perpetrators of technological progress.
- This image is beginning to change in the modernizing industrial sectors. Although the technological infrastructure of information transfer remains weak, awareness of its key role in the economy is on the rise. It is now widely understood that before nations can develop their own R & D sector, human resources and skills must be strengthened.
- In the public sector, the need for building a capacity for policy analysis through workshops and conferences has been recognized (Adamolekun 1990). It is not difficult to also make this argument with regard to information policies.
- In view of the large-scale privatization of public enterprises in developing countries, executive training programs are needed for the retraining of entrepreneurs in information management.

It is at the crossroads of these trends that locally generated innovation of information education is indispensable. The international seminar "Information Manpower Forecasting" (Dosa, Froehlich and King 1990), and a review of national information policy documents identified the following roles:

1. *Information counselors and other intermediaries* are needed to enable decision makers to identify, use and apply scientific, technological and socioeconomic data and to improve overall information literacy in society.
2. Information-related activities in organizations must be organized by competent *information resources managers* into systems and services that form the information infrastructure necessary for each country's development plan. Information policies and laws as well

as cultural norms should be part of the information resources manager's education.

3. *Specialized data managers* and *data systems designers* are essential for development planning to work in such areas as the construction of social and development indicators, technology assessment and impact studies, environmental and resource planning, and risk management and forecasting.

4. Information specialists in developing countries need a strong foundation in *communications for the crosscultural transfer of knowledge*. Communication techniques are needed for the support of emerging public participation movements (Bamberger 1988). The range of other needs includes multimedia production, information dissemination through extension programs, and interpersonal communication in information retrieval. Whether it takes place through oral history or new computer applications, technology transfer operates at two levels: From research into action (decision making and practice), and from country to country. At both levels the quality of communications largely determines the outcome.

5. Information science as an academic study rests on theories that have been developed with the analytic tools of several disciplines, although they uniquely pertain to the phenomenon of information. We need *information science researchers* to define and build the discipline. Because information transfer is not only an economic activity but also a culturally determined human process, developing countries need indigenous scientists who can contribute to universal science at the same time when they study the social, economic and technical applications of information science. Skills are needed also for the evaluation of information needs and for the assessment of the effect of information services on development (Chapman and Boothroyd 1988).

6. *Training the trainers* in both formal and nonformal programs is one of the most worthwhile directions information education can take. Some schools already specialize in continuing education; others endeavor to teach basic training and demonstration skills that can be used by information professionals in the workplace for in-house staff training and for orienting the users of information services in search strategies.

Feasibility Study

The feasibility studies solicited information from each of the ten schools by means of a questionnaire. Brochures and reports describing the schools' academic environment were obtained.

The introductory questions asked respondents how selected components of the information infrastructure (data and information, information professionals, information educators and education programs) contribute to national development. The next queries focused on the perceived effects information educators have on information policy and the corresponding effects information policies have on education. Questions 9–10 were concerned with the changing role of information professionals and their training.

The kinds of information that the various schools would like to receive over the electronic network were elicited by questions 11–13. The respondents were queried about desired content, form and services. Then they were asked to rate the potential benefits to their schools of the information content and of the sources of that information they wished to receive over the network. Questions 16–17 probed into the barriers that may impede the adaptation and use of information to be received from other countries, and into suggestions about overcoming these barriers or minimize their effects. Question 18 queried the kinds of assistance desired to adapt materials and information received over the network for local use.

Questions 19–20 were aimed at the kinds of training individuals who may use the proposed network will need, and asked who will provide such training expertise. Two further queries intended to establish if the schools had the resources and technical staff for the maintenance of network hardware and software and if potential users had prior and current experience with networks. The next questions inquired about specific telecommunications hardware the participating schools currently have, the kinds of individuals in each academic community who would make use of the proposed network, and the individuals in each academic community who would make use of the proposed network, and the anticipated effects of the network on academic programs. Respondents were asked to describe the information technology currently available at their institutions and to detail their need for hardware and software in order to participate in the network.

All ten questionnaires were completed and returned. The small sample size permitted a close inspection of the totality of the responses, so patterns and intentions could be inferred. Presented below are summaries of the conclusions drawn from the results of the analysis.

Results of the Feasibility Study

The overall impressions one gets from the responses to questions 1–10 are that (1) there is an important role for information professionals and information studies in national development; (2) perceptions of this role vary by country and by the socioeconomic characteristics of the country; and (3) there are different barriers which need to be reduced before information, information professionals and information educational programs can contribute more to national development. Since the situation in each country is different, the best approaches to "resolving" the barriers to national development must be found and implemented locally. Within such a context, the proposed electronic network can play a facilitative role.

Responses to questions 11–18 reflect considerable interest in being able to obtain many different kinds of information through the network. Though some of this information can be provided via formal channels, much of the information requested most frequently by the respondents is not available in this way. To accommodate the respondents' preferences for electronic mail and for the transmission of documents, it makes sense to base the proposed network on telephone linkages with computers and facsimile machines at each participating institution. Responses stress the need for both information from high-technology countries and information exchange among developing countries. Assistance essential to the successful introduction and continued use of the proposed network includes technical support and training.

Responses to questions 19–24 reinforce the well-known adage that one cannot simply put technology on someone's desk and expect it to be used over time, or even used at all. Plans for the proposed network must include mechanisms and resources for training. Given the expected availability of the proposed network to more than just a few individuals in each school, it is essential that the system be designed for many first-time and infrequent users. It is also evident that at this time the participating institutions do not have easy access to electronic networks which have links to other countries and permit the transmission of the types of information being considered for this project.

A fundamental question undergirding the entire project is whether the proposed network will be worth the effort and resources involved. While it is easy to paint an optimistic picture of how the network can help the participating institutions and their programs, it must be remembered that all technologies have negative as well as positive consequences. To determine the relative trade-off between positive impacts and negative consequences requires a long-term, carefully designed evaluation program—part of which is incorporated in the overall plan for the proposed pilot study. Even though the "final" assessment of the network has to wait for the completion of the evaluation process, it was useful to learn from the participants about their expectations of what the network could do for them. They anticipate

- increased awareness of the importance of information for development

- enhanced capabilities and skills of information professionals and the services they can provide through the network
- improvement in information education programs through better teaching, higher quality materials, and optimization of initiatives in information education in programs and institutions in the Third World
- greater utilization of technologies to strengthen the exchange of information
- changes in attitudes and skills for information sharing in an international context
- lower costs for information retrieval
- improved quality of research
- improved ability for keeping abreast of trends in scientific and technological information developments and learning innovations
- enhancement of the national technology transfer policy.

Findings and Implications

The feasibility study has identified the following international trends which form the background for educational policy planning:

- As new data and communication systems are introduced in developing countries, they create a profound need for the evaluation of their social impact and their relevance to sustainable development.
- Advances in telecommunications are creating new challenges in the form of transborder data flows (TDFs) which tend to widen the gap between data producing and data poor regions.
- The need for the cooperation of various disciplines and sectors is evident and should be supported by information and experience sharing networks.
- A growing number of policy makers urge development of a core of indigenous researchers in information and communication technology, but researchers lack basic literatures and contacts with counterparts abroad.
- Interactive communication and learning processes, previously overshadowed by large-scale modernization projects, are gaining importance but are hampered by a lack of access to information resources.

Respondents believe that it is not uncommon for new technology to lead to changes in people's attitudes and improvements in work effectiveness. It is expected that the proposed network will affect different groups of individuals (e.g., faculty, students, and professionals), and different academic activities (e.g., curriculum design, research, and teaching) and have an effect beyond their institutions on national development and on educational programs in other countries in the region. Responses suggest that there is a need for locally developed solutions to the challenge each country faces in terms of meeting information needs and supporting national development. This, in turn, depends upon information of various kinds from many sources, at many levels, and in different formats. The sharing of this information would be significantly facilitated by an informal network that connects the academic institutions with one another and with a coordinating member and offers electronic mail and document transfer.

Conclusions

The feasibility study investigated the potential of a new approach to technical assistance by the provision of timely and relevant information. DISTANCE TECHNICAL ASSISTANCE (DTA) was proposed as a specific form of development support. This model does not necessitate the creation of numerous separate, on-site technical aid projects. By the use of an electronic network linking schools of information studies in various countries, it may be feasible to provide two kinds of DTA:

- The dissemination of problem-solving information to educators, researchers, administrators and students in these programs to strengthen their effectiveness
- Provision of a multiplier effect to support national development and South-to-South cooperation by empowering the schools to share experience and knowledge within and outside of their countries.

The difference between Distance Education (DE) and Distance Technical Assistance (DTA) is that the former normally broadcasts formal programs from one source to numerous recipients, while the latter offers information support on an informal one-to-one basis. Another difference is that DE brings together teachers and students by the use of media whereas DTA connects colleagues with each other and with students.

To introduce DTA as a new form of development assistance is in accordance with the experience of development specialists who argue that technical assistance must be part of an overall learning process. Some projects in the past have presented "difficult problems which remain to be solved and their solution is inhibited by programming procedures better suited to large capital development projects than to people-centered development" (Korten 1980, p. 482). By sponsoring the feasibility study, UNESCO/PGI has provided a source of information on the perceptions, needs and plans of some information education programs in developing countries. The empirical data demonstrated that institutions in developing countries are interested in continuing and expanding the mutual support activity through networking after the termination of the pilot project.

In the course of the study, we have identified research problems that may form a conceptual framework for further empirical investigations. One of the foremost needs we have recognized on the basis of experience with evaluation approaches is the study of assessment methodologies applicable to a network carrying crosscultural information (Katzer, Cook and Crouch 1990). Other potential research areas include the relationship of information policies and professional education in the development environment; the impact of transnational network politics on information sharing; alternative carriers of information usable in areas where telecommunication facilities are weak; and factors affecting successful innovations by information science schools.

In conclusion, we want to emphasize the philosophy underlying the feasibility study. It professed that the creativity, talent and ideas at work in developing countries represent the capital of the future. We were enriched by our interactions with colleagues in geographically distant places. The purpose of our study was to see their leadership fully enfold.

References

Adamolekun, L. (1990). *Issues in Development Management in Sub-Saharan Africa*. Washington, DC: The World Bank (EDI Policy Seminar Report 19).

Altbach, P.G. (1987). *The Knowledge Context*. Albany, NY: State University of New York Press.

Bamberger, M. (1988). *The Role of Community Participation in Development Planning and Project Management*. Washington, DC: The World Bank (EDI Policy Seminar Report, 13).

Bell, S. (1986). Information systems planning and operation in less developed countries. *Journal of Information Science*. Part I, 12, 231–245. Part II, 12, 319–331.

Chapman, D.W. & Boothroyd, R.A. (1988). Evaluation dilemmas: Conducting evaluation studies in developing countries. *Evaluation and Program Planning, 11, 37–42*.

Choi, H.S. (1988). Science policy mechanism and technology strategy in the developing countries. *Technology Forecasting and Social Change,* 33, 279–292.

Cooperation South, the Magazine of Technical Co-Operation Among Developing Countries (TCDC). (1988). New York, NY: United Nations Development Programme, No. 1.

Dosa, M., Froehlich, T.J., & King, H. eds. (1990). *Information Manpower Forecasting. Papers Presented at the FID/ET Seminar, Espoo, Finland, 1988.* Paris: UNESCO/PGI.

Dosa, M. & Katzer, J. (1990). Innovation and Human Resource Networking: Feasibility Study Submitted to the United Nations Educational, Scientific and Cultural Organization, General Information Programme. (Manuscript). Syracuse, NY: Syracuse University, 1990.

Ghosh, P.K. ed. (1984). *Technology Policy and Development, a Third World Perspective.* Westport, CT: Greenwood Press.

Howell, R.C. (1988). International telecommunications and the law: The creation of Pan African satellites. *Howard Law Journal,* 31, 575–641.

Katzer, J., Cook, K., & Crouch, W. (1990). *Evaluating Information.* Third ed. McGraw-Hill.

Korten, D.C. (1980). Community organization and rural development: A learning process approach. *Public Administration Review,* 40(5), 80–511.

Korten, D.C. (1986). "Strategic organization for people-centered development." In Ickis, J.C. et al., eds. *Beyond Bureaucracy: Strategic Management of Social Development,* 233–256. West Hartford, CT: Kumarian Press.

Lucas, B.G. & Freedman, S. (1983). *Technology Choice and Change in Developing Countries.* Dublin: Tycooly International.

Montviloff, V. (1990). *National Information Policies.* Paris: United Nations Educational, Scientific and Cultural Organization.

Perrett, H., Letham, F.J. (1980). *Human Factors in Project Work.* Washington, DC: The World Bank, (WB Staff Working Paper, 397).

Redclift, M. (1987). *Sustainable Development, Exploring the Contradictions.* London: Methuen.

Samarajiva, R. (1989). Appropriate high tech: Scientific communications for small third world countries. *The Information Society,* 6(1/2), 29–46.

Sauvant, K.P. (1986). *International Transactions in Services: The Politics of Transborder Data Flows.* Boulder, CO: Westview Press (Atwater Series on the World Information Economy, transactions, No. 1).

Scott-Stevens, S. (1987). *Foreign Consultants and Counterparts: Problems in Technology Transfer.* Boulder, CO: Westview Press.

Shields, P. & Servaes, J. (1989). The Impact of the transfer of information technology on development. *The Information Society,* 6(1/2), 47–57.

Stewart, F. ed. (1987). *Macro Policies for Appropriate Technology in Developing Countries*. Boulder, CO: Westview Press.

Vernon, R. (1989). *Technological Development: The Historical Experience*. Washington, DC: The World Bank. (World Bank EDI Seminar Paper, 39).

Part III

Problem Solving and Information Counseling

8

Environmental Information Transfer

Introduction

This paper reviews major trends in the transfer of environmental information in the United States with implications for international information exchange, and offers observations on problem analysis, communications, and information use in formal and informal settings.

"If you want to converse with me, define your terms," demanded Voltaire. Both "environmental information" and "information transfer" are associated with a wide range of meanings and interpretations, depending on their context. The term information is particularly elusive and resistant to any generally acceptable definition. In various applications it has been referred to as symbol, message, phenomenon, natural resource, commodity, and tool. One of the mathematician Leo Szilard's pioneering papers, published in 1929, treated "what would now be called information theory: the relation between knowledge, nature and man" (Bronowski 1973, p. 65). A more pragmatic interpretation was offered at the Symposium on Problems Relating to Environment:

> Information includes the total complex of data and facts which people receive from outside and which contribute towards their knowledge. It may be said that information creates opinion about an object in a given environment . . . According to this line of thinking, the promotion and dissemination of information constitute an integral part of education (United Nations Economic . . . , p. 192).

The same symposium demonstrated that not only the terminology of environmental information research but also international attitudes toward the relationship of education, information and communications were unsettled and conflicting. In the context of the environmental movement, some societies objected to mass education as undue influence over people's values and behavior; others utilized the information dissemination function of mass education as a path to social transformation. This controversy permeated all intercultural discussions of environmental education and information transfer. Although the emotional force of the ecological movement peaked in 1972 at the time of the United Nations Conference on the Human Environment at Stockholm, communications in this field are still influenced by value judgments and cultural beliefs.

We are still somewhat at a loss to follow the historical development from early botany to the present ecological awareness of our mass culture. It is generally accepted that the term ecology (based on the Greek oikos-) may be traced back to its first scientific usage in 1869 by the German biologist and zoologist Ernst Haeckel, where it denotes a whole range of scientific activities. When the 1960s transformed this field into a broadly based, multidisciplinary, highly publicized concern for the quality of human life, the search for a relevant new definition began. "Environmental science" was defined as "basic and applied inquiry about changes in environmental quality resulting from the activities of man" (Metcalf and Pitts 1969, vol. 1, p. 1). In international debates, the reference to "the activities of man" conjured up a vast vision of complexity and controversy. Environmentalists and politicians in developing countries argued that their nations should not be held responsible for the large-scale natural resource exploitation by industrialized nations. The following definition is more indicative of, and sympathetic to, the psychological and social orientation of the field:

> Like any science, ecology provides an inclusive and consistent structure for perceiving the world; but, unlike other sciences, it also attempts to account for the behavior of man within the world structure (Finding . . . 1968, p. 23).

The Role of Human Communications

In one of his poems the Russian poet Gumilev tells of a bewitched violin. Those who start to play it must go on and on, without stopping, because they will be pursued by hungry wolves and monsters. As soon as a player stops, the beasts attack and devour him. A young man, intoxicated by dreams of his future, refuses to recognize the danger. He gets hold of the mysterious instrument. Now he will have to look into the eyes of monsters, he is told, and at the end he will die a "horrible and glorious" death.

There is in this tale a dark fascination with unknown danger, a hint of the moribund beauty of an inevitable, violent end. In the image of the postmodern individual created by the prophets, poets and philosophers of the ecological movement, rampant speed of life and alienation from nature represent the bewitched violin. A nameless sense of insecurity drives the individual into a search for enclaves, groups, microcultures in society—whether based on race, religion, ethnicity, age or other forces of cohesion (Kanter 1972). "All of us are both running scared and longing for community" (Bohannan 1972). In the process of running—playing the bewitched violin—we constantly increase the complexity of both of our worlds, the large-scale culture of institutions, organizations, networks, and political and professional relationships, and the microculture of our own chosen enclave.

If we accept the assumption that each of us—information user as well as information provider—tends to move back and forth between two worlds often without even realizing their separateness, what does this do to our carefully developed abstractions of formal information transfer? Envision the microcosm of an information exchange. Two individuals face each other, one just beginning to formulate an information query, the other watching for clues to better understand it. At this point they both are assumed to be part of the same structured and overt world. They communicate. But indeed, do they? A facial expression, or an almost imperceptible change in the cadence of a voice may stimulate, antagonize, or otherwise affect the other person, immediately conjuring up responses from that "other" hidden and tribal level. We may assume that this shift from the formal to the informal frame of reference does not interrupt the cognitive process; information gathering continues in the mind consciously or subconsciously. However, interpersonal tensions in communication are likely to undermine the potential creativity of the informal information gathering process.

Characteristic Trends Determining Needs

Environmental science, management and social institutions form the framework in which environmental information and ideas flow among individuals. The following examples attempt to illustrate characteristic trends in this emerging field.

A Problem-Focused Field. Research related to conditions of the environment is seldom based on knowledge emanating from one discipline. The insights and skills of several disciplines have to focus on any one target. "Problem-focused research is responsive to, and to some extent depends on, social needs, which determine its scope; it is focused on the problems which call for scientifically informed action" (Bie 1970, p. 579). For example, the program in urban geometrics at the Massachusetts Institute of Technology conducts research in computer-based planning for traffic flows, public transportation services, and new approaches to neighborhood renewal. Implementation is in the hands of contracting local governments and professional practitioners. We see two different sectors of a problem-centered field at work, each with its own methodologies and channels of communication: the community of researchers, and the community of practitioners. Borderlines between the two are neither clear-cut nor static. The same individual may play more than one role: landscape architect, regional planner, researcher or lecturer. But such individuals are rather rare, and their private worlds are growing enormously complex. Although they are linked by conferences, projects, training programs, and advisory groups, researchers and practitioners, moved by different motivations, inhabit separate planets. Their information gathering generates separate and sometimes divergent sets of knowledge.

Data resulting from research are imbedded in laboratory notes, in-house memoranda, grant proposals and reports, maps, aerial photographs, survey analyses, and many other sources. Information users not familiar with the "tribal" customs of researchers in a certain specialty usually have a difficult time detecting where and in what form data have been gathered and stored. Information generated by practitioners is needed but not easily located by researchers. At every turn of a professional's daily routine, at every phase of an organization's work, some form of information is produced. Hearings held by legislative and regulatory bodies, standards and specifications, procedure manuals, field reports, case studies and teaching aids represent environmental information sources created by practitioners.

The need for vigorous information flows—research findings interpreted for and by the practitioner and the professional experience of practice disseminated to researchers—has often been stressed in the literature. The need is obvious to the extent that the perceptions of researchers and practitioners of the information they need from each other should be collected as evaluation criteria for information systems. What is the relationship, if any, between the testing and analysis of an environmental problem and current methods used in practice to alleviate the same problem? Are regulatory agencies, special interest lobbyists and public interest groups aware of alternative approaches to a solution? Do organizations maintain information dissemination programs that act as switching mechanisms between the research community and the public? These and similar questions will have to be answered before we can formulate meaningful expectations of environmental information services.

Ideologies and Behavioral Patterns

Conflicting views of the relationship between technoeconomic development and the quality of life are clearly discernible in environmental scholarship, management, and social activism. Historian Lynn White, Jr., equated "the distinctive Western tradition of science" with what he called man's destructive dominance over nature. "By destroying pagan animism, Christianity made it possible to exploit nature in a mood of indifference to the feeling of natural objects" (White 1967, p. 1203). Microbiologist Rene Dubos retorted: "The theory that Judeo-Christian attitudes are responsible for technology and for the ecological crisis is at best a historical half-truth" (Dubos 1973, p. 56). John Maddox, editor of *Nature* and author of *The Doomsday Syndrome,* charged that "the United Nations Conference . . . seems to . . . have been a splendid expose of the inconsistencies with which the environmental movement has lumbered itself in the past few years" (Maddox 1972, p. 820).

While ideological conflicts between technological development and natural resource protection continued in industrialized countries, resulting in national legislation for technology assessment, the environmental movement became also a symbol of social class differences. Its "elitist" nature drew criticism from planners and activists at a national conference on The Environment of the Open Society. Participants rejected the "growing use of the rhetoric and symbols of the environmental movement by those who seek to confine minorities and poor people to the environment of the ghetto" (*New York Times* 1973, p. 22). Delegates from developing countries at the World Assembly of Non-Governmental Organizations Concerned with the Global Environment, held in Geneva in 1973, made the following formal statement:

> We are deeply convinced that environmental discussions should be people-oriented; the worst aspects of environmental degradation are the annihilation of so-called primitive peoples, apartheid, the obliteration of traditional cultures irrespective of their inherent values, and the growing disparity between the rich and the poor nations and, within nations, between the elite and the mass of the people (World Assembly, 1973, p. 1).

Public Interest Advocacy

The twin drives of consumerism and ecology, magnified by the mass media, produced keen public curiosity about environmental legislation, regulations and court cases. Several kinds of public-interest organizations have emerged in all industrialized regions and in a few developing countries. Their activities include critical reviews of environmental action, mobilization of public opinion, interpretation of technical information for the public, and representation of various consumer groups. The explosive growth of these organizations demonstrates the upsurge of both public and scientific concern. It has been especially difficult for the public to keep up-to-date with institutional changes, rearrangements of political alliances, and regrouping of projects. The International Union for Conservation of Nature and Natural Resources in Morges, Switzerland, responded to this need by creating the Operations Intelligence Centre, which is open to questions from the membership and the public at large.

At the First National Environmental Information Symposium in the United States, legal information became a topic of high profile pursued by almost all elements of the environmental movement (United States. Environmental . . . 1973). Since tangible improvement of existing conditions starts with bill-drafting and lobbying, it is crucial for citizen groups to become politically informed. Environmental impact statements, not yet required by the federal government, are receiving growing support from scientists. Statutes, regulations, and judicial opinions need condensation and interpretation for public use. What used to be the prerogative of the legislator and the professional lobbyist, is now demanded as a basic consumer right by different strata of the public.

Changes in Academic Programs

During the 1960s, colleges of agriculture and forestry across the country have moved from a narrow focus on the scientific and technical aspects of their own disciplines toward a broader interpretation of interdisciplinary relationships. Forestry was called upon to deal with resource allocation among competing land uses, the utilization of timber, mining practices, industrial and residential development, open space preservation, and recreation. In the wake of changing academic curricula and research goals, schools of conservation and forestry transformed themselves into schools of environmental science. The new programs required new, broadly conceived information services reflecting the changing terminology and the demand for data in elusive, unpublished resources.

History courses revised their approaches, particularly to early American history. "Suddenly all the scholarly assumptions about the frontier have changed as students look with a fresh consciousness at the Indian, the Mexican-American, the pioneer woman and the environment destroying 'hero' " (Lamar 1972, p. 9). In the early 1940s Yale had acquired the libraries of six great collectors of Western Americana. By the 1970s, the nature of inquiry into these manuscripts, newspapers, paintings, maps, and rare books underwent a significant change.

> Ten years ago the student probably would have reported on New Deal Indian policy; 20 years ago he would have talked about an Indian war or Custer's 'Last Stand.' In less than 10 years Indians have become in white eyes—and in history courses—peoples, societies and cultures (Lamar 1972, p. 9).

At Cornell, a crisis in undergraduate education in population studies prompted the university to reassess the relationship between demography and environmental issues, to restructure the curriculum and to start a publication program for the dissemination of new research. Not everybody on the faculty welcomed the revisions. A Cornell document is characterized by the occasional bitter and ironical tone of the time:

> Traditionally, the study of human population dynamics, including causes and consequences, has been "reserved" for demographers trained in the social sciences . . . with some selected aspects of this general area reserved for geneticists and various kinds of ecologists. Recently, however, it seems . . . that the "rules" governing this academic division of labor have become inoperative and that anyone, either with an advanced degree or a soapbox, feels competent to discuss the intricacies of population dynamics (Marden 1972, p. 10).

Similar examples can be found in practically all disciplines and professions. As the visions of innovators in these fields expand, curricula change, new journals and conferences surface, and students and faculty become political activists.

Traditional Approaches to User Studies

Traditionally, a study of information transfer includes information users, information resources, and information transfer mechanisms. Each of these components should be examined in the context of trends, communication patterns, and institutional relationships. It can be argued that in order to do justice to the versatility, changeability and dynamics of information that moves in and out of the private world of an individual, an additional element should be introduced into the study of information transfer: the "information problem/context." This concept will be further discussed following a brief overview of information user groups.

Researchers have devoted extreme attention, with uneven results, to the needs, demands, habits, and information seeking and use patterns of the information clientele (Lin and Garvey 1972). This body of research promised the benefits of a multidisciplinary social science perspective emphasizing structures, relationships, communications of scientific communities and their impact on communications. However, narrow conceptualization of the information user and tired and inflexible methodologies applied in some studies hindered the fulfillment of this promise. Nevertheless, this research represented the foundation of many subsequent efforts. The majority of studies delineated user groups by such factors as the subjects' organizational affiliation, discipline or profession, project task, or research orientation. Some of these perceptions can serve as possible departure points for studies of environmental information.

Organizational Affiliation

The information use habits of scientists working for government, industry and educational institutions have been tested. R&D laboratories, product engineering departments, university science departments and professional schools served as settings. This approach provided some insights into the ways scientists as information users are affected by their immediate environment. The ecological movement has created new institutional relationships and organizational settings which would lend themselves for similar investigations.

Discipline or Profession

Well-known studies have been carried out on information use by physicists, psychologists, chemists, medical researchers and others. A number of these projects were originated by professional associations as preliminary steps toward changes in the formal communication system of a particular discipline or profession. On the basis of such models it would be interesting to inquire into the poorly understood information requirements of the recently emerged environmental scientist.

Mission, Project or Task

Numerous investigations in this category concluded that identification with a particular task influences information use behavior. Because of the multidisciplinary nature of mission-focused areas, this type of investigation is most relevant to environmental information research.

Professional Role

What differences can be detected between the information/data requirements of basic, applied, and problem-oriented researchers, decision makers, practitioners, and educators? Each of these roles and activities can be conceptualized in the context of environmental science and management.

Research Methodology and Style

It has been shown that individuals engaged in different types of research display different attitudes toward the acquisition of data. Research styles affecting the ways people look for and use information range from archive-based historical research through quantitative surveys, laboratory tests, and field observations to the collection of qualitative information.

Three further research trends are relevant to ways information exchanges and sharing may be facilitated for environmentalists. First, studies on the interpersonal communication patterns of scientists identify the "invisible college," an undefined group in a particular research field whose members, often living at great distances from each other, depend on this peer group for recognition and awareness of new research (Crane 1972). The second trend probes scientists' interest in information outside of their specialties (Baker 1970). The third includes research on the diffusion of knowledge across national boundaries by scientists and other individuals with special communication skills who have been somewhat misleadingly termed "gatekeepers" (Allen, Piepmeier and Cooney 1971).

New Audiences, New Needs

The environmental information clientele is usually divided into general and specialized user categories. General users play a significant role because they (1) often form the target of public educational programs and publicity campaigns, (2) represent the membership of public interest groups, and (3) are likely to influence the development of future information systems designed to provide scientific, technological and legal information in popularized form. Specialized users are understood to include mainly scientists and engineers. However, this type of division does not accommodate the wide range of information needs and requirements. A few examples will show the variety of potential information-seeking groups:

Researchers in a well-defined discipline of basic science
Researchers in a well-defined discipline of applied science
Social science researchers
Researchers in a multidisciplinary area
Philosophers, authors of books, religious leaders, cultural analysts
Decision-makers, policy planners, managers
Legislators, regulators, legal experts
Professional practitioners in science and technology
Skilled paraprofessionals
Educators at all levels of the educational system
Students at all levels of the educational system
Members of special interest organizations, public interest groups, lobby groups, neighborhood organizations
Opinion leaders, gatekeepers, communication specialists
Journalists, columnists, other media personnel.

The Protean Information User

The kaleidoscopic character of our society has often been identified with complexity carried to its extreme. Today even this term is becoming too weak to express a sense of interrelatedness of all things in constant motion. "The term *complexity,* which belongs to a static, state-describing vocabulary, needs to be supplemented, if not yet supplanted, by a dynamic, process-describing equivalent as implied in the term *complexing*" (Landau 1972, p. 608). Versatility and flux permeate the information scene. Both the human process of information exchange and its social-technological mechanisms are fragmented and convoluted. Although changes in recent years "have greatly improved the potential (and, in some cases, the actual) performance of the technological information system, they also vastly complicated its structure and use" (Knox 1973, p. 415).

The scientist stands at the intersection of innumerable invisible lines, each potentially leading to a social, professional, institutional or cultural communication system. Dare we assume that in the midst of continuous societal and psychological alterations, their priorities, motivations, and habits remain unchanged? Are they still identifying with traditional values such as formal professional rewards implying ever-increasing pressures and demands on their privacy, or are their interests shifting to the new, unmeasurable value systems of any one of the emerging subcultures, be it a social group, a movement, a form of political activism or an avocation? More reflective insight and research into the individual as a whole system is needed before we could answer such questions.

A compelling model of a new perceivable psychological style is offered by Lifton. He speaks of a new kind of individual, symbolized by the form-changing Proteus. Elements of the Protean profile include

> changing and fluctuating life style and habits, penchant for experimentation and exploration, search for new forms, attitudes, approaches, beliefs, fragmented impressions and spontaneous reactions, tendency to defy categorization and generalization, readiness to embrace, abandon and reembrace sets of values and priorities (Lifton 1969, p. 15).

The terms "character" and "personality" cannot describe the Protean individual. Lifton prefers the term "self-process," suggesting motion and changeability. For it is quite possible

> that even the image of personal identity, insofar as it suggests inner stability and sameness, is derived from a vision of a traditional culture in which man's relationship to his institutions and symbols are still relatively intact—which is hardly the case today (Lifton 1969, p. 15).

The idea of the Protean information seeker is disquieting and challenging enough to suggest that one must search for new ways to conceptualize individual information use.[*]

The Information Problem/Context

It has often been said that the success of information acquisition depends on the provider's responsiveness to the seeker's ultimate purpose. How

---

[*]Robert Jay Lifton's model was also published in *The Protean Self: Human Resilience in an Age of Fragmentation*. New York, NY: Basic Books, 1994. (Author's note).

do information systems become aware of the inquirer's motivation that, in most cases, is not spelled out in the query addressed to the system? Question negotiation will usually detect the client's topical interest, professional frame of reference, mission or task, time and cost constraints, and even personal preferences as to form or depth of material. However, information providers tend to avoid the question: "What use will be made of this information?" Let us assume that working on the basis of interaction models used by other service professions we can build a case for professional counseling, a process that leads to the client's revelation of the ultimate purpose of the query. The complexity of the environmental arena challenges the information provider to seek this new path to service.

What the client intends to do with the data or other information may, in a consumer-oriented system, determine the best form or "package" in which the information should be delivered, as well as the depth, speed and mode of delivery. Queried about a region's flood-vulnerable land at a time of rapid spring thaw, a regional planning office will probably supply specialized technical maps to an engineering consultant firm, and a set of general aerial photographs to the local press. An instructor from a local college would use the same set of photographs for a class in photojournalism. Moreover, the same information user may need data and documents for different purposes at different times. Maps may be used by the instructor for dramatic visual illustration of reportage, or for demonstrating the technical precision of a photograph. The intention may be to reproduce the information by copying it, making a blow-up, using it as an illustration in a textbook, or converting it into a slide. Objectives may be educational, political, social/environmental or scientific, and they may be work-related or personal. In each case a number of legal, ethical, economic or technical constraints might apply.

Let us call the purpose for which the information is being obtained the PROBLEM/CONTEXT. This new element is added to the traditional model of an information system that had originally included user, resources, and information transfer mechanism (Figure 8.1).

The PROBLEM/CONTEXT of an information query is affected by the user's (1) broad environment (e.g. occupation, activity, personal situation), and (2) function within that occupation, activity or situation (e.g. manager, researcher, student). The PROBLEM/CONTEXT of the query is a combination of the user's (1) area of interest (e.g. demonstration media or reportage techniques in photojournalism), and (2) the intended use of the acquired information (e.g. critical evaluation, referral to people, or teaching visual interpretation).

An approach to the identification of and planning for information needs on the basis of the PROBLEM/CONTEXT can bypass the current dependence on generalized information user categories when designing information systems. The benefit for the user may be more individualized service.

Figure 8.1
The Information Problem/Context

Information Environment

Occupational Attributes
Agriculturist
Architect
Economist
Educator
Forester
Journalist
Lawyer
Physicist

Functional Attributes
Applied researcher
Basic researcher
Community activist
Manager
Politician
Regulator
Student
Text illustrator

Intended use of Information
Awareness raising
Backgrounding
Critical evaluation
Description of object or process
Interpreted data analysis
Learning about activity
Literature search
Locating documents
Raw data analysis
Referral to people
Repackaging information
Teaching interpretation

Area of Interest:
Photojournalism
Cost Studies
Demonstration media
Historical Study
Image interpretation
Legal aspects
Marketing
Professional aspects
Reportage techniques
Technical data use
Textual analysis

Information problem/context

Information Transfer Mechanism

Information User

Information Resources

Formal Information Resources

Informal Information Resources

Organizations
Agencies
Individuals
Documents
Data
Other Media

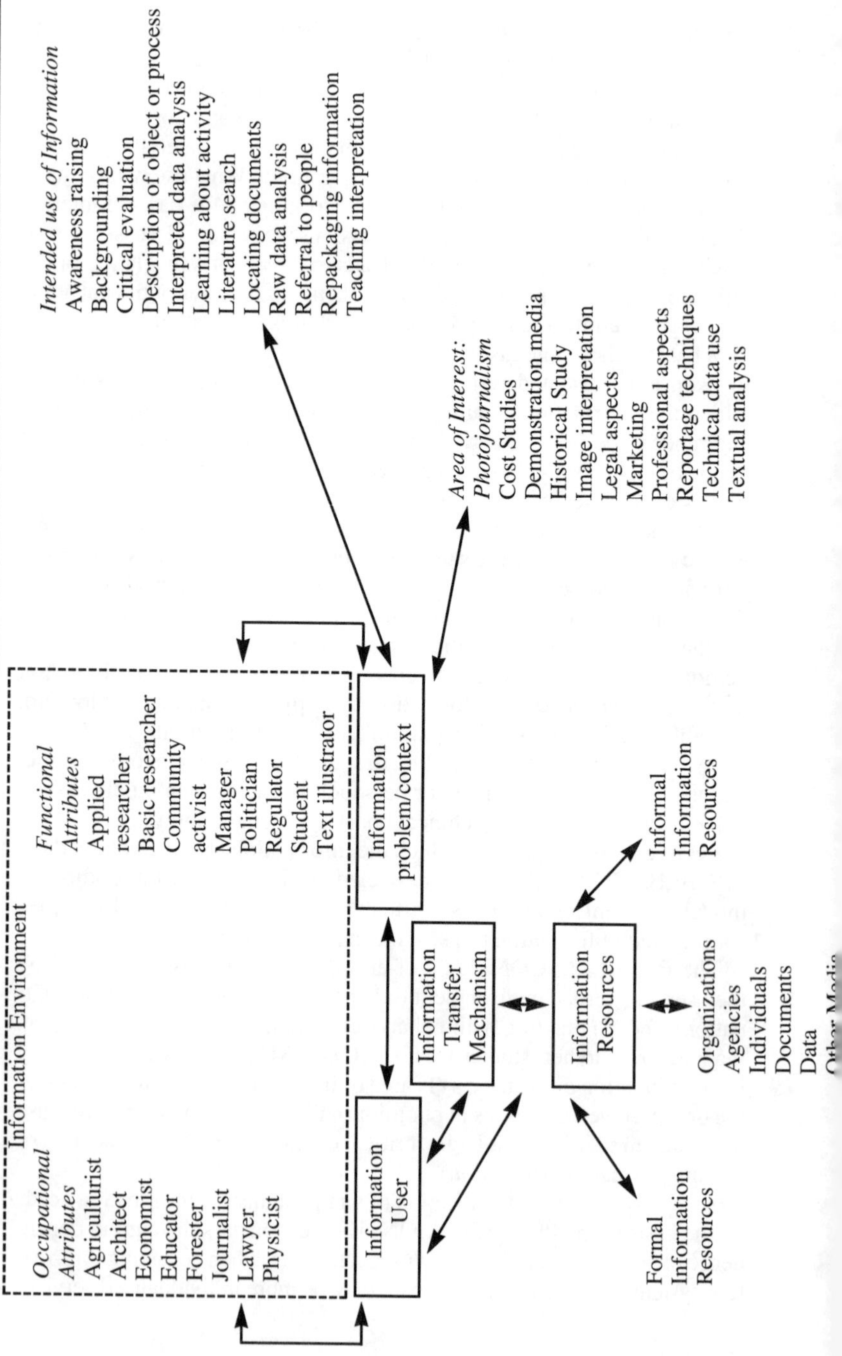

Information Resources

How can we systematize knowledge in a new field that hovers at the crossroads of science, technology, society and the individual and touches upon all human activities? Traditional schemes of organization fail because environmental concepts and their interpretations, cutting across all disciplines, are still in turmoil, and their interrelationship with other concepts are unclear.

Although there are some indexing/abstracting services and databases covering general environmental information, users frequently turn to sources in their own specific disciplines by habit. To assist in the formulation of a simple basic strategy, the entire knowledge field may be divided into (1) problem areas and (2) disciplines and professions that bring their own concepts and methodologies to bear on the problem areas. A partial list will suffice to illustrate this integrating approach:

PROBLEM AREAS	DISCIPLINE/PROFESSION-ORIENTED APPROACHES
Air pollution	Agriculture
Conservation	Architecture
Energy	Economics
Food, nutrition	Education
Land use	Forestry
Marine pollution	Law
Noise pollution	Medicine
Population control	Planning
Thermal pollution	Science
Visual pollution	Sociology
Waste disposal	Technology
Water pollution	

For example, a search on the "effects of air pollution on the respiratory tract" may start in a problem-oriented tool focusing on the "pollution" aspect, or in a discipline-oriented tool emphasizing "health" as a topic. This two-dimensional approach has the advantage of flexibility and expansiveness. "Problem Areas" and "Disciplines/Professions" may be added to the list depending on a search's objective.

Superimposed on the problem area and discipline or profession relationship are three broad categories of information resources: (1) Informal exchange of information between individuals through meetings, conferences, telephone calls, and other personal contacts, (2) unpublished information sources that pass through informal channels, and (3) data in raw and interpreted form. Characteristically, these are unevaluated sources of diverse quality. Their use and application must necessarily be based on the recipient's trust in the source. Information intermediaries who refer users to personal expertise should be aware of both the user's objective and the quality of the source, because in this process they become partners in the information gathering enterprise. Familiarity with unpublished and unevaluated information resources may be built through an understanding of the types and nature of information produced by organizations and by individuals within organizations.

Institutions and Individuals as Information Sources

The role nongovernmental organizations (NGOs) play in international environmental cooperation has been subject to studies in political science and other fields, but the extent of information dissemination by NGOs is still poorly understood. Although the contribution of a few large NGOs to the success of international environment programs is widely known, the impact of the majority of scientific, professional and voluntary organizations on the availability of environmental information has never been assessed. The problem is that many international organizations that have official consultative status with the United Nations Economic and Social Council (ECOSOC), and thus are eligible to provide formal input into the planning of member countries, have general agendas rather than specific environmental expertise. On the other hand, many NGOs exclusively concerned with the environment have no consultative status with ECOSOC, because they are considered national organizations even if they have international memberships.

In spite of these institutional barriers, the collective thrust for citizen participation in public affairs at the national level and for NGO participation in international affairs is beginning to produce some results. The United Nations Environment Programme (UNEP) has initiated a number of meetings of organizations with environmental commitments. The Union of International Associations (UIA) has called on the United Nations and other intergovernmental bodies "to help build recognition of voluntary and NGO groups as constituting a 'Third World' in organizational terms . . . which needs to be developed for balanced social change" (Judge 1973, p. 400).

Specialized information resources, particularly measurement-related intelligence for environmental assessment, present considerable hurdles to information seekers. The most trusted and viable resource for such information is the informal contact with an organization or person. Figure 8.2 and Figure 8.3 indicate types of information produced by organizations and individuals. Just as we understand an information need in a deeper sense by knowing the purpose of the query, we can better assess an organizational or personal information product by understanding the motives and constraints of its creation. This type of information can be obtained only by contact with its source. In multidisciplinary fields the trend toward reliance on individual expertise is indicated by the increasing use of "human resource guides" and "people's yellow pages" circulated informally within peer groups. Such guides are of special value when they show an individual's availability for consulting, public speaking, or discussion groups.

Information Transfer Mechanisms

Information providers and educators are partners in every effort to create informing processes. "The information system must bear the burden of responsibility for adaptation and not force this burden on the potential user." At the same time, "the educational system must prepare potential users to take full advantage of the information resources available to them" (Organization . . . 1971, p. 46). This partnership has to be particularly effective in emerging multidisciplinary fields.

Figure 8.2
INSTITUTIONAL RESOURCES

INFORMATION PRODUCTS	*MOTIVES AND CONSTRAINTS*
Archives, records	Client preferences
Conferences, meetings, symposia	Competition
Contracts, agreements	Cultural influences
Cost analyses	External power groups
Decisions	Financial situation
Designs	Funded research
Developmental plans	Information overload
Educational materials	Innovation
External communications	Institutional goals
Forecasts	Internal power groups
Impact statements	Internal priorities
Information systems, databases	Lack of information
Internal communications	Laws, regulations
Multimedia	Leadership impact
Operational measures	Market forces
Operational policies	Opportunity
Patents, copyrights	Policy direction
Press releases, marketing	Politics
Process descriptions	Problem solving
Research data	Proprietary information
Staff manuals	Publicity
Standards, specifications	Research & Development
Statistics, indicators	Social environment
Strategies, plans	Traditions, customs

Two types of information systems, relevant to environmental information seekers, will be discussed below.

Data Centers and Data Banks

In the past, data on the genetic effects of drugs, food additives, the toxicity of pesticides or hydrological observations were thought of as elements in the research apparatus of scientific investigation, while information expressed in textual form came under the purview of the information professions. None of these arbitrary lines of division can hold in the face of increasing need for data applications to policy, practice, and public action. The new data centers in environmental science require a convergence of different strains of professional talent and a commitment to cooperation by scientists, managers, policy makers, activists and information specialists.

Figure 8.3
INDIVIDUAL RESOURCES

INFORMATION PRODUCTS	*MOTIVES AND CONSTRAINTS*
Collection of samples	Behavioral traits
Collection of specimen	Change orientation
Compounds	Creativity
Document collection	Disciplinary goals
Engineering designs	Economic incentives
Expertise	Friendship
Field observations	Funding, sponsorship
Formal publications	Influence by peers
Human resource networks	Information overload
Ideas	Intergroup relations
Informal communications	Lack of information
Invisible colleges	Leadership
Laboratory observations	Mission orientation
Lectures	Need for privacy
Letters, memoranda	Personal commitments
Maps	Priorities
Methods	Professional goals
Office files	Professional tradition
Personal databases	Power building
Processes	Project support
Proposals	Research trends
Research data	Special skills
Special products	Status rewards
Statements, opinions	Technical know-how
Translations	
Unpublished papers	

Environmental indicators represent a data category of growing importance. It has often been stated by development specialists that conceptualizing and measuring the quality of life and the changes in quality introduced by projects in a developing country are among the most difficult tasks in project planning and evaluation. Problems of constructing environmental and quality of life indicators include identifying the appropriate methodology and fitting it to the project's cultural climate. The United States government is no exception with regard to the struggle for better environmental measurements and criteria. Train (1973, p. 121) wrote that " . . . there are conceptual questions that must be answered . . . Good indices depend on good data, but the environmental data now being collected are deficient in many respects."

Information from data centers emanates either as untreated, raw data or as aggregated sets of data analyzed, evaluated and organized to facilitate use. The latter repackaging activity has created the information analysis center. What is lacking is clear, straightforward guidance for users to (1) locate data facilities relevant to their needs, (2) find out about legal, institutional and technical constraints that govern access, and (3) learn about special services such as current awareness mechanisms, the publication of evaluated and condensed data in tabular form, and user's manuals. To locate data centers, potential users and intermediaries must consult a large number of fragmented sources published in different professional guides and journals, announcements of research-in-progress, and directories of all types of information sources.

There seems to be a great need for reflective conceptual analysis of problems relating to data services. What happens in the process that transforms raw data into information? For example, analyses of water samples taken at a local sampling station on certain dates produce data elements that may be compared with values established by water quality standards. Results of the comparison should be synthesized, summarized and packaged for use by water engineers, regulatory agencies, planners, and public groups. Is there a demonstrable benefit to summarizing technical data for popular announcement services? This and similar questions call for the attention of researchers.

Information Referral Services

Referral services established by international organizations, national governments and research institutes refer the user to specialized individuals and organizations prepared to respond to inquiries. Scientific information referrals have been emphasized because of the international visibility and information demands of environmental researchers. A different model, "Information and Referral," has been developed for use by social service agencies, and is now beginning to play a role in local communities.

Two themes are discernible throughout the environmental information literature: increasing people-orientation in both information seeking and delivery, and use of innovative approaches, especially referrals to resource people and organizations. The United Nations Environment Programme (UNEP) is developing a pattern of interaction with experts in various countries. "In the field of the environment there are often no definite answers to questions, and those that exist are seldom transferable from one situation to another. Experts will have to be consulted in connection with the analysis and compilation of answers" (United Nations . . . 1974, p. 34). In a local American setting, a newspaper publisher asks:

> Suppose a newspaper confronts an environmental problem of some complexity. . . . What avenues exist for independent review? Could a university be an instant resource? Experts from its own ranks, from other universities, from newspapers, could be available for telephone discussion of the parameters of the problem. If an on-site inspection seemed warranted, a task force could assemble, examine the issue first-hand, and present a report through the newspaper to the public" (Romm 1973).

The above examples illustrate the need for information referral ranging from international agencies to small towns. Some environmentalists predict that decisions concerning technology assessment and the quality of communities will be handled at top decision-making levels without filtering to the grassroots except as token publicity campaigns. Others believe that environmental issues will be decided by citizen participation. Chances for the latter alternative would be enhanced by citizen groups and community organizations having a reliable and credible information base not limited to formal institutions and information systems. Community networks, including environmentalists in different fields who are willing to serve as sources of information, could assist local environmental planning and problem solving collaboratively.

If networking of resource people continued as a trend, basically five challenges confront the environmental information community:

- *The information seeker* whose complex and elusive needs can be understood only through awareness of new environmental attitudes and societal interrelationships
- *The information provider,* in many cases not sufficiently prepared to deal with either the behavioral aspects or the multidisciplinary nature of environmental information transfer
- *Information resources* and data centers which need to be adapted to new user requirements in the public
- *Invisible information,* including large quantities of data and reports accumulated by agencies, short-term programs and projects not accessible to users, and lacking referral services

- *Human resources,* groups and individuals who have specialized knowledge and who would be willing to share it through community networks.

Concluding Note

Even in this sketchy map of the environmental information field we can sense its changeability, complexity, and fragmentation. There are indications that in the future the management of the environment will be based on measurements and indicators rather than on romanticized assumptions and opinions. However, even when the emotional tenor of the movement quiets, ideological and social factors can be expected to influence decisions about life in a world of diminishing resources. Because of its underlying stark reality, environmental information will become more and more personal for individuals. This fact- and data-oriented, yet deeply personal approach to knowledge that is both scientific and philosophical, will place a heavy responsibility on those who generate, use and transfer information. There must be open communication, cooperation and a mutual appreciation of personal views. Otherwise we may see environmental decisions made on the basis of information that is irrelevant to human needs.

References

Allen, T.J., Piepmeier, J.M., & Cooney, S. (1971). The international technological gatekeeper. *Technology Review,* 73(5), 37–44.

Baker, D.B. (1970). Communication or chaos? *Science,* 169(3947), 739–742.

Bie, P. de. (1970). "Problem-focused research." In United Nations Educational, Scientific and Cultural Organization. *Main Trends of Research in the Social and Human Sciences.* Part 1, 578–644. Paris, France: UNESCO.

Bohannan, P. (1972). Our two-story culture. *Saturday Review,* 55(36), 40–41.

Bronowski, J. (1973). The principle of tolerance. *Atlantic Monthly,* 232(6), 60–66.

Crane, D. (1972). *Invisible Colleges: Diffusion of Knowledge in Scientific Communities.* Chicago, IL: University of Chicago.

Dubos, R. (1973). St. Francis versus St. Benedict (Excerpt from *A God Within.* New York, NY: Scribner). *Psychology Today,* 6(12), 54–60.

Finding the forest in the trees. (1968). *Yale Alumni Magazine,* 32(3), 23–25.

Judge, A.J.N. (1973). Inter-organizational relationships: in search of a new style. *International Associations,* 25(8/9), 398–402.

Kanter, R.M. (1972). *Commitment and Community, Communes and Utopias in Sociological Perspective.* Cambridge, MA: Harvard University Press.

Knox, W.T. (1973). Systems for technological information transfer. *Science,* 181(4098), 415–419.

Lamar, H.R. (1972). The new old West. *Yale Alumni Magazine,* 36(1), 6–15.

Landau, R. (1972). Complexity and complexing. *Architectural Design,* 42, 608–610.

Lifton, R.J. (1969). Protean man. *Yale Alumni Magazine,* 32(4), 14–21.

Lin, N. & Garvey, W.D. (1972). "Information needs and uses." In *Annual Review of Information Science and Technology.* V. 7, ed. by C.A. Cuadra, 5–37. Washington, DC: American Society for Information Science.

Maddox, J. (1972). Economic growth and the environment. *The Listener,* 87(2256), 820.

Marden, P.G. (1972). *Current issues in the teaching of population. Teaching Notes in Population.* Ithaca, NY: Cornell University, International Population Program.

Metcalf, R.L. & Pitts Jr., J.N. (1969). *Advances in Environmental Science and Technology.* New York, NY: Wiley-Interscience.

New York Times. (1973). Sec. 2 (January 21) 22.

Organization for Economic Cooperation and Development. (1971). *Information for a Changing Society: Some Policy Consideration.* Paris, France: OECD.

Romm, A.N. (1973). Remarks. Presentation at Syracuse University Newhouse School of Public Communications, February 16. (Unpublished).

Train, R.E. (1973). The quest for environmental indices. *Science,* 178 (4057), 721.

United Nations Economic Commission for Europe. (1971). *ECE Symposium on Problems Relating to the Environment, Prague 1971. Proceedings and Documentation.* New York, NY: United Nations.

United Nations Environment Programme. Earthwatch. (1974). Informal expert meeting on the International Referral System, Nairobi, Kenya, March 4–6, 1974. (Unpublished).

United States Environmental Protection Agency. (1973). *National Environmental Information Symposium, Cincinnati, OH, September 24–27, 1972.* V. 1. *Summary Report.* Washington, DC: EPA.

White, L., Jr. (1967). The Historical roots of our ecological crisis. *Science,* 155(3767), 1289–1293.

World Assembly of NGOs Concerned with the Global environment, Geneva. (1973). Proceedings. Geneva, Switzerland: United Nations. (Unpublished).

9

The Consultant as Information Intermediary

Focus on Intercultural Processes

The Organization for Economic Cooperation and Development (1981, v. 1, p. 24) defined "consultative services" as information producers. Such services "are primarily engaged in applying a pre-existent body of information to the particular needs of the 'client' or 'situation'." Implied in this description is the complex process of evaluating, interpreting, and reshaping both the content and the form of information. Consultants use this knowledge base, inextricably fused with their own insights and experience, as a tool of intervention in their clients' professional and organizational processes. Such interventions often affect not only the working environment but also the personal attitudes and expectations of the client. Thus the consultant as intermediary is not a passive conduit of knowledge transfer but an active innovator.

This paper is about a particularly demanding situation where several conditions interact to render the consultant's job highly sensitive: technical assistance in developing countries. The consultant is usually a member of a technologically advanced country. The process of professional and human interaction takes place in an intercultural setting. The technology introduced from one culture into another must be adapted to the recipient's society, economy and traditions.

Describing the model of process consultation, Schein (1969, p. 9), argues that "the various functions which make up an organization are always mediated by the interactions of people, so that the organization can never escape its human processes." This view moves the consultancy from the level of abstract development theories and planning documents to the level of cultural interpretation and personal influence. For consultants with a commitment to professional integrity, the responsibility involved in this role is immense.

Projects dealing with the design, management and evaluation of information systems or the development of information science curricula are especially dependent on the consultant's understanding of local conditions. Knowledgeable as they may be in their fields, technical advisors lacking practical experience with some countries' traditionally slow approach to change often become frustrated and impatient with their local counterparts. They have to be familiar with the peculiar imbalance between science and technological policies in developing countries where the influence of technology is much stronger than the prestige of science (Moravcsik 1982, p. 9). Another source of disappointment is that the absence of national information policies impedes the planning and implementation of projects. Long and exasperating delays can ensue. Consultants have been known to abandon projects aimed at the development of information systems or educational programs due to the lack of governmental guidelines and policies in the host country. In other cases, complicated regulations by foreign governments are a cause of confusion for consultants. For example, Lall (1984, p. 235) describes the restrictions that impede foreign investment and the licensing of foreign technology in India.

The following brief overview of current trends in development assistance and information policies will conclude with some hard questions concerning the effective application of innovations in developing countries. Considerations that may ensure a development project's survival after the departure of the consultants will be discussed.

The Consultancy Mystique

As a term for a conglomerate of activities in a growth industry, "consulting" is almost as broad and equivocal a label as communication or information transfer. One has to search through the guidelines and policy statements of international agencies before one sees the outlines of a formalized profession emerge. The World Bank (1974, pp. 2–3) uses the services of consulting firms for (1) preinvestment studies (e.g. priorities, policies, feasibility studies, resource inventories, surveys, cost estimates), (2) detailed "engineering and design" of a project (e.g. technical, economic, financial and social analyses), and (3) implementation (e.g. field projects, operations, coordination, institution building, management studies, training). Individual consultants are retained by the Bank for project preparation, appraisal and supervision, and for special economic and sectoral studies. Consultants may also be selected and employed by the borrowing country. Although brief technical and legal guidelines are available from the Bank for such cases, for a discussion of the cultural, professional and behavioral factors that affect the outcome of the consultative process one has to turn to case studies and journal articles.

In the past three decades a large volume of literature has been produced concerning the philosophies and strategies of technical assistance to the world's poorer countries (Ghosh 1984). First, attention was focused on economic and technical considerations. But the literature of the 1970s and 1980s showed increasing interest in communications and human factors in planning and management. Moravcsik (1982, p. 12) cautioned that the scientific activities of developing countries had to be assessed by "considering values stemming from a wide variety of aspirations, not only material or economic ones." It seems that the more a development project depended on its cultural and social environment for success, the more political the consultant's role became.

The international consultant or advisor is most often thought of as a technical expert from a technology-rich country who assists less industrialized countries in a particular aspect of development. Whether working individually or as a member of a team or consulting firm, contracted by an intergovernmental organization, a nongovernmental organization, or a national government, assigned to a short-term task or a long-term mission, the consultant is an active carrier of specialized information and technological skills from one culture to another.

Just who are the members of this mobile, heterogenous and undefined corps of knowledge carriers who probably have more influence on international cooperation at the professional level than the official delegates of scientific and professional societies? In the past, when technical aid to the newly independent countries of the world was aimed mainly at the development of infrastructures such as electric power, transportation, and irrigation, most technical advisors represented architecture or engineering. Much of the literature of the consultancy has been written in engineering and technological terms (Hardiman and Midgley 1978, p. 233). But following the rise of large-scale projects in rural development, agriculture, education and health, donor agencies began to recognize the value of the human element in development, and to hire a growing number of specialists in nonformal education, rural communication, community health, and the development of environmental conservation activities. At the same time, a movement toward the integration of economic and social planning and the strengthening of indigenous management capabilities brought a large number of planners into consulting activities. Interdisciplinary teams gradually became the preferred pattern in technical advising. A case study by Giles (1979) criticizing the overuse of economists in national governments is a characteristic example of the trend toward interdisciplinary development work.

Consultants to library and archival projects have been active in developing countries ever since the post–World War II period, when the United Nations Educational, Scientific and Cultural Organization (UNESCO) took on major responsibility for the creation or modernization of libraries and scientific/technical information centers. Consultants designed buildings, assisted in publishing programs, and planned children's reading rooms and higher educational curricula. National bibliographic centers, union catalogs and cooperative library programs were created with their help. These missions were usually politicized. The consultants' intermediary role took them out of the institutions into the public policy arena. Berninghausen (1969, p. 99) spoke to the point: "The key to changing or developing an overseas library isn't in the library. It's in the prime minister's or the general's office, the ministry of education, the office of the rector or the dean, or in the faculty or other committee meetings."

Today this situation has intensified. At the confluence of telecommunication and computing advances, the availability of powerful information technology poses a new challenge to consultants and their counterparts in developing countries. Whether the technical expert deals with agroclimate information systems or the processing of financial data, the readiness of technology and the absence of culturally relevant policies render the process of development more political than it was in the preceding decades. The advisor in a host country, identified with imported ideas, is the antithesis of political and social independence. The mere presence of consultants conjures up questions about the cultural integrity of rapid technical change. Dore (1984), for instance, probes into the sincerity of the movement toward technological self-reliance. The use of technological devices, foreign or domestic, applicable to a situation or not, is expected as a matter of prestige. Menou (1981, p. 7) recounts the following experience: "A few years ago, there were more computers than national programmes in an African country where we happened to work and computers are currently installed in places where the electric power distribution is rather hazardous." Foreign consultants are surrounded by an aura, a mystique of technological capability that makes them honored and at the same time resented. As visitors from distant technocratic societies they are often seen as potential sources of advancement for their colleagues in poorer countries not only in terms of professional growth but also in terms of social and economic gains.

Ascroft (1978) refers to the reticence that prevents nationals of many African countries from openly discussing with consultants the problems of a project as "a conspiracy of courtesy." Thus many projects either fail before completion or are left to wither away after the project's foreign personnel leave. The implication is that technical expertise is not sufficient to make intercultural professional collaboration successful. Working together to convince government officials and the field officers of donor agencies of the importance of integrated information policies, consultants and their national counterparts need new political savvy. Tell (1980) speaks of the "social intelligence function," a continuous scanning of the social and cultural landscape, as a new dimension of the information profession. It is exactly this function that seems to be lacking in many development projects.

The latent impact of information and knowledge that consultants bring to a developing country could be turned into a dynamic force in the service of national development. What is needed is a new direction for both indigenous and foreign consultants. This new direction should move us toward a clear understanding that the constructive application of new information technologies and skills to development is determined not only by government support and development strategies, but also—and probably most powerfully—by local cultural traditions.

The Consultant's Environment

Within the last decade technical assistance strategies underwent several revisions. Consultants played a major role in the reassessment process by conducting comparative studies in a number of developing countries; questioning the major economic tenets of development assistance; and scrutinizing project planning and implementation methods (Baranson 1981, Stewart and James 1982, Weaver and Jameson 1978). Although the controversy between comprehensive development (the "trickle-down" approach) and the basic needs policy (priority given to basic human needs in the least developed areas within each country) has subsided in the face of global economic aspirations, its mark on the innovating role of the consultant is unmistakable. The consultant is not only a technical expert but also a developmentalist who is expected to identify with one or another school of thought. The majority of consultants probably believe with Dell (1979, p. 293) that "the real issues between the basic needs strategists and those who favour comprehensive development policies lie not in the goal of social equity, which is common ground between them, but in the means for achieving that goal."

By the onset of the 1980s, the emphasis of development policy changed from selecting and importing appropriate technology to strengthening domestic production in order to improve the international bargaining position of developing nations. In this new equation, consultants with expertise in information systems gained added stature. They were expected to answer timely and critical questions: Is information technology different from other technological processes and commodities? How does technology change following its importation and use in the host country? Policy makers and researchers rejected the general economic planning for development assistance by international organizations, demanding new approaches of political economy which applied specifically to low-income societies (Fransman and King 1984, p. 26). It was argued that in developing countries "the order of the three terms of the simplest production function capital-labor-residual factor (including technological change) is practically reversed and reads as technology-capital-labor. Technology is considered as a driving force and a determinant of not only the rate of growth but the very pattern of development" (Hetman 1982, p. 51).

The orientation of a consultant toward particular strategies is likely to influence the information activities and sources that will characterize a project. Advocates of the basic needs direction may emphasize social and economic data concerning rural development, migration to urban areas and poverty levels. Decisions of local people in project planning and the integration of indigenous values in goals are stressed. Nonformal education, public library role in literacy programs, and the diffusion of self-help information are frequently highlighted. Information technology must be appropriate and its introduction through a communication project must utilize the labor and creativity of local people. On the other hand, as Cusack (1981) points out in his discussion of the misconceptions of technology transfer, many development specialists argue that appropriate technology is often a cover-up for obsolete models and techniques that will be more damaging than useful to the recipients. These examples point to the need to keep abreast of changing development trends in order to better understand their implications for the consultant's information activities.

The Consultant's International Resources

The consultants' effectiveness with peers and government officials in the host country often depends on how promptly they can obtain relevant information when it is needed to solve a particular problem or advance a political interest or relationship. The extensive experience of international organizations would be an excellent source for information acquisition, if all organizations were to make their knowledge bases available in a more systematic fashion. However, there are several problems associated with this body of mostly unpublished and semipublished reports, policy papers, and research studies. Many consultants share the reluctance of developing country nationals to accept these information sources as a true representation of development efforts. Even less trusted are social data on indigenous populations and conditions, if collected by foreign researchers. "International officials are drawn from the elite of many countries, including Third World countries, and they are well qualified in the conventional sense. It may be that their status, education and conceptual apparatus will make it difficult for international staff to comprehend the universe of poverty and to prescribe suitable remedies" (Gulhati 1977, p. 362).

With some exceptions, internal documents of large assistance agencies are accessible. Since each donor has a different administrative procedure, reporting practices vary from agency to agency, and often from department to department within the same organization. Pattison and Fratianni (1978) discussed the relationship between an organization's hierarchical nature and its lack of direct connection with national policymakers. The authors, like most other critics of development sponsors, overlook the consultant as a viable information intermediary. Usually less formal in organizational communication than the staff of large donor agencies and oriented toward a discipline or profession, the consultant often maintains close ties with colleagues in developing countries. Even though reservations about the dissemination of hastily compiled, unpublished reports, are especially strong where data analyses are concerned, consultants often act as effective brokers in information acquisition between donor agencies and projects in host countries.

Many technical assistance organizations distribute published reports to field officers, advisors, grantees and some host country institutions. Most of them also respond to requests for specific reports and referrals to internal experts. These practices depend on such factors as the organization's structure and size, the clarity of top-level administrative policy and legal, economic and political considerations.

In recent years, a certain kind of international assistance agency, the private voluntary organization (PVO), has been attracting attention for its successful approach to collaborative projects at the grassroots level. All three types of PVOs—the technical/professional organization, the general issue organization and the development assistance organization—place considerable emphasis on information sharing and dissemination. Subramanian (1986, p. 183) reports that a "small but increasing number of VAs [volunteer agencies] were not comfortable with their distance from the economically poor . . . these VAs were convinced that they had to reach the relatively weaker sections of society . . . Some of the progressive VAs collected evidence for this observation through informal studies and investigation." The private voluntary agencies challenge traditional organizational processes by legitimizing counter models, and instituting participatory planning, experimentation, and joint monitoring of project impact (Subramanian 1986, p. 185).

Information by and about PVOs is scattered in a host of newsletters, conference reports and occasional papers. While in the past ties between these diversified organizations were not particularly strong, cooperation has intensified in recent years, partly under the influence of the International Council of Voluntary Agencies. Down-to-earth skills in social organization and informal communication channels with field offices and project personnel enable the PVOs and their consultants to become excellent information appliers and disseminators.

Macro-Influences on Knowledge Transfer

Effective as their personal resources may be, consultants don't work in isolation, sealed into their own projects and protected from whatever tensions might prevail in international relations. On the contrary, a consultant who works in the rapidly changing and expanding world of information will not be able to avoid accusations of "information domination" and other current controversies. Some consultants respond with bitter disillusionment, others accept the situation with scientific objectivity and humanistic tolerance, understanding that nowhere in the world, neither in the smallest village nor in the most teeming metropolis, can information-related work be completely devoid of cultural interpretation. Information processes bring people, ideas and technologies into interaction. Should a consultant be prepared to deal only with the technology, the consultancy's responsibility for people and ideas would be forsaken.

We generally hold that it is not for the physician to ask which side of the battle front is responsible for the wound. It is not for the advisor engaged in the design of a scientific information system, a public library program, or a rural information dissemination network to become politically involved in the course of the work. But consultants who are aware of internationally volatile information policy issues will be able to better understand the emotional reaction to the notion of "information" by political and intellectual leaders in the host country. Once familiar with the issues, some consultants find continued neutrality untenable. Physicians are compelled by their Hippocratic oath-dictated professional values to treat wounds on either side of the enemy line. Consultants are not compelled to design information systems for factions whose ideas and activities are offensive to them. Consultants must be familiar with the project environment in order to make decisions in situations where their own values may conflict with the actions of their local sponsors.

Three controversial areas of policy might be cited as examples of disagreement: the international transfer of scientific and technical information, transborder data transmission, and international mass communication. In each area, the concept of information is interpreted in a different way. All three interpretations divide people. These divisions are macroinfluences that may impede the professional and social interactions of foreign consultants with decision makers in the host country. Many consultants are so absorbed in their specialty that they frown upon the mere mention of broad policy issues. However, it is only at the level of personal professional cooperation that the potentially divisive influence of policy concerns can be alleviated.

Scientific and Technical Information

In this area, the cause of international tensions lies in the disparate capabilities of technologically advanced and developing countries to produce and use scientific and technical information. While the published results of scientific research emanating from academic institutions in the industrialized world receive slow but fairly steady distribution worldwide, the availability of technological innovations is being hindered by more and more complex Western regulations (Stewart 1979). The consultancy as an international institution is generally seen as ineffective in easing the technological dependence of poor countries. It often fails outright to empower and promote endogenous research capabilities, although the transmission of skills necessary for local R&D is the key to the use of research for development goals (United Nations Educational . . . 1981, United Nations University 1981). Economically struggling countries need assistance in building information infrastructures; equal participation in international networks; increased utilization of communication technology; and organizational skills to strengthen regional cooperation. Consultants assisting in achieving any of these goals find that tensions tend to arise around several problems in intercultural interaction:

- Who manages whose S/T information resources?
- Who has access to what information resources?
- Who disseminates what information to whom?

Changes in information technology make it difficult for the consultant to evaluate and recommend what is "appropriate" in a particular place and situation. Policy researchers are concerned that in many countries national policies for science and policies for technology are thrown together into an overall framework, failing to provide guidance to development project management (Hetman 1982, p. 46). Care must be taken lest people interpret technology only as hardware. Not until the idea that technology must be adapted to people takes a firm hold will consultants become effective links in technology transfer.

Transborder Data Flow

Transborder data flow is a little known but troublesome issue in developing countries. The problem (for high-technology countries an opportunity) has evolved from the rapid growth of international data transmission including electronic networks of the airline, hotel, car rental, banking and computer service industries and other information-intensive businesses. International carriers now provide transmission capacity to companies located in developing countries that handle large quantities of data for inventories, production, marketing and financial records, and radio and television networks, teletype and facsimile services. Originally, the concerns of developing countries were divided between the impact of gigantic electronic information pools beyond their borders, and the need to build their own data processing and transfer systems. Data that had originated domestically were most often transmitted and stored in remote data banks and were subject to foreign regulations. Problems included the protection of personal information about nationals, and the lack of institutional and technological capacity to operate domestic data networks. Third World leaders warned that reliance on foreign technology will retard the growth of indigenous communication systems (Intergovernmental . . . 1981).

A number of countries have passed privacy protection laws, not only to ensure the privacy of indigenous individuals whose data are carried by transnational networks, but also to protect these countries' trade interests vis-à-vis the foreign data transfer industry. The United States perceived these instruments as barriers to free international trade and as restrictions of American multinational companies. On the other hand, many developing countries welcomed such restrictions as measures against international technology dominance. In its "Guidelines" the Organization for Economic Cooperation and Development (1981) proposed that its member countries avoid creating privacy protection policies which raise obstacles to transborder data flows.

Three questions illustrate the decision points where consultants in developing countries may encounter critical or outright hostile reactions:

- Who collects personal data about whom?
- What network carries whose data into whose country?
- What data network crosses whose border?

These queries represent a transition of policy concerns in developing countries from focus on personal data to focus on industrial data and related economic activities. The International Chamber of Commerce (1983, p. 359) summed up the areas where transborder data flows threatened national stability as "economic sovereignty, the vulnerability of a computerized society, the migration of employment and decision making." Three trends account for this change: (1) electronic services transmitting data internationally now become growth-industries, (2) data services are transforming the workings of industries, and (3) international trade in data is changing economic relationships (Sauvant 1986, p. 7). The information consultant to development projects, traditionally committed only to the improvement of general information facilities or scientific and technical information systems, has to deal now with the new significance of economic data networks spanning several distant countries.

The New World Communication and Information Order

In relation to the movement toward changes in the international communication and information regime, the interpretation of information shifted from "scientific research" and "transborder data" to "news." A critical aspect of the debate has been the capability of electronic news reporting (including collection, editing, selection and distribution) from and about developing countries by the media of industrial nations. In 1978, a "Declaration on the Mass Media" attempted to assemble all pertinent grievances of Third World countries, requiring that the indigenous news agencies in these countries be used more intensively, foreign journalists respect the laws of countries where they operate, and research and training in journalism be enhanced (Masmoudi 1979). The MacBride Commission, sponsored by UNESCO, warned that the benefits of instant international mass communications can be realized only "if the temptation to enlist the mass media in the service of narrow sectarian interests and to turn them into new instruments of power . . . is resisted" (International Commission . . . 1980, p. xiv). Another aspect of the debate was based on Third World shortcomings in the allocation of the electromagnetic spectrum and of the geostationary orbit by the International Telecommunications Union (Smith 1980).

Representatives of developing nations at international conferences argue that the global imbalance in communication technologies creates major political and economic inequities. Even unintentionally distorted images and "bad" news depicting a country's internal affairs widen the gap between those societies which have advanced information gathering facilities and those which are mere subjects of reporting. The MacBride Commission provided research data and a set of recommendations supporting the media policy expected by developing countries, including a proposal for the regulation of the press by national governments. Western countries viewed this proposal as an encroachment on basic press freedoms. The bitterness of the controversy spilled over into bilateral relationships and contributed to the termination of its UNESCO membership by the United States. Information consultants may contemplate the implications of questions ensuing in the wake of the debate:

- Whose news is reported by whose network for whom?
- Whose responsibility is it to strengthen communication systems in developing countries?
- Who will establish the balance between the free flow of international information and the preservation of its cultural identity by each country?

Rogers speaks of a dominant paradigm in development communications that assumed simply: "Introduce the technology in the less-developed countries and they will become relatively more developed." However, "development was not going very well in the developing countries that had closely followed the paradigm" (Rogers 1978, pp. 65–66). Some international consultants introducing modern systems to information-hungry countries still live by the old paradigm. Not prepared to acknowledge current concerns with the cultural adaptation of new technologies, they may have difficulties dealing with unexpected tensions in their collaboration with local experts.

The Consultant at the Project Site

Agricultural extension agents demonstrate a growing conviction that rural development specialists can learn from rural people. Korten (1979, p. 52) describes a striking outcome of the PUEBLA project in Mexico. Agricultural technicians deployed by the donor agency learned by coincidence about successful intercropping from local farmers. On the basis of this case, the Mexican government established a program for the joint training of agricultural researchers, extension agents and farmers, integrating local and foreign experiences.

The foreign consultant on site has to find innovative ways to involve local people in the project and to learn from their familiarity with existing conditions and attitudes. The resources of international agencies and industrial countries are either out of reach or irrelevant to decisions about project changes and unexpected problems. The characteristics of local information resources vary from country to country and, within each country, from one location to another. At a time of social change, these resources are in a state of flux. A search for timely and relevant facts requires a complex strategy. Because governments mainly support scientific and technical information activities, we are likely to assume that social data concerning populations, institutions, and lifestyles are not available. Actually an abundance of locally generated information resources exist in developing countries although usually in unpublished and unorganized form (Bax 1980, Oguara 1980).

The in-country acquisition of information depends on personal contacts a consultant is able to develop with institutions in the host country. Academic departments are potential sources of current staff studies even though they are usually located at a distance from the project site. Provincial government agencies and community organizations in the project's vicinity are repositories of local information accumulated in the course of their work. Such in-country information resources are difficult to access by foreign advisors. Consultants drawn from countries in the region may be more successful, but they have been known to avoid formal resources and rely on informal contacts and social networks. Nevertheless, for a project that seeks local participation, it would be a serious mistake to be concerned only with the immediate information needs of the project personnel only. Where all members of a project interact with local people, the process evolves into a mutually supportive exchange of information. Although the response to an array of disjointed and hard-to-access resources is often a keen sense of futility, a project without the capability to identify local information runs the risk of using irrelevant or obsolete data.

Recognizing that there are a great many variations in information resources depending on a country's historical tradition and socioeconomic status, nevertheless the consultant may develop contacts with some of the following institutions common to most developing countries:

National scientific and technical information center
National library and library network
Specialized information systems (e.g. agriculture, energy, tropical diseases)
National technology transfer center
Industrial documentation center
National social science data center
Information dissemination, communications and extension services
Education and training institutions

There are also many institutions in a developing country that serve as information resources, although they often lack libraries. Such institutions include:

National, provincial and local government agencies
Private organizations (e.g. professional societies, banks, cooperatives, community centers)
Universities, research institutes, technical schools, literacy programs
Data archives constructed by development projects
Nonformal education, information dissemination and extension services
The press, including the rural press and alternative journalism programs
Publishers, book distributors, producers of information-related technology and materials
Cultural activities, arts and crafts (e.g. craft centers, community theaters, museums)
Trade organizations; markets
Social networks.

Informal contacts are the preferred mode of information acquisition in most developing countries. "Who knows whom" is an important consideration when accessing libraries which often have elaborate systems to certify borrowers. The Bharat Sanskrit Khendra in Katmandu established the policy that "there is no deposit required when someone is sponsored by another member, a business, or a university . . ." (Foster 1979, p. 338). In Dakar, the Documentation Service of the Society for Agricultural Development and Extension initiated a network to exchange ideas. Face-to-face encounters are increasingly important. In the Bharat Sanskrit Khendra "an average of six hundred readers pass through . . . each day, some to read and others to meet friends" (Foster 1979, p. 337).

The consultant's role in knowledge transfer is particularly critical when a project draws local researchers into its data collection efforts. One of the critical tasks of a project is to measure the extent and nature of change that has been introduced. Should the information be collected in the form of statistics or in the form of human perceptions? The challenge is to conceptualize the development problem in relation to a cultural environment that is unfamiliar to the consultant. Conceptualization usually occurs during a discussion with indigenous researchers. Such group interactions are part advising, part practical assisting, and part training in methodology.

When Do Consultants Succeed?

Consultants use international and in-country data, records, documents and informal communication. In the course of their work, information passes to those around them. We do not know how this process takes place, we only know that it is embedded in the various interactions with project personnel, other consultants, local people, researchers, and government officials. Based on these exchanges, a typology of information transactions may be developed and analyzed by objectives, resources used, type of interaction, user involvement, user response and outcome. Problems of the communication process may be identified and remedies sought.

Most development specialists agree that a foreign aid program's attitude toward the local population is a strong determinant for success or failure. Attitudes and strategies usually reflect the consultants' style. Why do consultants have such potential to improve the quality and equity of information access in a developing country, and why are the examples of success so few and far between? Aráoz (1981) provides a set of case studies and poses interesting questions for research on the engineering consultancy. Much less information is available on information systems consultants. Should the performance of a consultant be measured only in terms of the end results, or also in terms of the political, administrative and social problems that had to be conquered? Even if we could find answers, none of these questions would bring us much closer to understanding why consultants succeed or fail in amalgamating new processes and technologies with a particular culture.

We may speculate that the key in knowledge transfer is the specific blend of messages, attitudes and creative interactions brought to certain situations. Let's say that a consultant in a developing country is attempting to introduce a research dissemination program in alternative energy sources. The tasks are clear: identify the scope of the research field, the audiences to be reached and their needs, sources of research information, dissemination channels, the technological configuration, and so on. Working through these tasks according to the best textbook knowledge will not necessarily guarantee success. That special blend of propensity, communicative power and creativeness that characterizes the consultant's work is determined by factors which are poorly understood.

Conclusions

We have an unfinished agenda at hand. The following is offered as a prelude to the future when the agenda may be completed by collaborative efforts. Strategies and information policy issues suggest a special challenge to the information systems consultant in a developing country: To adapt knowledge, skills and electronic devices to local needs and to assure the continuation of innovations after the life cycle of the project. The involvement of counterparts and target populations in project planning, implementation and evaluation is indispensable to the success of knowledge transfer. Multidirectional communication channels must be maintained by the foreign consultant in order to learn as well as advise.

A research agenda will identify and plan investigations that may lead to a better understanding of the international consultancy. Education and training programs and workshops are needed to assure development of a corps of consultants drawn from developing countries. Regional resource networks of consultants who work on information-related projects may be initiated by extracting information from current consultant rosters as well as searching for new talent through informal contacts.

Regional organizations and conferences provide opportunities for consultants to exchange ideas, experiences and new methods. A novel pattern of regional cooperation, urging conference participants to remain in contact with each other and exchange experiences gained in their own work, promises fewer futile resolutions at conferences and more action at home. A consensus seems to be evolving that the quality of the international consultancy, currently focused mainly on technicalities, depends not only on a change in policy direction but also on a new unifying interdisciplinary and humanistic spirit.

References

Aráoz, A. ed. (1981). *Consulting and Engineering Design in Developing Countries*. Ottawa: International Development Research Centre.

Ascroft, J. (1978). A Conspiracy of courtesy. *IDR/Focus [International Development Research]*, 3, 8–11.

Baranson, J. (1981). *North-South Technology Transfer: Financing and Institution Building*. Mt. Airy, MD: Lomond.

Bax, N. (1980). "Documentation in financial administration." In *Seminar on Information for Economic Planning and Development for the African Region, Legon, Ghana, 1978. Proceedings*. Legon, Ghana: University of Ghana, Department of Library Studies, v. 1, 128–136.

Berninghausen, D.K. (1969). The American library consultant overseas. *International Library Review*, 1(1), 97–105.

Cusack, D.F. (1981). The Transfer of computer-based technology in agroclimate information systems. *Interciencia*, 6(4), 261–267.

Dell, S. (1979). Basic needs or comprehensive development: Should the UNDP have a development strategy? *World Development*, 7(3), 291–308.

Dore, R. (1984). "Technological self-reliance: Sturdy ideal or self-serving rhetoric. In Fransman, M. & King, K. eds. *Technological Capability in the Third World*, 65–80. New York, NY: St. Martin's Press.

Foster, B. (1979). Special libraries in Katmandu. *Special Libraries*, 70(8), 333–340.

Fransman, M. & King, K. eds. (1984). *Technological Capability in the Third World*. New York, NY: St. Martin's Press.

Ghosh, P.K. ed. (1984). *Technology Policy and Development*. Boulder, CO: Westview Press.

Giles, B.D. (1979). Economists in government: The Case of Malawi. *Journal of Development Studies*, 15(2), 216–232.

Gulhati, R. (1977). A Mandate on behalf of the poor? *The Round Table*, 168, 351–364. (World Bank reprint 93).

Hardiman, M. & Midgley, J (1978). Foreign consultants and development projects, the need for an alternative approach. *Journal of Administration Overseas*, 17(4), 232–244.

Hetman, F. (1982). "From technology assessment to an integrated perspective on technology." In Srinivasan, M., ed. *Technology Assessment and Development*, 36–54. New York, NY: Praeger.

Intergovernmental Bureau for Informatics. (1981). *Transborder Data Flow Policies: Papers Presented at the IBI Conference, Rome, 1980.* Rome, Italy: IBI.

International Chamber of Commerce. (1983). "Information Flows: An International Business Perspective. Policy Statement Adopted by the Council of the International Chamber of Commerce." In Sauvant, K.P. (1986). *International Transactions in Services: The Politics of Transborder Data Flows,* 359–363. Boulder, CO: Westview Press.

International Commission for the Study of Communication Problems. (1980). *Many Voices, One World.* Paris, France: UNESCO and London, UK: Kogan Page.

Korten, D.C. ed. (1979). *Population and Social Development Management: A Challenge for Management Schools.* Caracas, Venezuela: Instituto de Estudian Superiores de Administracion.

Lall, S. (1984). "India's technological capacity: Effects of trade, industrial, science and technology policies." In Fransman, M. & King, K. eds. *Technological Capability in the Third World,* 225–243. New York, NY: St. Martin's Press.

Masmoudi, M. (1979). The New World information order. *Journal of Communication,* 29(2), 172–192.

Menou, M.J. (1981). Cultural Barriers to the International Transfer of Information. Paper Presented at the 18th Cranfield Conference on Mechanized Information Transfer, Cranfield, UK, July 21–24, 1981 (Unpublished).

Moravcsik, M.J. (1982). "Assessment of science in developing countries." In Srinivasan, M. ed. *Technology Assessment and Development,* 3–35. New York, NY: Praeger.

Oguara, E.T.A. (1980). "Information for banking in Africa: Needs, sources and organisation." In *Seminar on Information for Economic Planning and Development for the African Region, Legon, Ghana, 1978. Proceedings,* v. 1, 97–127. Legon, Ghana: University of Ghana, Department of Library Studies.

Organization for Economic Cooperation and Development. (1981). *Guidelines on the protection of privacy and transborder flows of personal data.* Paris, France: OECD.

Organization for Economic Cooperation and Development. (1981). *Information Activities, Electronics and Telecommunications Technologies: Impact on Employment, Growth and Trade.* Paris, France: OECD. 2 vols.

Pattison, J.C. & Fratianni, M. (1978). "International institutions and international progress." In N.M. Kamrany ed. *The New Economics of the Less Developed Countries,* 319–341. Boulder, CO: Westview Press.

Rogers, E.M. (1978). The rise and fall of the dominant paradigm. *Journal of Communication,* 28(1), 64–69.

Sauvant, K.P. (1986). *International Transactions in Services: The Politics of Transborder Data Flows.* Boulder, CO: Westview Press.

Schein, E.H. (1969). *Process Consultation: Its Role in Organization Development.* Reading, MA: Addison-Wesley.

Smith, A. (1980). *The Geopolitics of Information: How Western Culture Dominates the World.* New York, NY: Oxford University Press.

Stewart, F. (1979). *International Technology Transfer: Issues and Policy Options.* Washington, DC: World Bank. (Staff working paper 344).

Stewart, F. & James, J. (1982). *The Economics of New Technology in Developing Countries.* London, UK: Frances Pinter.

Subramanian, A. (1986). "Strategies for changing agency-centered development programs." In Ickis, J.C., et al., eds. *Beyond Bureaucracy: Strategic Management of Social Development,* 182–195. West Hartford, CT: Kumarian Press.

Tell, B.V. (1980). The Awakening information needs of the developing countries. *Journal of Information Science,* 1, 285–289.

United Nations Educational, Scientific and Cultural Organisation (UNESCO). (1981). *Domination or Sharing? Endogenous Development and the Transfer of Knowledge.* Paris, France: UNESCO (Insights series 5).

United Nations University. (1981). *Endogenous Intellectual Creativity and the Emerging New International Order.* Tokyo, Japan: UNU.

Weaver, J. & Jameson, K. (1978). *Economic Development: Competing Paradigms, Competing Parables.* Washington, DC: U.S. Agency for International Development.

The World Bank. (1974). *Uses of Consultants by the World Bank and Its Borrowers.* Washington, DC: WB.

10

Transfer and Adaptation of a Group Problem-Solving Model for Community Organizations

Ann P. Bishop and Marta Dosa

Inquiry about the impact of the group problem-solving process is a significant area of research that is beginning to receive more attention from information scientists. Group problem solving is an information activity potentially useful for improving the effectiveness of organizations. People from different professional backgrounds may form groups in order to resolve particular intra- or interorganizational concerns through the exchange of information, knowledge, and experience. Face-to-face meetings contribute to the creation of an ongoing information sharing network among participants that extends beyond the meetings themselves.

This paper describes the development of a model of informal information sharing processes used by community health professionals to analyze and resolve problems. That model has already been transferred from the original research site to a community setting in the health care sector. We suggest that the same model may be transferable to other domains where members of various community organizations are working on issues of common interest. One domain that appears hospitable to new approaches is information resources management (IRM). We conclude this paper with a proposal for testing the group problem-solving model in the IRM domain with members of community organizations.

The prototype group problem-solving process is appealing on both theoretical and practical grounds, given the dilemmas that face organizations at the community level. Typically, difficulties include budget cuts, scarcity of funding, communication barriers among and within organizations, and complex political and legal constraints. Testing the informal group problem-solving model and participants' perceptions of its effectiveness in different environments may provide some useful insights into the way community organizations deal with problems and work-related information flows. Further, it may also be helpful in designing new approaches to research on group problem solving.

Interdisciplinary Views of Problem Solving

Research in management science and cognitive studies has produced intriguing topologies of "the problem-solving space" that focus predominantly on the individual's approaches to problems, choices and decisions (Bartee 1973, pp. 440–441). Its intellectual tradition goes back to the earliest studies on the creation of scientific knowledge, which were concerned with both the process and the product of scientific problem formulation, analysis and synthesis. By the end of the 1960s, we saw several efforts by scientists themselves to analyze different cognitive approaches to scientific problems (Gordon and Morse 1969, Chakrabarti and O'Keefe 1977). This analytic direction of inquiry continued throughout the 1970s and produced more interesting insights than information use studies have generated. In extreme cases, this trend built on the theories of transactional analysis and Jungian personality types in order to study the behavior of individuals and organizations. Better interpersonal relationships, it was believed, would lead to more successful group problem solving (Mitroff and Mitroff 1979).

However, within a few years researchers were looking for new ways to analyze the problem-solving process (Huber 1986, Caplan 1984). The exploratory potential of research in cognitive science was dramatically increased by the more recent contributions of information science, computational linguistics and artificial intelligence (Walker 1981, Schell 1987/88). Attention to problem solving by researchers in artificial intelligence, for example the questioning of the rationalistic foundation of current problem-solving theories by Winograd and Flores (1986), has lent an entirely new significance to inquiries into that process.

A different tradition of research on problem solving has emerged from the areas of policy implementation, interorganizational relations and interorganizational networks (Regens 1988, O'Toole 1988). The concept of coordinative management of multiple organizations is especially relevant to the research context we are describing here, because it addresses problems that span agency boundaries (Mandell 1988). The interdependent organizations in such an unsystematic network are linked by tenuous information processes.

In describing the creation of community organizations, Sarason (1972) noted that planning, management, and problem solving were often hampered by the inability of administrators to act in a truly creative manner, and by the difficulty of breaking down traditional barriers in both interpersonal and interagency communication. He suggested that organizations operate *in* and *with* the community, not *for* the community, i.e., that they encourage and empower the community to take responsibility for working on its own problems. The implication Sarason draws from these conclusions is that new community organizations or programs should avoid as many of the institutional and bureaucratic trappings as possible. Reviewing a large body of research and charting a framework for dialectical interaction among organizations, Zeitz (1980, pp. 78–79) warned that when "creative actions" are transformed into "enduring patterns" by establishing a new program or organization, resources that involve material objects are likely to be highly constraining to organizational interaction. On the other hand, "networks of informal contacts among organizations are seen as facilitating work-related communication."

Changes in the Culture of Science

Currently, there are certain shifts in thought that call for a mode of problem solving that is more dynamic, informal and interactive. People and organizations in our society are searching for new ways to plan, coordinate and work. Many of the new ways they find concern the identification and use of knowledge. Nelson (1969, p. 126) observed that while in the past we viewed science (the generation and application of knowledge and solutions) as "a unique human activity unfolding in a rigorously logical way from its own internal logic," eventually we came to see science as "an aspect of the culture subject to forces and dynamics similar to those which affect other social activities or institutions." If the scientific enterprise is part of the culture, scientific knowledge should be more accessible, and more easily generated, shared and possessed than ever before.

Penman (1988, p. 393) traces the change from the philosophical view of foundationalism, that is, an individual's search for facts and other objective foundations upon which knowledge can be built, to the constructionist view which perceives the world "via an active cooperative enterprise in that we bring about our social realities and hence our understandings." The implications are that people can create their own social realities through groups and face-to-face meetings that enable them to participate in knowledge production. Group problem-solving sessions seem to represent to participants the feeling of effectiveness and influence they could not achieve alone.

Empirical Development of a Group Problem-Solving Model

The Health Information Sharing Project (HISP), funded by the National Library of Medicine from 1977 to 1982 as academic research, used empirical methods to study the informal information processes that link health professionals in a community (Dosa 1982, Dosa and Genova 1980). Today the program is part of the regular operations of a county health department. We saw the informal peer network evolve from small beginnings, pass through a period of uneven growth, and change from a network of organizations to a network of individuals. In the early years of the network, the chief executives of health care organizations designated contact persons to represent their organizations in information and experience exchange meetings. However, the meetings lacked vitality; the discussions lacked a certain spark.

In 1982 a radical change in meeting structure enabled HISP to find a unique voice and style. Designated participants were replaced by people who came of their own accord. Interaction became charged with the intense personal involvement of participants. The meetings, clustering around controversial health care issues, became living resources for health professionals. The network fostered self-learning and the formation of new interorganizational relationships in the community. When the program was transferred from the academic setting to the community, an analysis of the steps and phases enabled us to capture the generalizable features of the transfer process.

The style of the meetings has been unusual. There are no speakers and there is no audience in the traditional sense. In a group of 25 to 30 people, everybody participates. Problems are described, related experiences shared, and alternative approaches scrutinized jointly. From this problem-solving environment, we are learning about the information seeking and use behavior of health professionals.

We observed the following nonsequential and overlapping dimensions in the way HISP participants interact:

- An issue or concern exists, with its own set of circumstances and relationships
- Somebody becomes aware of this condition as a problem
- The awareness links the new experience or perception with past occurrences and related concerns
- Unless there is some urgency about it, the problem may sink back into semipassivity
- With new urgency, the dormant notion changes back into a problem, this time insisting on attention
- New motivation to attack the problem emerges
- Efforts are made to "do something" even before the issue is properly defined
- A discussion brings things into sharper focus
- The problem refuses to fade away; new implications for several situations are noted
- Clarification of the problem cannot be put off any more

- The problem turns into a tentative analysis and inquiry
- The inquiry, already controversial, is pursued
- Alternative solutions are discussed.

The meetings, and the day-to-day reliance on contacts first established at the meetings, are used in all aspects of problem resolution.

To summarize, the HISP model of group problem solving is an informal, interorganizational, multilevel, and interactive human network. Health professionals and their organizations are able to identify mutual problems through a mechanism that levies little financial burden. The informal network also subverts the need for formal interorganizational committees which are often difficult to assemble and lack the ability to act. It facilitates the efforts of individuals to generate alternative solutions, get advice, acquire needed information, and work toward problem resolution.

Transfer and Adaptation of the Model

This paper is concerned with two kinds of model transfer. The transfer of the research-generated prototype of an information sharing network from an academic setting to the county's health department has been accomplished with the active involvement of the community. Now we raise the question: Can the same model be applied, adapted and tested by another community and in another domain?

One possible testbed for the transferability of the HISP model to another community lies in the area of information resources management (IRM). In order to survive, community organizations must collect, organize, retrieve, and disseminate various kinds of data and information. Whether devoted to human services, economic development, the arts, or politics, most community organizations need to meet legislative and regulatory requirements, maintain records, and communicate with their constituents.

Analyzing information requirements and managing information resources and processes present particular challenges to community organizations. Staff members often lack the experience to perform formal analyses of their needs and to build information systems. Many community organizations require conceptual and technical advice for the acquisition, use and maintenance of microcomputers. Discussions of the benefits of computer applications to human service delivery have been characterized by a predominantly technical focus, neglecting social and philosophical issues (Murphy and Pardeck 1988). Could this situation be improved by the creation of an informal network of professionals concerned with these issues and by group problem-solving sessions based on the HISP model? Preliminary research was carried out in a small upstate New York community by Richard Entlich, who has extensive experience as a computer consultant and community volunteer. The purpose of the interviews was to elicit information resource requirements and problems from the participants. These data were used by Entlich and Bishop to explore possible models for offering technical assistance to community organizations.

The first step in initiating the model transfer process is to consider alternatives to the HISP prototype that emerge from the research literature as well as from professional practice in both the private and public sectors. For example, internal assistance to staff in solving computer-related problems may be provided by the creation of (1) cooperative change projects, (2) quality circles, (3) parallel organizations, (4) applied research, and (5) group techniques. Bushe (1988, p. 131) chose the setting of labor-management relations in unionized factories to study the pragmatic implications of introducing change into organizations by cooperative projects. A quality circle was defined as a "small group of employees who volunteer to meet regularly to work on solving problems." The "parallel organization" (also known as collateral organization) consisted of a set of problem-solving groups that operate parallel to the hierarchy. Bushe provided a review of the evolution of these practices and relevant theories, and described the outcome of his study as positive.

In the context of the not-for-profit sector, Burke (1987) and others argued that applied research can make valuable contributions to theories about organizational innovation. The focus of their argument was that research and community problem solving are not mutually exclusive. The introduction of group techniques in organizations to help scientists confront and deal with value-related rather than technical issues was discussed by Mitroff (1977).

Throughout the literature of organizational analysis a strong current of intellectual dissonance has been discernable. The exclusive dominance of the rational decision making school of thought was crippled, if not defeated, by natural system models and other nonrationalistic explanations of the organization. This dissonance seemed to be detrimental to unbiased organizational analysis, threatening to undermine the confidence in research of policy makers and practitioners. Consequently, several theorists sought to reconcile the strictly rationalistic and other views of organizations. For example, Bryman (1984, pp. 403–404) opened the door to unbridled flexibility in organizational studies by giving credence to researchers who argued that in some organizations, under some circumstances, rational and irrational features may coexist. Schmidt (1987) analyzed the major approaches to science which were deemed applicable to organizational analysis: The "lawlike" or purely quantitative paradigm; the systemic or closed systems of inquiry mixing quantitative and qualitative approaches; and historical and interpretive investigations, both using mainly qualitative methods. Schmidt (1987, p. 36) strove to defuse the controversy among competing perspectives and research frameworks by suggesting that

> the problem of rationality . . . could be resolved by conceiving of the . . . explanatory frameworks as if they were different cultures. For with this, we would be able to understand how researchers in one culture could, through translation, make sense of the work of researchers in other cultures.

Such conciliatory views support our approach to the transfer of a model in the reality of a social domain where interdisciplinary sympathies are essential. However, organizational analysis, in any explanatory context, deals mainly with the staff of the organization at different levels. We are facing the additional complexity of community organizations which often rely on external support to unravel their information resource problems. They frequently seek expert advice from local computer assistance centers, independent consultants, or vendors. One feature shared by these approaches is that, for the most part, they involve problem solving by individuals rather than by groups. They also require financial expenditures. There is a dearth of research that could help to guide and inform consideration of external assistance with computer applications available to not-for-profit organizations. According to anecdotal reports, independent computer consultants proliferate; they may be found in communities of all sizes. Communication with computer assistance centers or organizations in various parts of the United States reveals that this is a common model. These not-for-profit centers are typically located in urban areas and offer a variety of minimally priced services.

A number of institutional barriers militate against the success of any current scheme for providing help with information management problems, no matter which model is chosen. Potential clients may be unable or unwilling to alter relationships with their existing sources of technical assistance, share resources, give up their autonomy, or pay (either in terms of money or staff time) for consultation.

The HISP model offers community organizations an alternative to the more traditional means of recognizing and resolving their IRM problems. An information sharing network devoted to this end may be valuable in several respects:

- It allows participants to dissect, compartmentalize and treat problems through the sharing of ideas, opinions, data, knowledge, and methods.

- Its emphasis is on action, self-reliance, and mutual support.
- It encourages the participation of all community members willing to contribute their experience and time.
- In dealing with colleagues engaged in similar work, participants might shift the focus of their concerns from "acquiring and using technology" to improving the information-intensive functions in the organization that the technology is meant to serve (e.g., information and referral, program planning and delivery, marketing and education, evaluation and research).
- Informal meetings encourage the breakdown of institutional barriers; financial and legal requirements can be reduced to a minimum.
- Finally, works by Winograd and Flores, Nelson, Penman, and others suggest that useful solutions need not arise strictly from scientific or technical analyses of the problems at hand.

Conclusion

Any process transferring a model from one setting to another or from one domain to another consists of a combination of decisions, implementation strategies, and relationships among people and organizations. In the traditional empirical/experimental approach, each of these components may be tested in the context of potential factors that can be expected to affect the transfer process. However, the "factors affecting . . . " approach was criticized, probably justifiably, by Caplan (1984, p. 239) as not the most productive.

We suggest an alternative, perhaps more feasible, approach in which meetings based on the HISP model would be held with members of community organizations who have an interest in introducing, improving, effectively operating and better understanding information technology in their organizations. The group problem-solving sessions would be audiotaped, and the text would be submitted to analysis: (1) To elicit the categories of information requirements (explicitly stated), information needs (implicitly interwoven), and problem-solving behavior that could be used to guide the design of information systems for specific organizations, (2) to evaluate the extent to which information is shared and the extent to which sharing information facilitates the resolution of problems, (3) to explore participants' perceptions of the network model, and (4) to characterize more generally the information requirements, needs and problem-solving patterns of community organizations.

We believe that such research can contribute to the understanding of the group problem-solving process as a potential enhancement of individual and organizational effectiveness, and it can bring us closer to the understanding of how a process model might be transferred from one setting to another. In every research project, there is an element of uncertainty about the applicability of findings. How results could be used, by whom and at what expense, are perennial questions for research sponsors. Investigators are also often troubled by the issue of transferability. The HISP project's research utilization phase that institutionalized the model in the community addressed part of the problem. Testing the model in an entirely different domain may provide insights into the other complex facets of transferability.

References

Bartee, E.M. (1973). A Holistic view of problem solving. *Management Science,* Part 1, 20(4), 439–448.

Bryman, A. (1984). Organization studies and the concept of rationality. *Journal of Management Studies,* 21(4), 391–408.

Burke, J.A. et al. (1987). Problems and prospects of applied research: The development of an adolescent smoking program. *Journal of Applied Communication Research,* 15(1–2), 1–18.

Bushe, G.R. (1988). Developing cooperative labor-management relations in unionized factories: A multiple case study of quality circles and parallel organizations within joint quality of work life projects. *Journal of Applied Behavioral Science,* 24(2), 129–150.

Caplan, N. (1984). "Research on knowledge utilization: lessons and observations." In Proceedings of the 47th ASIS Annual Meeting, Philadelphia, PA. V. 21, 239–242. White Plains, NY: Knowledge Industry Publications, Inc.

Chakrabarti, A.K. & O'Keefe, R.D. (1977). A Study of key communicators in research and development laboratories. *Group and Organization Studies,* 2(3), 336–346.

Dosa, M. (1982). "Community networking in gerontology and health: A Centralized and a decentralized model." In *Special Collections,* 53–72. New York, NY: Haworth Press.

Dosa, M. & Genova, B.K. (1980). "Policy implications of health information sharing." In *Proceedings of the 43d Annual Meeting of ASIS,* 104–111. Anaheim, CA. White Plains, NY: Knowledge Industry Publications, Inc.

Gordon, G. & Morse, E.V. (1969). Creative potential and organizational structure. *Academy of Management Journal,* 12, 37–49.

Huber, O. (1986). "Decision making as a problem solving process." In Brehmer, B., ed. *New Directions in Research on Decision Making,* 109–138. Amsterdam: North-Holland.

Mandell, M.P. (1988). Intergovernmental management in interorganizational networks: A revised perspective. *International Journal of Public Administration,* 11(4), 393–416.

Mitroff, I.I. (1977). Some Unresolved issues in the psychology of science—A research agenda. *4S Society for Social Studies of Science Newsletter,* 2(3), 20–22.

Mitroff, I.I. & Mitroff, D.D. (1979). Interpersonal communication for knowledge utilization. *Knowledge, Creation, Diffusion, Utilization,* 1(2), 203–217.

Murphy, J.W. & Pardeck, J.T. (1988). Technology and human service delivery, challenges and critical perspective. *Computers in Human Services,* 3(1/2), 1–8.

Nelson, S.D. (1969). Knowledge creation, an overview. *Knowledge, Creation, Diffusion, Utilization,* 1(1), 123–149.

O'Toole, Jr., L.J. (1988). Strategies for intergovernmental management: implementing programs in interorganizational networks. *International Journal of Public Administration,* 11(4), 417–441.

Penman, R. (1988). Communication reconstructed. *Journal for the Theory of Social Behavior,* 18(4), 391–409.

Regens, J.L. (1988). Institutional coordination of program action: A conceptual analysis. *International Journal of Public Administration,* 11(2), 135–154.

Sarason, S. (1972). *The Creation of Settings and the Future Societies.* San Francisco, CA: Jossey-Bass.

Schell, G.P. (1987/88). A Primer for problem solving using artificial intelligence. *Journal of Educational Technology Systems,* 16(4), 365–382.

Schmidt, V. (1987). Four approaches to science and their implications for organizational theory and research. *Knowledge, Creation, Diffusion, Utilization,* 9(1), 19–41.

Walker, D.E. (1981). The Organization and use of information: Contributions of information science, computational linguistics and artificial intelligence. *Journal of the American Society for Information Science,* 32(5), 347–363.

Winograd, T. & Flores, F. (1986). *Understanding Computers and Cognition: A New Foundation for Design.* Norwood, NJ: Ablex Publishing.

Zeitz, G. (1980). Interorganizational Dialectics. *Administrative Science Quarterly,* 25(1), 72–88.

11

From Informal Gatekeeper
to Information Counselor:
Emergence of a New Professional Role

Introduction

The purpose of this descriptive study is to identify and synthesize some of the concepts and patterns in the application of the "information gate-keeper" theory. We have not attempted to cover all aspects of the topic in this preliminary synthesis. With very few exceptions, relevant findings in organization theory, decision science, cognitive psychology, and communication science are not included. Nor does the literature underlying this document do any justice to the universal nature of the gate-keeper concept and to its remarkable potential for crosscultural investigation. More examples might have been drawn from development studies and from the experiences of information professionals in developing countries. We recommend a research inventory on the relevance of the technological information intermediary to social and economic development.

Closely related to the gatekeeping function are phenomena such as research diffusion and utilization, technology transfer and adaptation, innovation management, and international consulting. Successful development project managers and technology brokers share some objectives, behavioral characteristics and essential skills with the information gate-keeper, and they have a similar potential for enhancing the effectiveness of information transfer. We will mention some of these research areas only tangentially. It is our hope that the present study and recommendations, in spite of their shortcomings, may stimulate discussion of and contributions to this international topic.

Conceptual Framework and Examples of Studies

What justifies the interest in the gatekeeper's role is its impact not only on a wide range of information users, but also on different information scanning, seeking, and browsing situations of users. Information is typically defined as the composite of messages, including signs, data, facts and narrative, that a human being receives from the outside world and applies to information situations such as problems, tasks, decisions, learning, reflection or leisure. We conceive of information as both formal/structured and informal/unstructured messages.

The study of the gatekeeper's role spawned an extensive and ambiguous terminology. To some scientists, "gatekeeping" means excluding rather than transmitting information. Other observers describe the gatekeeper as the focal point of informal communications. An analysis of selected studies concluded that this concept, albeit controversial, can attract research on adding value to audience-oriented information dissemination and services. Even if an active gatekeeping function in an organization does not represent a solution to all problems of information seekers, an effort to understand the ways gatekeepers access and disseminate information will be one step towards using knowledge effectively. An organization's decision to invest in this strategy and to lend policy support to it might lead to the recognition that gatekeeping processes are more effective and less expensive than some other options.

In recent decades, several research approaches led to the study of key communicators in organizations. Variously referred to as gatekeepers, change agents, linking agents, communication stars, and knowledge adaptors, these intermediaries have been described as relayers of problem-oriented or technical information. Gatekeeping is usually seen as an informal facilitating role rather than a formal position. Gatekeepers emerge through an organization's activities without systematic training, designation, and job description. They often perform their function in addition to their formally defined responsibilities. Locating information pertinent to innovation projects from the external environment and diffusing it throughout the internal research project are their strengths. In some situations, for example in interorganizational networking, these key communicators form networks of peers for information sharing outside of their organizations. Although applied researchers have tried to explore ways of semiformalizing the gatekeeper's approach, and some organizations have assigned to regular staff members well-defined responsibilities for internal and external networking, gatekeeping essentially remains an informal role.

The present document will introduce the concept of "information counseling" (IC) based on a composite model of earlier work on counseling integrated with "gatekeeping" attitudes and activities. The information counselor's role includes liaisoning, networking, advising, information filtering, transmitting, repackaging and applying activities, often carried out informally by gatekeepers. One could call the information counselor a "professional gatekeeper." This term consists of two contradictory meanings. If the greatest strength of gatekeeping were its informal nature, what could one achieve by formalizing it? To seek answers to this question, we propose that the characteristics of information gatekeeping, as observed in various studies, be mapped and studied. Instead of the controversial term "professional gatekeeper" we suggest "information counselor," a role that was conceptualized and described in the 1970s and early 1980s (Hershfield 1972, Debons 1975, Brindle and Dosa 1981).

Discussions of the nature and promise of information counseling are often followed by the comment: Information counseling is assumed to operate mainly in formal organizations, serving clients who work in professional or technical settings. May information counseling be applied in the community where the users are assumed to be general consumers or members of an amorphous public? Yes, information counseling may be structured for community settings with a great variety of diverse users. However, the present paper explores the transition from informal gatekeeper to formal information counselor only in organizations, projects, and other decision-making task environments.

In order to identify research trends and the implications of gatekeeping for the improvement of information systems and services, we offer a brief review of five selected areas: (1) Intermediaries in organizational information transfer; (2) the technological gatekeeper; (3) invisible colleges and other networks; (4) information professionals as players in informal communication flows, and (5) information professionals as gatekeepers. Our purpose is to find evidence of the potential applications of these research areas in developing countries.

Intermediaries in Organizational Information Transfer

Interest in the informal linking role of individuals in organizations led to empirical studies of vertical information flows and communication chains in the 1960s. Coleman, Katz and Menzel (1966), Katz (1961), and Menzel (1966) studied modes of diffusion and application in medical, scientific and technical innovation. Rogers and Schoemaker (1962) integrated thinking about communication patterns in innovation diffusion projects based on the major paradigm. During the next decade diffusion research evolved into "a single, integrated body of concepts and generalizations" (Rogers and Shoemaker 1971, p. 47). A few years later, a revision of the major paradigm and new approaches to diffusion were offered by Rogers (1978, 1983). Havelock (1969) made his main impact with research on informal networks and human linkages in the planning process. A theory developed by Granovetter (1973) proposed that networks thrived on "weak ties" representing relationships of people who can enrich a network by new ideas because they come from dissimilar backgrounds and intellectual traditions.

These studies identified the role of intermediaries who linked the originators of knowledge with knowledge users by bridging disciplinary and organizational boundaries. Other research efforts, with intellectual ties to management information theory and decision making under risk, formulated problems of information use by decision makers. Most studies dealt with processes in scientific and technological information. Holland (1974) termed an organization's special communicator "the key" to informal information sharing. Alter (1976) and Churchman (1964) probed into the manager's information seeking and use. Based on empirical investigation of political and social factors that affected policy makers' decisions in the Nigerian Civil Service, Aiyepeku (1982) reported on how this population conceptualized and used information and what barriers they encountered. Baker (1981) pointed to informal group communication as a management tool.

The picture of the gatekeeper's sphere of effectiveness would not be complete without reference to the considerable body of research on key communicators in human services and health care. While medical innovation is usually classed with the literature of science and technology, research on health care and human service management is predominantly a social science arena, including studies in health economics, quality of care, and consumerism. In this environment, the gatekeeper is a central information relayer in a community setting, in hospital management, in a social service agency, or in a local government program (Dunlap 1984, Greer 1977). The attributes of the activity treated by this strain of research, especially the interdisciplinary nature of health care teams, were significantly different from the characteristics of scientific and technical gatekeepers. Scrutiny of the international policy climate of health and environmental management led to the recognition that information intermediaries were needed for coordination and problem solving in these crossdisciplinary sectors (Schaefer 1981).

The results of research on informal communications within the organization and with its external environment began to bear fruit in the late 1970s. The field of education witnessed many of the applications in the form of information systems making research available to teachers, administrators and policy makers (Paisley and Butler 1983). Ogunniyi (1977) reported on a network in Africa attesting to the international interest in the networking paradigm.

The Technological Gatekeeper

Of the various types of the information intermediary, the technological gatekeeper is the most relevant to developing countries. Technological gatekeepers are individuals in firms who distribute external information internally, and connect foreign sources with indigenous users. In the American context, Allen, Piepmeier and Cooney (1971) found that technological gatekeepers or "communication stars" within an industrial organization played a central role in the international transfer of technology. These individuals were found to make significantly greater use of scientific and professional journals than other members of the firm. Their peers turned to them to speed up access to information. Technological gatekeepers were found also to develop networks among themselves, thus considerably expanding the range of contacts between the organization's staff and international information sources. Subramanyam (1977) reached similar conclusions in India. Having identified and examined four major phases in the continuum of communication as information generation, recording, surrogation/dissemination and utilization. Subramanyam concluded that large amounts of information are transmitted directly from sources to ultimate users through technological gatekeepers, bypassing formal channels.

A holistic approach to the relationship of social needs, knowledge, culture and technology compelled many researchers with international development experience to question the effectiveness of information transfer across cultural borders. Although Allen and Cooney (1973), Baker and Freeland (1972), and others provided useful approaches to optimizing information flows in innovation, these models are not necessarily applicable in other parts of the world. There are different kinds of institutional mechanisms in different countries to evaluate and adapt technology and social programs for local use, and there are different legal provisions for licensing, marketing, distribution and training. Following decades of a blind drive for new machinery and technical skills, developing economies are beginning to turn to technology assessment (Srinivasan 1982). Evaluation, choice, and, if necessary, rejection of foreign technology as inappropriate are processes in need of information undergirding. Even more critical is information support for the development of domestic research and technology production.

Invisible Colleges and Other Networks

While the gatekeeper is a central actor in organizational communication and information transactions, in networking the emphasis is on participants. While the effectiveness of gatekeeping hinges on individual personality traits and capabilities, international networking draws on skills in crosscultural communication for its existence. Merging these two processes may dramatically improve the quality of information transfer. Organizational gatekeepers may form new networks in their specialties or they may utilize existing networks for sharing experience, observations, documentation, data and opinion. Crane (1969, p. 338) observed that "scientific fields can be defined as broadly as a discipline or as narrowly as a problem area (a cluster of closely related problems)."

She tested the hypothesis of informal peer networks in science, and became the concept's major disseminator (Crane 1972).

Information sharing is a process by which individuals act as both information consumers and information providers. Transactions in an information sharing network include information acquisition, referral, resource identification, verification, and opinion exchange. Not only the continuous and overlapping processes of information seeking/finding and information providing/accepting, but also the nature and quality of the information content depend on individual cognitive and behavioral styles, personal circumstances, time-bound events, and the integrity and effectiveness of participants.

A review of research on the invisible college by Cronin (1982) covered historical and sociological perspectives, categories of studies by methodology, doubts expressed by researchers about the paradigm, and recommendations for future research. Several authors in the review had warned against attempts to formalize the patterns of informal communication. One of the early research findings by Price (1961) gave rise to the concern that in peer networks a few "core scientists" formed an elite group. Empirical data on scientists working in several narrow specialties supported these findings. Crawford (1971) investigated knowledge diffusion in sleep research and concluded that information gatekeepers may play a role in invisible colleges. Hayashi (1976) reexamined Crawford's conclusion by conducting a survey of communication flows among Japanese researchers who investigated the effects of manganese on human beings. Studying pertinent factors, he confirmed that some scientists showed a higher rate of communication activity than others.

In the 1970s, a few researchers working independently from each other addressed specific problems in communication with implications for networking. Both Athanassiades (1973) and O'Reilly (1978) were concerned with potential distortions of information in communication flows. In recent years, the perception of social networks as elitist, peer-dominated, scientific "clubs" gave way to a new vision of networks as constructive self-help tools for personal growth and community development (Ferguson 1980). Similar basic networks at the grassroots have been in operation in Africa, and one of the rural development models is said to be a version of informal information exchange (Durrani 1985).

We may conclude that in "horizontal" information exchange beyond the boundaries of the organization, just as in the "vertical" information transfer chain within the organization, some individuals play a special role that affects information access and dissemination in several ways. Models of the technological gatekeeper and the invisible college, while representing important findings, also raise questions about their applicability to information systems and services in developing countries.

Information Professionals as Players in
Informal Communication Flows

Traditionally, the information professions relied on recorded information in print and nonprint sources. In recent decades, source use and
channels of information acquisition have diversified in all types of institutions and communities. Information professionals who serve specialized user populations and often turn to informal sources to gather information in response to clients' requests tend to use a gatekeeper approach.
Flawell (1978) reported that librarians depended on the most accessible
sources such as colleagues and personal files before consulting formal
resources. Informal channels were said to filter out irrelevant or excessive information while formal systems were not able to provide filters.
Flawell conceptualized the difference between information resource and
channel or mode of access. He perceived a paradoxical relationship between source and channel and suggested that the librarians in the study
were "informally using the formal." Wilkin (1977), too, called attention
to the information professionals' growing use of informal networks and
to their interest in establishing working relationships with contact persons who act as important nodes of information in a variety of disciplines.

In a recent theoretical discussion Matta and Boutros (1989) listed
technological, economic, political and social factors that affect the use
of electronic mail in developing countries. From a managerial point of
view, social barriers, divided into individualistic, organizational, and societal types, were found to be the most difficult to overcome. Information professionals, not mentioned in the review, might recognize in this
situation an opportunity to act as gatekeepers in familiarizing people
with email at the workplace.

Information Professionals as Gatekeepers

This class of research includes studies of libraries and information
centers as communication facilities. Information professionals who are
effective communicators have a natural propensity for carrying out gatekeeping functions because they (1) are boundary spanning individuals
who can develop empathy with people in other institutions, disciplines
and types of work; (2) are traditionally service- and user-oriented and
thus can be expected to balance the need for public information with the
need for personal privacy and proprietary data; and (3) are open to new
technology and willing to explore techniques of "translating" and
"repackaging" information to fit specific use situations.

Suggesting that libraries be considered publicity-oriented "medial
channel systems," a concept derived from communication science,
Hagelwide (1980) emphasized the library's function as opinion leader

and the librarian's role as gatekeeper. Evans and Line (1973), who studied the characteristics of communication among social science researchers, proposed that information officers work in close proximity to their clients, maintain ongoing contacts with them, and become involved in the process of identifying research problems. Conference papers in 1978 analyzed the ways human intermediaries affect access to public administration knowledge and experience (Vasarhelyi 1978). It was recommended that information gatekeepers serve on administrative teams responsible for making decisions. Research on boundary spanning attitudes (Aldrich and Herker 1977), communication in bureaucracies (Bachruch and Aiken 1977), the problem of information overload (Jacoby 1984) and "the art of filtering" (Delaney 1979) produced findings of consequence to gatekeeping activities.

Research Reviews

Assessments of research are especially useful for identifying new trends in the interpretation of the gatekeeper's role. Intermediaries handling a large volume of direct or computer-mediated information transactions are called upon to handle problems of information integrity and quality, computer security, privacy of data, intellectual property, equity of access, and other policy issues. Monographs and review papers trace the evolution of an information practice or policy, or serve as sources for scenarios of future trends. For example, in a broadly based review of the philosophical perspectives of information science derived from universal scientific concepts, Maricic (1987) analyzed the relationship between an emerging discipline and classic paradigms. Craig (1979) reviewed differences in individual information processing styles. The evaluative review of research by Cronin (1982) and the case studies of information systems planning in developing countries by Bell (1986) filled gaps in the awareness of information professionals who knew little about the social impact of networking and technology transfer. Ng'ang'a (1987) addressed the improvement of services offered by intermediaries by studying user needs. Salasin and Cedar (1985) suggested that strategies for supporting information flows among researchers, practitioners and policy makers may be based on research on communication networks. They recommended that the difficulties of accessing knowledge be remedied by the appropriate packaging of information.

Observations Derived from the Literature Review

Based on the foregoing research summary, we identified four broad types of the gatekeeper in terms of professional background:

Specialized Researchers

Actively transmitting information, these researchers have no formal function in information services and, in most cases, no formal training in information or communication techniques. They approach data and information gathering from the framework of the problem solver, and this is their strength. They pass on information to colleagues because they believe in sharing. Many scientists start gatekeeping communications and participate in external information exchange networks in order to enhance their research base.

In the developing economies, institutional hierarchies are not conducive to informal information sharing, except within close-knit circles of scientists within the same discipline. Researchers facing resource shortages value information sources almost as personal assets. Leading specialists are usually active participants in international communications, make contacts at conferences and on study trips, and are somewhat isolated from their colleagues at home. The gatekeeper concept is not alien to these scientific cultures which are nourished partly by indigenous and partly by foreign influences. While it has limited applications at the present, it has potential for unfolding in the future.

Technologists

Usually involved in short-term innovation processes which pertain to small improvements in procedures and products, technologists or engineers are receiving more and more attention from the media and the public. As the relationship between technical advancement and the national economy is better understood, these members of companies and academic institutions are gaining in stature. Less naturally inclined to communicating information informally than research scientists, some technologists nevertheless become gatekeepers in their organizations' R&D programs based on personal interest in promoting collaboration.

Foreign direct investment in technology production in developing countries raises barriers to substantial information sharing because technologists working for foreign companies develop intensive competitiveness among themselves. On the other hand, the trend toward emphasizing and promoting indigenous technology serves as an incentive for creating new technical resource networks.

Managers of R&D Programs

Less visible in the extraorganizational environment than the scientist and the technologist but holding more decision-making responsibility within the organization, R&D managers formally transmit information as part of their jobs. Practices in governmental bureaucracies and private enterprises are considerably different, the latter tending toward more unstructured communications. Some managers distribute information informally within their laboratories and departments, and participate in external networks to enhance the organization's goals as well as their own effectiveness. International organizations funding managerial training programs sometimes present organizational networking models which are difficult to match to local organizational customs.

Similarly, foreign managers in transnational corporations located in various developing countries need information gathering and disseminating skills, but feel constrained in using them. Referring to empirical evidence, Hofstede (1980, p. 63) argued that "for managers who have to operate in an unfamiliar culture, training based on home-country theories is of very limited use and may even do more harm than good. Of more importance is a thorough familiarization with the other culture, for which the organization . . . can develop its own program by using host-country personnel as teachers." Both indigenous and foreign managers might improve their working relationships by the gatekeeping function, if used appropriately.

Information Professionals

With or without managerial responsibility in the organization, information professionals actively transmit information in their official capacity. Tasks similar to those of the scientific, technological and managerial gatekeepers might be included in the formal job or might be personally initiated and informally pursued. Communications are carried out mainly within the organization and, at the present, are seldom considered gatekeeping.

Information professionals in developing countries participate in external networks whenever networks formally serve the goals of the organization. Both systems of information centers and consortia of libraries create opportunities for informal information exchange. Information professionals are interested in the gatekeeping concept and sometimes introduce dissemination projects which are likely to function in ways more formal than their initiators had hoped.

Use of the Informal Information Source

The controversy about the effectiveness of informal communication flows is longstanding and still unresolved. Over the years studies have recognized enough advantages in the informal networking and gatekeeping patterns to recommend further research (Mitroff and Mitroff 1979). Both benefits and problems of these communication modes stem from the informality of the operation. Formalization of some or all functions has often been attempted on the premise of earlier research findings and the experience of practitioners.

The trend towards the systematic utilization of informal communication gathered momentum in the 1970s. Allen and Cooney (1973) opened the door to new debates when their previously mentioned study of R&D scientists and engineers in Ireland concluded that interpersonal contacts among scientists, engineers and "international gatekeepers" can be effectively managed. The study prompted both protests against and support for the notion that informal scientific and technical activities may be improved by managerial streamlining. Simultaneously, organizations began development of databases of specialists, particularly in crossdisciplinary problem areas such as resource management, population studies, and nutrition. The proliferation of knowledge/resource registers was acknowledged by a British survey of indexes to personal expertise (Barry 1976).

The controversy regarding the formalization of informal communication brought to the forefront the following questions:

1.   How do researchers and professional practitioners react to attempts to formalize gatekeeping? Cronin (1982, p. 227) cautions that one should not fall into the trap of thinking that "by tampering in some unspecified way with the essential features, a formalized and enhanced model of the information system will emerge . . . " However, he believes that further investigation of the informal communication phenomena would be fruitful.
2.   How do we distinguish between individual expertise and organizational expertise? Greer (1977) reviews theories of knowledge diffusion falling into three categories: Adoption of innovation by individuals, organizational attributes affecting adoption, and knowledge dissemination based on specific decisions. Conclusions imply that organizations might not be as flexible and useful in information exchange as are individuals.
3.   What kind of impact do informal networks and gatekeeping activities have on managers and information intermediaries? Would formalization improve information provision? In light of current global imbalances in the availability of information, amelioration of communications in the developing regions is imperative. Information intermediaries in government, industry, and university have to deal with the interplay of technological and social factors. As Elmandjra (1985, p. 5) asserts: "The information revolution is creating totally new ethical, political, legal and economic problems the implications of which are not yet fully apprehended by decision makers." Organizations are seen as open-ended learning systems where managers

must absorb new strategies and skills throughout their working life (Ajuogu 1981). Information professionals are called upon to broaden their sociological understanding and be "knowledgeable about the channels of communication through which knowledge is generated and communicated" (Ng'ang'a 1987, p. 73).

4. How does informal communication affect the international distribution of knowledge? Analyzing the dissemination system of publishing and scholarship, Altbach (1987) defines conferences, scholarly journals, professional associations, and publications as institutionalized elements of the invisible college, with editors, publishers and other knowledge workers acting as gatekeepers. "Third World researchers are at a particular disadvantage because they are not only distant from the centers of scholarly power but they frequently lack the resources to fully participate in the knowledge system of the invisible colleges" (Altbach 1987, pp. 177–178).

Research on gatekeeping and interpersonal networking as well as documented attempts to formalize these activities lead us to believe that the time has come to consider development of a new intermediary model including the best elements of the gatekeeper and invisible college models. Is it likely that these roles have not been successfully formalized because systematization destroys their informal nature? We need to seek empirically based answers to this question. Should their optimal features be integrated with the model of information counseling, the three paradigms together might create an effective new mode of communicating information informally and advising users in a formal counseling process.

Shifting the Emphasis to User Involvement

Information scientists have been searching for an answer to the puzzle of high quality yet underutilized information retrieval systems. Designers of systems have been criticized for concentrating on supply aspects rather than on user demand. Innovative and elegant solutions seem to be no guarantee against users' frustration.

One of the explanations suggested by researchers is that when the objectives of a system are formulated, designers too often work without significant contact with expected users. A thorough understanding of a proposed system's context and potential consumer group is extremely difficult to achieve (Stamper 1988, Segura 1985). Few designers conceptualize the difference between information requirements (expressed wants) and needs (not always expressed or perceived wants). The applicability of operational and logistic processes to the technical problems of information systems is more readily understood than the cognitive and behavioral dimensions of human choices and problem resolution or compromise that the information system or dissemination program should support (Winograd and Flores 1986).

Information gatekeepers have been particularly active in organizations where specialized information users such as decision makers, scientists, technologists and mass media specialists work. The environment of each of these user groups forms the context in which gatekeeping activities may be reconfigured as the tasks of information counselors.

Decision Makers

Many research efforts in recent decades were targeted on this heterogenous and ill-defined user population. Studies of decision makers as information users have been based on the notion that in any organization or society, the gathering, transmittal and utilization of intelligence will have an impact on the performance of the organization or society. It has been suggested that in the firm each level of management function and decision making—operational, administrative and strategic—requires differently structured and transmitted information (Kost and Rosenzweig 1985). Pursuant to recommendations by researchers, improvements have been made in the design of management information systems and decision support systems (Cooper 1988).

New approaches to the study of decision making eventually overshadowed earlier findings. Disillusioned with widespread assumptions that decision making is a rational and structured cognitive process, researchers turned from individual to organizational settings. Each new approach created a change in the information user's image. Today, decision making is being studied with the assumption that, in most cases, it is not a systematic, textbook-like process, but an intuitive and often unpredictable human phenomenon (Faust 1982, Riesbeck 1984, Kuhl 1986). Utterback (1986) suggested a "wide holistic appreciation" of innovation as a creative human activity that we understand only in a fragmentary way. Cronin and Gudim (1986) proposed that the linkages between R & D and technological innovation be traced.

Scientists

In a team, scientists and technologists work together and share the motivation for designing new products and processes. They write joint research reports and papers, and use information for their teamwork. They also play a joint role in public policy development. However, to the extent that one can generalize, scientists and technologists differ considerably in their priorities, approaches to problem solving, work habits and use of information. Scientists may contribute to the process of discovery and innovation or to the interpretation and synthesis of existing knowledge. Researchers need a policy environment that (1) stimulates and supports creativity and systematic investigation, (2) maintains the infrastructure necessary for scientific development, (3) promotes long-range goals and recognizes results that may be evaluated over a lengthy period of time, (4) fosters human resource development, and (5) facilitates contacts with scientists and organizations in other countries.

Within all scientific disciplines, there are traditional and renegade groups which possess constantly changing information requirements. In some disciplines we can still distinguish between the basic researcher in theoretical and experimental work and the applied investigator whose objective is to contribute to the solution of specific problems or to particular improvements of services and products. Each group has clearly identifiable data and information demands. In spite of new fields of specialization, there are shared values and beliefs that form strong bonds among scientists. The identity of the scientist based on a belief in the universality of science is one of the most forceful ties. From this philosophical foundation arose the principles of objectivity, collectivity, and the cumulative nature of knowledge. However, these values have been questioned by scientists who deem them to be "Western" in cultural origin and not globally applicable (Moravcsik 1982).

In applied research and development, the team consisting of different specialists forms the basic unit of organizational structure. Innovative teams which are more autonomous and work on new products have been found to be more active communicators and information users than operational teams because the former type deals with more complex tasks (Tushman 1979). It is possible that the integration of an information counselor into an innovative team would lead to the exploration of new fields of knowledge, a decrease in the risk of duplicating work done elsewhere, and the enrichment of the team's work by information from extra-organizational sources.

Technologists

National technology policy in each country is designed to (1) stimulate the generation of knowledge and skills for the solution of problems identified by industry, (2) motivate research directly applicable to improvements in the economy and the quality of life, (3) support the utilization of research results, (4) address the education and training needs of technologists, and (5) foster short-term objectives and the rapid assessment of results. The potential information user group of technologists includes all individuals who use technological information in the course of their work, such as engineers, development specialists, technology transfer specialists, industrial planners and managers, the legal experts and economists of technology, those involved in trade and business investment decisions, and educators specializing in various aspects of technology. Many of these potential users also originate information, although they are not as clearly identified with writing and publications as are scientific researchers. The advice and assistance of information counselors would be particularly appropriate for this group of users for three reasons. The concept of the informal technological gatekeeper originated in this environment. Second, technological information services tend to benefit from the work of experienced intermediaries because of the need to locate crossdisciplinary economic, legal, and social information pertinent to technology production and impact. Third, contrary to their reputation for being secretive, industrial and technical organizations have much nonclassified information flowing in and out (Mautort 1983).

Mass Media Specialists

The largest user group is comprised of journalists, television and radio programmers, and other mass media practitioners. The specialists of educational media, corporate media, agricultural extension services, and small businesses have their own characteristic information gathering and production habits. The popularizers of scientific and technological events interpret and repackage source material for their audiences. Mass media specialists need not only the assistance but the partnership of information counselors who can identify and obtain scientific and technical reports, translations, tables and graphs, maps and video programs and reorganize appropriate elements into digestible formats without error or distortion.

Information counselors may assume at least two further tasks in cooperation with media specialists. First, counselors can help to spread the benefits of information technology. As the MacBride Commission's report indicated, "the amount of information available to those with access to present-day technologies has been immensely increased by developments in the new science of informatics" (International Commission . . . 1980, p. 12). But this situation is also marked by uneven access and lesser opportunities for those who are on the outside of the advanced technological loop. It might be improved by information dissemination projects in cooperation with distance education programs and mass media campaigns. The second task is to participate in the informal social networks of journalists and science writers. One of the purposes is to identify information gathering needs that could be met by augmenting the services of libraries and information centers through referrals, and by establishing liaison with resource organizations. Another goal is to assist members of these user groups to recognize possible collaborative relationships beyond their immediate circles.

In spite of intensive R&D efforts to render information systems more user-friendly and economical, the infrastructure, encompassing telecommunication and computer systems in interaction, is a rapidly expanding maze. Moreover, a trend toward privatization in developing countries is expected to increase competition and the number of information enterprises and products, and to lead to a more pronounced need for information intermediaries (Bande 1985). A recent study illustrates the complexity of selecting the most appropriate databases for search in response to a particular query (El-Shooky, Roboz and Vasarhelyi 1988). A set of decision points and selection criteria is identified. It is also useful to review the research perspective on factors that affect online searching (Fidel and Soergel 1983). Following retrieval, the user faces another set of decisions concerning the proximity, timeliness, relevance, credibility, appropriateness, affordability, applicability, and usability of the retrieved information.

Currently, researchers believe that most of these postretrieval decisions can be made only by the user, and that some cannot be made by a step-by-step decision process at all. Other information scientists conjecture that neither of these processes can be separated from individual ways of thinking. It is not likely that users will be prepared to accept all these time-consuming decisions. The principle of "user involvement" should not compel the user to make information-related decisions in a vacuum. In this respect, a partnership between user and information counselor who is familiar with human processes as well as resources holds considerable promise.

Trends that Necessitate the New Role

The information society might be described as complex, technologically sophisticated, rich in information transactions, media and resources, but poor in terms of the human capacity to understand, filter and use information to meet social and personal needs. Countries which are referred to as "rapidly industrializing," are beginning to accumulate similar characteristics (Hobday 1985). Although some requirements for experience-based information have been met by knowledge processing systems, as one area of need is met, another, usually higher level need for analyzed, reordered and synthesized information, appears. There are indications in the research literature that human intermediaries will be needed for a number of intellectually challenging tasks likely to fall into three main domains: (1) The coordination and evaluation of the products and services of the multitudes of information systems in the context of each seeker's situation, (2) formatting, repackaging, disseminating, and otherwise adding value to information, and (3) supplementing formal information systems by ad hoc informal channels and resources which are often indispensable for diffusing an information problem.

In response to managerial shortcomings that often result in the chaotic or wasteful creation of information systems without any provisions for their utilization, information resource management (IRM) is being taught and implemented in several countries. Informal gatekeepers are active partners of information managers in fulfilling strategic tasks. Horton (1982, p. 18) suggests that information counselors in companies "can help bring some order out of chaos by resolving disputes, clarifying technical issues, explaining needs and communicating effectively."

Research in development science and related disciplines indicates that the confluence of several trends, briefly charted below, is creating institutional needs for information gatekeeping activities in developing economies (Ghosh 1984, Nankani 1988, Pratt and Manheim 1988, Singer and Ansari 1988, Stevenson 1988).

- A new perception of information as economic commodity, human resource, and national asset by policy makers
- Convergence of telecommunication and computer technologies in the evolving national information infrastructures
- The need for coordinated information strategies and consideration of information economics at the organizational, national and international levels; the need for a corps of policy-oriented information professionals in each country
- The change from emphasizing the importation of foreign technologies to creating favorable conditions for the development of indigenous technology production
- Growing complexity of information resources; lack of user-oriented, one-step information services; the need for information intermediaries who can communicate with diverse groups of information seekers
- Increasing number of specialized information users in research, development and management in crossdisciplinary areas such as environmental preservation, population studies and development science
- The need for research skills applicable to the assessment of new information and communication tools and techniques, and the evaluation of information system performance on the basis of users' perceptions
- The importance of avoiding information overload and redundancy, and the need for filtering, repackaging and disseminating research findings for policy makers and practitioners.

Although researchers generally fail to find connections between economic growth, social well-being, and informatics, development science has created a framework for such research. Keen interest in indigenous involvement in development projects (Bamberger 1988) has led to new thinking and methods that focus on the impact of change on people. This current development model is eminently relevant to user-centered information planning.

The Roots of Information Counseling

Information counseling (IC) is an intensive mode of human interaction to assist the user not only in locating, but also in organizing, absorbing, and applying information. It has been defined as

> the interactive process by which an information practitioner (a) assesses the information needs of an individual or organization, (b) determines the optimal ways to fill such needs, and assists the client in information use, (c) assures systematic follow-up and feedback in order to evaluate the effectiveness of counseling. Information counselors can optimize their effectiveness by accessing, on behalf of their clients, not only formal information systems but also support networks and human resource networks (Brindle and Dosa 1981, p. 31).

The IC model emanates from concepts embedded in the research literatures of four crossdisciplinary areas. KNOWLEDGE UTILIZATION addresses the transmitting of research results to practitioners, policy makers or consumers. Key questions in this field focus on organizational and personal factors leading to change following the use of information (Larsen 1980). In the study of the DIFFUSION OF INNOVATIONS, the early model of dissemination to decision makers was replaced by social networks to facilitate change (Rogers 1978). Network analysis, the favored methodology for at least two decades, addressed communication structures and relationships in a system and among systems. Another development underlying the IC model was the convergence of communication studies and INFORMATION RETRIEVAL studies. Researchers in both fields were interested in problems of cognitive style and behavior evident in problem solving. A variety of user-oriented interface systems for online searching have been studied. Hendler (1987) brought together a number of papers on the design, development, and impact of expert systems. The fourth area includes research on the applications of INTERPERSONAL COUNSELING (Hoffman 1979). In these studies there is generally a deeper understanding of the possibilities and fallacies of human interaction than in information science research.

Composite Model of Information Counseling

For purposes of future research, a preliminary model of information counseling will be described based on the gatekeeping and informal peer networking (invisible college) paradigms, and drawing from research on information intermediary roles in both high-technology and low-technology countries.

Strategic Role

Some elements of the information counselor's participation in the organization's strategic planning and management emerged from the gatekeeper studies. Other aspects of this role were identified or proposed by research on the use of informal information resources and the reorientation of organizational information services towards the user. The role outlined below assumes that the most important capability of the information counselor is skilled coordination of formal and informal information processes in terms of organizational culture, staff relationships, and technological applications.

- Assisting management in the formulation of information policies in the organization by identifying problem areas such as fee structures, privacy protection, copyrights, patents, or new technical standards; making management and staff aware of national information policies
- Increasing the involvement of users in information systems planning and evaluation by acting as a link among researchers, user groups and system analysts
- Assessing and interpreting the value of products and services offered by information providers and systems for various user groups
- Improving the quality of formal and informal information transfer in relation to organizational goals and the needs of specialized users by decreasing information overload and increasing personalized information usability
- Bringing information managers, scientists, systems designers, and librarians together to optimize the effects of cooperation in planning information services and policies.

Specific Tasks

It would be premature to speak of a job profile of the information counselor because only further research can lead to the development and testing of job characteristics and professional attributes. However, some expectations are implied by the findings of previous research. For example, it is obvious that any individual in the role of the information counselor should have sufficient influence in the organization to work in partnership with managers, scientists and engineers. Some information professionals achieve stature through specialization and work on research teams. Others develop an interdisciplinary understanding of the organization's goals, and thus play a boundary spanning role in R&D and innovation projects. The responsibilities of an information counselor may vary from society to society, and even from organization to organization within the same country, because informal information processes are shaped by the immediate cultural surroundings. The following examples of tasks represent a composite projection from the findings of several studies on the information gatekeeper and related concepts.

- Coordinating with the goals and objectives of the organization; liaison with management, technical and research staff and external users; identifying the ethical and legal implications of counseling
- Providing in-depth technical assistance to users in solving problems, and completing tasks; logging each information transaction and user feedback concerning the quality and consequences of counseling
- Analyzing information needs and requirements on the basis of the users' background and current tasks; developing an understanding of people's ways of thinking about problems and tasks, and skills for working with users in partnership
- Cooperating with informal gatekeepers in the organization; involving users in sharing their experience with each other; developing a database of expertise and a network for information and experience exchange; scanning the environment for social and economic trends, new information products, and opportunities for collaborative research projects
- Evaluating, filtering, and repackaging information in the form of summary reports and policy briefs; deciding about alternative formats of dissemination (newsletter, electronic bulletin board, public forum) in cooperation with users
- Assisting user groups and management in evaluating and improving information systems and policies.

Transition to the New Role

Strategies for transforming informal gatekeeping into formal information counseling may be initiated by the management in any part of the organization. In most cases an innovation project or R&D unit provides a hospitable setting due to its demonstrated acceptance of change and experimentation. The extent of change might range from a slight revision (with the least disruption in existing informal information flows) to the introduction of a substantial policy change. The function of all four players in gatekeeping described earlier—the specialized scientist, the technologist, the project manager, and the information professional: should be analyzed to establish their relevance for the composite model of the information counselor. The extent of formality and informality in applying the model will change from organization to organization. The following processes might take place simultaneously or in phases:

- Discuss informal gatekeeping processes and the potential of information counseling in the organization at staff meetings and discussion groups to raise awareness and improve communications.
- Information counseling will remain a "role" rather than a "job." Use an existing position in the information unit of the organization or create a new position for this role, to consolidate selected gatekeeping/counseling tasks. Information professionals characterized by attitudes and skills for effective interpersonal and intergroup communications are the most likely candidates for information counseling.
- Identify and bring together scientists, technologists, managers and subject specialists who have been acting as informal gatekeepers and invite suggestions for overall coordination.
- Analyze activities of gatekeepers. Select those informal functions which are the most innovative and useful, and introduce them in staff discussions exploring their possible transfer into the formal job responsibilities of the information counselor.
- Consider possible benefits and problems of adopting information counseling as a pilot project, integrating it with gatekeeping elements.
- Collaborate with other organizations in order to test the composite model or parts of it, in order to observe its implications for the organization, for information users, and for the information professions.
- The information counselor might begin with a small internal database and network of specialists whose expertise has promising implications for the R&D or innovation project where the information counseling was initiated. Evaluate this pilot experiment with the involvement of users.
- Introduce policies for information counseling in the organization if the results of the pilot project and staff discussions warrant such change.

At the time the IC role is introduced in the organization, discussions should include its impact not only on intraorganizational communications and cooperation, but also on information services, products, and pertinent costs. The impact of an information activity represents a certain value to the user which depends on the extent to which the acquired information contributes to the success of a work-related task, idea, decision, or action. Each message has a different information value for the receiver, and the quality of the same message is perceived differently by different users, and by the same user in different situations. Information is usually characterized by the attributes of relevance, timeliness, accuracy, cost, origin, form, and so on. Enhancement of any of these attributes is expected to increase the value of information to the user, but such changes in value have not been measured and documented. Information counselors may therefore play an important role in this respect.

The information counselor has to respect and support the informal information flows which exist both among users and between a user and multiple information resources. The counselor is a partner in information and experience sharing networking. Therefore, the counseling process should be neither dominating nor subordinate to the information user. To recognize the point at which informal contacts turn into formal counseling demands the most significant skills of the counselor. Participation in both electronic networking and face-to-face discussions within the R&D or innovation team and with external resources is a way to unobtrusively market the counseling function.

The value of acquired information can be increased by understanding the requirements and needs of information seekers, selecting the most appropriate resources, and identifying the optimal application of information. Information resources, in particular computerized databases, have different structures, utilize different search languages and allow for the use of different search strategies. Awareness of the limitations, coverage and search characteristics of different information systems will enable the information counselor to select the most appropriate databases and to translate the user's requirement and need into the most efficient search strategy. An increase in relevance could be achieved also through the filtering out of irrelevant items and matching the information with the background and experience of the users, their previous knowledge and the problem at hand.

One of the most important attributes of information is its timeliness. Delays in processing may significantly reduce information usefulness. Counselors familiar with the time frame underlying the user's inquiry can make sure that the information received is not outdated. The value of information to users may be enhanced also by repackaging it into the most effective form. For example, quantitative data may be displayed by tables, graphs, and charts. Information may also be presented in qualitative form as in the use of categories and classifications. The choice of the medium is important: computer print-out, typeset sheets or microfiche.

Information could be displayed on slides, screens, tapes, and disks. The analysis and synthesis of several documents, and the aggregation of data presented in tables found in different sources, might be more appropriate than full documents.

To some extent, the accuracy of information depends on the reliability of its original source or the credibility of its transmitter. Researchers and decision makers obtain data from both known and unknown sources. Information counselors might be in the position to evaluate the reliability of an information source by examining its lineage and the medium transmitting it. While the benefits of information are difficult to assess, cost estimates are measurable. Information counselors may not only enhance the value of information but also decrease its cost to the user by comparing database royalties, maximum and minimum price schedules, or transmission costs.

The introduction of information counseling in an organization affects the entire staff. Open discussion of expected benefits, costs, and limitations will prepare the staff, in particular information professionals, for actively participating in the adaptation process.

Strengthening the Evaluation Process by Information Counseling

It is widely acknowledged that system planning should include the goals, criteria and methods of assessment. The conceptualization of evaluation measurements should make it clear that evaluation is more concerned with the effectiveness than with the efficiency of services.

> The literature of project appraisal commonly gives the impression that the goal is to produce a number or set of numbers that tells whether a project is good or bad. In reality, it is not the numbers themselves that are important, but rather the appreciation of the project's relative strengths and weaknesses that is gained in the course of appraising it (United Nations Industrial . . . 1978, p. 6).

Several approaches are used to avoid the usual weaknesses of the evaluation process: (1) Cost-benefit analysis, (2) analysis of "value added" features, (3) content analysis of feedback from users, (4) retrospective assessment of user perceptions of the performance, effectiveness and impact of the service and the information content. Human factors influencing information utilization are considered critical (Taylor 1986).

In view of the overall unsettled state of evaluation studies in information science, it is useful to explore the experience of development scientists. A World Bank staff paper reports that at the outset of each project, criteria for evaluating each phase are built into the plan. This "monitoring and evaluation" process assumes flexibility and adaptability on part of the project. Perceptions of local populations are elicited not only retrospectively but also at periodic intervals throughout the project (Cernea 1979).

The concern for transferring inappropriate evaluation criteria and methodologies from industrial to developing countries must be considered. Program evaluation is a sociocultural process and it should be developed in cooperation with nationals in the host country. An evaluation model for developing countries was recommended by Fall and O'Sullivan (1982). An experienced information counselor might contribute to the strengthening of feedback from users and to enhancing its impact on the system. Activities may consist of searching for new methodologies, including software, testing the "monitoring and evaluation" approach in a pilot setting, and disseminating results of the experiments. Users who are often reluctant to participate in evaluation exercises are likely to appreciate the involvement of a local intermediary as an impartial interface with the system.

Informal gatekeeping is characterized not only by positive features but also by problems. Critics of the gatekeeper and invisible-college paradigms often refer to the elitist nature of information dissemination and exchange, because unstructured and informal communication flows tend to favor individuals who are knowledgeable, influential, and effective communicators. It is likely that whenever participants are selected for the exchange of ideas and the process is left to the dynamics of an uncoordinated network, the benefits of information sharing will go to individuals who are most likely to reciprocate with innovative and useful suggestions. In contrast, the partial formalization of gatekeeping activities into information counseling may lead to substantial improvements in the distribution of information access opportunities.

Information Policies

The tasks of the information counselor require both a general understanding of the organization's policy environment and policy analysis skills for specific needs. Research has demonstrated that the quality and effectiveness of decisions most often depend on the manager's grasp of the interrelationships among various policies (Ayub and Hegstad 1987, pp. 95–96, Rondinelli 1983, pp. 1–22). Helping managers and other users to relate sometimes contradictory ideas in different information policies to each other, the counselor will operate in an internal organizational policy environment and in an external, national and international policy context. The implications of this dual role have not yet been explored.

Organizational Information Policies

As online searching of databases is increasingly performed by end users, information counselors may shift their emphasis to advising users about complex infrastructures and resources, cooperative relationships in information and data exchange, and the consequences of policies for information seeking. Data transfer policies draw on expertise in economics, law, innovation management, development science, and public administration (Pavlic and Hamelink 1985, Schaefer 1981, United Nations Department . . . 1985). Although an information counselor cannot become a specialist in all these areas, the ability to identify linkages among different fields and to locate resource persons is indispensable.

Probably the most difficult task of an information counselor is to delineate ethical issues which affect the integrity of the information intermediary. A balance between professional and personal ethics must be established. Some counselors will assume that they can remain neutral in providing advice; others will admit that an attitude towards the information they deliver has to be formed in each situation. In any case, information counselors ought to be cognizant of a research insight in mass communications that touches upon the dilemma of all types of human intermediaries:

> It is the goal of all sources to influence decisions by changing the stock of information upon which those decisions are based. Since the public is generally only marginally involved in the determination of public policy . . . sources have greater incentives to use the press to *define* public opinion than to influence it directly (Gandy 1982, pp. 13–14).

Interesting perspectives of the gatekeeper concept, with ethical and ideological aspects of the responsibility of making information-related choices for other people may be found in a series of research studies started by White (1964).

With the direction of policy negotiations changing from emotional politics to economic and trade interests, information counseling has to pay particular attention to the following trends: (1) The progress in many developing countries toward privatization and South-South cooperation among private enterprises (United Nations Centre . . . 1987, Marsden and Belot 1987), and (2) the growing interest in indigenous creativity and management skills demonstrated by transnational corporations. As Bartlett and Ghoshal (1987, p. 48) observed:

vital strategic information now exists in many different locations world-wide . . . Furthermore, the growing dispersion of assets and delegation of responsibilities to foreign operations have resulted in the development of local knowledge and expertise that has implications for the broader organization.

These trends augur a strengthening of mutual support among developing countries in information policy matters, as well as improved relations between industrial and developing countries. Constant alertness to the emergence of unifying rather than divisive information policies cannot be expected from information users. Rather, it has to become an important part of the information counselor's tools.

Global Information Policies

Policies may be embodied in formal instruments such as laws, rules, standards, treaties and codes of conduct, or they may be informal, expressed by norms, tradition, customs and beliefs. Whether policies are formulated by a government, a professional association, or an institution, they may be of two kinds. Some policies are made in response to a suddenly felt need or crisis, while others are the result of long-range planning. Information policies are plans and strategies for information infrastructures, services, research, and education. Although the growth of technologies is way ahead of society's understanding of their impact, most governments concentrate their policies on the unquestioned development of information technology. The need to study the balance between the cost of technology-based systems, the information they deliver, and the effect of that information on societies is a more recent recognition on the part of policy makers. In the light of this new approach, in many countries efforts are under way to revise and coordinate a number of separate policies relating to informatics and telematics (United Nations Educational . . . 1985). Developing nations are striving to strengthen specialized human resources, research facilities, and information dissemination to wide strata of the population.

Information managers in developing countries often voice a need for the following strategies in support of policies:

- Surveying information needs and resources in various sectors of the economy
- Developing an indigenous workforce for information management and information science, often referred to as research on the implications of informatics and telematics
- Strengthening indigenous information research capabilities and closer interaction between the research, practice and educational sectors

- Disseminating information more effectively to industrial enterprises and rural areas
- Developing networks and specialized information clearinghouses in each region
- Expanding the concept of scientific and technical information to cover the economic, social and legal aspects of sustainable development
- Gaining skills in evaluating the connection between information supply and development

In order to influence resource allocations and programs to advance these efforts, information managers need to participate in the formulation of national policies which define information as a significant resource, and in programs that establish tangible measurements of the value of information to national development plans. The information counselor would be a new asset in this process.

Computer equipment and software production, telecommunication facilities and data services are concentrated in a few areas of the world. In countries lacking a diversity of devices and the means to produce or acquire them, inventories of national data and information production are needed. Transborder data flow "should be dealt with by clearly analyzing what we could call 'Intraborder Data Flows' (IDF), since the phenomenon of the transfer of information between one country and another is closely linked to the internal phenomenon of the production and consumption of data within countries" (Villaveces 1986, p. 71). These issues are interwoven not only with trade interests but also with cultural identity and independence.

Governments of different countries responded to the uneven trend of technological change in different ways. In the 1970s, a series of national laws and regulations in industrialized countries, protecting the personal privacy of citizens, provided that data processing must meet certain standards and remain within domestic industries. Such legislation and regulations were seen by international observers as nontariff barriers to information flows, serving both privacy protection and domestic industry protection. Several newly industrializing countries (NICs) turned to openly protectionist trade policies to build up self-sufficiency in telecommunications (Mowlana 1985, Rada and Pipe 1984, Hobday 1985). At the same time, low-income countries began to participate in international discussions of data and cultural communication at the political level. In recent years, through a reorientation from the political to the legal and economic framework of discussions, a potential rapprochement began to take shape (Sauvant 1986). In spite of tensions caused by the politicization of data transfer, the international cooperation of scientists, educators and information professionals aims to maintain continuity in contacts and information exchange.

Granelli (1984, p. 341) stated that "informatics development will very probably be one of the dominant factors in mankind's development and progress during the decades to come." To a considerable extent, advances in informatics will depend on the sound state of information policy issues which will expand the sphere of responsibilities for information counselors. The following are a few examples of these issues.

- The position of each country in *international economic and trade relations* determines that nation's access to markets and data resources.
- *National security and sovereignty,* two primary goals of development, are supported by transborder data transmission under favorable economic conditions but may be undermined when a country lacks control over international electronic communication (Finch and Dougall 1984).
- *Technology transfer* embraces machinery, information necessary for domestic development, and technical expertise. Technology transfer and transborder data flow issues are inseparable. In many countries domestic R&D and technology assessment systems remain weak because of the lack of scientific and economic data (Hattori 1986, Alkhafaji 1986, Lucas and Freedman 1983).
- One of the main benefits of technology transfer is the strengthening of *domestic research* for social goals (United Nations Educational . . . 1981, 1986).
- A global concern about *scientific and technical information (STI)* has resulted in cooperative information systems developed by nongovernmental organizations. A study of international access to online databases made several recommendations for strengthening the capability of developing countries in this respect (United Nations Centre . . . 1982).
- *Individual privacy* has been defined as a sociocultural issue with legal implications (International Consultative . . . 1986). The two main aspects of privacy legislation include (1) the prevention of disclosure of personal data in a database to others than the subject of the data, and (2) the right of individuals to know about data collected about them and to correct errors and misrepresentations.
- In the North-South debate on the effects of international data transfer, *cultural issues* are the ones most exploited for political arguments. As countries rediscover the value of indigenous heritage, customs and languages, external influences on these genuine domestic resources are viewed with resentment. Cultural issues pertain to spillover from foreign broadcasting, imported radio and

television programs, films, and other products of the entertainment industries. Remote sensing is also seen as a potential threat to developing countries because of their lack of control over the use of data collected by satellites.

- Arguments about *mass communication* as a divisive policy issue culminated in the report of the MacBride Commission (International Commission . . . 1980, Indian Institute . . . 1983). Developing nations viewed as detrimental the sensationalist treatment of news about Third World countries by a handful of major international news agencies. The response of Western countries was a rejection of any interference with the press (Stevenson and Shaw 1984).
- The prevailing international policy for allocating use of the *electromagnetic spectrum* and of the *geostationary orbit* has been challenged by representatives of most developing economies. Both are resources of mankind, but are used predominantly by countries with superior technological capabilities. The International Telecommunication Union (ITU) maintains treaties with various countries for radio frequency allocations that can be renegotiated every twenty years. At the last World Administrative Radio Conference (WARC) in 1979, developing countries sought allocations of the spectrum, upon which radio, television, and computer messaging by satellites depend, on a systematic rather than on a first-come-first-served basis. The current use of the geostationary orbit by communication satellites (e.g. Direct Broadcast Satellites) was challenged by a similar argument at "Space WARC" meetings. Two policy issues represented the core of the debate: A new mode to allocate the geostationary orbit by the ITU, and the concern about the content of the DBS messages beamed into countries which have no influence over them (Mowlana 1985, pp. 33–44).

Over the years, the objective of negotiations has been to develop guidelines for a comprehensive international agreement on data transfers. Such an agreement, "enabling a fair and correct control of transborder data flow, and taking into account all the needs, could become a factor of utmost importance in relations between countries and could considerably contribute to detente, to stability, and to world peace" (Granelli 1984, p. 342). Although such agreement on TDF policies has not been reached, some progress may be observed (Jussawalla and Cheah 1987).

Implications for Education and Training

Formalized job descriptions are usually created by workplace requirements, professional standards agreed upon by groups, employment policies, or the analysis of job content. None of these conditions exists in the case of information counseling. We believe that, for the time being, information counseling will remain an important "role" rather than a "job." This section will focus on areas of particular strength of an information counselor, and suggestions for capabilities which could further enhance these strengths.

It is important to distinguish between information science (a research discipline) and information counseling (a form of professional practice). Information science encompasses the propositions for and concepts of the phenomena and behavior of information produced by research. Vickery and Vickery (1987, p. 1) defined information science as "the study of the communication of information in society" and added that "this meaning is only beginning to emerge from its practical background, the social activity of facilitating information transfer."

We can differentiate between the sciences and the professions also by their historical roles. Traditionally, science has been described as having a universal and unifying character and pursuing long-term goals, while the professions are said to be guided by social demand, public policy, national priorities and client expectations. Today, science is affected by immediate national goals, and the service professions, drawing on the resources of an impressive array of technologies, are shaping public policy and client needs rather than being guided by them.

As the development of the information workforce is becoming a national policy issue in most countries, there is a critical need for closer cooperation among information scientists and information professionals. Crossnational cooperation is especially important in (1) organizing seminars on the relationships that link information, technology, and national development, (2) identifying research areas for comparative investigation, (3) promoting educational exchange programs, and (4) gaining more understanding of global information policies.

There are many efforts worldwide to revise curricula in view of national policies and development trends (Neelameghan 1984, International Federation . . . 1985). Some of these trends are technology-driven and lack emphasis on the human aspects of information transfer. Others prompted new courses with direct application to the needs of the information counselor. Research on decision making and problem solving provides road signs for new forms of information support for these activities (Brehmer 1986).

The following areas in information education and training will enhance the process of information counseling.

Analytical capabilities

Systems planning and design; methodologies for need assessment and evaluation research; data-, word-, and information-processing; benefit-cost analysis; budgeting; analysis of organizational hierarchies and processes; technology assessment; information analysis; search strategies; and basics of information market analysis.

Policy-related capabilities

Identifying relationships between the components of national information and communication infrastructures; review of policy instruments; recognizing national and international policies that affect local information processing; development, review and adaptation of information policies within the organization; decision-making skills; use and dissemination of policy research.

Technological capabilities

Knowledge of information and telecommunication technologies and applications; rapid orientation to emerging technologies; selection of software; use of microcomputers for innovation; word and information processing; fundamentals of data base management; networking; cooperating with other units in the organization in technology applications.

Communication capabilities

Interpersonal communication; group techniques; planning meetings and conferences; leadership skills; supervision of staff; interdisciplinary work; application of communication skills to information marketing and dissemination; oral and written presentations; demonstration using audiovisual techniques; user training; repackaging information for purposes of the end user.

Many other skills and competencies were identified by a survey aimed at ultimately strengthening the dissemination of information in support of development (McDowell and Baney 1983).

Conclusions

In order to identify and test the potential contributions of the information counseling model to the quality of information transfer, it is suggested that pilot research and demonstration projects be carried out. Settings where the model could be best tested include research institutions, government agencies, the research and development divisions of industrial organizations, and academic departments. As part of the pilot projects, there will be a need for inventorying user demands, gathering data on query answering, and collecting qualitative information about user perceptions of information counseling.

An international seminar may consider a job profile and its attributes, based on user demand inventories. The proposed job description may be transmitted to professional associations in various countries for discussion and comment. The model should be adaptable and flexible, in order to be adjusted to the information environments of different countries. Guidelines for information counseling will be necessary for the review and consideration of professional associations. The final report of the seminar and results of research and demonstration projects may signal the future course of information counseling.

References

Aiyepeku, W.O. (1982). Mapping the information environment of policy-makers: Some empirical findings from Nigeria. *Social Science Information Studies, 2*, 79–91.

Ajuogu, M.O. (1981). Technology dynamics in lifelong education and development of managers in developing economies. *International Review of Administrative Sciences, 47*(1), 71–76.

Aldrich, H. & Herker, D. (1977). Boundary spanning roles and organizational structure. *Academy of Management Review, 2*(2), 217–230.

Alkhafaji, A. (1986). Technology Transfer: An Overview as Related to LDCs. *Journal of Technology Transfer, 11*(1), 55–66.

Allen, T.J. & Cooney, S. (1973). Institutional roles in technology transfer: A Diagnosis of the situation in one small country. *R & D Management, 4*(1), 41–51.

Allen, T.J., Piepmeier, J.S. & Cooney, S. (1971). The International technological gatekeeper. *Technology Review, 73*(5), 37–44.

Altbach, P.G. (1987). *The Knowledge context.* Albany, NY: State University of New York Press.

Alter, S.L. (1976). How effective managers use information systems. *Harvard Business Review, 54*(6), 97–104.

Athanassiades, J.C. (1973). The Distortion of upward communication in hierarchical organizations. *Academy of Management Journal, 16*(2), 207–226.

Ayub, M.A. & Hegstad, S.O. (1987). Management of public industrial enterprises. *The World Bank Research Observer, 2*(1), 79–101.

Bachruch, S. & Aiken, M. (1977). Communication in administrative bureaucracies. *Academy of Management Journal, 20*(3), 365–377.

Baker, H.K. (1981). Tapping the power of informal groups. *Supervisory Management, 26*(2), 18–25.

Baker, N.R. & Freeland, J.R. (1972). Structuring information flow to enhance innovation. *Management Science,* 19(1), 105–116.

Bamberger, M. (1988). *The Role of Community Participation in Development Planning and Project Management.* Washington, DC: The World Bank. (Economic Development Institute EDI Policy Seminar Report 13).

Bande, A.B. (1985). Privatization: The Missing link to developed countries. *Telephony,* 209(26), 42–43.

Barry, S.G. (1976). *Indexes to Expertise: An Examination of Practical Systems.* London, UK: The British Library. (British Library Research and Development Report 5314).

Bartlett, C.A. & Ghoshal, S. (1987). Managing Across Borders: New Strategic Requirements. *Sloan Management Review.* Part 1, 28(4), 7–17. Part 2, 29(1), 43–53.

Bell, S. (1986). Information systems planning and operation in less developed countries. *Journal of Information Science.* Part I, 12, 231–245. Part II, 12, 319–331.

Brehmer, B., ed. (1986). *New Directions in Research on Decision Making.* Amsterdam, Netherlands: North-Holland.

Brindle, E.A., & Dosa, M.L. (1981). "An exploration of some areas of research on information needs and networks and their applicability to Puerto Rican Aging." In *Working Conference on Puerto Rican Aging: Research Needs, Priorities and Utilization.* San Juan, PR, 1981, 105–137. Proceedings, ed. by W.M. Beattie and A.M. Pacheco. San Juan, PR: University of Puerto Rico.

Cernea, M.M. (1979). *Measuring Project Impact: Monitoring and Evaluation in the PIDER Rural Development Project, Mexico.* Washington, DC: The World Bank. (Staff working paper 332).

Churchman, C.W. (1964). Managerial acceptance of scientific recommendations. *California Management Review,* 7(1), 31–38.

Coleman, J.S., Katz, E. & Menzel, H. (1966). *Medical Innovation: A Dissuasion Study.* New York, NY: Bobbs-Merrill.

Cooper, R.B. (1988). Review of management information systems research: A Management support emphasis. *Information Processing and Management,* 24(1), 73–102.

Craig, R. (1979). "Information systems theory and research: An Overview of individual information processing." In *Communication Yearbook,* 3, New Brunswick, 99–121.

Crane, D. (1969). Social structure in a group of scientists: A Test of the invisible college hypothesis. *American Sociological Review,* 335–352.

Crane, D. (1972). *Invisible colleges, diffusion of knowledge in scientific communities.* Chicago, IL: University of Chicago Press.

Crawford, S. (1971). Informal communication among scientists in sleep research. *Journal of the American Society for Information Science,* 22(5), 301–310.

Cronin, B. (1982). Invisible colleges and information transfer. *Journal of Documentation,* 38(30), 212–236.

Cronin, B. & Gudim, M. (1986). Information and productivity: A Review of research. *International Journal of Information Management,* 6(2), 85–101.

Debons, A. (1975). "An educational program for the information counselor." In *American Society for Information Science. Proceedings of the 38th ASIS Annual Meeting.* Boston, MA, v. 12, 63–64. White Plains, NY: Knowledge Industry Publications. Inc.

Delaney, W.A. (1979). The Art of filtering. *Supervisory Management,* 24, 9–12.

Dunlap, D. (1984). Resource networking in rural health education. *Health Education,* 15(6), 40–42.

Durrani, S. (1985). Rural information in Kenya: Rural information and advice services (and) information services in Eastern Pilbara. *Information Development,* 1(3), 149–168.

Elmandjra, M. (1985). "Communication, informatics and development." In *Development, Seeds of Change,* 1, p. 5.

El-Shooky, H., Roboz, P. & Vasarhelyi, P. (1988). *Guidelines for selecting the most appropriate data base in relation to a particular information request.* Vienna: United Nations Industrial Development Organization.

Evans, S.M. & Line, M.B. (1973). A Personalized service to academic researchers: The Experimental information service in the social sciences at the University of Bath. *Journal of Librarianship,* 1, 225–235.

Fall, M. & O'Sullivan, E. (1982). Importing program evaluation by developing nations: A View from Senegal. *International Journal of Public Administration,* 4(1), 1982, 39–63.

Faust, D. (1982). A Needed component in prescriptions for science: Empirical knowledge of human cognitive limitations. *Knowledge,* 3(4), 555–570.

Ferguson, M. (1980). *The Aquarian Conspiracy: Personal and Social Transformation in the 1980s.* Los Angeles, CA: J.P. Tarcher.

Fidel, R. & Soergel, D. (1983). Factors affecting online bibliographic retrieval: A Conceptual framework for research. *Journal of the American Society for Information Science,* 34(3), 163–180.

Finch, J.H. & Dougall, E.G. eds. (1984). "Computer security: A Global challenge." In *Proceedings of the Second IFIP International Conference on Computer Security, 1984.* New York, NY: Elsevier Science Publishing.

Flawell, S. (1978). Informally using the formal: Coming to terms with informal channels of communication. *Australian Special Library News,* 11(2), 46–49.

Gandy, Jr., O.H. (1982). *Beyond Agenda Setting: Information Subsidies and Public Policy.* Norwood, NJ: Ablex Publishing Company.

Ghosh, P.K. ed. (1984). *Technology Policy and Development: A Third World Perspective.* Westport, CT: Greenwood Press.

Granelli, L. (1984). Information assets: National development indicators. *Transnational Data Report,* 7(5–6), 341–342.

Granovetter, M.S. (1973). The Strength of weak ties. *American Journal of Sociology,* 78, 1360–1380.

Greer, A.L. (1977). Advances in the study of diffusion of innovation in health care organizations. *Milbank Memorial Fund Quarterly,* 55, 505–532.

Hagelwide, G. (1980). The Library as an object of communication research. *Bibliothek, Forshung und Praxis,* 4(3), 215–224.

Hattori, T. (1986). Technology transfer and management systems. *The Developing Economies,* 24(4), 314–325.

Havelock, R.G. (1969). *Planning for Innovation Through Dissemination and Utilization of Knowledge.* Ann Arbor, MI: Center for Research on Utilization of Scientific Knowledge.

Hayashi, M. (1976). Informal communication among scientists in the study of manganese effects on human beings. *Library and Information Science,* 14, 145–170.

Hendler, J.A. ed. (1987). *Expert Systems: The User Interface.* Norwood, NJ: Ablex Publishing.

Hershfield, A. (1972). "Information Counselors: A New Profession?" In Atherton, Pauline, ed. *Humanization of Knowledge in the Social Sciences,* 29–34. Syracuse, NY: School of Library Science.

Hobday, M. (1985). The impact of microelectronics on developing countries: The case of Brazilian telecommunications. *Development and Change,* 16(2), 313–340.

Hoffman, J.C. (1979). *Ethical confrontation in counseling.* Chicago, IL: University of Chicago Press.

Hofstede, G. (1980). Motivation, leadership, and organization: Do American theories apply abroad? *Organizational Dynamics,* 9(1), 42–63.

Holland, W.E. (1974). The special communicator and his behavior in research organizations: A Key to the management of informal technical informatications. *PC-17*(3/4), 48–53.

Horton Jr., F.W. (1982). The Emerging Information Counselor. *Bulletin of the American Society for Information Science,* 8(5), 16–19.

Indian Institute of Mass Communication. (1983). *News Agencies Pool of Non-Aligned Countries.* New Delhi, India: Allied Publishers Private Ltd.

International Commission for the Study of Communication Problems.

(1980). *Many voices, one world*. Paris, France: United Nations Educational, Scientific and Cultural Organization. London, UK: Kogan Page.

International Consultative Commission for Transborder Data Flows Development. (1986). *Inaugural Meeting Proceedings, Rome, 18–20 September 1985*. Rome, Italy: International Bureau of Informatics.

International Federation for Information and Documentation. (1985). *Curriculum Development in a Changing World. Proceedings of the Seminar of the Education and Training Committee of the International Federation for Documentation (FID/ET), The Hague, September 17–20, 1984*. The Hague, Netherlands: FID.

Jacoby, J. (1984). Perspectives on information overload. *Journal of Consumer Research*, 10, 432–435.

Jussawalla, M. & Cheah, C-W. (1987). *The Calculus of International Communications: A Study in the Political Economy of Transborder Data Flow*. Englewood, CO: Libraries Unlimited, Inc.

Katz, E. (1961). The Social itinerary of technical change: Two studies on the diffusion of innovation. *Human Organization*, 20, 70–82.

Kost, F.E. & Rosenzweig, J.E. (1985). *Organization and Management*. 4th ed. New York, NY: McGraw-Hill Book Co.

Kuhl, J. (1986). "Human motivation: From decision making to action control." In Brehmer, Berndt, ed. *New Directions in Research on Decision Making*, 5–28. Amsterdam, Netherlands: North-Holland.

Larsen, J.K. (1980). Knowledge utilization. *Knowledge*, 1, 421–442.

Lucas, B.G. & Freedman, S. eds. (1983). *Technology Choice and Change in Developing Countries, Internal and External Constraints*. Dublin, Ireland: Tycooly International.

Maricic, S. (1987). Information science as interfaces of the cognitive sphere and society. *Information Processing and Management*, 23(1), 33–43.

Marsden, K. & Belot, T. (1987). *Private Enterprise in Africa: Creating a Better Environment*. Washington, DC: The World Bank. (World Bank Discussion Papers 17).

Matta, K.F. & Boutros, N.E. (1989). Barriers to electronic mail systems in developing countries. *The Information Society*, 6, 59–68.

Mautort, R.T. de. (1983). Ambivalence of technological information. *International Forum on Information and Documentation*, 8(1), 33–35.

McDowell, E. & Baney, L. (1983). A Survey of communication skills needed and communication methods used in the dissemination of development information. *Journal of Technology Transfer*, 8(1), 59–67.

Menzel, H. (1966). Scientific communication: Five themes from sociology. Reprinted in: Griffith, B.C. ed. *Key papers in information science*. Washington, DC: American Society for Information Science, 1980, 58–63.

Mitroff, I.I. & Mitroff, D.D. (1979). Interpersonal communication for knowledge utilization. *Knowledge*, 1, 203–217.

Moravcsik, M.J. (1982). "Assessment of science in developing countries." In Srinivasan, Mangalam, ed. *Technology Assessment and Development*, 3–35. New York, NY: Praeger.

Mowlana, H. (1985). *International Flow of Information: A Global Report and Analysis*. Paris, France: United Nations Educational, Scientific, and Cultural Organization. (Reports and Papers on Mass Communication No. 99), 45–53.

Nankani, H. ed. (1988). *Techniques of Privatization of State-Owned Enterprises: Selected Country Case Studies*. V. 2. Washington, DC: The World Bank.

Neelameghan, A. (1984). International and regional cooperation in human resource development for information services in developing countries: A Case study. *Education for Information*, 2, 191–208.

Neelameghan, A. & Pascua-Cruz, M.D. (1983). Online access to remote data bases: An Experiment in user sensitization. *Journal of Information Science*, 7, 107–115.

Ng'ang'a, J.M. (1987). "Information and users: How to bring them together—The Intermediary role of the professional." In Hutteman, L., ed. *Librarianship and Documentation Studies, A Handbook of Teaching and Learning Materials*, 67–79. Bonn, Germany: Deutsche Stiftung für Internationale Entwicklung.

Ogunniyi, O. (1977). Network of educational innovation for development in Africa (NEIDA). *Innovation*, 13/14, 3–4.

O'Reilly, C.A. III. (1978). The intentional distortion in organizational communication: A laboratory and field investigation. *Human Relations*, 31(2), 173–193.

Paisley, W.J. & Butler, M. (1983). *Knowledge utilization systems in education*. Hollywood, CA: SAGE Publishing.

Pavlic, B. & Hamelink, C.J. (1985). *The New International Economic Order, Links Between Economics and Communications*. Paris, France: United Nations Educational Scientific and Cultural Organization.

Pratt, C.B. & Manheim, J.B. (1988). Communication research and development policy: Agenda dynamics in an African setting. *Journal of Communication*, 38(3), 75–95.

Price, D.J. De S. (1961). *Science Since Babylon*. New Haven, CT: Yale University Press.

Rada, J.F. & Pipe, G.R. eds. (1984). *Communication Regulation and International Business*. Amsterdam, Netherlands: North-Holland.

Riesbeck, C.K. (1984). Knowledge reorganization and reasoning style. *International Journal of Man-Machine Studies*, 20, 45–81.

Rogers, E.M. (1983). *Diffusion of Innovations*. 3rd ed. New York, NY: The Free Press.

Rogers, E.M. (1978). The Rise and fall of the dominant paradigm. *Journal of Communication*, 28(1), 64–69.

Rogers, E.M. & Shoemaker, F.F. (1962). *Diffusion of Innovations*. New York, NY: Free Press.

Rogers, E.M. with Shoemaker, F.F. (1971). *Communication of Innovations: A Cross-Cultural Approach*. New York, NY: Free Press.

Rondinelli, D.A. (1983). *Development Projects as Policy Experiments*. London, UK: Methuen.

Salasin, J. & Cedar, T. (1985). Person-to-person communication in an applied research/service delivery setting. *Journal of the American Society for Information Science*, 36, 1985, 94–115.

Sauvant, K.P. (1986). *International Transactions in Services: The Politics of Transborder Data Flows*. Boulder, CO: Westview Press.

Schaefer, M. (1981). *Intersectoral Coordination and Health in Environmental Management, An Examination of National Experience*. Geneva, Switzerland: World Health Organization (Public health papers 74).

Segura, E.L. (1985). *Guidelines for Evaluating the Management Information Systems of Industrial Enterprises*. Washington, DC: The World Bank.

Singer, H.W. & Ansari, J.A. (1988). *Rich and Poor Countries: Consequences of International Disorder*. 4th ed. London, UK: Unwin Hyman.

Srinivasan, M. ed. (1982). *Technology assessment and development*. New York, NY: Praeger.

Stamper, R. (1988). Analyzing the cultural impact of a system. *International Journal of Information Management*, 8(2), 107–122.

Stevenson, R.L. (1988). *Communication, Development, and the Third World: The Global politics of information*. New York, NY: Longman.

Stevenson, R.L. and Shaw, D.L. eds. (1984). *Foreign News and the New World Information Order*. Ames, IA: The Iowa State University Press.

Subramanyam, K. (1977). A didactic model for science communication. *Indian Librarian*, 31(4), 157–167.

Taylor, R.S. (1986). *Value Added Processes in Information systems*. Norwood, NJ: Ablex Publishing Co.

Tushman, M. (1979). Impacts of perceived environmental variability on patterns of work related communication. *Academy of Management Journal*, 22(3), 482–500.

United Nations Centre on Transnational Corporations. (1982). *Transborder Data Flows: Access to the International On-Line Data-Base Market*. Amsterdam, Netherlands: North-Holland.

United Nations Centre on Transnational Corporations. (1987). *Arrangements Between Joint Venture Partners in Developing Countries*. New York, NY: UNCTC (UNCTC Advisory Studies No. 2, Series B).

United Nations Centre on Transnational Corporations. (1987). *Transnational Corporations and Technology Transfer: Effects and Policy Issues*. New York, NY: UNCTC.

United Nations Department of Technical Cooperation for Development. (1985). *Modern Management and Information Systems for Public Administration in Developing Countries*. New York, NY: UNCTC.

United Nations Educational, Scientific and Cultural Organization. (1985). *Guidelines on National Information Policy: (Scope, Formulation and Implementation)* by I. Wesley-Tanaskovic. Paris, France: UNESCO.

United Nations Educational, Scientific and Cultural Organization. (1981). *Societal Utilization of Scientific and Technological Research*. Paris, France: UNESCO (Science Policy Studies No. 47).

United Nations Educational, Scientific and Cultural Organization. (1986). *Strategies for Endogenous Development*. Paris, France: UNESCO.

United Nations Industrial Development Organization (UNIDO). (1978). *Guide to practical project appraisal*. New York, NY: United Nations.

Utterback, J.M. (1986). Innovation and corporate strategy. *International Journal of Technology Management*. 1(1/2), 119–132.

Vasarhelyi, P. (1978). The role of information gatekeepers in computerized public administration. Paper presented at the Conference on New Technologies in Public Administration. Vienna: European Coordination Centre for Research and Documentation in the Social Sciences (Manuscript).

Vickery, B. & Vickery, A. (1987). *Information Science in Theory and Practice*. London, UK: Butterworths.

Villaveces, J.P. (1986). "TDF in Colombia." In *International Consultative Commission for Transborder Data Flows Development. Inaugural Meeting Proceedings, Rome, 18–20 September 1985*. Rome, Italy: International Bureau of Informatics.

White, D.M. (1964). "The Gatekeeper: A case study in the selection of news." In Dexter, L. & White, D.M., eds. *People, Society, and Mass Communications*. 160–172. New York, NY: The Free Press.

Wilkin, A. (1977). Personal roles and barriers in information transfer. *Advances in Librarianship*, 7, 257–297.

Winograd, T. & Flores, F. (1986). *Understanding Computers and Cognition: A New Foundation for Design*. Reading, MA: Addison-Wesley.

12

Thoughts on the Social Implications of Information Theory

Introduction

It seems presumptuous to share one's thoughts on a topic that merits in-depth examination. I am nevertheless prompted to do so by my belief that even the humblest approach to speculate about the links between research in information science/informatics and its social consequences may be forgiven because information, a unique and so far undefinable phenomenon of life, is wide open to formal and informal reflection.

At the 46th Conference and Congress of the International Federation for Information and Documentation, held in Omiya, Japan, Prof. Shizuo Fujiwara (1994) called for the cooperation of researchers in different fields. With emphasis on the regional interaction of researchers and policy makers, the process of interdisciplinary cooperation can be set in motion. Because today regionalism is a leading and widely debated theme in economics and development science (Cernea 1994, Wong 1994), it is challenging to view the role of information science/informatics research in this framework.

The title of this brief paper does not refer to the scientific discipline of Information Theory as introduced by Shannon and Weaver (1949) addressing the measurement of the physical movement of information from one point to another. Rather, "information theory" here stands for all theories and models, relevant to information, that have been created by basic and applied research in a wide range of disciplines. Generally, theories are meant to serve either the understanding or the prediction of the behavior of information. They have been constructed using various approaches including exploratory, experimental, statistical, comparative, descriptive, case study and other methods. "Theory" is used here in the singular as it denotes collectively all unintegrated, unsystematized, and often unrelated products of information-related research brought forth in recent decades.

Theory is the result of an inquiry based on certain assumptions, the investigation of conceptual relationships in a certain context, and ensuing insights into new meanings. The social implications of theories are determined by those areas of human activity where relevant new insights imbedded in theories are adopted, tested, and applied. Since there is no consensus in either the scholarly community or in the arena of economic

225

and social activities on a conceptual definition of "information," both research and the use of research in practical terms are wide open to interpretation. The ambiguity of a discussion of information theory is intensified by the proposition—upon which there is wide and unequivocal agreement—that as thoughts expressed by language may be understood only in the context of their cultural associations, information may be understood only in the cognitive context of its creation, movement and use (Holland and Quinn 1987, Savolainen 1993).

Information Theories: The Process of Fragmentation

The international development of information science, informatics and related fields does not have an undisputed beginning point in intellectual history. Some reviewers trace its origin to the date when a particular professional organization was founded, others attach more significance to the publication of landmark research. Historians have described the evolution of national information systems in several separate countries or entire regions, and are now beginning to record the emergence of national information infrastructures (Moore 1993, Zulu 1994). In the global economy the place of each nation is determined by its relation to international trade through its growing "information society" (Organization . . . 1992).

Science is lagging way behind this technological momentum. Research in development science, economics, education, and the communication, computer, information, and management sciences is far from the capability to empirically, or even descriptively, assess the consequences of innovations for the developing economies (Foster and Rosenzweig 1993). What is the impact of information flows on the poor, on nationalistic movements, environmental planners, urban sprawls or rural needs? Where are the researchers who will provide the theories and tests in this living complexity?

Even the landscape of research in one country presents a vast picture of fragmentation. Theoretical fields ranging from mathematical and engineering specialties and cybernetics through logic, cognitive science and artificial intelligence to economics and decision sciences have contributed to the change of focus from information-handling processes to theory building. A rich assemblage of theories exists now in the intellectual realm, but the words of Heilprin (1989, p. 343) still ring true as he identified

a consensus of opinion that although many laws, theories, hypotheses and speculations about information have been proposed, adequate scientific and epistemic foundations for a general science of information have not yet appeared.

Heilprin suggested a "fundamental open framework" of theoretical findings into which "the contents can be fitted when discovered" (Heilprin, 1989, p. 343). Such a framework is still in the making. Instead of becoming more definitive, the borders of participating disciplines are constantly broadening and overlapping with each other. As Kitagawa (1972) warned, theories of information probably cannot be organized into a systematic body of knowledge until better channels of communication have opened up among researchers in all physical, biological and social sciences and the humanities.

Relationships between Theories and Applications

In his discussion of the contribution of research to society, Dubin (1978, p. 16) posed the question "whether the ability to make such [a] contribution depends upon being a scientist . . . or on the product of being a good reporter." In the United States, decades of intensive federal funding for systems to disseminate the reported results of scientific research answered this question. Entire subdisciplines came to crystallize into new research communities: Knowledge utilization, research communication, and the diffusion of innovations, among others. New theoretical models were built by multidisciplinary research teams. Eventually, also the motives and interactions of such teams became the targets of research attention. Large bodies of literature have clustered around the processes of creativity and productivity; investigators, indeed, have searched in vain for measurable connections between these two sociopsychological phenomena.

Systems in information science/informatics are expected to assist other disciplines and professions in improving the effectiveness of research dissemination. In the past, actually their only mission was to serve national economic and military interests by playing a support role to other sciences. Only in the last two decades has governmental and industrial attention in high-technological countries shifted to information-centered research itself. "Information" is usually defined in its broadest sense to include telecommunications and computer applications. Thus, under the influence of the media and public debate, the borderlines among information-related fields have become even more blurred. What is clear is that the public expects research (romanticized as invention and discovery) and policy to join forces and to solve all current problems. In the background of this expectation lurks the invisible problem of making the connection between theory and its social application stronger and more transparent.

In a far-reaching effort to identify factors that produce and affect real connections between information and development, the International Development Research Centre has conducted a project on measuring the impact of information on development. Three assumptions were suggested as the basis of assessment indicators: Assumptions about the nature and role of information, and the concept of indicators. Following a preliminary theoretical framework of assessment and recommendations for future research, the project report indicated the key attributes of this line of research:

> A number of theoretical questions underlie the concepts, criteria, framework, and methods for impact assessment presented in this report. To a large extent, assessing the impact of information implies that the value of information is defined, which will lead to some definition of information itself. How to move from the model of discrete messages, where information theory has been deadlocked, to an acceptable representation of a plurality of messages and uses, which is the common experience of individuals and groups, is probably the more significant and challenging of the problems (Menou 1993, p. 112).

Characteristics and Implications of Information Theories

The concept of the social implications of information theories can be narrowed to the proposition that theoretical knowledge may (or may not) improve the ways information is made useful for people. The optimism of science suggests that theoretical models will first affect peers and then might find their way to success in industry, the professions and society. We can contemplate these possibilities only by beginning to identify the main characteristics of information theories.

Politicians, the media, and information professionals know that part of the theory-transfer and popularization process is the critical task of "translation," condensation, and integration into the social fabric. Here, again, we need to understand the characteristics of information theories in order to speculate on their implications for those who disseminate, those who add value, and those who eventually apply them. I will limit my discussion to four examples of characteristic issues relating to research in information science/informatics.

Multidisciplinary/Multicultural Context

Characteristics of Models.

Research does not take place in a vacuum but in the framework of disciplinary, professional, and cultural assumptions. "Scientists operate within a background of belief about how things are. This background in-

visibly shapes what they choose to do and how they choose to do it"
(Winograd and Flores 1986, p. 24). The ambiguous nature and multidisciplinary perspectives of information science/informatics produce
elusive theoretical models that are difficult to interpret. Moreover, development projects sponsored by international organizations bring together researchers from different cultures, adding to the complexity of
theoretical work and outcomes.

Social Implications

Philosophers and behavioral scientists have found that the self is a
powerful filter of observations. Based on their study, Gudykunst and Kim
(1992) reported that cultural, sociocultural, psychocultural, and environmental factors form people's views of reality. Researchers in developing
and industrialized countries make very different assumptions when they
formulate a problem and plan a project (Scheuch 1989). Although theoretical models may aspire to universal validity, in practice one cannot expect a concept's interpretation, a policy, or a social institutional model to
fit smoothly into another culture (Narula and Pearce 1990).

In recent years, researchers observed that a shift in the ways people of
different backgrounds perceive the world has taken place. Penman
(1988, p. 391) describes this change with reference to communications:

> Foundationalism refers to all those ways of thinking that search for . . .
> some certain foundation or some infallible fact upon which knowledge can
> be built . . . In contrast, constructionism sees the world as we know it as the
> product of a cyclic, hermeneutical process in which knowledge is ex-
> pressed and created in social practice.

In an international research team both verbal and written communications reflect the cultural perceptions of each team member (Day, Dosa
and Jorgensen 1995). From problem formulation to the interpretation of
analytic findings, the sources of misunderstanding can go well beyond
language barriers to the cognitive diversity of participants. We can only
speculate about the extent to which theoretical results are affected. Differences in professional "cultures" may have similar impact, especially
when information theories are adopted by systems designers.

On the other hand, multidisciplinary and multicultural research has a
great potential for creative richness, wherever open communications
help to minimize barriers. Increased cooperation among scientists and
information system designers might be one of the answers. Zeisel (1981,
p. 32) observed that

> Cooperation is fostered when designers and researchers decide they want
> to use the other discipline as a tool . . . to solve more broadly defined prob-
> lems than they can solve alone.

The same might very well be true for researchers and practitioners with different cultural backgrounds.

The "Theory into Practice" Quandary

Characteristics of Models

Information and development professionals have been questioning whether links between theoretical models and practical applications really exist (Boon 1992, Cernea 1991, Makovetskaya and Bernadsky 1994). It seems that the analysis of models in order to identify elements of usability and specific needs for adjustment is especially problematic in information science/informatics where models are often descriptive and too general.

Social Implications

The successful use of research results in the real world depends on the investigator's interest in making results understandable and on the applier's willingness to bring unbiased receptiveness to a research effort. Projects serving specific needs are more amenable to understanding by practitioners than abstract inquiries. Unfortunately, specific applied research projects are often restrictive and inflexible in research design (Choguill 1994, Nelkin 1984). Consequently, many researchers are disturbed by a sponsor's "guided research" program. Others admit that studies supporting economic and social improvements in developing countries must conform to national development plans and to the sponsor agency's strategies in order to be effective (Palvia, Palvia and Zigli 1990).

An unusual approach to justifying research, which needs to be subordinated to particular political and policy objectives in the interest of development, is the concept of the economics of ideas. Romer (1993, pp. 63–64) explains that while in the economic analysis of patents the uniqueness of ideas has always been recognized, in policy models ideas are most often ignored. In his view the reason is that the contribution of ideas to development cannot be quantified and measured. However, the new appreciation of creative ideas shifts the emphasis to the qualitative evaluation of development projects. Romer insists that an open social discourse about ideas, although not quantifiable, is a powerful development model. "The logic behind the economics of ideas supports the new development orthodoxy that a policy of openness . . . offers the potential for large gains in poor countries" (Romer 1993, p. 65).

Similarly, an active flow of communication between researcher and practitioner is essential in order to transform conceptual models into working strategies. The resentment scientists often feel against guided applied-research projects may be ameliorated by a sense of moral responsibility for meeting human needs, a sense frequently shared by researcher and practitioner.

The Formal-Informal Information Dichotomy

Characteristics of Models

Most information retrieval and use models have been created with formal information systems in mind. How do computers and people communicate? How do users formulate problems? Even in research addressing information seeking not mediated by a person or system, usually the purpose is to understand how people (who are classed into certain categories) ask questions (which are assumed to pertain to the inquirer's information needs). Information seeking is conceptualized as a rational activity that can be simulated by computer programs. Informal communication among people who are not looking for information yet finding it in spontaneous ways is seldom studied by information science/informatics.

Social Implications

Information professionals have borrowed models from other disciplines which have studied interaction patterns of people within or outside organizations. However, even the theories produced by this strain of research are based on the image of the communicator as a well-defined person (health care provider, physicist, student, listener, consumer) driven by a certain purpose. We have also witnessed remarkable advances toward changing the orientation of research from information systems to information users, but even these efforts address mainly people who purposefully seek information (Cole 1994). In contrast, Lifton (1994) speaks of the "Protean" individual who is multidimensional, changes purposes and interests frequently, and is motivated by different frames of reference in different situations. The "Protean" individual defies categorization.

Studies of informal information flows among people would do well to take the Protean model into account to arrive at a more realistic conceptualization of the individual. An inquiry into spontaneous and unstructured information exchanges among people, including chance remarks and unplanned digressions, might shed considerable light on their multi-dimensional "Protean" interests and reveal unspoken information needs indirectly. Such studies would probably produce theories upon which future research could be built.

From Linear to Cyclic Innovation Processes

Characteristics of Models

Reexamination and testing of information-related theories is difficult because information behaves differently under different conditions. One example is information as a component of the innovation process. In the traditional linear model of innovation (from problem perception through experimentation and testing to implementation of the change), information was assumed to behave at every point in predictable ways (abundant, scarce, inaccessible, accessible, etc.). Researchers thought that these ways could be observed and measured (Stern 1982). Since information did not follow expected patterns, theories based on the linear model of innovation included some characteristics which defied reexamination and testing.

Social Implications

We cannot expect that innovations in organizations or societies will normally be well-planned and systematic. Problems may interfere with the flow of events, or breakthroughs may occur in unexpected ways. Many changes in the direction of planning, risk-taking, or experimentation are spontaneous. Innovation resembles a cyclical rather than linear process. In the firm, different dimensions of the activity (scanning the competition, formulating criteria for testing, entering a creative research phase, or exploring the market) interact and overlap with each other to the extent that sometimes a chronology of steps is impossible to construct. This fluid state of affairs sometimes saves the innovation from becoming stagnant and failing.

Under these conditions, information processes are unstandardized and unpredictable. Several phases and events happen simultaneously, different units of the organization gain or lose influence, and information needs peak and fall like waves. Bartlett and Ghoshal (1987) found through their empirical research project that in corporations the management of the flow of intelligence, ideas and knowledge is an enormously complex task. Radosevic (1991, p. 68) warns that "intelligence failures, caused by an exclusive technological orientation" are not rare.

Social innovation, in particular, is the realm of fluctuations where new trends demand the involvement of more players in the change process than ever. The evaluation of social change is information-intensive, calling for new approaches to data gathering and analysis (Kumar 1993). The planning of new information infrastructures may be assisted by lessons from the past, or by an intuitive envisioning of the future. Melody (1986, p. 57) reports that "important—and totally overlooked in the great majority of studies—is an examination of the information and communication networks being used prior to the introduction of new technologies. Without knowing the prior information flows and communication relations, one has no base case against which to compare the new, changed relations . . . " Mytelka (1993) urges consideration of "innovation networking" in the effectiveness of development processes, while Ruth and Gouet (1993), reporting on an empirical project in Chile, identify the study of scientific network users as a neglected research domain.

Reexamining and testing theories that had been constructed around the traditional linear image of the innovation process in the real, unpredictable organizational and social environment is an exciting task for the information scientist.

Concluding Note

The rendering of a research model socially useful is a form of technology transfer. It is easier to speculate about this process than to identify criteria to assess the extent, nature, and validity of the model's usefulness. To recognize and evaluate factors that may assist or hinder the application of the model is even more intractable.

However, information science/informatics cannot turn away from this research need. Four reasons account for this responsibility. Information is essential for

- recognizing opportunities and coping with problems in *individual* life
- preparing *societies* for meaningful transformations
- using *environmental* resources wisely
- making the right choices in *technology*.

In this broad framework, the open-endedness and flexibility of theoretical knowledge in information science/informatics can work to the advantage of the social impact of information theories. It can attract researchers from different disciplines. It can accommodate the diversity of future research on the role of information in individual-society-environment-technology relationships, and it may produce models relevant to the changeable world of reality.

References

Bartlett, C.A. & Ghoshal, S. (1987). Managing across borders: New strategic requirements. Pt. 1. *Sloan Management Review,* 28(4), 7–17.

Boon, J.A. (1992). Information and development: Some reasons for failures. *The Information Society,* 8(4)227–241.

Cernea, M.M. (1994). Environmental and social requirements for resourcebased regional development. *Regional Development Dialogue,* 15(1), 186–198.

Cernea, M.M. (1991). *Using Knowledge from Social Sciences in Development Projects.* Washington, DC: The World Bank.

Choguill, C.L. (1994). Implementing urban development projects: A search for criteria for success. *Third World Planning Review,* 16(1), 26–39.

Cole, C. (1994). Operationalizing the notion of information as a subjective construct. *Journal of the American Society for Information Science,* 45(7), 465–476.

Day, D., Dosa, M., & Jorgensen, C. (1995). The transfer of research information within and by multicultural teams. *Information Processing & Management,* 31(1), 89–100.

Dubin, R. (1978). *Theory Building.* Rev. ed. New York, NY: The Free Press.

Foster, A.D. & Rosenzweig, M.R. (1993). "Information flows and discrimination in labor markets in rural areas in developing countries." In *Proceedings of the World Bank Annual Conference on Development Economics, 1992.* Washington, DC: The World Bank.

Fujiwara, S. (1994). Introductory Remarks to this Special Issue. *Japanese Journal of Information and Knowledge,* 6(1), 1–3.

Gudykunst, W. & Kim, Y. (1992). *Communicating With Strangers: An Approach to Intercultural Communication* (2d ed.). New York, NY: McGraw Hill.

Heilprin, L.B. (1989). "Foundations of information science reexamined." In *Annual Review of Information Science and Technology.* Ed. by M.E. Williams, v. 24. Amsterdam, Netherlands: Elsevier Science Publishers.

Holland, D. & Quinn, N. eds. (1987). *Cultural Models in Language and Thought.* Cambridge, UK: Cambridge University Press.

Kitagawa, T. (1972). "Information science and the era of cybernetics." In *Proceedings of the First Japan-United States Conference on Li-*

braries and Information Science in Higher Education, Tokyo, 1969, 234–245. Ed. by T.R. Buckman. Chicago, IL: American Library Association.

Kumar, K. (1993). *Rapid Appraisal Methods.* Washington, DC: The World Bank.

Lifton, R.J. (1994). *The Protean Self: Human Resilience in an Age of Fragmentation.* New York, NY: Basic Books.

Makovetskaya, D. & Bernadsky, V. (1994). Scientometric indicators for identification of technology system life cycle phase. *Scientometrics,* 30(1), 105–116.

Melody, W.D. (1986). "Learning from the experience of others: Lessons from social experiments in information technology in North America." In *Proceedings of the Conference on Social Experiments with Information Technology, Odense, Denmark, 1986.* Luxembourg: Commission of the European Communities, FAST Programme (Document No. 83).

Menou, M.J. ed. (1993). *Measuring the Impact of Information on Development.* Ottawa, Canada: International Development Research Centre.

Moore, N.C. (1993). *Information policy and strategic development: A framework for the analysis of policy objectives.* ASLIB Proceedings, 45 (11/12),

Mytelka, L.K. (1993). Rethinking development: A role for innovation networking in the other two-thirds. *Futures,* 25(6), 694–712.

Narula, U. & Pearce, W.B. eds. (1990). *Cultures, Politics and Research Programs: An International Assessment of Practical Problems in Field Research.* Hillsdale, NJ: Lawrence Erlbaum Associates, Inc.

Nelkin, D. (1984). *Science as Intellectual Property. Who Controls Research?* New York, NY: Macmillan.

Organization for Economic Cooperation and Development. (1992). *Integration of Developing Countries into the International Trading System.* Paris, France: OECD.

Palvia, P., Palvia, S. & Zigli, M. (1990). Models and requirements for using strategic information systems in developing nations. *International Journal of Information Management,* 10(2), 117–126.

Penman, R. (1988). Communication reconstructed. *Journal of the Theory of Social Behavior,* 18(4), 391–409.

Radosevic, S. (1991). Techno-economic intelligence in the 1990s: A development policy perspective. *Social Intelligence,* 1(1), 55–71.

Romer, P.M. (1993). "Two strategies for economic development: Using ideas and producing ideas." In *Proceedings of the World Bank Annual Conference on Development Economics, 1992.* Washington, DC: The World Bank.

Ruth, S.R. & Gouet, R. (1993). Must invisible colleges be invisible? An approach to examining large communities of network users. *Internet Research,* 3(1), 36–53.

Savolainen, R. (1993). The sense-making theory: Reviewing the interests of a user-centered approach to information seeking and use. *Information Processing & Management,* 29(1), 13–28.

Scheuch, E.K. (1989). Theoretical implications of comparative survey research: Why the wheel of cross-cultural methodology keeps on being reinvented. *International Sociology,* 4, 147–167.

Shannon, C.E. & Weaver, W. (1949). *The Mathematical Theory of Communication.* Urbana, IL: University of Illinois Press.

Stern, B.T. ed. (1982). *Information and Innovation.* Amsterdam, Netherlands: North Holland.

Winograd, T. & Flores, F. (1986). *Understanding Computers and Cognition: A New Foundation of Design.* Norwood, NJ: Ablex Publishing Corporation.

Wong, S.Y. (1994). Globalization and regionalization: The shaping of new economic regions in Asia and the Pacific. *Regional Development Dialogue,* 15(1), 3–17.

Zeisel, J. (1981). *Inquiry by Design: Tools for Environment-Behavior Research.* Cambridge, UK: Cambridge University Press.

Zulu, S.F.C. (1994). Africa's survival plan for meeting the challenges of information technology in the 1990s and beyond. *Libri,* 44, 77–94.

Part IV

Information Policies

13

A Future Perspective on Information Policy Research Needs

Introduction

One of the major problems in the use of research results by policy makers is the stereotyped image researchers and policy makers have of each other. The researcher is often seen as a reality-alien academic with little understanding of the actual challenges and struggles in the field. Conversely, many researchers believe that decision makers conclude all negotiations by politicized choices based on ideological or personal bias, without consideration of data on alternatives (Churchman 1964). The theory-practice gap may stem from an oversimplification of both the research and policy-formulation processes. This distortion of images might very well be the result of inadequate communications among key players in the two groups. The problem is greatly aggravated in projects carried out in developing countries where research results often stem from a foreign culture, and decision makers are operating in the political environment of meager resources and nationalistic interests.

The information society, a new technological powerhouse-image, is an ideal in developing countries that is drawing many top policy makers towards the introduction of information policies within national development plans. The goal is to create a national information infrastructure as the backbone of the information society, dominated by improved, frequently privatized telecommunication services. Technology transfer, or the importation of research-based knowledge and experience-based skills, plays a key role in this attractive scenario. What is seldom recognized is the connection between two major problems: The need for high-level information policies for development on the one hand, and the theory-practice gap on the other. Neither imported nor domestically generated research can support the design of new policies without ongoing active communications between researchers and decision makers. Therefore, one of the primary justifications of information policy research is the need to better understand the implications and potential solutions of this problem.

This brief descriptive paper offers a preliminary framework of research needs related to information policies in the development environment. Since information production and policy implementation are integral parts of national advances, concepts and studies in development science serve as guidelines for this paper's themes. The suggested simple framework will include research on (1) policy processes, (2) policy issues, and (3) policy methodologies.

Dimensions of Development Information

In every discipline and profession, four activities are in continuous dynamic interaction: Practice, research, education, and policy formulation. In the information professions, practice and education/training have long commanded much more attention than research and policies. However, without the latter two dimensions receiving more support by international organizations and national governments, the four dominant activities in the information field could not be in proper balance. This is especially true in international relations where a lack of empirically founded understanding of the gross information inequalities between low-technological and high-technological countries hinders both the balanced development of domestic information infrastructures and effective professional cooperation.

In the international perspective, new initiatives are required for the amelioration of the precarious interactions among practice, research, education, and policies in order to forestall frequent failures in technology transfer. In his research policy proposal Madu (1990), expanding the classification of Van Gigch (1988), recognizes structural, technological, and behavioral failures or malfunctions in the transfer of appropriate technology. His remedy is a rationalistic policy-formulation model for developing countries that has dubious promise for application under difficult and unstable conditions.

Madu's assumptions explain the nature of his model. He describes technology transfer as "the acquisition, development, [and] utilization of technological knowledge by a country other than that in which this knowledge originated" (Madu 1990, p. 932). The definition harbors its own pitfalls. Where does technological knowledge originate? In the scientific relationships that produce it, in the industrial companies that need to apply it, in the diffusion process, or in the integration of knowledge within the new culture? Madu (1990, p. 933) points to "modes of production in a particular country" that increase domestic economic stability and competitiveness. However, the early decades of international assistance to developing countries have demonstrated that growth in industrial production without simultaneous evolution in understanding the comprehensive (rather than fragmented) process of small innovations through learning will not bring about overall social changes in the current atmosphere of economic insecurity. Hetman (1982, pp. 46–52) illustrates the direction in policy research towards recognizing the value of unspectacular steps in technology handling. He calls for policies in support of "intellectual activities connected with scientific discovery, on the one hand, and with the inventive development of new ways of doing things, on the other." Indeed, small innovations are new ways of doing everyday simple things. Information policies, therefore, cannot be built on the basis of existing models that target major national innovations, rather than conditions that allow small innovations at the organizational and grassroots levels. If strengthened and harmonized, practice, research, education and policy-making in the information professions may become the determinants of success or failure of such small-scale transfer and distribution of knowledge.

Concepts and Cultural Implications

In the context of development, what can research do to meet the needs of information policy design and implementation? This is the focal question of this paper. In the following, the beginnings of a conceptual undergirding for considering (1) development, (2) information policies, and (3) research will be outlined.

The World Commission on Environment and Development (1987, p. 24) defines sustainable development as the process which "meets the needs of the present without compromising the ability of the future generations to meet their own needs." The characteristics of economic imbalances between the North and the South have been well documented elsewhere (Laird and Nogues 1989, Redclift 1987, Singer and Ansari 1988). But research in political development is particularly relevant to this paper, because today information is intensely politicized. O'Leary (1987) reviews political studies of development from postcolonial paternalistic attitudes through the pessimism of the dependency literature to the current critical realism of political science investigations of popular trends such as the mobilization of local participants by development projects.

The combination of economic progress with central authority in the newly industrializing countries (NICs) is of keen interest to political development research. McCord (1986) identifies in these countries openness to foreign influence, emphasis on education, wide-scale introduction of high-technology lifestyle, and a simultaneous movement for retaining traditional symbols and values (O'Leary 1987, p. 13). The NICs represent a curious contradiction: Their striving for advances in telecommunications and computing includes little interest in the professional aspects of information science and management. For example, policy support by the central state to information education is a fairly recent development.

To say that an information policy is a plan for the development of information and data resources, services, and their optimal utilization, would be an inadequate statement because it ignores the importance of information science research and education/training. Furthermore, no country has a single comprehensive national information policy. Instead, usually there is a fragmented set of laws, regulations, decrees, codes of conduct, and standards, each dealing with a different aspect of information handling or a different technology (United Nations Centre . . . 1988). More valid definitions can be derived from the experience of development specialists whose observations about development policies fit well information policies. Stewart (1987, p. 2) suggests that "macropolicies go beyond the normal macropolicies of economic textbooks . . . [they] are used to describe this great variety of policies to indicate that they apply to the whole spectrum of microdecision-making." Rondinelli (1983, p. 3) questions the validity of normative strategies: "Rarely . . . have development policies been carried out in the prescribed ways, and this disparity between theory and reality is at the heart of recurrent debates over the effectiveness of development planning and administration."

Policy research includes studies using scientific methodologies to analyze and describe needs, institutions, players and instruments, and to identify relationships among them. Applied research may focus also on a specific problem that needs to be better understood before its solution can be attempted at the policy level. Scientific thought, creativity, and analytic skills are human resource assets seen by development strategists as essential for the process of sustainable development. Consequently, policy analysis is an activity on the rise in developing countries (McFarland, Jr., 1989, p. 207). Most analytic methodologies have been borrowed from industrial countries, while indigenous talent capable of developing them is neglected.

Human assets are imbedded in a society and should be nourished by local cultures rather than be patterned on imported models. A multiplicity of cultures characterize the environments in which social and economic changes occur as a result of gradual development. Without understanding the historical interaction of cultures in a particular country, we cannot decipher research needs. This cultural orientation is alien to many research consultants who bring predesigned blueprints of approaches to their work in the developing regions. However, a direction urging the acknowledgement of intuitive creativity and a holistic vision in problem solving is discernible in the literature in both the North and the South. Zeisel (1981, p. 32) suggests interdisciplinary communication between researchers and architectural designers in order to introduce flexibility in projects, a perspective that may also address information science researchers and systems designers:

> Research and design cooperation grows out of the variability of social reality: Boundaries of problems change, situations differ, viewpoints are flexible, and people grow . . . cooperation is fostered when designers and researchers decide they want to use the other discipline as a tool . . . to solve broadly defined problems that they cannot solve alone.

Development economists who conceptualize the role of institutions in development in broad social terms warn that informal factors such as "ethnicity, religion, and nationalism are much more influential than their place in the policy literature implies" (Van Arkadie 1990, p. 173).

Potential Classifications of Information Policy Research

Just as we speak of information-rich and information-poor economies with a wide range of newly industrializing countries in between these two extremes, we can observe a high visibility of information policy needs in some countries and low priority accorded to information-related problems in others. However, no nation can ignore the problems of international technology transfer in the form of electronic information and data networks. The rapid transmission of data influences trade relations and economic progress as much as mass communication affects cultural values and customs. In view of overarching political changes in the world, issues of global information access can be expected to intensify (Fisher 1989, Howell 1988).

One may consider future research needs related to information policies in several contexts:

- *Geopolitical structures* (nations, economies, societies, regions)
- *Administrative structures* (local, provincial, state-level, regional, international hierarchies)
- *Economic structures* (centralized economies, decentralized economies; public sector, private sector, hybrid organizations)
- *Professional structures* (information science, librarianship, archives/records management, information resources management)
- *Sectoral structures* (agriculture, business, education, energy, environment, health, population, urbanization).

Each of these and several other categories of research needs offer a foundation from which a research program could be evolved. The following discussion uses the themes of policy processes, policy issues, and policy methodologies, a framework suggested at the beginning of this paper.

Research on Policy Processes

The formalistic process of policy formulation includes a review of existing policies, need assessment, data collection, negotiations, decision making, implementation, inclusion in national development plans, operation, and evaluation. Montviloff (1990) provides practical descriptions of the process in developing countries. But Mingat and Tan (1988, pp. 3–4) cautions that many research-generated approaches to policy analysis are too abstract to put into operation in the education sector. It is difficult to locate the data required to assess "the value which society attaches to each of its principal objectives." In education-centered research, efforts are made to balance goals of efficiency and goals of equity in providing access to educational opportunities. This formula augurs well for application to research on information policies, specifically the efficiency and equity of information resources and services guided by such policies.

With the maturing of information and data infrastructures, the following research problems might become crucial within each developing country:

- The nature and quality of the domestic information policy process and its relation to international agreements
- In-country capabilities in policy, research, need assessment, and in the evaluation of existing policies
- Communications among policy makers and researchers; the role of educators and practitioners; ways the communication flows may be improved.

The process-oriented research program will have to begin with some basic surveys, inventories, and plans for the use of their results:

- A survey of government agencies and nongovernmental organizations bearing on national information, data, and telecommunication policies
- Analysis of existing national laws, decrees, regulations, norms, and international treaties and agreements
- Assessment of gaps in existing policies, and collection of qualitative and quantitative data on information users' and professionals' perceptions of needed policies

- Dissemination of survey and research results to policy makers, practitioners, educators and user groups for comments and recommendations.

Research on Policy Issues

The issues identified here are merely examples. A fuller inventory of research needs may be evolved from local situations in each country. In one country, probing into the relationship between rural areas and central ("core") organizations would identify technological factors that affect information flows (Swinth and Alexander 1990); in another setting where perhaps strengthening business decision making is a priority, attention would focus on testing strategic information systems (Palvia, Palvia and Zigli 1990). Each of the categories listed below present a challenge to the formulation of research questions.

1. INFORMATION TECHNOLOGY AS THE MAJOR DRIVER OF THE DEVELOPMENT OF INFORMATION SYSTEMS, SERVICES AND RELATED POLICIES
   - The relative effectiveness of ways of information technology acquisition (in-country research and development, purchase, licensing, joint ventures, technical assistance)
   - Applications and uses of electronic and satellite communications (direct broadcast satellites, electronic mail, bulletin boards, videotex), and lack of access by those unable to pay
   - Policies on public information systems and services; the information marketplace; the privatization process.
2. SOCIAL AND ETHICAL IMPLICATIONS OF NEW INFORMATION SYSTEMS AND SERVICES
   - Quality of resources and channels that point to data and information; barriers to access due to inequality problems; conditions of the information poor
   - Effect of international data transfer on social development and economic conditions in different sectors
   - Policies on information dissemination to different population groups: new entrepreneurs, rural dwellers, women's organizations, adult educators.
3. THE ROLE OF DATA AND INFORMATION IN SOCIETY'S CAPACITY TO INNOVATE
   - Innovation as an information process; the role of indigenous talent; ways of public participation in policy innovations
   - Leadership of information professionals in the country's development processes

- Information policies that support or impede innovation in information systems and services.
4. IMPLICATIONS FOR WORKFORCE DEVELOPMENT
   - The extent to which support for education and training for new responsibilities in information handling is included in national development plans
   - Ways information professionals participate in the process of public policy making; ways to intensify participation
   - Education and training on information policies: concepts, resources, analytic skills.

Research on Policy Methodologies

The previous two sections alluded to methods used in policy analysis. In the following, the emphasis is on research needs relevant to the design and methodology used in policy-related exploratory and experimental studies intended to elicit perceptions of policy makers, information producers and users.

In recent years concern about the appropriateness of transferring theories developed in the North to the South has been growing (Chapman and Boothroyd 1988, Pratt and Manheim 1988, Scott-Stevens 1987). Research design depends on the creative merging of reflection and measurement, one a culture-based, the other a universal scientific concept. Reflection draws its vitality from the psychological and social environment, while measurement relies on internationally agreed-upon standards. The balance between them is critical to the integrity of the inquiry.

To study the connection between theorizing and method, more research orientation and capability are required in developing countries. Policy problems in need of clarification and resolution are difficult, if not impossible, to investigate by using foreign models. The building of domestic research strength has been impeded by economic pressures and a number of less known forces. The failure of some policies has been blamed on poor design due to the lack of analytic skills (Ingraham 1987). Inappropriate paradigms used in studying the role of technology in economic, social and political integration have been identified as partial reasons for poor research results (Samarajiva and Shields 1990). Exogenous consultants were described as "itinerant advisers who may be well informed about 'success stories' [in development] but not about the specific origins of the observed success or the relevant informal characteristics of the setting to which the model is to be transferred" (Van Arkadie 1990, p. 156).

Remedies for the weak social system of science have been suggested in the areas of research administration, funding, the education of scientists, the indigenous development of methodologies, the dissemination of research to policy makers, and the upgrading of the economic and social status of the researcher (Lee 1988). Participating in the development process, albeit not in the political arena, the information professions offer their own remedies (Dedijer and Jequier 1987). Parallels between development and information policies suggest that developing countries need an increasing corps of skilled policy researchers in the information domain. Schools of information studies are challenged by this need. Roberts (1987, p. 167) suggests that "if a school has a positive approach to using research in teaching, and also troubles to develop a formal research policy, the scene is set for a lively interplay between research and curriculum."

Development and information scientists seem to agree that one of the priorities in strengthening research is in the area of evaluation methodologies. Potential research topics include not only the use of various methods, but also the responsibilities, resources, and politics of the research process:

- Alternative approaches to policy analysis; comparative study; criteria for the selection of the approach
- Appropriateness of different methodologies to determine the need for new policies: exploratory, experimental and descriptive studies; the combination of qualitative and quantitative methods; participatory and action research
- Social and ethical responsibilities of policy researchers
- The politics of funding for policy research
- Dissemination of research findings; reaching bureaucracies and newly privatized services.

Implications for the Future

To achieve a productive balance of practice, research, education, and policy in the information field, the information professions have to start with some courageous changes. We have to strip away the escalating complexity of our professionalism. To bring the four dimensions into harmony and foster communication among practitioners, researchers, educators, and policy makers, we have to rise to the most genuine simplicity. We have to reconceptualize "information" in human terms. We used to say that information was a support system for decision making, that information was a support system to development. Then we said that information was the decision-making process. Collective and applied information was the development process.

Now we have to say: Information is the expression of a person. Collective and applied information is the expression of a society. Today each individual can be an information producer and provider. Therefore, the quality of information is only as good or bad as the person who generates it. We are concerned that information systems are not responsive to information needs. Maybe this is because people are not responsive to people.

What is the prognosis for the future of information policy research? If current trends continue, growing information and computer literacy will enable most everybody to produce, transmit and consume information. New ethical and legal problems will arise due to intended or unintended inaccuracies and distortions. Every society hopes for the proliferation of personal computers, desktop publishing, electronic mail and bulletin boards. But then, we should recognize that the traditional top-down policies will be even less of a guarantee of information quality than they are today. Personal decisions will exert the main impact on the credibility and validity of information.

Once the world discovers that information technology in itself is no solution for the multifarious ills of societies, that information-integrity is only as solid as people's integrity, there will be a desperate search for ethical considerations to guide information processes. Laws and regulations can govern published and computer-generated products and the formal statements of people, but not the quality of information that passes informally from person to person. Only a new ethics permeating politics, economies and social relationships could form the foundation upon which the information policies of the future can be built. Research needs are the most dire wherever information flows outside of formal systems. The misuse of personal power, magnified by technology and its distributive capabilities, will be the most effective—and also the most dangerous—in informal processes.

Conclusions

This paper viewed information infrastructures and information policies as continuously changing elements in national evolution. Information-related advances were not conceptualized here as supports for development, but as the movements of people in development. The need for using research patterns and findings in development science is recognized. Themes that signal research needs include the measurement of information impact on indigenous innovation, human resource upgrading, public choice, the privatization of public services, the economics of skill (rather than knowledge) distribution, and the relationship of information to societal learning. These research themes are interwoven with national decision-making agencies, industrial enterprises, and rural communities. But the most crucial and challenging research needs exist in situations where people talk with each other, that is, exchanges that carry information not recorded anywhere.

A modest and workable proposal at this point envisions the initiation of plans in developing countries for surveys of government agencies with jurisdiction for information policies, and reviews of national laws, regulations, and other policy instruments. A new international working group of social scientists, legal experts and information professionals drawn partially from developing countries and partially from international development-assistance agencies would identify ways to support indigenous research on information policies. The most important responsibility of the working group would be the establishment of standards for high quality research. The most difficult task would be the preliminary selection of research priorities. Since at the present there is no international consensus concerning information policy issues and methodologies that need research attention, the list of priorities ought to be drawn up with the participation of as many developing countries as possible. This proposed effort itself represents the first research priority.

References

Adamolekum, L. (1990). *Issues in development management in Sub-Saharan Africa*. Washington, DC: The World Bank.

Chapman, D.W. & Boothroyd, R.A. (1988). Evaluation dilemmas: Conducting evaluation studies in developing countries. *Evaluation and Program Planning*, 11, 37–42.

Churchman, C.W. (1964). Managerial acceptance of scientific recommendations. *California Management Review*, 7(1), 31–38.

Dedijer, S. & Jequier, N. eds. (1987). *Intelligence for Economic Development: An Inquiry Into the Role of the Knowledge Industry*. Oxford, UK: Berg.

Fisher, B. (1989). *Electronic Highways for World Trade: Issues in Telecommunications and Data Services*. Boulder, CO: Westview Press.

Granelli, L. (1984). Information assets: National development indicators. *Transnational Data Report*, 7(586), 341–342.

Hetman, F. (1982). "From technology assessment to an integrated perspective on technology." In Srinivasan, M. ed. *Technology Assessment and Development,* 36–54. New York, NY: Praeger.

Howell, R.C. (1988). International telecommunications and the law: The Creation of Pan African satellites. *Howard Law Journal,* 31(4), 574–641.

Ingraham, P.W. (1987). Toward more systematic consideration of policy design. *Policy Studies Journal,* 15(4), 611–628.

Laird, S. & Nogues, J. (1989). Trade policies and the highly indebted countries. *The World Bank Economic Review,* 3(2), 241–261.

Lee, C.O. (1988). The role of government and R&D infrastructure for technology development. *Technological Forecasting and Social Change,* 33, 33–54.

Madu, C.N. (1990). Prescriptive framework for the transfer of appropriate technology. *Futures,* 22, 932–950.

McCord, W. (1986). *Paths to Progress: Bread and Freedom in Developing Countries.* New York, NY: Norton.

McFarland, Jr., E.L. (1989). "Conclusions." In *Successful Development in Africa, Case Studies of Projects, Programs, and Policies.* Washington, DC: The World Bank.

Mingat, A. & Tan, J-P. (1988). *Analytical Tools for Sector Work in Education.* Baltimore, MD: The Johns Hopkins University Press for the World Bank.

Montviloff, V. (1990). *National Policy on Information: Handbook on Formulation, Approval, Implementation and Operation of National Policy on Information.* Paris, France: United Nations Educational, Scientific, and Cultural Organization.

O'Leary, J.P. (1987). Toward an intellectual history of development: Notes on contemporary research. *Teaching Political Science: Politics in Perspective,* 15(1), 10–14.

Palvia, P., Palvia, S. & Zigli, M. (1990). Models and requirements for using strategic information systems in developing nations. *International Journal of Information Management,* 10(2), 117–126.

Pratt, C.B. & Manheim, J.B. (1988). Communication research and development policy: Agenda dynamics in an African setting. *Journal of Communication,* 38(3), 75–95.

Redclift, M. (1987). *Sustainable Development, Exploring the Contradictions.* London, UK: Methuen.

Roberts, S.A. (1987). Education and training in the information fields: Curriculum and research. *Education for Information,* 5(2/3), 157–168.

Rondinelli, D.A. (1983). *Development Projects as Policy Experiments: An Adaptive Approach to Development Administration.* London, UK: Methuen.

Samarajiva, R. & Shields, P. (1990). Integration, telecommunications and development: Power in the paradigms. *Journal of Communications,* 40(3), 84–106.

Scott-Stevens, S. (1987). *Foreign Consultants and Counterparts: Problems in Technology Transfer.* Boulder, CO: Westview Press.

Singer, H.W. & Ansari, J.A. (1988). *Rich and Poor Countries: Consequences of International Economic Disorder.* 4th edition. Boston, MA: Unwin Hyman.

Spacy, J. et al. (1971). *Science for Development.* Paris, France: United Nations Educational, Scientific, and Cultural Organization.

Stevenson, R.L. (1988). *Communication, Development, and the Third World: The Global Politics of Information.* New York, NY: Longman.

Stewart, F. ed. (1987). *Macro-Policies for Appropriate Technology in Developing Countries.* Boulder, CO: Westview Press.

Swinth, R.L. & Alexander, A. (1990). Power and dependence between the core and rural communities: Participating with major actors in solving local problems. *Journal of the Community Development Society,* 21(1), 71–82.

United Nations. (1987). *Popular Participation Policies as Methods for Advancing Social Integration.* New York, NY: UN.

United Nations Centre on Transnational Corporations. (1988). *National Legislation and Regulations Relating to Transnational Corporations.* V. 6. New York, NY: UNCTC.

United States. Office of Technology Assessment. (1989). *Critical Connections: Communication for the Future.* Washington, DC: U.S. Government Printing Office.

Van Arkadie, B. (1990). "The role of institutions in development." In *Proceedings of the World Bank Annual Conference on Development Economics, 1989,* 153–175. Washington, DC: The World Bank.

Van Gigch, J.P. (1988). Diagnosis and metamodeling of systems failures. *Systems Practice,* 7(1), 31–45.

World Commission on Environment and Development. (1987). *Our Common Future.* Oxford, UK: Oxford University Press.

Zeisel, J. (1981). *Inquiry by Design: Tools for Environment-Behavior Research.* New York, NY: Cambridge University Press.

14

The Regional Professional Association: A Key to Global Cooperation

Introduction

"The survival of mankind will depend to a large extent on the ability of people who think differently to act together." With these words Hofstede (1980), the Dutch social psychologist, introduced his massive research on the impact of cultural differences on human values at the workplace. Ten years later, a world immersed in political and economic changes could do no better than to adopt his vision.

The transformations we are witnessing today display a curious tension between the forces of national politics and international economic aspirations. As the people of East Europe succeed in their struggle for self-determination, they also move into participation in global trade relations. The Soviet Union, shedding its extreme ideological ballast, strives to hold its people together by meager economic reforms. The emerging Europe of 1992, a challenge to world trade, consists of strongly divergent national interests. South Africa is caught in the grip of a human drama while the international community watches, weighing the potential role of economic sanctions. And then there are the developing countries, each stunningly unique in culture, creative expression and human aspiration, but classified according to its level of economic status in an international scheme. The newly industrializing countries (NICs) have become proud players in world business while nations burdened by high external debt and mired in poverty worry about competition for international development aid (Krueger 1986, Rushing and Brown 1986, Smith and Cuddington 1985). So many people, thinking so differently, are so far from acting together.

Patterns of the Regional Approach

Yet a pattern of co-action is more and more discernable. International trade relations form a fabric of humanity largely divided into regions. Nations within each geopolitical region struggle to act together. Historical animosities between neighbors still threaten cooperation, and in some areas occasionally erupt into warfare, but the economic advantages of coexistence are difficult to ignore. A region creates a feeling of a shared past and of a future of possibilities, a sphere of joint planning and the reality of joint compromises. Regional schemes support the coordination of communication networks and information policies (Mattelart and Schmucler 1985, Wang and Dissanayake 1984), and share both problems of slow technological growth and returns of progress in local technological innovations (Mytelka 1989). Bereznoi (1990, p. 194) notes that observers in industrialized countries tend to underestimate the "innovational potential" of Third World multinational companies which are expanding within and beyond their own regions. Cultures and languages within the region may be divisive, but efforts to develop information, technology applications communicate themselves across borders.

The representation of needs and expectations toward the international political community is more persuasive when it comes from a regional organization. The Association of South-East Asian Nations (ASEAN); the Caribbean Community (CC); the Latin American Economic System (SELA); and the Organization of African Unity (OAU), whose member states launched the Lagos Plan incorporating the development of a Pan African satellite network, have been successful (to different degrees) in creating regional identities. With the objective to advance informatics for national development, particularly in the poorest countries, the Regional Informatics Network for Southeast Asia and the Pacific promotes training, research, infrastructure development, software design and policies in member countries.

In many parts of the world the cohesion within a profession, first generated by the establishment of national organizations, is legitimized and represented worldwide by regional professional associations. Considerable research effort in various disciplines has been devoted to the evolution of international agencies (Paul and Israel 1991), but little attention has focused on the attributes and processes involving the regional professional association.

Professional associations (including scientific and technical societies) form a subset of nongovernmental organizations (NGOs) falling inbetween the categories of trade organizations and voluntary organizations. Researchers underscore the lack of theoretical models, the ambiguity of definitions, and the problems of gathering and analyzing data for the study of these organizations (Lindblom 1990, Powell 1987). International voluntary agencies, widely praised for their work in developing countries, present particular difficulties in performance evaluation, because altruism, the assumed motivation of their members, their reward system expressed in reciprocity, and their informal activities do not lend themselves to empirical assessment (Bratton 1989, Brown and Korten 1989).

Professional associations wield considerable influence through their normative, interventive, and monitoring powers concerning professional credentials, standards, employment conditions, and codes of ethics (Freidson 1986). Topical conferences and annual meetings of professional associations have a longstanding history of disseminating knowledge through traditional media, and a more recent role in communicating through teleconferencing (Oseman 1989). Professional associations often spearhead a review of the profession's relationship to the economy and social health, and lead the regeneration of an entire field in order to meet new demands (Caldecote 1986). In the international arena, the regional professional association has great potential significance, for it can link the culturally determined national organizations with the more remote and abstract international bodies. This connecting role requires from the association's leadership sensitivity to cultures and traditions in the region as well as sweeping perspectives of international professional developments.

Implications for Information Professionals

Problematic issues in technological information flows, trade relations concerning data goods and services, and intellectual property rights urge upon information professionals the necessity to reach out for more imaginative cooperation. At a time when negotiations at the General Agreement for Tariffs and Trade (GATT), the International Telecommunications Union (ITU), and other international forums for the legal solutions of problems are intensive and adversarial, professional associations have a special mandate to increase their contacts with each other across different regions. Such contacts serve to bring about joint meetings and symposia, research initiatives and inventories, and informal networking among information scientists worldwide. The politics of official negotiations in international conference rooms must be balanced by open communications at the professional level.

The American Society for Information Science (ASIS) has a remarkable track record in initiating cooperation with professional associations in many countries as well as with intergovernmental organizations (IGOs) and international nongovernmental organizations (NGOs). As this important activity continues, the appropriate bodies of ASIS, in conjunction with the Canadian Association for Information Science (CAIS), might consider development of an information exchange and collaboration scheme with regional associations representing communication, computing, and information professionals in various parts of the world. As electronic communications reach larger and larger areas, the linking of ASIS and CAIS with distant associations which, in turn, have a ripple effect on professional developments in their own regions can grow into a significant project. The primary objective is to enhance not only the exchange of ideas about the international applications of informatics, but also pragmatic ways of collaboration through projects. Research shows evidence that NGOs are interacting with a growing number of indigenous institutions and innovations (Jussawalla and Hughes 1984, Montgomery 1988). The information exchange network of regional professional associations thus would identify career opportunities, team research, and joint training possibilities in participating countries. The exchange program would support also the twinning of institutions, or the establishment of a professional relationship between an institution in a developing country and a counterpart elsewhere, which is valued for its ability to integrate training and technical assistance during prolonged periods of collaboration (Cooper 1984).

In addition to bringing regional professional associations in contact with each other and with ASIS and CAIS, this activity would provide new perspectives on (1) the international transfer of information technology, (2) developments in the information service sector, (3) private entrepreneurship and information consultation, (4) international research projects in information science, and (5) the role of regional associations with regard to information policies. Regional professional organizations may also share experience in such applications as videotext services to PC users, advances in data interchange between different email systems, new developments in rural information dissemination, and policy-related activities in the different regions.

Why Regional Professional Associations?

A few years ago the International Federation for Information and Documentation (FID) began a major move to establish contacts with regional professional associations in information science, information management and informatics. The entire FID membership benefited by what was learned through these contacts. Regional organizations translate research carried out by international projects into practicable ideas to allow experimentation at the regional and local levels. They also have the potential to channel local and regional talent, motivation and energy into international activities. Their main functions are to create multidirectional discussions and stimulate regional cooperation in order to strengthen the effectiveness of information professionals in development projects.

In recent years the thinking about professional associations has been changing. Formal structure is minimized in favor of a dynamic system, and the impact of organizational processes is defined in terms of communication among the different components of the system and with the external world. Many regional associations are unable to implement such changes as they lack the means to keep their staff updated. Others are still in transition. Because the membership of national professional associations depends on the effectiveness of the regional body, development of the analytical, managerial and communication capabilities of the regionals is crucial. In many parts of the world, recognition of this reality is lacking.

The Learning Society

In a rapidly changing world, the ideal goal of international cooperation is to find new ways to originate, transmit and use knowledge in the service of peace. As ideas about the information society have spread in both high-technology and low-technology countries, people have either come to depend on information and data services, or they are growing impatient in localities where these services are lacking. In any case, few understand the magnitude of investment in human resources, research, education, and technology assessment necessary to maintain user-oriented information services. One gets a sense of information-talk fatigue. It seems that people are tired of hearing about supersystems and superproducts, they just want the right information when they need it. Although the steady advancement of technological knowledge and its applications has unequivocal merit and deserves broad public support, claims of superiority have penetrated international professional language too deeply, and often appear to be a mockery of severe prevailing societal problems in every corner of the world.

Cooperation with regional professional associations can give us a sense of the wondrous diversity of cultures, human efforts, and social transformations, and help us to evolve a new perspective on the global information society. The learning society, as the learning organization, is characterized by the kind of ongoing communication that does not try to impose ideas on people but is open to mutual learning in the course of all societal or organizational processes (Korten 1987). Maybe this concept can lead us to an understanding—indeed a welcoming—of the diversity of life in our time. We need to sustain the capacity to think differently but to act together when professional action is needed.

References

Bereznoi, A.V. (1990). *Third World Newcomers in International Business*. Delhi, India: Ajanta Publications.

Bratton, M. (1989). The Politics of government—N.G.O. relations in Africa. *World Development,* 17(4), 569–587.

Brown, L.D. & Korten, D.C. (1989). *The Role of Voluntary Organizations in Development.* Boston, MA: Institute for Development Research.

Caldecote, V. (1986). Engineers in the 21st century. *International Journal of Technology Management,* 1(1/2), 31–34.

Cooper, L. (1984). *The Twinning of Institutions, Its Use as a Technical Assistance Delivery System.* Washington, DC: The World Bank. (Technical Paper No. 23).

Cowhey, P.F. (1990). The International telecommunications regime: The Political roots of regimes for high technology. *International Organization,* 44(2), 169–199.

Freidson, E. (1986). *Professional Powers: A Study of the Institutionalization of Formal Knowledge.* Chicago, IL: The University of Chicago Press.

Hofstede, G. (1980). *Culture's Consequences: International Differences in Work-Related Values.* Beverly Hills, CA: Sage Publications.

Jussawalla, M. & Hughes, D.L. (1984). "The Information economy and indigenous communications." In Wang, G. & Dissanayake, W. eds. *Continuity and Change in Communication Systems: An Asian Perspective,* 251–266. Norwood, NJ: Ablex.

Korten, D.C. (1987). Third generation NGO strategies: A key to people-centered development. *World Development,* 15 (Supplement), 145–159.

Krueger, A.O. (1986). Aid in the development process. *The World Bank Research Observer,* 1(1), 57–78.

Lindblom, C.E. (1990). *Inquiry and Change: The Troubled Attempt to Understand and Shape Society.* New Haven, CT: Yale University Press.

Mattelart, A. & Schmucler, H. (1985). *Communication and Information Technologies: Freedom of Choice for Latin America?* Norwood, NJ: Ablex.

Montgomery, J.D. (1988). *Bureaucrats and People: Grassroots Participation in Third World Development.* Baltimore, MD: Johns Hopkins University Press.

Mytelka, L.K. (1989). The Unfulfilled promise of African industrialization. *African Studies Review,* 32(3), 77–137.

Oseman, R. (1989). *Conferences and Their Literature: A Question of Value.* London, UK: The Library Association.

Paul, S. & Israel, A. (1991). *Nongovernmental Organizations and the World Bank: Cooperation for Development.* Washington, D.C.: The World Bank.

Powell, W. (1987). *The Nonprofit Sector: A Research Handbook.* New Haven, CT: Yale University Press.

Rushing, F.W. & Brown, C.G. eds. (1986). *National Policies for Developing High Technology Industries: International Comparisons*. Boulder, CO: Westview Press. (Special Studies).

Smith, G.W. & Cuddington, J.T. eds. (1985). *International Debt and the Developing Countries*. Washington, DC: The World Bank.

Wang, G. & Dissanayake, W. eds. (1984). *Continuity and Change in Communication Systems: An Asian Perspective*. Norwood, NJ: Ablex.

15

New Challenges
to the Information Professional

Living with Complexity

Being attuned to society's wavelengths is the essence of all information-related work. Neither the design of information systems and networks nor the delivery of library services can claim true user-centricity without an understanding of the multifaceted psychological environment of people. The greatest challenge to the information professional is the accelerating rate of change in every dimension of life.

What do we know about the world we live in? What turbulences, transformations and undercurrents shape the knowledge needs of today? It appears that complexity—in the way we live, work, learn, think, play, and communicate—affects our thoughts and actions more powerfully than we realize. The complexity of the political process, social problems, scientific inquiry and technological possibility, entrepreneurship and competition in trade, is the underlying characteristic of the present information environment. We have to learn to live with complexity in order to strengthen the positive forces in societies and to fight persistent problems by all available tools of knowledge.

The style of inquiry by which we seek knowledge is intensively studied in several fields. Zeisel (1981, p. 3) noted that both research and design are difficult to grasp because they include "so many intangible elements such as intuition, imagination and creativity." In recent years, the linear approach to problem solving has given way to the recognition that all things are connected in complex relationships. Three examples may illustrate this point.

First, the Gaia hypothesis, proposed by Lovelock in 1969 and restated in his book *Gaia: A New Look at Life on Earth* (Lovelock 1979), created a brief but passionate controversy in the scientific community. This total systems view conceives of all living things on our planet interacting with chemical and geophysical processes to sustain atmospheric conditions suitable for life. Indeed, teams of scientists are studying the interrelationships of all phenomena in the oceans, climate, land, living organisms, and atmospheric changes.

Secondly, changes in perceptions in cognitive science are likely to affect the design and use of information systems. Winograd and Flores

(1986) illustrate the connectedness of all things by the image of the computer not as a piece of technology, but as a component in a social network of institutions, actions, meanings and interacting processes. This complexity also characterizes the environment of problem solving. The authors reject the long-standing assumption that decisions are made by rational choices: "We conclude that models of rationalistic problem solving do not reflect how actions are really determined, and that [computer] programs based on such models are unlikely to prove successful" (Winograd and Flores 1986, p. 12).

Thirdly, the study of corporate cultures has entered a phase where the concept of interrelatedness is dominant. Drucker (1988, p. 45) bore witness to the change: "The traditional sequence of research, development, manufacturing, and marketing is being replaced by synchrony; specialists from all these functions work together as a team from the inception of research to a product's establishment in the market."

In the context of turbulent trends, what challenges face the information professional? Of the far-flung pattern of changes that mold the information environment, I will select a few examples.

Information Technology

Advances have been so swift and potent that our awareness of new processes and tools has long surpassed our understanding of their consequences. The availability of technology underscores our lack of insights into the kinds of public and corporate policies needed to maximize the benefits of systems. For example, the proliferating use of commercial and scientific data transfer internationally gave rise to an entangled pattern of standards, regulations, and security and privacy protections in various countries. Superimposed on this global pattern are the measures of intergovernmental organizations, reflecting political and economic negotiations. The user of electronic mail and bulletin boards, indulging in the new speed and richness of information acquisition and in instant personal communications across continents, tends to ignore their legal and ethical complexity.

Who will be responsible for establishing criteria for quality control? Where are the advocates of equity in access? These policy questions must be confronted by information professionals because they are related to professional decisions and the evolution of national information policies in the context of economic and social systems. Hanson and Narula (1990, p. 13) expressed this challenge: "There has to be a positive relationship between technology and cultural development enriching the cultural resources and respect for cultural diversity."

Globalization

In international relations, economic and trade information is matching or surpassing the significance of ideological and political communications. The rapid transmission of information—from minute by minute satellite news to the financial data of transnational corporations—has all but obliterated the division between domestic and global messaging.

Research has shown that the current dependency relationship of low-income countries with other areas of the world has been aggravated by their inability to exploit local resources to support modern production. Sauvant (1986, pp. 7–9) asserts that data products and services are the major components of international trade. Nations lacking adequate telecommunication infrastructures and access to international trade continue to exist under debilitating conditions. Some developing economies, however, are in various stages of introducing communication and information technology (Jussawalla 1992). The privatization of public telecommunication utilities and the appearance of South-to-South transnational corporations call for the strengthening of human resources, entrepreneurship, and skills to manage innovations (Greenaway and Milner 1990).

Trends suggest that the capability of modernizing societies to enter and compete in international markets will result in sound internal growth only if concomitant concern for social conditions and the quality of life exists (Castells 1991). These issues cannot be localized or regionalized any more. Development specialists with a long-range perspective argue that now is the time to reinforce the ties of cooperation among the scientific/professional communities of low-technology and high-technology countries (Redclift 1987). Sharif (1992, p. 382) urged that nations promote "the exchange of information through networking—international, regional, and subregional networks may be organized for the exchange of experiences . . . " Thus, in industry as well as in the public sector, information professionals have to respond to the challenge of global cooperation.

Multicultural Information User Groups

Populations of active or potential information users are becoming ever more diversified and richly pluralistic. Transnational corporations expanding to several countries employ local workers and managers in order to increase productivity and cost-effectiveness. Positive relationships in such situations can be maintained only by communications based on cultural sensitivity. The traditional protocol of face-to-face international conferences is overlapping with the new "rules" of computer conferencing and the still unformulated etiquette created by the rapidly spreading practice of electronic mail.

In communities we are witnessing the self-organization and self-assertion of distinct cultures not only by ethnicity, religion and gender, but also by such groups as the handicapped, the aged, or the consumer of certain goods. In these enclaves of people-gathering, there is a new meeting of high-technology and personal or neighborhood information. Multimedia databases of cultural heritage, oral history, storytelling, and contemporary skill-based experiences are being created in communities. Information is becoming the organizational tool for grassroots movements, new enterprises and political negotiations at all levels. The information professional needs to note especially the phenomenon of social organization at the local level where enhanced communication channels and information dissemination are basic necessities. Many developing nations are experiencing a burgeoning of popular participation in planning for change (Annis and Hakim 1988, Montgomery 1988). And at the global level, neither technology transfer nor scientific cooperation in fighting disease and poverty can succeed without intercultural communication.

Interdisciplines

One of the most constructive answers to economic and social problems has been the emergence of interdisciplines, such as environmental science, management science, population studies, rural development, and technology assessment that integrate the conceptual approaches and professional skills from several fields of research and applications.

Fiedler et al. (1988, p. 49) observe that "it is no longer enough that a manager be good at a specialized skill. Increasing demands of the job force are the cultivation of a wider perspective." How does information affect the decision making of teams whose members have disparate backgrounds? "The . . . desirable property of information is synergism. Simply put, if the information is organized and presented in just the right way for a particular problem, the individual pieces reinforce each other and the decision-making process improves greatly."

Today, questions that originate in an interdiscipline and challenge information services include the following:

- Who is doing research; on what aspects of the field?
- What is the social configuration of policies, research support, development, workforce preparation, education and training in this field?
- How can national and international databases, networks and li-

braries pertaining to each of the subdisciplines and to the interdiscipline as a whole, be accessed?
- What channels are used, if any, for disseminating research results to the public?
- Which national agencies, intergovernmental organizations, and scientific or technical societies are engaged in developing standards and regulations?

Managing Complex Information Flows

The capability to manage information provision and usage effectively by matching needs with multimedia resources and multichannels has been expanding due to research and innovation in software engineering, information resources management (IRM), systems design and evaluation, and communications. The challenge is now to reach beyond structured information systems and tap the largely unmapped abundance of informal information flows.

The image of a world where information moves from well-organized formal resources — databases, corporate files, clearinghouses, libraries — through systems and networks to recipients, is relatively comfortable. On the other hand, the environment of information flows external to systems — personal expertise, peer communications, group problem solving, "the learning organization," desktop publishing, electronic mail and bulletin boards — is rich in unexploited information, but intricate and demanding from the point of view of the user. Disturbing questions have emerged, largely from the scientific and policy sectors, concerning the source, intent, credibility, validity, appropriateness, value and security of the message. Information managers are called upon to deal not only with the ever-changing technology and user requirements, but also with emerging policy and research needs. They have to find ways to assess the value of information to the social system, the community, the organization, the individual. They have to define information ethics and incorporate ethical consideration into decisions (Glastonbury and LaMandola 1992).

The managers of information who recognize and provide access to information flows outside of traditional systems have to be innovators with a vision.

The Enabling Function

People use information for choices, learning, research, creating new goods, enjoyment, power, and many other reasons that prompt them to find out. We tend to forget that one of the basic motivations for information use is creative curiosity. Personal development implies an increase in a person's ability to cope, work, and contribute to the quality of life. It is the primary task of the information professions to increase the possibilities of people and societies to develop. This is the enabling function of information. Whether we apply supercomputers or oral history to this task is only a question of the information environment and its optimal tools. Consequently, the common goal of education and training for the information professions is to foster the enabling function and to provide the best intellectual, technological and behavioral tools for this purpose.

In technology-rich and research-rich situations we can observe a tendency of information professionals to believe that gateway and front-end software interfaces will replace human intermediaries. These transparent systems indeed offer features such as selecting databases, uploading problem statements, performing steps in the search, and sorting, ranking and downloading citations. There is a great deal of the user-enabling function in these interfaces. What, then, is the challenge to the information professional?

In a complex world, active and potential users need a human intermediary who has both the imagination and technical competence to evaluate information systems in the context of cultural use (Stamper 1988). Complexity mandates the "mentor" and "interpreter" who can coordinate all types of access to not only formal systems but also to informal channels to expertise, unpublished research and the "gray" literature; translate clinical, legal and scientific information into the language appropriate to the use situation; and disseminate research findings to various populations. Legal and ethical consideration and the illumination of relevant policies form part of this role. The paradigm of information counseling has been developed by drawing on the best features of several models of guidance. Information counseling provides in-depth and personalized advice in the cost-effective acquisition, use and application of data and information. An interactive process by which the counselor determines the optimal way and resources to meet the information requirements and needs of individuals, groups and organizations, it assures follow-up in order to assess the effectiveness of the advising.

The challenge of the enabling role can take the information professional into a new partnership relation with users which will make it possible for people to overcome both information scarcity and overload.

The Outlook

In the context of current trends, information education and training programs, similarly to all branches of professional education, can expect growing economic and social demands calling for cost cutting and, at the same time, for innovations (Schon 1987). To the well-established need to prepare information practitioners for productive work and to endow them with the capability to pioneer services, we must add the responsibilities of enhancing research, formulating and implementing information policies, and disseminating information to interdisciplinary and multicultural user groups.

Rewards, too, can be expected in the dynamic and competitive information handling arena, but only if the various types of information professionals can learn to work together, acknowledging and supporting each other's role. Individuals will need to form priorities and harmonize their personal and professional value systems to be able to make the necessary commitments to cooperation. International and regional joint projects will play an important role. These can identify problems related to information access, validate innovative approaches, and develop models of long-distance teamwork addressing practical, policy-related, educational and research issues. Today the notion that equitable access to information technology will support a sounder economic and social balance is widely accepted. The challenge now is to recognize that the equitable application of information and knowledge worldwide depends on synergy across the information professions as well as across cultures.

References

Annis, S. & Hakim, P. eds. (1988). *Direct to the Poor: Grassroots Development in Latin America.* Boulder, CO: Lynne Rienner Publishers.

Castells, M. ed. (1991). Transnational corporations, industrialization, and social restructuring in the ASEAN region. *Regional Development Dialogue,* 12(1), 1–65.

Drucker, P.F. (1988). The Coming of the new organization. *Harvard Business Review,* 88(1), 45–53.

Fiedler, K.D. et al. (1988). Managing complex decisions. *Information Executive,* 1(1), 49–53.

Glastonbury, B. & LaMandola W. (1992). *The Integrity of Intelligence.* New York, NY: St. Martin's Press.

Greenaway, D. & Milner, C. (1990). South-South trade: Theory, evidence, and policy. *The World Bank Research Observer,* 5(1), 47–68.

Hanson, J. & Narula, U. (1990). *New Communication Technologies in Developing Countries.* Hillsdale, NJ: Lawrence Erlbaum Associates.

Jussawalla, M. (1992). Telecoms in Southeast Asian division of labor. *Transnational Data and Communications Report,* 15(5), 31–37.

Lovelock, J. (1979). *Gaia: A New Look at Life on Earth.* Oxford, UK: Oxford University Press.

Montgomery, J.D. (1988). *Bureaucrats and People: Grassroots Participation in Third World Development.* Baltimore, MD: Johns Hopkins University Press.

Redclift, M. (1987). *Sustainable Development, Exploring the Contradictions.* London, UK: Methuen.

Sauvant, K.P. (1986). *International Transactions in Services, The Politics of Transborder Data Flows.* Boulder, CO: Westview Press.

Schon, D.A. (1987). *Educating the Reflective Practitioner: Toward a New Design for Teaching and Learning in the Professions.* San Francisco, CA: Jossey-Bass Publishers.

Sharif, N. (1992). Technological dimensions of international cooperation and sustainable development. *Technological Forecasting and Social Change,* 42, 367–383.

Stamper, R. (1988). Analyzing the cultural impact of a system. *International Journal of Information Management,* 8(2), 107–122.

Winograd, T. & Flores, F. (1986). *Understanding Computers and Cognition.* Norwood, NJ: Ablex.

Zeisel, J. (1981). *Inquiry by Design: Tools for Environment-Behavior Research.* Cambridge, UK: Cambridge University Press.

Part V

Education, Training and Professional Development

16

Conceptual Issues in Environmental Information Education and Training

Introduction

What is the rationale for singling out the environmental knowledge field for special attention by educators and researchers? It might be because in any scientific discipline there must be a conceptual foundation upon which the principles of theoretical education are built. Conversely, in any professional practice there must be a philosophical foundation upon which experience and competency are built. In education for environmental information work, these two strains merge and present a unique challenge.

The purpose of this brief presentation is to review conceptual issues inherent to this challenge. The assumption underlying the review is that in environmental management, where many disciplines and fields of practice contribute to the information base, the information professions have to reinvent their role in order to become proactive. The rhetoric, so abundant today, must be stripped away so that questions that plague the information policy and dissemination process can be addressed.

Information science demands, above all, three human qualities: The creativity of the innovator, the realism of the economist, and the humility of the philosopher. There are few fields where the complexity of problem solving is as prevailing as in environmental information work. Changes are rapid, societal interests are contradictory, and scientific and professional responses must be prompt and unfailingly accurate. Indeed, environmental information management needs bold creativity to construct a theoretical foundation, keen realism to assess the appropriateness of services for the information need situations of people, and the humility of wisdom to face the limitations of any one discipline, any one economic sector, and any one country managing this complexity alone.

Critical Relationships

International environmental policies hinge mostly on the relationship of sustainable development, technological and social innovation, environmental risks, and the quality of human life (Figure 16.1). To have adequate information and data to measure the level of balance or imbalance between these four dimensions is essential for a country's environmental planning. These values, however, can be interpreted only in the context of the culture which influences people's perceptions and expectations (Wolfgang 1979). Information that emanates from research, community advocacy, and learning about environmental changes is shaped by cultural factors. In every country, education and training programs are needed for information professionals who can fit technological and research solutions to culturally determined environmental problems and knowledge needs.

International educational planning rests on the fulfillment of certain prerequisites which enable educational policy makers to take into account diverse, sometimes contradictory, human and cultural needs (Butlin 1981). One of the most important requirements for coordinated global planning for the information workforce is the assessment of specialized career needs in the framework of cultural, social, economic, and political realities. In many cases, information workers trained in countries other than their own are exposed to theories and skills which have little or no applicability in their own professional settings. Increased cooperative planning can be expected to ameliorate this situation.

Another factor affecting educational planning consists of those characteristics of environmental information transfer that require special attention in curriculum development. Usually we divide learning objectives for courses and workshops into acquiring (1) conceptual understanding, (2) areas of competency, and (3) specific skills. This paper covers only the first category which is dominated by a great richness of interdisciplinary themes describing the characteristic features of envi-

Figure 16.1
Life-Long Learning

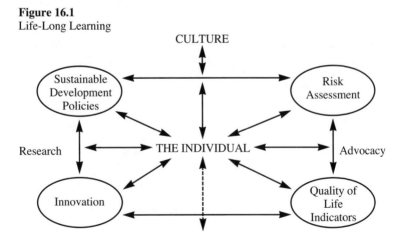

ronmental information. These themes are indispensable for the understanding of environmental information needs, and form the foundation for competencies and skills.

Main Themes for the Curriculum

Environmental policy issues, including data and information use for planning, management, and assessment, fall into three groups:

(1) *Global issues* include such examples as pesticide residues due to foreign agricultural technology or changes in climatic patterns.
(2) *Regional and national issues* may be concerned with river development and protection, decertification, and transnational air pollution.
(3) *Local issues* are growing in importance as more and more community groups take the initiative to halt the indiscriminate exploitation of natural resources.

Problems of the human environment originate in many sources including poverty, climatic conditions, and ignorance of ecological fragility (Critchfield 1981). All problems, interventions, and preventive measures are interrelated, and thus information requirements and queries are multifaceted, in need of analysis and the ability to relate unlike ideas to each other.

The knowledge base of environmental policies may be envisioned in three dimensions (Figure 16.2). These are (1) the areas of environmental problems, research, and policies (atmosphere and climate, land use and misuse, wastes), (2) different aspects of each problem area (theories, legislation, measurements), and (3) institutional experience and knowledge pools (international NGOs, multinational corporations, university departments). This approach helps the student of environmental policies to expand thinking and exploration into three directions, with more dimensions added as discovered.

Information and data requirements change from country to country and are determined by the forces of nature, the relationship between development and environment, political and social priorities, level of technology use, economic conditions, and other factors. For example, the World Bank's Office of Environmental Affairs reported that tropical countries are more vulnerable to environmental degradation than developing countries in the temperate zones. The same report warned that under conditions of poverty, environmental changes (e.g. over-grazing, erosion, deforestation, surface water pollution, toxic substances, vector population in stagnant irrigation areas) endanger not merely the quality of life but life itself (The World Bank 1979).

Environmental data and information resources include a wide range of quantitative and qualitative tools generated by:

- *environmental assessment* (e.g. monitoring, evaluation and review, sector-specific research, research utilization and dissemination),
- *environmental management* (e.g. planning, financing, legal aspects, conservation, development, technology transfer),
- *environmental education* (e.g. special, technical, public, formal and informal), and

Figure 16.2
THE KNOWLEDGE BASE OF ENVIRONMENTAL POLICIES

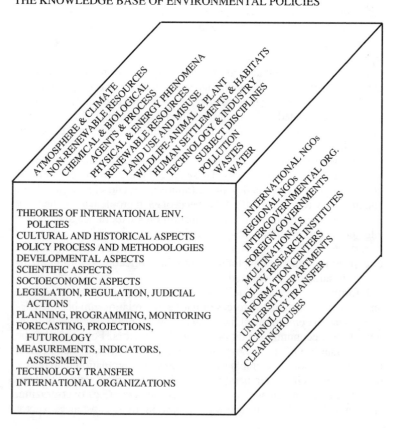

- *environmental communication* (e.g. literature, polemics, mass media, visual and performing arts, advertisement for tourism museums and culture centers).

Environmental literature is culture-bound. Societal and individual attitudes toward environmental issues are often determined by tradition, value-orientation, beliefs and customs. Reviews need to distinguish opinion-literature from scientific and technical information (Beres and Targ 1975).

The measurement and comparison of various levels of environmental deterioration present a formidable problem. Length of time, degree of severity, reversibility, and social impact combine to render environmental problems hard to quantify. Linkages to health, housing, work and other conditions prompted national governments, academic institutions and international organizations to experiment with the construction of quality-of-life indicators (Hyman 1981).

Access to domestic and international legal, regulatory, judicial and treaty information is a high priority need (Emerging . . . 1981). Sources on the relationship of economic measures (subsidies, charges, tax incentives) to governmental regulations on the one hand, and to market structures on the other, are especially difficult to identify and interpret.

Key Roles

At the present, in most countries environmental information work is not a full-time responsibility, and it must be skillfully integrated with the entire range of information activities and specialties (O'Hare 1980, Schoenfeld 1981). However, as governments in developing countries strive to make industrialization and environmental management more compatible, there is a need to begin long-range planning for programs, curricula and workshops to meet the following anticipated needs:

Increasingly, *environmental policy makers* will be required who have an understanding of environmental information as a national resource. High-level seminars will need to be organized jointly with academic programs of public administration to orient decision makers concerning the role of the environmental information infrastructure in relation to environmental law, economics, politics, sociology and technology assessment (Mann 1979). Policy makers need to develop more sensitivity to differing needs for machine-intensive or labor-intensive information systems in developing countries.

There is a growing role for *environmental information management* that encompasses information need assessment, planning, system design, implementation and evaluation. Information managers will increasingly benefit from skills in constructing information sharing networks among specialists, institutions, environmental research centers, information systems and libraries. Interaction among managers now often includes the exchange of information about the location and availability of data sets.

We need to come to some imaginative agreement concerning the role of *information liaison officers and counselors* who act as intermediaries between the user and the whole range of interdisciplinary information resources. Currently our understanding of the theoretic foundations of the intermediary role is fragmentary. Intermediaries in environmental information services will have to be cognizant of economic trends and international political relationships, environmental assessment methodologies and international sources of indicators. The information content of sources and systems will have to be "translated" for users at different levels, and often it will have to be condensed in order to transmit it through human resource networks.

The function of enabling people to learn, to make choices, and to interact with others, is not unique to information professionals. Other kinds of intermediaries, each perceiving and interpreting the world in a different way, include the scientist, the environmental interpreter, the writer, the actor, and the educator (Figure 16.3). Information intermediaries need to identify with the vision and creative imagination undergirding all these human interaction roles.

There is a growing role of importance for *educators* in environmental information use. The new generation of educators in information science and management will have to develop innovative courses for interdisciplinary knowledge, and will have to use available technology for new applications. We can anticipate a growing need for education and training in the use and interpretation of environmental data as well as data for risk assessment.

New or strengthened roles in *information science research* will need to be developed in regard to environmental information. Quantitative and qualitative methodologies complementing each other would assure more reliable data on information needs and use patterns. But technical skills in research will not suffice. The ability to identify and conceptualize research problems will be needed as well as the capacity to work in interdisciplinary research teams and write lucid research reports. Programs will be needed also for information scientists who synthesize research results in several disciplines, extract findings relevant to international environmental decisions, and disseminate this information to policy makers and practitioners in the appropriate media and form.

Figure 16.3
COGNITIVE INTERMEDIARY ROLES

SCIENTIST	EDUCATOR	WRITER	ACTOR	ENVIRONMENTAL INTERPRETER	INFORMATION INTERMEDIARY
Interprets observations of the world	Interprets experience and the written word	Interprets experience and observations	Interprets the written word	Interprets the environment	Interprets data and information
into **data information knowledge meanings**	into **information** and **meanings**	into **written word** and **meanings**	into **experience** and **meanings**	into **perceptions** and **meanings**	into **information knowledge** and **meanings**

Conclusion

These are only tentative outlines of some of the educational and training requirements we might see emerging in the near future, forming but one step toward meeting anticipated challenges. Future needs for information workforce development include specialized work areas emerging in industrial companies, research institutes and government agencies. These needs call for an intensified exchange of ideas among educators and researchers who are focusing on the future availability and usefulness of environmental information.

References

Beres, L.R. & Targ, H.R. (1975). *Planning Alternative World Futures: Values, Methods and Models*. New York, NY: Praeger.

Butlin, J.A. ed. (1981). *Economics of Environmental and Natural Resources Policy*. Boulder, CO: Westview Press.

Critchfield, R. (1981). *Villages*. Garden City, NY: Anchor/Doubleday.

Emerging international environmental law. (1981). *Stanford Journal of International Law,* 17(2), 229–412.

Hyman, E. (1981). Uses, validity, and reliability of perceived environmental quality indicators. *Social Indicators Research,* 9(1), 85–110.

Mann, D.E. ed. (1979). *Environmental Policy Formation: The Impact of Values, Ideology and Standards*. Lexington, KY: Lexington Books.

O'Hare, M. (1980). Improving the use of information in environmental decision making. *[Environmental Impact Assessment] EIA Review,* 1(3), 229–250.

Schoenfeld, C. (1981). Educating for integrated resource management. *The Environmentalist,* 1, 117–122.

Wolfgang, M.E. ed. (1979). The environment and the quality of life: A world view. *Annals of the American Academy of Political and Social Science,* 444, 1–127.

The World Bank. (1979). *Environment and Development*. Washington, DC: The World Bank.

17

Informatics, Technology, and Education

Introduction

"Development must be seen within the context of each nation's goals, values and aspirations. The origin of many present problems faced by African countries can be traced to their failure to heed this essential lesson" (Obudho and Salau 1979). These words, written almost a decade ago, still sound somber but less ominous. Policy makers in Africa today are thinking in terms of national identity, leadership and telecommunications as indispensable elements of economic growth. Development is the effective integration of economic, technological, and social changes into the cultural patterns of society. The effectiveness of integration depends on factors that have come into focus only recently:

- Economic growth measured by improvements in the life of the entire population rather than in the life of certain population groups
- Scientific advances in research that came forth as the results of indigenous creativity, and, at the same time, are in the mainstream of the international flow of scholarship (Bell 1984)
- Technological strength based on indigenous productivity rather than on the continuous importation of foreign goods and processes
- Physical, institutional and telecommunication infrastructures based on an assessment of national requirements
- Policies that anticipate future conditions and needs in human and natural resources
- A view of development as a learning process that allows the simultaneous creation and testing of new knowledge, dissemination mechanisms and applications (Soedjatmoko 1985)
- Strategies designed to build national capacity for international cooperation, in order to reduce dependency relations with industrialized countries.

The changes introduced by development are both qualitative and quantitative, and affect the entire range of individual and societal activities. Each society, and within each society each subculture, deals with transformations in its own way. Drastic and abrupt implanting of foreign constructs of thought and lifestyle may evoke neotraditionalist reactions. On the other hand, attempts to thwart change result in uneven and slow development or stagnation. In respect to informatics, Elmandjra (1985, p. 3) suggests that:

> Culture is by definition dynamic and any culture which does not deal actively and consciously with change is destined to disappear. The best way to protect cultural identity . . . is by making culture one of the key motors of the development process and by encouraging an endogenous and creative use of the new information technologies.

Informatics denotes the technological processes and products of creating, supplying, using, and applying information—that is, both the supply and demand (user) sides of the electronic information economy. The use of "informatics" synonymously with "information technology," often noted in the literature, is oversimplified and incorrect. The concept of informatics, as expressed in the activities of the Intergovernmental Bureau of Informatics (IBI) and other policy-oriented agencies, is much broader than the concept of information technology. As one observer of international communications formulated it, informatics includes "the organization of the equipment for the new information services: Marketing, investment, research, manufacturing which results in a society being provided with the means to collect and use information" (Smith 1980, p. 126).

In each country, the relationship of informatics, technology and development is defined either by the presence of information policies or by the lack of them. The characteristics of the relationship range from gradual and coordinated evolution through haphazard spurts of legislation and regulations to a chaotic state of ambiguous information use and misuse. The establishment of productive links between informatics, technology and development plans is based on subjective and political perceptions. This is the personal domain of policy making. How these links are forged and maintained is a question of group strategies. This is the institutional domain of policy information. Personal and institutional patterns of information development can be brought together only by ongoing communication between politicians, scientists, industry leaders, technology innovators, and catalysts of informatics.

This paper will discuss (1) the characteristics of information as commodity, (2) the process of informing, (3) research on informatics, (4) education for informatics, (5) information policies, and (6) an idea sharing network in support of education programs in developing countries.

Information as Commodity

The concepts and approaches which have contributed to our understanding of informatics have developed in a fragmented way. Research has been carried out in several disciplines and interdisciplinary fields. The diversity of assumptions and definitions frequently acts as a deterrent to the international utilization of research results produced in different countries.

The nature and function of information may be perceived in many ways, but currently the two most frequently applied interpretations of its role in economic growth and technological progress are information as a commodity and information as a culturally determined process. Information becomes productive when it forms a link in the knowledge acquisition chain, that is, when data are organized and processed for use as information, and thus form the basis for knowledge.

In the 1960s and early 1970s several economists became preoccupied with the statistical representation of information activities in the nation, and with constructing models of the market-related behavior of information and knowledge in the firm. The emphasis was on expanding economic rather than information theory (Lamberton 1971, p. 10). Information analysis was constructed upon economic assumptions about choice and uncertainty, a conceptual framework in which information was treated as content-free message and could be quantified. However, the decisive importance of the content of information could not be denied for long. Jenner (1971, p. 87), who studied information in pure or perfect competition (a case when no firm is assumed to be able to control the conditions under which a new product reaches the market), stated that "a product that has been created through human effort may be said to have a certain information content."

Simon (1964, p. 94) suggested that machines and equipment were external evidences of a technology rather than the real core. Subsequently researchers and policy makers came to recognize the content of information as the "core of technology" whether the content was scientific, technological, market-related, or social intelligence.

The most persuasive expression of considering information and knowledge to be the central elements in a technology is found in studies on international technology transfer. Marton (1986, pp. 4–5) referred to what is known as embodied technology: "Where technological knowledge is embodied in machinery and equipment, information on machinery operations would itself constitute transfer of operational technology." Such "packages" contain techniques and specialized know-how necessary for developing products or services: Drawings, blueprints, formulas, patents, and managerial expertise (Lall 1982, pp. 11–12). Recipient firms in developing countries may "unbundle" or "unpackage" imported technology, analyze its elements, and substitute local experience and skills for foreign methods. Unbundling may take place in any of the industrial technology importation processes such as turnkey projects, licensing, and consulting.

The rise and convergence of the computational and telecommunication industries vastly increased the commercial value of the "core of technology," or information and knowledge. The expanding parameters of competition in the informatics market can be captured and measured only inadequately. Changes in technologies and applications are so rapid that a common framework for the statistical investigation of all information, electronics, and telecommunications activities will be outdated as soon as it is established (Organization . . . 1981).

The imbalance in technology and knowledge production between the developing and the industrialized areas of the world led to an intensifying political struggle concerning the flows of electronic data and information across national borders as well as the barriers erected by protectionist measures. These events signalled to many governments in developing countries the need for investment in human capital, research and development, and efforts towards the establishment of indigenous computer and telecommunication industries. South-to-South technology transfer arrangements, and the formulation of national information policies became political priorities (United Nations 1985, Singer 1982). By the early 1980s it was widely believed that informatics, or the application of information to economic, social and political problems, was bringing to developing countries the conceptual tools and mechanisms for the acceleration of this trend.

The Process of Informing

The assumption underlying the second major aspect of information planning is that disjointed and disorganized data become information only when accessible at the level, and in the form, quantity and communication mode most appropriate to the particular information seeking situation of the user. Much has been written about the process of informing (oneself or others) in the literatures of scientific research, decision making, and interpersonal communication. In the Western world, the emphasis has been on formal information transmittal from source to user or audience by human or electronic intermediaries. The information content is usually assumed to be instructive or at least informative, and it is expected to contribute to the recipient's knowledge or know-how. However, the process of informing takes place also in countless other situations.

One example of the critical role of the informing process is the development project. Effective project planning, implementation and evaluation skills are required whenever a new technical aid project is being considered by a national or provincial government. International sponsoring agencies require complex plans and reports supported by data. In the 1970s, management information systems (MISs) promised to solve many of the data processing problems. "Critical decision categories" within a project were identified as (a) development objectives including indicators of success, (b) project components, (c) management arrangements, and (d) resource commitments (Weisel and Mickelwait 1978).

By the end of the 1970s, disillusionment began to set in. The decision support that project managers received from MISs was criticized for unnecessary complexity, lack of selectivity in data collection, and emphasis on efficiency rather than on effective decisions. An analysis of case studies pointed to two predominant problems with MISs in rural development projects: Data overload and lack of feedback to rural populations from whom the data were collected (Mickelwait et al. 1978). Most observers agreed that where communication with users was concerned, MISs had many problems, although under skilled management these systems have contributed to project performance.

The informing process has also been hampered by uneven, and often very poor, use of research-generated knowledge in developing countries (Guha 1985). In pursuing short-term economic and social goals which presuppose fast returns on investments, it is critical to disseminate the findings of researchers to the fields of application as rapidly as possible. In developing countries, even basic researchers are more aware of the necessity of communicating results than most of their counterparts in more affluent societies. Studies provide ample evidence that knowledge utilization is most often seen as a one-way process from the vantage point of either the researcher (production, interpretation, dissemination, evaluation) or the research user (search, finding, application, implementation) (Beyer and Trice 1982, Gerstenfeld and Wortzel 1977). Feedback from practitioner or policy maker is rare, and it exists mainly in the framework of special conferences or symposia. However, a link is still missing from most models, even if they represent two-way or networking processes: The acceptance of information and/or knowledge by the recipient.

Information acceptance is based on a relationship between disseminator and user that is characterized by trust and interaction. In many countries, the mental distance between the researcher and the practitioner in education, agriculture, health and social care or entrepreneurship is aggravated by the fact that the scientist has often been educated in a foreign country and has a communication style different from that of the practitioner. Due to advances in disciplines as well as in society at large, both the professional knowledge gap and the generation gap represent hindrances in communication. Information sharing through workshops and newsletters can build the kind of trust that contributes to the acceptance and use of information.

The same need exists in extension services. Information dissemination to farmers, enterprises and distant learners is an important activity in developing countries. Educators planning and conducting non-formal education programs report a wide range of experiences with participants. In countries where strong indigenous social structures and oral tradition exist, a culture-based approach to education and training and the use of folk theatre, puppet shows, poetry and other traditional media tend to succeed more than foreign-produced instructional technology (Kidd and Colletta 1980).

Research on international technology transfer and assessment provides useful clues for a better understanding of the information process in the firm. In developing countries clarity of concepts is particularly important because there are fewer research institutes and industrial research units to experiment with different interpretation than in the West. Bell (1984, p. 188) distinguishes between the flow of information (for example feedback about a system's performance) and the flow of knowledge (how to affect change in the system). After transferred technology is introduced, six different kinds of information and knowledge processes are identified in the firm (Bell 1984, pp. 190–191):

- Learning by completing tasks and operating systems ("learning by doing")
- Learning by introducing changes (better understanding the form and principles of the technology)
- Using system performance feedback (generating, recording, reviewing, interpreting the experience)
- Learning by training (attending in-house or external programs)
- Learning by hiring (acquiring "ready-made technology" through new employees or consultants)
- Learning by searching for information about improvement practices in other firms (scanning the external environment).

Technology adaptation specialists, similarly to information professionals, have difficulty assessing the contribution of information and knowledge flows to change in the performance of the firm. Bell (1984, p. 195) notes that "the extent to which a flow of information adds to the change-capacity of a firm depends on the prior availability of skills and knowledge to analyze and interpret the information generated." Bell (1984, pp. 200–201) draws the following conclusions from his study: Multifirm comparisons are needed to even approximate evaluation of the connection between the firm's learning and its performance. Local knowledge systems need to be examined to identify their ways to adapt technology to development needs. These recommendations have direct implications for research on the informing process and the process's connection to development.

We have seen that information as a commodity is a key element in development. However, information must be organized for use and transmitted by an informing process that depends mainly on communication and trust.

Research on Informatics

One of the societal capabilities that is said to contribute to the development of technology is indigenous research (United Nations 1979). If informatics were expected to accelerate progress, research on its characteristics, its relationship to educational and communication technology and its potential social impact, is an essential activity. But data for informatics assessment and forecasting are as difficult to obtain as data for social assessment and forecasting. Problems of social measurements in other contexts have been identified by development specialists (Hicks 1982, Pearce-Batten 1980).

The construction and use of indicators is seen as both a conceptual and a methodological problem. The choice of criteria for measuring social (or information-related) conditions and expectations is surrounded by controversy about assumptions (Griffin 1986). How do we define information equity, free-flow, access or information sharing? Interpretations change from situation to situation, and even internationally standardized terms may fail when used in a different culture.

There are convincing conceptual constructs which underscore the influence of culture on field research. Bartee (1973) developed a "problem-solving chronology" in four phases: (1) Personalization or individual problem solving, (2) collaboration or data exchange and joint use, (3) institutionalization or problem-related decision making in organizations, and (4) socialization or the introduction of changes in social attitudes and norms. To these processes, Bartee added diffusion. Each of these dimensions of problem solving requires an understanding of assumptions in the context of a culture. In research on informatics and technology, the need for taking the social and cultural environment of users into account is further heightened by the dominant role of the informing process. We are thus led to the conclusion that investigations of informatics-related questions in a developing country should be conducted by indigenous researchers rather than consultants. National information policies must take this necessity into consideration and support resource allocations for the development of domestic research capability.

Research approaches have been classified into "basic" and "applied," which is another source of difficulty whenever investigators try to fit their studies into one or the other category. Two other modes of conducting experimentation may be more applicable to social research in developing countries and should be considered by information scientists seeking to better understand the social impact of new technologies. Action research is effective especially when researchers advocate on behalf of their subjects and want to return the benefits of the results to them (Stromquish 1984). Problem-focused research, which originated in Europe but has considerable potential for developing countries, is the approach "where questions of theory and utility mingle in varying proportions. In this area, the desire for knowledge is to a certain extent linked with the desire for action" (Bie 1970).

Once a basic conceptual framework is identified and agreed upon by researchers and policy makers, assumptions and interpretations which are quite different in different countries can be clarified. The role of governmental or external financing might influence the investigation. The shortage of high-quality researchers may threaten all efforts to get a project under way. However, without recognizing that research on the impact of informatics is a national resource, information technology may not become integrated with the country's overall development goals.

Education for Informatics

Creativity is the most precious resource for development. Without it, a society can become neither productive nor self-reliant. Davies (1967) refers to the role of accident, scientific wild-catting, and serendipity in the innovation process as some of the expressions of creativity. Leadership and policies are needed to recognize and nurture creative talent and to apply it to national needs. What is the balance between risk-taking through responsiveness to new ideas and the continuity essential for the stability of society? Probably the only way to approach an answer, upon which both humanistic and technocratic thinkers can agree, is through education and training. Knowledge may be defined as the fusion of information, intuition and experience. This view of knowledge places a great responsibility on national planners and educators, because it professes that the development of human resources (formal and nonformal education and training) should be assisted by information flows to people from a multiplicity of innovative and traditional sources and information flows among people. Indeed, information and knowledge in this context become the powerful conduits of imagination, participation in policy processes, and action.

Learning and informatics are inseparable. However, it has been stated that "in no other area is the dependency of the Third World as great as in that of information; and in no other field is the concept of self-reliance so neglected" (Elmandjra 1985, p. 4). Low-economy countries suffer also from shortages in analytic and technical skills. Not surprisingly, education, together with indigenous research, has risen to join technological growth as national goals. Therefore, it is necessary "to relate the whole system of education at all levels to the concrete problems of the country" (Singer 1982, p. 88).

In rapidly changing fields of professional practice, the roles of practitioners tend to diversify to the extent that it is increasingly difficult to perceive the original goals of the profession. People who have developed the habit of exchanging and using information are the ones who usually span boundaries of specialization. In countries with a well-developed information infrastructure, it is not unusual to see information scientists, managers and technologists attending the same professional meetings. Information professionals who can link systems and, more importantly, human resources into networks, are widely sought. And when extreme specialization results in fragmentation, it is professional education that provides the mental discipline and social context for self-analysis and clarification.

In countries where information infrastructures are at the beginning of development, information handling activities and roles are less multifarious. At this stage, national information policies can bring coordination into play and assure the planned development of the workforce. Low-income countries are severely hindered in this by resource constraints, lack of educational opportunities, a shortage of teachers and teaching materials, reluctance to take the risks associated with educational innovation and brain drain. However, in some countries, even these acute problems have been overcome by creativity and determination (Ghosh 1984). With the assistance of international organizations, curriculum revision and the development of new programs are under way in many places. Activities include the assessment of workforce requirements, the design of new programs; the training of information workers at different levels through workshops; the formulation of new standards for qualification and testing; coordination for resource sharing; and the organization of regional conferences. Professional preparation is being planned for several roles in the information workforce, for example:

Researchers in information science, informatics and telematics
Planners and managers
Systems analysts
Data processors
Intermediaries for information retrieval, analysis and reference
Intermediaries for repackaging information for popular dissemination
Educators and trainers
Educational administrators
Paraprofessionals
Specialized technicians.

Continuing education is of utmost importance to enable current information personnel to deal competently with increasing managerial and technological responsibilities. Ajuogu (1981, p. 76) suggested that "organizations need to review their development needs occasionally in order to provide their managers with more fundamental and more analytically based training that would help them to continue to learn throughout their career path." This is true also for information managers.

Special courses are required in the areas of the training of trainers; management, planning and marketing; assessing, acquiring and using new technology; research methodologies; dissemination and extension; information policies; and information entrepreneurship. The information professions need to develop a capacity to become more relevant to national goals. But how can the contributions of information work to development be measured? The answer might lie in the analysis of value-added processes in solving information problems, database development, information repackaging, training in new technology, and other activities in order to demonstrate the outcome of information work in terms of productivity. However, in view of human development goals, probably the most important area of training and continuing education is in information dissemination to policy makers, small enterprises, and rural areas.

Information Policies

Following rounds of debates at international and regional conferences, technology and knowledge transfer became the key issues at the United Nations Conference on Science and Technology for Development (UNCSTD) held in Vienna in 1979. Five main concerns were incorporated in the recommendations: Policies, infrastructure, development, information utilization and global networking. A framework for information policies was to be formed by cooperative action. The Intergovernmental Committee on Science and Technology for Development has selected only information systems for science and technology for examination by an international panel (United Nations 1985). This framework suggested for information policies strikes us today as too narrow and restrictive. It has become obvious that without equal emphasis on information and data systems for science, technology, and social development, the information infrastructure provides an unbalanced planning base (United Nations Educational . . . 1985, Solomon 1985).

The cooperation of government officials, industry leaders, and information scientists needs a framework broad enough to accommodate policy issues arising from the economic and political aspects of telecommunications and computer networks. The principles of national autonomy and of unhindered transnational information exchange are in conflict. There is evidence that the current situation is only the beginning of international tensions in informatics. Jussawalla (1985) projected that the equitable dissemination of information will become as serious a problem for policy makers as the equitable distribution of income.

With the recognition that the scope and objectives of national information policies vary from country to country, a preliminary framework can bring together those themes which most often appear in national plans, statements and memoranda. Information policies are generally expected to aim at the following functions:

- Coordinate or integrate information and data transfer, informatics and telecommunication (telematics) policies
- Create economic incentives to produce information and knowledge applicable to national development
- Guide national informatics and telematics plans which are based on current and anticipated economic and social objectives as well as on cultural heritage
- Provide for resource allocations, infrastructure development and the coordination of all types of information resources in terms of their management and user services
- Establish a framework for the dissemination, repackaging and utilization of information
- Provide resources for research on information-related needs and problems and for education and training at all levels
- Develop a framework for the economic valuation of information and information work and for the transfer and indigenous production of informatics technologies
- Deal with questions of access to information, privacy, intellectual property rights, and other problems heightened by the use of informatics technologies
- Create mechanisms for the assessment of different informatics technologies in the context of the country's requirements; develop priorities for technology selection use and popularization
- Establish a framework, based on economic, cultural and legal considerations, for participation in international informatics relationships.

A Network for Informatics Education

When a planner, manager, researcher, educator or other worker needs international information, an overview of available resources is almost always impossible. The fragmentation of the information transfer process has led to informal information sharing among peers located in different countries. "Informal information sharing" refers to the exchange of scientific papers, reports, educational tools, data files, and other materials that are normally not available through libraries. A growing number of specialized information clearinghouses around the world serve as the exchange points for professional cooperation in resource sharing. Above all, such networks enable educators in the field of informatics to exchange ideas and new initiatives.

Based on discussions with informatics educators in a large number of countries, the Education and Training Committee of the International Federation of Documentation (FID/ET) has developed a nonelectronic network of informatics educators and researchers in developing countries. Members of the network are sending education and training materials to the Clearinghouse of the committee, to be used as resources when information queries are received. Since the Clearinghouse emphasizes service to developing countries, a project designed to change the traditional communication mode into an electronic network has begun to explore a new mode of development assistance by linking informatics education programs in developing countries with international professional organizations and clearinghouses.

The project represents Distance Technical Assistance (DTA), a term coined at the FID/ET Clearinghouse. This is a specific form of professional cooperation that provides information to educators and researchers through the personalized service of the Clearinghouse. The term has been patterned on distance education (Sewart et al. 1983, p. 8). The objective is to bridge the gap between informatics education programs in developing and industrialized areas. Distance Technical Assistance is needed in the following areas:

- *Curriculum* revision and *instruction;* the organization of continuing education programs; the acquisition of appropriate teaching materials and evaluation tools
- Educational *administration* and policy formulation; development of the information work force; planning and evaluation; funding sources
- Growth of an indigenous *research* sector; research applicable to educational improvements; dissemination methods
- *Professional developments;* standardization of degrees, qualifications and measurements; professional communications
- The accumulation of *experience* and "know-how" that may be found in reports, studies, analyses, test models, software and other tools, not available through the formal literature

- The choice of *informatics technology including hardware, software, assessment methods,* application modes, procedures, etc.

The project's goal is the testing of the feasibility and usefulness of Distance Technical Assistance and knowledge sharing through a network. Technological limitations present no barriers to active participation. For each institution, the Clearinghouse and its network will use the communication mode (electronic or traditional) most appropriate to the given environment.

Conclusion

This paper described trends and problems in the relationship of informatics, technology, and education in the context of development. Development is intervention in social patterns, and informatics can facilitate or hinder effective intervention. To fully appreciate this key function of informatics, current views of information as a commodity and as a process have been reviewed. Each of these aspects of informatics affects the utilization of information resources and international cooperation. Research should test whether a network for peer information sharing can assist information research, education/training and policy making in developing countries. As Davies (1967, p. 320) suggested, we need a "symbiotic advancement of learning and the development of the spirit of open-ended inquiry."

References

Ajuogu, M.O. (1981). Technology dynamics in lifelong education and development of managers in developing economies. *International Review of Administrative Sciences,* 47(1), 71–76.

Bartee, E.M. (1973). A holistic view of problem solving. *Management Science.* Part 1, 20(4), 439–448.

Bell, M. (1984). " 'Learning' and the accumulation of industrial technological capacity in developing countries." In Fransman, M. & King, K. eds. *Technological Capability in the Third World,* 187–209. New York, NY: St. Martin's Press.

Beyer, J.M. & Trice, H.M. (1982). The utilization process: A conceptual framework and synthesis of empirical findings. *Administrative Science Quarterly,* 27, 591–622.

Bie, P. de. (1970). "Problem-focused research." In United Nations

Educational, Scientific and Cultural Organization. *Main Trends of Research in the Social and Human Sciences.* Part I, 578–644. Paris, France: United Nations Educational, Scientific and Cultural Organization.

Davies, D. (1967). "A scarce resource called curiosity." In Lamberton, D.M. ed. *Economics of Information and Knowledge,* 83–108. Harmondsworth, Middlesex, UK: Penguin Books, Ltd.

Elmandjra, M. (1985). Communication, informatics and development. *Development, Seeds of Change,* 1, 3–5.

Gerstenfeld, A. & Wortzel, L.H. (1977). Strategies for innovation in developing countries. *Sloan Management Review,* 19(1), 57–68.

Ghosh, P.K. ed. (1984). *Appropriate Technology in Third World Development.* Westport, CT: Greenwood Press.

Griffin, J. (1986). *Well-Being: Its Meaning, Measurement, and Moral Importance.* Oxford, UK: Oxford University Press.

Guha, B. (1985). (1985). *Study of the Language Barrier in the Production, Dissemination, and Use of Scientific and Technical Information with Special Reference to the Problems of Developing Countries.* Paris, France: United Nations Educational, Scientific and Cultural Organization.

Hicks, N.L. (1982). Sector priorities in meeting basic needs: Some statistical evidence. *World Development,* 10(6), 489–499.

Jenner, R.A. (1971). "An information version of pure competition." In Lamberton, D.M. ed. *Economics of Information and Knowledge,* 83–108. Harmondsworth, Middlesex, UK: Penguin Books, Ltd.

Jussawalla, M. (1985). International telecommunication policies. *Development,* 1, 64–66.

Kidd, R. & Colletta, N.J., eds. (1980). *Tradition for Development, Indigenous Structures and Folk Media in Non-Formal Education.* Bonn, Germany: German Foundation for International Development.

Korten, D.C. (1980). Community organization and rural development: A learning process approach. *Public Administration Review,* 40(5), 480–511.

Lall, S. (1982). *Developing Countries as Exporters of Technology: A First Look at the Indian Experience.* London, UK: The Macmillan Press.

Lamberton, D.M. ed. (1971). *Economics of information and knowledge.* Harmondsworth, Middlesex, UK: Penguin Books, Ltd.

Marton, K. (1986). *Multinationals, Technology, and Industrialization.* Lexington, MA: D.C. Heath & Co.

Mickelwait, D.R. et al. (1978). *Information for Decision Making in Rural Development.* Washington, DC: Development Alternatives, Inc. 2 vols.

Obudho, R.A. & Salau, A.T. (1979). Development and planning in Africa in the 1970s. *African Urban Studies,* 4, 1–5 (New series).

Organization for Economic Cooperation and Development. (1981). *Information Activities, Electronics and Telecommunication Technologies.* Paris, France: OECD. 2 vols.

Pearce-Batten, A. (1980). New measures of development. *Development Digest,* 18(1), 75–94.

Sewart, D. (1983). *Distance Education: International Perspectives.* London, UK: Croom Helm.

Simon, H.A. (1964). "Decision making as an economic resource." In Seltzer, L.H. ed. *New Horizons for Economic Progress,* 69–95. Detroit, MI: Wayne State University Press.

Singer, H. (1982). *Technologies for Basic Needs.* Geneva, Switzerland: International Labour Office.

Smith, A. (1980). *The Geopolitics of Information: How Western Culture Dominates the World.* Oxford, UK: Oxford University Press.

Soedjatmoko. (1985). Alienation or creation in informatics—is there a choice? *Development,* 1, 15–16.

Solomon, E.S. (1985). *Social Science Methods, Decision Making and Development Planning.* Paris, France: United Nations Educational, Scientific and Cultural Organization (Socioeconomic Studies 8).

Stromquish, N. (1984). Action-research, a new sociological approach in developing countries. *The IDRC Reports (International Development Research Centre),* 13(3), 24–25.

United Nations. (1985). *Scientific and Technological Information for Development. Proceedings of the Ad-hoc Panel of Experts on Information Systems for Science and Technology for Development, Rome, 1985.* New York, NY: UN.

United Nations Department of International Economic and Social Affairs. (1979). *Improving Social Statistics in Developing Countries: Conceptual Framework and Methods.* New York, NY: UN (Studies in Methods, Series F. No. 25).

United Nations Educational, Scientific and Cultural Organization. (1985). *Applicability of Indicators of Socioeconomic Change for Development Planning.* Paris, France: United Nations Educational, Scientific and Cultural Organization (Socioeconomic Studies 7).

Weisel, P.F. & Mickelwait, D.R. (1978). *Designing Rural Development Projects: An Approach.* Washington, DC: Development Alternatives, Inc.

18

The Management of Innovation
as an Integrating Theme in the Curriculum
for Industrial Information Officers

Background

Much has been written in recent years about the need for innovative concepts and techniques in technological development and industrial production. Interest in the factors that enhance and motivate scientific creativity has been renewed. New concerns, such as industry-university cooperation, the creation of "centers of excellence," the use of research for technological innovation, and the administration of team projects, have been added to existing themes (Child and Bate 1987; Perkins, Nieva and Lawler 1983; Shaw and Gaines 1982; Twiss 1980). The transfer of technology to developing countries in the form of products, processes, or know-how has become an intense international economic and cultural issue (Knoppers 1984, International Labor . . . 1985). Nations in various stages of economic development seek to formulate strategies that stimulate domestic projects for innovation. The tension between the private value and social benefit of inventiveness has been studied in the context of economic theory and in relation to the scientists' freedoms and limitations in research activity (Hirshleifer 1971, Kanter 1983, Nelkin 1984). Research, conferences, and massive theoretical studies have been devoted to the relationship between science, technological innovation, and economic productivity.

In this broad and open-ended field, at least three domains have direct bearing on the education of information professionals: (1) innovation management, (2) information utilization, and (3) information resource management.

Institutions everywhere have constantly been tested by economic and social stresses. Consequently, researchers and policy makers have given much attention to the management of creativity and inventiveness. Investigations into information systems that may support this management function have been widespread in a number of disciplines (Brinberg 1983, Eveland 1985, Levinson 1986, Stern 1982). This body of work has implications for industrial project management, which is often the vehicle for the innovation process. Thus, effective information systems and services in industry become an integral part of innovation management.

Levinson (1986, p. 355) argues that "while several themes have emerged from the plethora of writings in this area . . . , the most critical theme by far is the importance of effective information flow both within an organization and between the organization and key organizations in its environment." Levinson examines factors which may affect information system design.

Other research, generally referred to as information-use studies, addresses the interface between information and innovation (Wersig and Windel 1985). What information do innovative people need or use? This has been the quest implied but rarely pursued in depth in most of these investigations. Serious questions have been raised about the quality and momentum of user studies and about their relevance to the application of information to problem solving (Cronin 1981).

The vision that guided the emergence of research in knowledge utilization was both futuristic and history oriented (Boulding and Senesh 1983). Rich (1979, p. 15) states that "the notion of adapting knowledge to the needs of society dates back to the Greeks and is a theme running through much of Western thought." Controversial, yet steadily growing in significance, the conceptual area of knowledge utilization, focusing on the diverse applications of information, holds promise for information education programs in an environment where the understanding of the interaction among data, information, and knowledge is crucial. The "knowledge center" is a recent model that goes beyond knowledge utilization by merging the functions of research production and management with the training of research and development personnel in one unit of the organization (Dror and Bnaya 1984).

Before the theoretical constructs of innovation management and information use could be integrated, a third approach emerged: information resources management (IRM). Variously defined as professional practice, national-level policy, or a new paradigm for systems analysis, IRM may become all these things once it passes its formative phase. The concept and its applications have been described in legislative and regulatory documents, industrial journals, education programs, and the literature of organizations (Lytle 1986, Marchand and Horton 1986). Essentially, IRM is the management of all types of information as a national, organizational, and individual resource. Education programs entirely or partially devoted to IRM concepts and practices exist or are being developed in several countries.

Different directions in the voluminous literature are converging to support the argument that the knowledge base for industrial innovation, essential for development, can be planned and managed at the national level. In the organization, both the maintenance of creativity and the continuous search for opportunities are inseparably linked to viable information resources.

Objectives

The intent of this paper is to raise questions and stimulate discussion about international education programs for managers of information and data in organizations. Currently, "industrial information officer" is the term most widely used for this role in the international literature. The reflections below are based on the following propositions:

- Information officers in industry work in a team with the company's management in its search for new opportunities and in the planning, operation, and evaluation of innovation projects.
- The role of the industrial information officer is not one of support service but of a partner in the entire process of the enterprise.
- The information officer is responsible for the continuous assessment of the organization's information needs, systems, and resources and for the selection of the right time and opportunity for introducing changes.
- Since the management of innovation draws on a wide knowledge base, a master's level course and a series of continuing education seminars are needed to prepare industrial information officers for the previously described roles.
- To move into the front line of developments, this education program should include a research component, in order to explore the information requirements of innovation projects.

Some Definitions and Interpretations

One of the problems of understanding the intellectual and administrative mechanisms that generate innovations is that, in spite of many years of work by research programs, governments, and international agencies, basic tenets are still controversial. "The researchers in this field have been properly concerned not to make definitive statements concerning a process which is imperfectly understood and which they are unable to prove with the rigour expected in research reports" (Twiss 1980, p. xxii). Three major dimensions of innovative activity, innovation in private life, in organizations, and at the societal level, will be considered below.

Innovation in Personal Life

Because the drive to seek improvements in the human condition is part of everyday life, many people consider change, like creativity, a personal matter. In this context, the innovation process has been interpreted as self-help, including the seeking and use of information. Srinivasan (1977) proposed that in every society people need "access to opportunities" in order to better their lives, and that levels of poverty could be measured by the lack of access to opportunities. He suggested that unless a society provides organized information channels, the search for self-improvement will remain a haphazard matter favoring the educated, who are better equipped to "find out." These concepts are especially relevant to the improvement of information services in developing countries where much industrial activity takes the form of small entrepreneurship.

Equal access to education and information is one of the principles of technical assistance by international organizations. In some development projects, information is being used not only as the necessary technical support to the project team, but also as know-how. It is perceived to be one of the basic human needs of the recipient population, together with adequate food, shelter, clothing, essential services provided for the community, and freely chosen employment (Hope 1982). Information literacy thus becomes one of the major goals of development aid.

Industrial innovation in developing countries may be evident in indigenous enterprises, small industry, tourism, artisan workshops, cooperatives, and markets. Alternative technologies and techniques might be introduced in cement block production in Kenya and in shoe manufacturing in Malaysia (Bhalla 1985). Information exchanged by informal interactions may be more useful than formal systems in economies where there are many small manufacturing firms (Page 1979). Recognizing this reality, more and more technical aid providers link people and small local organizations into human resource networks in order to increase motivation and basic skills training (Kidd and Colletta 1980).

Three observations about innovation projects in developing countries seem to be justified here. First, studies of the effectiveness of technical aid have shown that neither factories nor housing developments nor manufacturing process improvements will be accepted by local populations as changes introduced in their interest unless local people are involved in project-related decisions and planning (Scott-Stevens 1987). Second, the diffusion of information creating opportunities and innovations in small enterprises often depends on kinship and social networks. Cooperatives and marketplaces, well known as information exchange points, provide connections, sources of employment, partnerships, investment opportunities, and other indirect benefits. Third, it is essential to remember that in poor countries the chances of the entrepreneur or small industry to bring about changes are often destroyed by major disasters such as drought and famine. Poverty traps people in unproductive conditions that sap their energy. Dawson (1978) saw the reluctance or inability of the poor to take risks as perhaps the greatest barrier to innovation.

Innovation in Organizations

Technological innovation in medium or large industry requires the information officer's analytic and communication skills because of the professional diversity of people—production workers, managers, engineers, researchers, and marketers—involved in a system. Organizational innovation depends mainly on creative individuals. Innovation has been defined as "the process by which problems are identified and solved, needs are met, materials are made available, and new concepts are added to society" (United States 1978, p. 4). This definition implies the interaction of ideas, people, and technologies, and views innovation as a collective problem-solving effort. Since the contribution of new concepts is intellectual production, the definition also indicates a relationship between industrial innovation and productivity.

In the industrial environment, innovation is usually understood to mean the introduction of a new process, product, or technology as distinguished from invention, defined by the U.S. Office of Technology Assessment as the development of a new idea. However, a further aspect is essential: "Innovation is more than discovery and theorizing, more than speculation and invention, and more than engineering design. For until the new know-how is incorporated into what is done, innovation has not occurred" (United States 1978, p. 5). Assuming that the activating element in the relationship between a new process and its application, or between a new product and its use is information, the question arises: Is the role of information as a link between innovation and productivity reflected in national policies?

In recent years, the formulation of national policies for the promotion of innovation and productivity has addressed mainly scientific research and technological development. Science and technology, linked to industrial R&D, have been seen by developing countries as almost the only means to rapidly modernize societies. In most cases, national policies for the establishment of research centers, the advanced education of the talented young abroad, and the development of the physical infrastructures were formed with industrial innovation in mind. The impact of information on productivity has not been determined by empirical studies.

As developing countries achieve various levels of technological capacity, policy makers find that social relationships and structures are still shaky, and the distance between the well-to-do and poor populations still exists and, in some cases, is increasing. Because economic and technical data do not explain the persistence of social ills, governments are recognizing the importance to development of such information sources as are found in social accounting, quality of life indicators, and indigenous cultural systems (United Nations . . . 1985). Data on industrial technology in transnational companies, personnel, services, and products are often processed outside of a developing country without any benefits to the home economy. International observers now refer to a new global imbalance between developing and industrialized countries: the imbalance in data production and the availability of data resources (Baark 1985, Perrin 1984).

These trends indicate that the links between innovation, productivity, and human well-being are multiple, requiring research and education that span numerous disciplines. Changes in policies will require a reassessment of information systems planning by governments and industrial organizations. Social science data that might be useful for understanding the relationship between innovation and the quality of life are dispersed and inaccessible. Improvements will be needed not only in social science data collection and organization, but also in the information professional's ability to design multidisciplinary data systems.

Innovation at the Societal Level

Another kind of innovation affecting industrial information services is a national policy change in such areas as export-import activities, raw materials, wages and prices, working conditions, environmental impact of industrial affluents, and industrial safety. In several countries, for example in Canada, government subsidy of innovation projects aims to promote private sector investment in research and development (Tarazofsky 1984). The result is usually a small and highly specialized information service that must be managed with full understanding of both governmental and industrial policies. Cooperation between industry and academic research centers is another trend that creates new patterns and relationships in information sharing (Eveland 1985). Policy changes may be prompted also by rural development needs, including special incentives, agroindustrial reform, cooperation in technology use, and by the shifts of population groups from rural areas to urban fringes (International Labor . . . 1986). It is doubtful that today's information dissemination systems can respond effectively to new requirements created by changing human conditions.

Some information officers make serious efforts to keep abreast of economic and industrial policies, laws, standards, and international agreements. This practice must be strengthened in order to enhance the information manager's ability to use external sources of policy information. Trade legislation, patent policies, or technical standards often serve as unique information sources on new production or market trends. It is generally held that the quality of information services in industry improves when the information center's goals are coordinated with the goals of the organization and with the external influences on the organization.

Dimensions of the Innovative Activity

The process of innovation or the introduction of something new in an organization's life is not as linear as one tends to think. Rather, the different aspects of the activity interact with each other and overlap to the extent that sometimes it is difficult to recognize the beginning of an idea's travel through research laboratories, industrial R & D, academic seminar rooms, government-sponsored research projects, and field testing. Designing information systems in support of innovation would be easier if the process of innovation were more predictable. As it is, information managers must depend on intensive participation in projects, communication, and negotiations within the organization and with its external environment. Innovation projects with interdisciplinary R & D teams are likely to demand more complex communication processes than do general staff interactions.

Understanding the innovation process is useful to information officers designing user-oriented information systems. Social scientists in recent decades produced several models that raised significant issues concerning the relationship between science policy and economic productivity. According to one theory that is losing influence today, the process of innovation begins with basic or applied research, the results of which lead to the development of a new device or process. This model, sometimes referred to as "science push" (a version of "technology push") was subsequently overshadowed by the theory of "market pull." Empirical studies suggested that the flow of invention moved from the identification of a need or problem in the work environment to the generation of research expected to lead to a new technology or improvement in the old. Schmookler (1966) used patent statistics to interpret technological change and concluded that economic factors such as market potential greatly influenced the production of innovations. The term "social pull" indicates a pattern of social science research demonstrating social needs and generating experimentation with new problem-solving approaches (Agnew 1980). All the above representations of the innovation process take the view that innovation activities occur in a linear, phased progression.

As a consequence of a research trend that rejected such linear models of innovation, a school of thought is emerging that seeks to support the theory of simultaneous movements of activity where economic factors, scientific knowledge, and technological or social inventiveness interact. Within this broad school of thought, however, a number of scholarly and professional disagreements exist. Levinson (1986) describes the difference between two approaches to conceptualizing innovation: Quinn's and Drucker's. Following an in-depth international study, Quinn (1985) envisioned successful innovation as a chaotic progression of events driven by "visionary individuals who often possess the technical expertise and integrative idea power" that is needed for carrying out an innovation project (Levinson 1986, p. 359). On the other hand, Drucker (1985) represented the "more rational side" and postulated that "most innovations . . . especially the successful ones, result from a conscious, purposeful search for innovation opportunities which are found only in a few situations (Levinson 1986, p. 357).

International studies on technological choices and change tend to support the interpretation of innovation as a nonlinear, nonsystematic process. Stewart (1984) divides the extensive literature of technical change into four categories: Empirical case studies, the neoclassical approach, the political economy approach, and institutional explanations. Stewart (1984, p. 93) saw as the major contribution of this theoretical and empirical work the evidence of a "multiplicity of causal factors [for innovation] and interactions between them," and urged research on this complex theme rather than on any one of its components.

Innovation Transfer

The communication of innovation-related information and experience from country to country is probably the most sensitive aspect of technology transfer. Transmission of innovation takes place when an organization or individual shares with or sells to persons in another country know-how that is either new or in the testing process. Information about evidence that the new prototype product or method had been pretested in the recipient country would be of great benefit to the industrial organization that anticipates its introduction by licensing or purchase (Calhoun and Bendekgey 1987). The literature refers to many cases in which production processes, techniques, or information systems that had been recommended by foreign consultants were inappropriate for the new user group. New technology might be too advanced or too obsolete for its intended users (Cusack 1981, Lucas and Freedman 1983). More than a few technical assistance projects have failed because of the assumption that a device or method designed for one environment will work in another culture.

What can the information community learn from the experience of "false transfers" reflected in the development literature? First, the large-scale innovation projects of the past attracted much criticism in developing countries. For example, the change to a new production process or worker education program normally requires extensive institutional support in the new environment. An administrative structure created by external specialists cannot be readily integrated with the recipient culture. Second, the psychological and technological gap between a foreign assistance team and local counterparts cannot always be closed. Without continuous efforts to involve indigenous managers in the planning and operations of innovation projects, the new techniques and tools might not be accepted by the local population for long-term use.

Managing Information for Innovation Projects

Since the late 1970s, reports of international organizations have emphasized the need for analytic methods and other management skills in R & D and other innovation projects. The capacity to coordinate and use a large number of different information resources was identified as one of the attributes of the effective manager (Stern 1982, Twiss 1980). Information resource management might solve some problems for project management if its effects on the work of researchers and technologists could be better understood. The following questions represent the beginning of probing that the proposed education and research program should attempt.

- Issue 1: How is new knowledge produced in industrial innovation projects?
  - Through an unexpected breakthrough or discovery that takes place during the course of a project pursuing other goals
  - Through an unexpected discovery caused by chance rather than by much creativity and inventiveness
  - In the course of systematic, well-planned, and steadily sustained R & D efforts, which are said to produce most of the industrial innovations
  - By taking risks and changing the course of research or attempting something new without the benefit of long-range planning
- Issue 2: What does information do for the innovation process?
  - Input to the process, providing support, stimulus, and continuity
  - Output generated by the innovation activity in the form of research findings, know-how developed in the course of the work, and links to the appliers of the research
- Issue 3: What are the relationships among the following kinds of information?

- Internal administrative records
- Scientific research results
- Technological assessment
- Risk assessment
- Marketing information
- Socioeconomic data and indicators
- Bibliographic and textual information
- Heuristics accumulated through problem-solving processes
- Communications for the diffusion of innovation
- Personal, culturally determined, and unevaluated information passing through informal networks

Other areas to be explored may be signaled by such questions as: How can the impact of information on the innovation be assessed? What approaches will optimize the effectiveness of information for the innovation? In other words, how can one increase "good" information, eliminate "bad" information, and distinguish between the two kinds? What kind of education and research program would be responsive to the needs of information officers in industry and would be flexible enough to be adapted to the requirements of each country?

Educational Needs

At least two major kinds of information resources must be organized and managed: The formal, structured, and institutionally available information resources, and the informal, unstructured, intuition-based sources of knowledge, available mainly through personal contacts. The human response to the rapidly growing array of information resources is often a keen sense of futility. In the face of information richness, the industrial researcher, technologist, and project manager sense a maze of sometimes overlapping and sometimes grossly inadequate information channels. It seems that the successful transfer of information depends on many formal technological and administrative factors, but the effective use of transferred information depends mainly on informal interaction between people.

To achieve both the technological and the communication dimensions in professional preparation, several new programs have been designed in and for developing countries (Beilke and Thompson 1987, Cook 1986, Neelameghan 1984). Programs with an emphasis on management are taking off in four directions: (1) Teaching information-related courses to managers, (2) teaching general management principles and techniques to information professionals, (3) developing a completely new program for an integrated approach to information resource management, and (4) offering workshops on selected aspects of managing information.

With rapid changes in the technological capabilities of industrial societies and the need of developing countries to close the technological gap, industrial organizations everywhere are under pressure to produce, to perform, and to innovate. The lack of qualified information professionals has been identified as one of the constraints in scientific and technological information transfer to and among developing countries (Baark 1985). Industrial information officers need to prepare for a dual responsibility: Providing support to the organization's innovation projects, and making decisions about the continuous upgrading of information systems and services.

Proposed Program

A new approach to the understanding of the innovation transfer effort through research and curriculum design is primarily concerned with (1) the conceptual clarification of innovation transfer and (2) the techniques of field testing new procedures or tools before recommending their application.

The new curriculum identifies three interrelated activities: (1) hardware or process transfer, (2) information transfer (data and documentation, standards and specifications, maintenance or process implementation guidelines, and licenses), and (3) knowledge transfer (concepts, paradigms, management skills, technical know-how, measurement criteria, analytic models, evaluations of impact, and training manuals). Suggested objectives and content of the course must be flexible and adaptable to various national and cultural goals. The principle that educational planning is at its best if integrated with economic and social planning is to be observed.

As a remedy against a mismatch between need and innovation in development projects, adaptive field testing has been used as a project tool, allowing for experimentation with new approaches without drastic consequences (Olson 1978). A program on innovation management would consider administrative, ethical, technical, and policy-related issues that surround a choice of method for the field testing of an innovation proposed for a developing country.

Administrative considerations may include the following: Should field testing be carried out by the staff of the innovation project or by outside consultants? Are local experts available? Who will cover the costs? How can the risks be assessed? What will be the consequences if the proposed innovation is not accepted for application? Is the documentation of the system or process adequate?

Probably the most difficult task is posed by the *ethical issues* that surround each change proposed for intercultural implementation. Have all human and cultural implications been considered? Who will be affected? How can the effects be communicated? What interests motivated the innovation? Will the innovation provide equally distributed benefits, or will it favor a few groups or individuals? Have the educational aspects been worked out so that all users or participants will have enough understanding of the innovation to make decisions about it?

Technical aspects that the new curriculum will have to address will be numerous. Will the introduction of the new technology or technique strain the existing communication infrastructure? Is enough information about maintenance costs and methods available? How much local expertise will be needed to institutionalize the proposed change? Will technical training of users be feasible?

Some examples demonstrate the essential role of *policy-related issues* in the transfer of innovations: Who owns the prototype process or new device? Should a license be purchased? What are the social controls that will affect the use of the innovation? Is the proposed change socially and professionally relevant? Will the new application require modification? What should the appliers know about its long-range consequences?

An education program seeking to probe not only into management issues but also into the psychological and social dimensions of innovation may encounter a real challenge in covering such topics as creativity, motivation, and inventiveness in research and development. While many studies are exploring the relationship of these human phenomena to successful innovation and productivity, the linking role of information has received less attention.

Preparation for New Responsibilities

As partners in R & D projects, industrial information officers must be prepared to:

- be aware of the state-of-the-art of innovation research and literature
- assist in the identification and evaluation of new technical ideas
- be alert to new developments in copyright and patent legislation and other laws, regulations, and standards affecting industry
- be familiar with the goals of different projects within the organization, give information support to each, and protect their proprietary information
- be knowledgeable about economic factors in information provision and use

- understand the use of computer and telecommunication technology and the need for data security in the context of projects that deal with sensitive proprietary information
- provide information counseling to researchers, engineers, project managers, and other members of the team by identifying potential research issues, processes, methods, and resources as needed
- develop systems and procedures for information requirement assessment, auditing, current awareness service, decision support, database management, evaluation, and user education as appropriate to project management.

The Course

The objectives of a suggested master's level course (Figure 18.1) are to (1) bring together concepts and techniques of fostering innovative activities at the organizational and national levels, (2) investigate the role of information professionals and systems in the innovation process, and (3) review worldwide, interdisciplinary research, institutions, conferences, and publications that are pertinent to this area of knowledge.

A powerful benefit one might expect from the course is a synthesis of concepts of scientific and technological policies, economic development planning, cultural relevancy, creativity and productivity. Such synthesis can form the basis of a research program.

The course should be offered in seminar style to allow for discussions and individual, original projects by participants. It could also be structured as a series of workshops for practicing industrial information officers. The outline does not intend to serve as a model because each country and each cultural environment requires changes and adaptations in both content and practical examples of applications.

Industrial information officers must contribute creatively to the applications of information to research, development, and project management. Preparation for this professional role includes understanding the meaning of change and innovation in personal life, in the organization, and in society. Such understanding may be derived from a multitude of experiences, for example, becoming aware of various schools of thought concerning the relationship of research, invention, and the market in the innovation process; analyzing the cultural and technical problems in transferring a new product or process from one country to another; and working with case studies of information requirements and innovation management in industry.

The proposed master's level course is aimed at bringing together industrial information officers with diversified professional backgrounds.

Figure 18.1
Master's Level Course in Information for Innovation

1. Is innovation a management problem, an academic concept, or a personal experience?
   - Can one "teach" anything about innovation?
     Examples of current approaches in different countries
   - Concepts, definitions, and terminology
   - The management of research and development projects in industry
   - Cases of industrial innovation:
     Small enterprises
     Innovation projects in large companies
   - The requirements of developing countries
2. Information support for the innovation process
   - Identifying the role of information and data in project-related decisions
   - Review of theoretical models of the innovation process
   - Bridging the gap between theory and practice
   - Professional ethics and information handling
3. Information resources for R & D projects
   - Informal contacts, networks, meetings
   - Organizations, programs, projects
   - Print and electronic text, video images, graphics, audio
   - Print and electronic data
   - Research tools, processes, results, interpretations
   - Technological forecasts, assessments, indicators
   - Patents, licenses, standards, specifications
   - Statutes, regulations, decisions, contracts, agreements
4. The information professional as member of a project team
   - Introducing Information Resource Management (IRM)
   - Information services to support phases in research activities
   - Information to facilitate research dissemination
   - Information services for technological applications
   - The information professional as catalyst and communicator in the organization
   - Information counseling, new interpretation and techniques of a professional role
5. The innovation process at the national level
   - National development plans
   - Scientific, technological, economic, and social policies
   - The importance of know-how at the entrepreneurial and small industry level
   - Technology transfer and information resources related to the process
   - The information professional's responsibility for and participation in infrastructure planning
6. Determining the need for innovation in information systems and services
   - The role of information science research
   - Financial assessment of changing information procedures
   - The impact on the staff and human relations
   - Managing the transition to an information technology
   - Appropriateness of information system innovation in different countries
   - Keeping up-to-date on innovations in information science and services
7. Critical evaluation of the literature on decision support systems, expert systems, and related developments

It is intended to provide a framework for study, discussion, and research. Educators and industrial information officers in other countries may change the content and the examples according to local requirements. No international education program can be complete without offering both the vision that synthesizes a diversity of concepts and the flexibility that allows for independent applications.

References

Agnew, J.A. ed. (1980). *Innovation Research and Public Policy.* Ann Arbor, MI: University Microfilms.

Baark, E. (1985). "Constraints on the flow of scientific and technological information: A review of issues with particular reference to developing countries." In *Scientific and Technological Information for Development,* 107–112. New York, NY: United Nations.

Beilke, P.F. & Thompson, V.A. (1987). Improving the quality of library and information science education in countries other than Canada and the United States: An investigation concerning regulations and guidelines. *Education for Information,* 5(4), 295–310.

Bhalla, A.S. ed. (1985). *Technology and Employment in Industry.* 3d ed. Geneva, Switzerland: International Labor Office.

Boulding, K. & Senesh, L. eds. (1983). *The Optimum Utilization of Knowledge.* Boulder, CO: Westview Press.

Brinberg, H.R. (1983). Contributions of information to economic growth and development. *International Information, Communication and Education,* 2, 5–20.

Calhoun, A.D. & Bendekgey, L. (1987). International software licensing: Basic legal and business issues. *Information Management Review,* 2(3), 55–62.

Child, J. & Bate, P. eds. (1987). *Organization of Innovation: East-West Perspectives.* Berlin, Germany: Walter de Gruyter.

Cook, M. (1986). *Guidelines on Curriculum Development in Information Technology for Librarians, Documentalists and Archivists.* Paris, France: United Nations Educational, Scientific and Cultural Organization.

Cronin, B. (1981). Assessing user needs. *Aslib Proceedings,* 33(2), 37–47.

Cusack, D.F. (1981). The Transfer of computer-based technology in agroclimate information systems. *Interciencia,* 6(4), 261–267.

Dawson, A. (1978). Suggestions for an approach to rural development by foreign aid programmes. *International Labour Review,* 117, 391–404.

Dror, I. & Bnaya, D. (1984). Knowledge centers: A technology and engineering hybrid. *R&D Management,* 14(2), 81–90.

Drucker, P.F. (1985). The Discipline of innovation. *Harvard Business Review,* 63(3), 67–72.

Drucker, P.F. (1986). *Innovation and entrepreneurship.* London, UK: Heinemann.

Eveland, J.D. (1985). *Communication Networks in University/Industry Cooperative Research Centers.* Washington, DC: U.S. National Science Foundation.

Gerstenfeld, A. & Wortzel, L.H. (1977). Strategies for innovation in developing countries. *Sloan Management Review,* 19(1), 57–68.

Glaeser, P.S. ed. (1983). *Data for science and technology. Proceedings of the Eighth International CODATA Conference, Jachranka, Poland, 1982.* Amsterdam, Netherlands: North Holland.

Hirshleifer, J. (1971). The Private and social value of information and the reward to inventive activity. *American Economic Review,* 61, 561–574.

Hope, K.R. (1982). The New international economic order, basic needs and technology transfer: Toward an integrated strategy for development in the future. *World Futures,* 18, 163–176.

International Labor Organization. (1986). *Rural development: Report II, 12th Conference of American States Members of the ILO, Montreal, March 1986.* Geneva, Switzerland: ILO.

International Labor Organization. (1985). *Technological change, the tripartite response, 1982–85.* Geneva, Switzerland: ILO.

Kanter, R.M. (1983). *The Change Masters: Innovation for Productivity in the American Corporation.* New York, NY: Simon and Schuster.

Kidd, R. & Colletta, N. eds. (1980). *Tradition for Development: Indigenous Structures and Folk Media in Non-Formal Education.* Bonn, Germany: German Foundation for International Development and International Council for Adult Education.

Knoppers, J.V.T. (1984). Transborder data flow issues and technology transfer. *Journal of Technology Transfer,* 9(1), 1–14.

Levinson, N.S. (1986). "Information requirements in managing innovation: Implications for systems design." In Hubner, H. ed. *The Art and Science of Innovation Management.* Amsterdam, Netherlands: Elsevier Science Publishers.

Lucas, B.S. & Freedman, S. eds. (1983). *Technology choice and change in developing countries, internal and external constraints.* Dublin, Ireland: Tycooly International.

Lytle, R.H. (1986). *Information Resource Management: 1981–1986. Annual Review of Information Science and Technology,* 21. Williams, M.E. ed. White Plains, NY: Knowledge Industry Publication, Inc., 309–336.

Marchand, D.A. & Horton, F.W. Jr. (1986). *Infotrends, Profiting from Your Information Resources.* New York, NY: Wiley.

Neelameghan, A. (1984). International and regional cooperation in human resource development for information services in developing countries: A case study. *Education for Information,* 2, 191–208.

Nelkin, D. (1984). *Science as Intellectual Property, Who Controls Research?* New York, NY: Macmillan.

Olson, C.V. (1978). *Adaptive Field-Testing for Rural Development Projects.* Washington, DC: U.S. Agency for International Development.

Page, J.M., Jr. (1979). *Small Enterprises in African Development: Agenda.* New York, NY: Praeger.

Perkins, D.N.T., Nieva, V.F. & Lawler III, E.E. (1983). *Managing Creation.* New York, NY: Wiley.

Perrin, J. (1984). The Production of knowledge and obstacles to its transfer. *Prospects,* 14(4), 479–488.

Quinn, J.B. (1985). Managing innovation: Controlled chaos. *Harvard Business Review,* 63(3), 73–84.

Rich, R.F. (1979). The pursuit of knowledge. *Knowledge, Creation, Diffusion, Utilization,* 1(1), 15.

Schmookler, J. (1966). *Invention and Economic Growth.* Cambridge, MA: Harvard University Press.

Scott-Stevens, S. (1987). *Foreign Consultants and Counterparts: Problems in Technology Transfer.* Boulder, CO: Westview Press.

Shaw, M.L.G. & Gaines, B.R. (1982). Tracking the creativity cycle with microcomputer. *International Journal of Man-Machine Systems,* 17, 75–85.

Smith, W.E., Letham, F.J. & Tholen, B.A. (1980). *The Design of Organizations for Rural Development Projects, a Progress Report.* Washington, DC: The World Bank. (Staff Working Paper 375).

Srinivasan, R.N. (1977). Development, poverty and basic human needs: Some issues. *Food Research Institute Studies,* 16(2), 11–28.

Stern, B.T. ed. (1982). *Information and Innovation.* Amsterdam, Netherlands: North Holland.

Stewart, F. (1984). "Facilitating indigenous technical change in Third World countries." In Fransman, M. and King, K. eds. *Technological Capability in the Third World,* 81–94. New York, NY: St. Martin's Press.

Tarazofsky, A. (1984). *The Subsidization of Innovation Projects by the Government of Canada.* Ottawa, Canada: Government Printer.

Twiss, B. (1980). *Managing Technological Innovation.* 2d ed. New York, NY: Longman.

United Nations Educational, Scientific, and Cultural Organization. (1985). *Applicability of Indicators of Socioeconomic Change for Development Planning.* Paris: UNESCO. (Socioeconomic Studies 7).

United States Office of Technology Assessment. (1978). *The Health of the Scientific and Technical Enterprise*. Washington, DC: OTA.

Wersig, G. & Windel, G. (1985). Information science needs, a theory of information actions. *Social Science Information Studies,* 5(1), 11–23.

19

Recruitment of International Students: Suggestions from Syracuse

Introduction

A few years ago Dr. Mahesh Bhave, then an international student at Syracuse University, wrote:

> I struggle each time I have to relinquish the stability of one established path and explore, appreciate and reconcile differences. Each battle won brings quiet joy, and also leaves a scar, as it were, of additional loneliness. Not many, unfortunately, have the opportunity to straddle different worlds and make personal peace with each one (Bhave 1986, p. 2).

How many international students can make peace with unavoidable conflicts between their own cultures and new academic and community environments? What role do educators play in the process of individual adjustment? We can hardly discuss academic recruitment techniques without facing these fundamental questions that underlie my observations throughout this paper.

I use the words "suggestions from Syracuse" reluctantly, because I don't want to pretend that we have the answers. International students, knowingly or unknowingly, are intermediaries in a process of intercultural technology transfer. Even as we make the first contact with a potential student, we have to recognize that the transfer or, rather, the exchange of ideas will involve their minds and cognitive approaches, their cultural attitudes and memories, their emotions, indeed, their entire image of and relationship with the world. Developing effective links with these fragile human bridges with foreign cultures is a more complex and less understood task than we care to admit.

My comments will reflect my own experience and thinking rather than any official message from Syracuse, and they are based not only upon our school's recruitment practices, but also upon a broad perspective on international academic relationships in which I have been involved as the chair of the Education and Training Committee of the International Federation for Information and Documentation (FID) from 1983 to 1988 and now as the director of the FID International Clearinghouse for Information Education and Training. My participation over the years in joint projects with colleagues and international students across several continents has inspired the considerations and beliefs that have flowed into my counseling of international students at Syracuse. I have learned that we have some academic policies we can trust, but also that our challenges are always ahead of our answers.

Trends Characterizing
the Recruitment Environment

In order to identify some solutions to the recruitment puzzle, we need to better understand the environment of populations which give us international students, that is, the interplay of trends in global economic, political and cultural relations. Among the major issues are *technology transfer, intercultural communications, international scholarship,* and the concept of *the learning organization* that has emerged from development studies. What follows is a brief glimpse at these issues.

It is the crucial need for *technology transfer* and innovation that prompts foreign governments, universities and national, regional and international funding agencies to send students to American universities. The literature of information science is vocal on the need of societies in various phases of economic development for the acquisition of not only computers and telecommunication equipment, but also of information (about processes, policies, software, operational approaches, techniques and analytic tools) and of knowledge (research results, data for analysis, scientific and technical reports, computer mediated and face-to-face conferences, and consultation).

The questions that emerge from this literature aim at adaptations that are required for the transmitted models, for example curricula or research paradigms, in order to render them applicable in the recipients' environment. Are education and training programs adequate mechanisms for the introduction of innovations in culturally different societies? Are there applied research approaches and problem areas that should be emphasized in order to better understand the creativity of the indigenous change process and its impediments?

Some of the above questions were raised at a Syracuse University Symposium on Technology Transfer to Developing Nations. One of the main objectives was "to challenge and reformulate the premises and assumptions that underlie current technology transfer policies and, by implication, the role of American institutions of higher education in training graduate students who will become agents for the transfer of technology and know-how" (Symposium/Workshop 1991, p. 1). The discussions identified the sustainability and replicability of innovation as fundamental to the success of international education at American universities

(Greenblatt 1991). The conference ended with a commitment by the university administration and faculty to build a database of relevant studies and conduct a continuous examination of the university's role in preparing international students as future change agents in their societies.

Knowledge transfer can be defined only in its social context. The trend is towards a mutual rather than a one-way process and towards increased attention to communications at the local level in the participating country. Several international organizations, such as the United Nations Development Programme (UNDP), favor South-to-South knowledge transfer that promotes the discovery and use of indigenous talent.

American universities hope to create and maintain optimal conditions for technology transfer through international scholars and students. Two policy recommendations stand out in the literature: (1) the transfer, through study or consultation, should be in the economic and social interests of the recipient country, and (2) it should be consistent with national objectives (Scott-Stevens 1987, pp. 32–33). It is also noted that "culture shock, a psychic and physiological phenomenon which affects the ability of people to work and adapt to a different culture, is an obvious constraint in the transfer of technical knowledge" (Scott-Stevens 1987, p. 102). Do we recognize the effects of culture shock when international students have problems?

The study of *intercultural communication* produces a broad interdisciplinary vista, international trade being a powerful determinant in changing communications into competitive postures. Stobaugh and Wells (1984) note the case of American multinational companies with subsidiaries in developing countries where communications between local and expatriate managers tend to be strained. On the other hand, in situations where executives of the parent company work with executives of the host country who had the opportunity to work at company headquarters, the acculturation process is more effectively managed. Mowlana (1985) is less concerned with the communication process itself than with the quality and reliability of interpreting information in the new context after it had been transmitted.

Communications across cultures and the various interpretations of messages are phenomena to which international students have been exposed first in their home countries and then in their new American communities. As educators, we need to be aware of the ambiguity of the ideological interpretation of relationships between high-technology and low-technology societies. At home, many of these students heard and read about two conflicting needs of their countries: On the one hand, their people expect more information and data from industrialized countries in support of development; on the other, politicians and intellectuals express resentment of cultural domination by the North. We should not be surprised that these students are not always clear as to the potential effects of their own studies on their societies at home.

International scholarship and professional cooperation tend to have an idealistic ring in the brochures of American recruiters. However, Altbach (1987) presents a picture of grossly uneven international distribution of scholarly activities and products. The researcher/ educator suggests that developing countries failed to become full participants in the benefits of global scholarship due to such factors as intellectual property laws, textbooks that are irrelevant to "the vast hinterland of consuming nations," and journals that feature only the advances and concerns of the North (Altbach 1987, p. xii). Publishing is affected by the economic and political constraints raised by the industry's networks, especially by the author-editor-publisher relationships which tend to hinder the emergence of new fields by ignoring untested creative talent. Nor is research always considered an essential part of academic culture in developing countries where library and computer facilities are often lacking (Altbach 1987, pp. 20–21).

American education of foreign students will contribute only to the one-way diffusion of scholarship and professionalization, unless we involve students in interactive learning, encourage them to share their memories and new ideas with us, and invite them to critically assess the applicability of studied material to their future professional work in the home environment. This understanding should be the premise of recruiting and the topic of frequent faculty discussions in order to clarify a school's role in the international flow of scholarship.

As we recruit with the assumption that we will prepare our best international students to be leaders in their profession in their home country, we have to keep learning ourselves. Three assumptions guide us toward the adoption of Korten's model of the learning organization for international development programs: (a) In view of the failures of many past programs which had considered the production of goods to be their primary goal, current programs are expected to concentrate on people; (b) bureaucratic management usually serves the latter purpose poorly; and (c) strategic management builds an organization's capacity to be responsive to rapid changes in the environment (Korten 1987, p. 232). With this paradigm in mind, recruitment plans should include a self-monitoring process and enough flexibility for review and adjustment as our experience with international students and their needs change and grow.

The Dilemma of Recruiting

A targeted mode of marketing education programs, the recruiting of international students is an information exchange process between the university and the potential consumer. Marketing for products and services usually includes research on the customer's environment and preferences, strategic planning, a communication and public relations plan, the transaction of information, and evaluation. The focus is on satisfying customer needs and identifying the needs of noncustomers. Although the difference between the social marketing of not-for-profit organizations and commercial marketing cannot be overlooked, the two practices have a great deal in common. Not-for-profit social service and educational institutions which, in the past, had considered themselves exempt from the tensions of the marketplace, are recognizing the growing need for well-planned marketing techniques (Kotler and Andreasen 1987). Products and services should be continuously updated to serve current demand, and consumers should be included in the review and planning process.

How do these widely known characteristics fit the marketing of information and library studies for international consumers? The question may be answered only if we understood the motivation of institutions to internationalize education programs. Three kinds of incentives have been identified in the literature: Self-interest, a commitment to contribute to international scholarship and professional improvement, and, in the case of students from economically developing countries, the desire to provide education as a form of development assistance. Herein lies the dilemma of ambiguous motivations for recruiting. Many educational institutions are still reluctant to openly admit to self-interest as the dominating factor in international recruiting. Many administrators and faculty members, who seemingly welcome foreign students, begrudge the extra time these students sometimes require. New students are not unaware of this attitude. Disoriented by abrupt immersion in a different culture and often able to communicate only with difficulty, they face the additional discomfort of feeling stigmatized and being treated, however subtly, as a burden.

The self-interest motive was described as a potentially positive incentive by an empirical study sponsored by the Institute of International Education and carried out by two professors from Duke and Harvard respectively:

> We sense a need in the United States for the public, who are the ultimate "policy influentials," to understand fully the value to the nation of international education . . . The training of foreign students does in fact stimulate bilateral trade, investment, economic cooperation, and economic and political development of the less-developed world . . . There is a pronounced danger that if the American people do not come to appreciate their overall self-interest in the education of carefully selected foreign students, they may neglect this function to their own loss and that of the students (Goodwin and Nacht 1984, pp. 47–48).

The study, based on interviews with graduates of American higher education programs currently working in Brazil, recognizes the fact that development assistance, like most other international enterprises, is mainly motivated by self-interest.

Going several steps further, Firebaugh (1990, pp. 67–70) advocates joint research in developing countries. In her description of the Collaborative Research Support Program funded under the United States Foreign Assistance Act she suggests that

> a strong rationale for the expansion of research abroad, is its potential contribution to the knowledge base of the field of study . . . The challenge of conducting research abroad, especially in Third World countries, makes faculty more knowledgeable about difficulties that can be encountered. Their experience-based advice to both domestic students who plan to conduct research abroad as well as international students can be particularly realistic and beneficial.

A substantial argument for international education in the interest of American academic institutions can be made on the basis of rapidly expanding worldwide markets for information managers and information scientists. "Developing nations will see much faster growth in their network spending, as they seek to modernize and expand communications networks, according to the 1990 International Review and Forecast conducted by Telephony's Market Research Department (Wilson 1990, p. 33). As new or upgraded telecommunication infrastructures are put in place in numerous countries, there are reports of a parallel increase in the need for skilled information and data handling (Duzs 1990).

The market of international education is in constant flux. Recruitment cannot be planned without awareness of factors that shape global conditions such as revolutions, civil wars, boundary shifts, national debt, rise of new leadership, or economic blocks. The impact of the European single market of 1992 on research funding and telematics development is already felt (Cowhey 1990, Philip 1990). The European Community is attracting a growing number of African and Asian students by scholarships and new programs in informatics. Students in the former Soviet Union and the East and Central European region who aspire to attend schools in the United States have a great variety of complex educational requirements including management, environmental data handling, parliamentary information systems, and telecommunication policies (Duzs 1990). In the past, the needs of Asian countries for library and information skills predominated throughout the subject selections of foreign students in American library and information studies schools (Oliveira 1990, p. 46). Today, there is an urgent need for information technology management in the newly industrialized countries (NICs) of Southeast Asia. In spite of the national debt problem in some of these countries, they are demonstrating dramatic advances in international trade and are creating high-technology societies. In Africa, struggling with multiple resource problems, there is a serious need for training programs "both

for information providers and for organization directors and managers"
(National . . . 1989, p. E2).

Cognizance of the competition faced by American programs is essential; innovations by information education institutions in other countries
are on the rise (Beilke and Thompson 1987). The recruitment dilemma
presents at least two pressing demands to each American information
studies program: (1) Identifying the real motivation for internationalizing the curriculum and following up with innovations in view of identified long-range goals, and (2) continuously reviewing the competition in
other parts of the world in order to make informed choices of changes.

Previous Work on International Student Issues

The recruiter's "desktop collection" on the topic is mainly recent in origin and open-ended in scope. Growing experience and understanding
based on both direct observation and feedback from current and former
international students may be categorized as (1) the history of foreign
students in the United States, (2) programs of international and national
organizations and professional societies, (3) research in this domain, (4)
conferences, and (5) relevant guides and handbooks.

1. The historical perspective offered by Oliveira (1990) leads from the
1920s to the present through a survey of the national origin, enrollment
statistics, institutional affiliations, admission criteria and concerns of
foreign library school students in the United States. The author thought-
fully reminds us in his conclusion that in order to offer a relevant curriculum to foreign students, schools "must assess beforehand the LIS
knowledge most needed by students from those countries" (Oliveira
1990, p. 46). He does not propose that with the vast expansion of transnational information and data systems and their social and legal implications for information users, curriculum designers should pay close attention also to courses and independent study projects that will take
students beyond librarianship into the practice, management and research of information use in any setting in society.

2. Cooperative efforts by international organizations towards flexible
and adaptable programs of information education and training, including the training of the user, are best illustrated by the programs of the
United Nations Educational, Scientific and Cultural Organization
(UNESCO). The examination of curriculum models that are the results
of joint deliberation by educators from diverse countries can assist recruiters of international students in assessing education needs (Cook
1986, Fontaine and Bernhard 1988, Large 1987). The ever-present expectation to prepare nationals of developing countries for leadership in

their societies calls for covering international information and telecommunication policies in American curricula. A handbook by UNESCO on national information policy formulation, with an emphasis on developing countries, is a key resource in this regard (Montviloff 1990).

Conference papers and other publications by international nongovernmental organizations (e.g. The International Communication Association, the International Council on Archives, the International Federation of Information and Documentation, the International Federation of Library Associations and Institutions) treat the issues of transmitting knowledge through formal and nonformal education and joint research extensively. In the proceedings of these professional bodies foreign educators frequently discuss the benefits and problems of their American or British educational experiences. Others concentrate on the emergence of new professional roles in developing countries, implying a variety of academic and work-related training needs. Highlighting the role of the individual in development, Paez-Urdaneta (1990) of Venezuela defines the new information professional as a social agent for change who participates in the management and diffusion of social intelligence and ensures the utilization of informatics technology. At the institutional level, the American Library Association (1989) is building up rich experience in international professional cooperation through its Library/ Book Fellows Program.

3. Empirical research on international students' perceptions of their American education experience in a variety of fields has helped us to better understand the tensions between expectation, frustration and achievement (Amoh 1987, Tallman 1990). Findings of an investigation of the impact of American library studies on the foreign student's home country may be used as indicators of potential consequences of recruiting students to our programs. Bornsztein's dissertation, although not specifically oriented towards library and information studies, places us into the frame of mind of prospective international students as they struggle with the choice among American graduate schools (Bornsztein 1987).

Conceptual papers based on an analysis and assessment of the literature rather than on empirical data can contribute exquisite insights to our view of the international student. Such papers clarify definitions, identify and evaluate existing theories, provide a framework for the organization of assumptions, and formulate research questions. With respect to developing countries, barriers to electronic mail (Matta and Boutros 1989), Western dominance of knowledge generation and dissemination (Selvaratnam 1988), and factors in the impact of transferred information technology on development (Shields and Servaes 1989) are some of the problem domains emphasized by international observers.

4. Although appreciation of the value of computer conferencing is growing, a face-to-face exchange of ideas among specialists, who need

a unifying context because their assumptions originate from different cultures, is the preferred mode of interaction. Conferences play a particularly important role in linking people with each other at the personal level, as here language barriers seem to matter less than in print or computer interaction. A study by Guha (1985) on the language problem in scientific and technical information use helps to explain the frustration of non-English speaking individuals in the face of proliferating English-based information systems (Guha 1985). Following personal exchanges at a conference, informal networking—an excellent mechanism for reaching potential international students—tends to be a more significant resource than published proceedings.

Recommendations at conferences have been known to lead to active international cooperative programs. Other results of meetings may include the identification or reinforcement of trends which have not yet crystallized in the formal literature. For example, the International Doctoral Student Conference at the School of Library and Information Science at the University of Pittsburgh concluded that "Library and information science education for international students should be directed towards developing leadership competencies. Developing countries need leaders as well as technocrats who can direct international technological development" (Tallman and Ojiambo 1990, p. 199).

5. The publication of guides, manuals, directories and the production of databases of use to international recruiting programs have accelerated in recent years. One of the most fundamental tools is the growing set of general and specialized references on potential funding sources for foreign students. Administrative manuals such as that of Harvey and Carroll (1987) are especially useful when they include examples of policies.

Based on experience, suggestions in the literature and unpublished documents of international meetings, five broad areas of information educational needs in developing countries have been identified:

- Information technology, its assessment and factors affecting transfer
- Information management and ethics of decision making
- Basic and applied research, especially methodologies and ways to adapt them
- Education for the information professions
- International and national information policies.

Included in recruitment pamphlets, newsletters, and electronic messages, these broad fields of study map the currently emerging education needs of the developing areas.

Who Are the Potential International Students?

In this paper we have looked at a few characteristic trends in the international environment of recruiting. There is another way to envision potential international students. What do they expect from the American education experience? We can assume that there are many kinds of expectations depending on personal orientation and prediction. Although we cannot predict all the various motives that prompt young individuals in other countries to seek an American education, we can discern their attitudes soon after they enter our schools. It may be helpful to international student advisors to anticipate at least some behavioral patterns. For example, do you recognize the following profiles?

- *The Technology Buff* who "walks" through American programs enthusiastically learning about computer systems and telecommunication networks, trying to avoid all other subjects
- *The Socially Conscious* who wants to be a pioneer and innovator of information services in order to improve conditions in the home country
- *The Future Corporation CIO* gobbling up courses and internships for the management of technology preparing for a job at home in a national bank or multinational corporation
- *The Cosmopolitan,* aiming at a job in an international agency or nongovernmental organization where crossnational contacts are made and exciting
- *The Policy Oriented* coming from the national elite of a country already established in a fairly influential position at home where participation in the national and regional policy process is expected
- *The Service Provider* with an undergraduate library education and a few years of library experience. A better job upon returning home, with somewhat more authority to initiate community information services or to improve existing library programs, is anticipated.
- *The Quiet One* who struggles through assignments, exams and term papers, patiently passing course after course without participating in class discussions, and who will return home and do an excellent job.
- *The American Job Hunter* who wants to become skillful and Americanized in order to stay on in this country.

There is no recruitment plan that can anticipate these and many more individual differences. And should there be one? Can we ever individualize programs to the extent that we accommodate all kinds of attitudes and dreams? Hardly. However, schools have an unequivocal responsibility to close the gap between promise and fulfillment. For example, if the recruitment literature advertised "individualized learning," international students may expect to succeed in the program without exposure to behavioral modification that compels them to conform to the American institution's style and tradition. The stress of making daily choices between their own cultural norms and the expectations of their new surroundings could weaken their capacity to learn with a creative and open mind.

A School's Assumptions

Recruiting methods of a school are mostly based on assumptions made by the faculty and administration about international education. At Syracuse we made the following assumptions:

- Most international students are up to the challenge of the American educational system; they do not expect and should not be granted any double standards.
- Transition to the new education system can take its toll. We want to give our best effort to each student, American or international. This means being available for advising, discussion and individual attention, even if it takes extra faculty time. It also means preparedness before problems arise. Orientation sessions at their best include not only faculty advising, but also peer advising.
- The educational experience includes a basic body of knowledge and skills for all students. Individual needs can be met by independent study, course projects, internships, and small group and personal discussions.
- We are not only givers. The relationship with international and all other students is a multidirectional configuration. Their rich culture, background, and creativity enhance our programs.
- The responsibility we have for our international students is formidable. We must not impose values, but show the way to professional choices and how to assess them.

A Philosophy of Recruiting

Based on assumptions and experience, a philosophy emerges over the years. Although there are no written policies, the shapes and tones of these values are discernable in the activities of most schools.

- No pressure for increasing the enrollment must be allowed to create a climate for "recruiting at any cost." High standards must be kept intact, as high as in domestic recruiting and admission programs.
- We should never make false promises. What a school teaches is what attracts the student, and how teachers think and act about intercultural relations is what makes the difference.
- We cannot consider American education to be a favor to the whole world. Excellence in scholarship and professional values is what one offers, no more, no less. To claim superiority in every sense is to undermine the excellence itself.
- One must accept the fact that often more time is needed to implement a two-way learning process across cultural and language boundaries than within the domestic academic experience.
- Feedback from international alumni should be taken seriously. Partnerships, cooperative projects, and joint evaluation efforts should come into play.

Recruiting Strategies

1. Most academic marketing techniques apply except face-to-face recruiting. This is a loss. What makes up for this loss is the quality of the literature a school disseminates. Catalogs, newsletters and reports sent to alumni and colleagues abroad have an impact. Literature sent to international scholarship organizations has a fighting chance to draw attention.
2. International presence of a school's teachers, researchers, administrators and students is vital. Faculty performance at conferences, consulting and projects is the single most powerful direct recruiting power. Work with international organizations creates effective communications.
3. We often overlook the impact of faculty publications on readers thousands of miles away. It is in research papers, reports, articles, even brief communications that potential students abroad find matching interests and desirable goals. It is in faculty publications that a school's scholarship and human value systems are expressed. Publications are indeed read, and they create dynamic linkages.
4. Many American universities have programs abroad. Syracuse's Division of International Programs Abroad (DIPA) is a bridge to international audiences in several countries and beyond.
5. Visiting scholars at our universities, both in our schools and in other disciplines, carry home the message of who we are and what we

represent. Moreover, they will remember us at international meetings. Networking with current or former visiting scholars is an excellent recruiting strategy.

Conclusion

Recruiting international students may be seen in a context much broader than just another academic activity. We are dealing with an extremely diffuse and complex process: intercultural technology transfer.

Technology transfer includes the international transference of knowledge, information, and machines. Many students come from less technologically developed areas of the world to learn about designing databases, building systems, and using microcomputers for a variety of applications. They come for the skills. But will skills alone help them to become effective leaders at home? Will skills alone help them to evaluate and select the kinds of systems most suited to their needs? Will skills alone help them to participate in formulating information policies?

It is up to the American schools to offer the whole range of options in the intricate informing process, from knowledge generation through knowledge transfer to policy analysis. Students will react to such a range of curricular opportunities according to their needs and predilections.

Building international relationships is a continuous process. There are prerecruiting activities (mailings, telephone interviews, email) and there are postgraduation responsibilities such as a teacher's continuing interest in the graduate's career, successes or problems. This dynamic process of ongoing interaction with former students is actually the criterion for any effective recruiting of new students. It will work once we believe that we learn from the interaction as much as we give.

At the beginning of this paper, I raised a question about the role of American educators in the adjustment process and creative learning of international students. This question may be answered with one word: commitment. Without being committed to making every effort to bring out the best not only in our international students but also in ourselves in this relationship, recruitment will be a hollow exercise.

References

Altbach, P.G. (1987). *The Knowledge Context*. Albany, NY: State University of New York Press.

American Library Association. (1989). *The Information Ambassadors: The Library/Book Fellows*. Chicago, IL: ALA.

Amoh, K.O. (1987). Newly Arrived Foreign Students at a U.S. University: Their Adjustment Difficulties and Coping Strategies. Minneapolis, MN: University of Minnesota. (Ph.D. Dissertation).

Beilke, P.F. & Thompson, V.A. (1987). Improving the quality of library and information science education in countries other than Canada and the United States: An investigation concerning regulations and guidelines. *Education for Information,* 5(4), 295–310.

Bhave, M. (1986). Learning acceptance: Thoughts about study in a foreign country. *Newsletter on Education and Training Programmes for Information Personnel,* 8(1), 1–2.

Bornsztein, B. (1987). Why Did They Come? A Study of the Foreign Student's Decision to Apply for Admission to Selected Graduate Schools of Education in the United States. Minneapolis, MN: University of Minnesota. (Ph.D. Dissertation).

Cook, M. (1986). *Guidelines on Curriculum Development in Information Technology for Librarians, Documentalists and Archivists.* Paris, France: United Nations Educational, Scientific and Cultural Organization.

Cowhey, P.F. (1990). The international telecommunication regime: The political roots of regimes for high technology. *International Organization,* 44, 169–199.

Duzs, J., ed. (1990). *Information Management: Practice and Education. International Seminar Held in Budapest, 1990. Proceedings.* Budapest, Hungary: International Information Management Foundation and the International Association for Information Management Schools and Programs. 2 vols.

Firebaugh, F.M. (1990). Expanding research abroad. *Phi Beta Delta International Review,* 1, 66–75.

Fontaine, F. & Bernhard, P. (1988). *Guidelines for Writing Learning Objectives in Librarianship, Information Science and Archives Administration.* Paris, France: United Nations Educational, Scientific and Cultural Organization.

Goodwin, C.D. & Nacht, M. (1984). *Fondness and Frustration, the Impact of American Higher Education on Foreign Students with Special Reference to the Case of Brazil.* New York, NY: Institute of International Education.

Greenblatt, S.L. (March 23, 1991). Personal Communication.

Guha, B. (1985). *Study on the Language Barrier in the Production, Dissemination and Use of Scientific and Technical Information with Special Reference to the Problems of the Developing Countries.* Paris, France: United Nations Educational, Scientific and Cultural Organization.

Harvey, J.F. & Carroll, F.L., eds. (1987). *Internationalizing Library and Information Science Education: A Handbook of Policies in Administration and Curriculum.* Westport, CT: Greenwood Press.

Korten, D.C. (1987). "Strategic organization for people-centered development." In Ickis, J.C., et al., eds. *Beyond Bureaucracy, Strategic Management of Social Development,* 233–256. West Hartford, CT: Kumarian Press.

Kotler, P. & Andreasen, A.R. (1987). *Strategic Marketing for Nonprofit Organizations.* Englewood Cliffs, NJ: Prentice Hall.

Large, J.A. (1987). *A Modular Curriculum in Information Studies.* Paris, France: United Nations Educational, Scientific and Cultural Organization.

Matta, K.F. & Boutros, N.E. (1989). Barriers to electronic mail systems in developing countries. *The Information Society,* 6, 59–68.

Montviloff, V. (1990). *National Information Policies.* Paris, France: United Nations Educational, Scientific and Cultural Organization.

Mowlana, H. (1985). *International Flow of Information: A Global Analysis and Report.* Paris, France: United Nations Educational, Scientific and Cultural Organization. (Reports and Papers on Mass Communication).

National Research Council. (1989). *Board on Science and Technology for International Development. Science and Technology Information Services and Systems in Africa. Report of a Workshop Held in Nairobi, 1989.* Washington, DC: National Academy Press.

Oliveira, S.M. de. (1990). Foreign students in American LIS schools: A Historical and statistical survey. *Journal of Education for Library and Information Science,* 31(1), 33–48.

Paez-Urdaneta, I. (1990). National Information Policy and Modernization of Development: A Redefinition of the Information Professional in the Third World from the Point of View of Education and Social Action. Paper presented at the International Federation for Information and Documentation, Education and Training Committee Seminar, Havana, Cuba.

Philip, G. (1990). Deregulation of telecommunications in the EEC. *International Journal of Information Management,* 10, 67–75.

Rochester, M.K. (1981). American Influence in New Zealand Librarianship as Facilitated by the Carnegie Corporation of New York. Madison, WI: University of Wisconsin. (Ph.D. Dissertation).

Scott-Stevens, S. (1987). *Foreign Consultants and Counterparts: Problems in Technology Transfer.* Boulder, CO: Westview Press.

Selvaratnam, V. (1988). Higher education cooperation and Western dominance of knowledge creation and flows in Third World countries. *Higher Education,* 17, 41–68.

Shields, P. & Servaes, J. (1989). The impact of the transfer of information technology on development. *The Information Society,* 6, 47–57.

Stobaugh, R. & Wells, L.T. (1984). *Technology Crossing Borders.* Boston, MA: Harvard Business School Press.

Symposium/Workshop on Technology Transfer to Developing Nations,

Syracuse University, Syracuse, NY. (March 23, 1991). *Program.* Syracuse, NY: Syracuse University, Office of International Services.

Tallman, J.I. (1990). Library and Information Science Programs in the United States: International Student Perceptions of their Academic Adaptation Process. Pittsburgh, PA: University of Pittsburgh. (Ph.D. Dissertation).

Tallman, J.I. & Ojiambo, J.B., eds. (1990). Translating an International Education to a National Environment. Papers Presented at the International Doctoral Student Conference . . . at the University of Pittsburgh School of Library and Information Science, 1988. Metuchen, NJ: Scarecrow Press.

Wilson, C. (1990). New markets developing. *Telephony,* 218(4), 30–67.

20

Training the Trainers in Information Management: Overview and Recommendations

Introduction

"Training the trainers," a phrase often used in international development projects, illustrates a trend toward intensive short-term programs designed for the preparation of national leadership to meet specialized training needs in various countries. Such programs range from in-service experiences to advanced academic seminars, all sharing certain characteristics. Topics usually represent a rapidly emerging field in a key sector of the economy, in which many people need swift upgrading of perspectives and techniques. Such training programs have to be based on already existing experience and familiarity with the subject of the participants who are expected to become the next wave of trainers in this particular field. Consequently, programs for "training the trainers" (TRT) have to integrate not only specialized practical knowledge and skills, but also the ability to experiment, lead and convey a change process without creating a painful confrontation between the old and the new. At their best, TRT workshops and seminars tend to promote evolutionary rather than drastic and abrupt change. Policy support and national-level planning are indispensable factors in their success.

This paper, focusing on developing countries, gives an overview of the need for training the trainers in information management, and of typical attributes of programs. The second part proposes an international cooperative planning meeting and a series of regional workshops, indicating potential audiences, principles, objectives and methods. The planning session will identify priorities and training needs in each region. The regional workshops will be designed to create a corps of information management trainers in each participating country in the region. The preparation, direction, and follow-up of each workshop will be supported by an electronic network accessible to participants before their workshop attendance as well as following their return to their home countries. Those who are not electronically connected would not be left out of the communications flow, but would be reached by alternate means. With qualitative and quantitative evaluation criteria and measurements built into the entire training process, each workshop's ripple-effect across a region may be expected to result in a well-documentable contribution to development.

Training vs. Formal Education

This paper will adopt some definitions used by the United Nations Educational, Scientific and Cultural Organization (UNESCO) for the different levels and methodological branches of education (United Nations Educational . . . 1984, p. 35). *Formal education* is defined as "the education system with its hierarchic structures and chronological succession of grades, from primary school to university . . . " *Non-formal education* or *training* includes "all those educational activities that are organized outside the established formal system . . . " And *informal education* denotes "the lifelong process . . . whereby each individual acquires attitudes, values, skills and knowledge through everyday experience . . . " In many countries the formal education system was based on models derived from former colonial powers and had to undergo many slow phases of indigenization and modernization. Nonformal modes of education are influenced by both local and foreign approaches, while informal education is embedded in indigenous values and customs.

Public mass education, described as activities that carry messages in print, sound, image and electronic media to large groups of people, may be added to the UNESCO categories. Objectives range from basic awareness-raising through opinion modification to direct instruction in topics relevant to work and self-help. In developing countries, public mass education is employed especially in such areas as preventive health, environment, small business practices, and rural communities (Servaes and Arnst 1992). Future trainers in information management need to be knowledgeable about current concerns with the need in developing countries to strengthen a feeling of cultural identity in society (United Nations . . . 1987, pp. 43–44). Utilizing channels of mass education forms part of the future trainers' pool of skills.

Training or nonformal education may be organized into short-term and specialized programs such as workshops, seminars, tutorials, discussion sessions, demonstrations, distant learning, self-teaching, and other interactions. Training and retraining are major mechanisms to teach new skills and ways of thinking necessary in a society that is in many ways in transition. There is a great need in all sectors for retraining technicians and professionals who have been in the workforce for years, have built up important experience, and now need to reorient themselves toward new techniques and technologies. It is essential to stress that "retraining" should not imply that professionals who have worked in their jobs for years do not have important knowledge and skills to offer. At their best, retraining workshops are designed for interaction and mutual learning among experienced and experimenting professionals. Members of each group bring their visions to the workshop and by exchanging ideas, they reinforce each other's assets.

The Need for Training the Trainers

This paper centers on training the trainers in information management (TRT/IM) in low-income countries where poverty is a way of life and any contribution IM may make to improvements by supporting development decisions and productivity is desperately needed. The World Bank (1991, p. 149) reports that "industrial countries with only one-fifth of the global population account for four-fifths of world output, more than four-fifths of world trade, and almost all exports of capital and technology." The rest of the world struggles toward development.

Development means quantitative and qualitative improvements across society. Development indicators combine measurements of economic, social and cultural transformations (Bunge 1981) and, increasingly, are supplemented by indicators of environmental quality and people's perceptions of individual and social well-being. Some researchers, including Moravcsik (1982, p. 12), conceptualize development not only as a society-wide process, but also as personal fulfillment, that is, "the course of action taken by an individual or a group of individuals in order to achieve a greater realization of their aspirations." This view brings learning into the central current of development.

It is now widely recognized that training in the form of workshops, seminars, on-the-job training and distance education is an effective way to introduce change (United Nations 1985). But what kind of change? For positive social transformation to occur, it is necessary to acknowledge that not all transformation is beneficial; one has to carefully identify in what sectors, activities, attitudes and processes one needs to bring about change in order to witness improvements across society.

Then we have to ask: How is the innovation going to be introduced and sustained? Agriculture, business, education, health care, transportation, and other sectors of the economy in a developing country show a trend toward using specialized training to foster and sustain technical advances. This trend offers an opportunity to information professionals for seeking out sector specialists (e.g. agriculturists, business managers, educators, health care administrators, transportation planners) and for creating partnerships for the organization of workshops and information exchange through networks. The challenge to information professionals is to train interdisciplinary groups to apply information use techniques (data acquisition, evaluation, comparisons, policy review, dissemination of proposals for policy change, involving people in making a choice, etc.) to various sectoral problems.

Partnerships bring together information managers with members of other professions to jointly address the information requirements of different specialized fields. Information managers learn how other groups work on solving problems, and other professionals experience the usefulness of selecting and combining information, data and knowledge at various levels of depth. Research and information transfer are now considered integral parts of the sustainable development process not only by information scientists and educators, but also by economists. In the view of a development economist, "we know a great deal about the distribution of income . . . but the lack of hard quantitative evidence on the effect of social sector interventions in health, literacy, nutrition, and so forth is striking . . . it is not unreasonable to ask for information on what can be accomplished through social sector programs" (Summers 1990, p. 11).

Assumptions Concerning Information Management

When stated explicitly, assumptions and preconceptions can be useful for illuminating the meaning of definitions (Zeisel 1981, p. 22). However, in spite of the considerable body of research in the cognitive, psychological and communication sciences, little is known about the ways personal assumptions affect human interaction (Brown and Hendrick 1986; Hofstede 1980; Holland and Quinn 1987). When personal assumptions act as biases they are seen as barriers to be removed by cognitive restructuring, that is, by learning to look at a situation in new ways (Schein 1987, pp. 105–114). When assumptions are undogmatic and open they promote discourse. The following are my thoughts about information management as it relates to this paper, offered here to facilitate discussion.

Assumption 1

The management of information has been practiced throughout history under different names, at different levels and in different institutional contexts.

Assumption 2

Today, information management (IM), covering a number of data-, communication-, and technology-related activities, is interpreted differently by different professional groups. In comparison, information resources management (IRM) is a more specific professional field which has been formalized and institutionalized since the late 1970s. Both IM and IRM are professional roles within a huge, evolving, multidisciplinary field (Figure 20.1).

Assumption 3

Information management (IM) and similar functions address formal information processes and, at the present, do not attempt to deal with informal information flows which are being increasingly sought out as sources by the users. We may expect that the paradoxical relationship between management and informal information processes will pose the next big challenge to information management.

Assumption 4

We must create and test a conceptual chart of the social and institutional maturing of the information professions that would enable people to define and represent their own branch of activity without feeling defensive about it, an attitude often manifested at international meetings and conferences.

Assumption 5

In each country, a corps of information management trainers, prepared as part of a national human resource development program, can significantly contribute to the education and development goals.

Information Management

The emergence of the information sector in the developing economies necessitates intensifying efforts for information management in the context of technology assessment and adaptation, entrepreneurship, and the privatization of telecommunication and other public services. The development of human resources has become a major policy thrust, and as organizational effectiveness grows into a central policy issue, so does the management of human communications and information transfer as a factor of innovation (Van Arkadie 1990, Altbach 1987, The World Bank 1992).

The very relationship of information to national planning is changing. We used to see it described as a support service to development decisions. Recently, one can sense a shift from the view of "information as development support" to the perception of "information as development." In this case we see the transfer and use of data, information and knowledge described as integral elements of the development process itself (Hanson and Narula 1990, United Nations Educational . . . 1991). A growing international literature asserts that as information is part of sustainable development, information management is an indispensable activity in research, public policy, fiscal planning, private enterprises, and grassroots movements. Today we recognize that we must establish criteria and measurements to assess the impact of information and information management training on society and social equity. A similar process attempts to evaluate the effect of investment in education (Coombs and Hallak 1987). In this light, training the trainers in information management becomes a national resource.

To be fulfilled, the above assumptions depend on three conditions. First, both the context and the assumptions upon which an information management training plan rests must be clearly defined. Are the trainers going to illuminate the management of resources which contain and move information, the management of the technological facilitators of information, the management of people who provide information, or the information content? These clarifications will help define not only the

Figure 20.1
EMERGING MULTIDISCIPLINARY FIELD

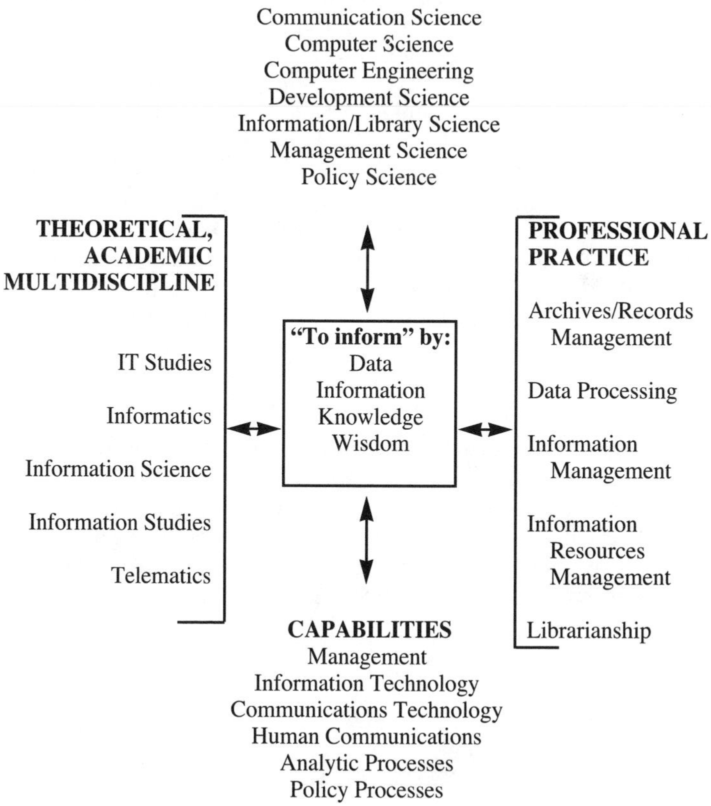

Communication Science
Computer Science
Computer Engineering
Development Science
Information/Library Science
Management Science
Policy Science

**THEORETICAL,
ACADEMIC
MULTIDISCIPLINE**

IT Studies

Informatics

Information Science

Information Studies

Telematics

"To inform" by:
Data
Information
Knowledge
Wisdom

**PROFESSIONAL
PRACTICE**

Archives/Records
Management

Data Processing

Information
Management

Information
Resources
Management

Librarianship

CAPABILITIES
Management
Information Technology
Communications Technology
Human Communications
Analytic Processes
Policy Processes

topics and goals of each training program but also the ways issues and problems will be analyzed (Mingat and Tan 1988, p. 15).

Second, we have to acknowledge that the economic, cultural and social environment of each training site will require different applications of information management skills. Training models will have to be scrutinized for relevancy and adapted to local needs and conditions. Although the analysis by Lynton and Pareek (1978) of a broad training approach in support of development makes as much sense today as it did in the late 1970s, each developing country has to examine Lynton and Pareek's model in the light of its own priorities. Wholly transplanted training models which do not allow for local initiative are seldom welcome by host countries, because encountering and encouraging new talent and leadership is one of the significant benefits of regional workshops.

Third, we should not forget that information management does not deal with abstractions but with people who often display spontaneous attitudes and actions. Since spontaneity may be a rich source of original ideas, informal and personal expression of information must be acknowledged as a valuable resource, especially when workshop participants come from a number of countries and informal information exchange draws upon several cultures. A better understanding of the role spontaneous and "organic" information plays in human and organizational life may lead information managers to a clearer picture of the relationship between information system design and user. Other professions have undertaken this search. In the words of Frank Lloyd Wright, to whom a building was the expression of the relationship between design and inhabitant, "if architecture has any future more than revival or passive reform, we must speak of future architecture as organic" (Wright 1953, p. 319).

TRT in Information Management: A Proposal

This section describes potential audiences, principles, objectives, methods and expected benefits of a program designed for preparing a corps of information management trainers in participating countries. The program's approach, involving national governments, nongovernmental organizations (NGOs), private voluntary organizations (PVOs), and professional associations, has the advantage of drawing energy and imagination from both local initiatives and regional cooperation. The goal is to achieve long-range local impact and replicability, with adjustments, of the training program. The success of the proposed model depends on the interaction of seven program elements:

1. INTERNATIONAL PLANNING MEETING with representatives from all regions
2. Creation of a TRT DISCUSSION GROUP using the Internet, supplemented by other modes of communication where network connection is not available
3. COLLABORATIVE PREPARATION OF THE TRT WORK-SHOPS in information management (TRT/IM) using the network or more traditional channels for the discussion of objectives, selection of topics, decisions on multimedia teaching materials, and setting of evaluation criteria
4. Building the TRAINING TEAM; recruitment of participants; preliminary discussions and networking with participants
5. REGIONAL TRT/IM WORKSHOPS held in several locations
6. During the FOLLOW-UP PHASE evaluation feedback obtained through the network and other channels; workshop project completed by participants in their home countries by integrating learning with local situations and needs.
7. Continuity of idea and experience exchange among former and future participants secured by ongoing communications and networking.

All seven elements have to be linked by an uninterrupted learning process in order to create a program with lasting impact. While most international training opportunities conclude when a workshop ends, the unique feature of this program is its continuous sharing of experiences and personal reactions following the workshop.

Potential Audiences of TRT/IM Workshops

Technological advances in developing countries have increased the tendency toward specialization and the need for skills in all sectors of the economy. Along with specialization, we have witnessed the rise of the threat of obsolescence in every field where new, mainly imported approaches, machines and techniques require the acquisition of new technical knowledge. A decade ago engineering was seen as the integrating discipline, "its purpose being to reunite compartmentalized areas of knowledge and to combine them with machines and qualifications" (United Nations Educational . . . 1984, p. 26). Today it is the various forms of information use—in systematic or informal ways, through structured information searching or serendipitous discovery, by individual initiative or synergy—that bridge the different fields. While engineering spanned divergent disciplines and professions by addressing the universal need for technological methods, information management can accomplish integration by addressing the interdependence of cognitive processes, human actions and technological capabilities.

Two groups of participants would particularly benefit by attending the regional TRT/IM workshops together: Information professionals and members of other professional communities (e.g. small business managers, teachers, government officials, regional planners). Although today there are many excellent training programs delivered either in face-to-face or distance education modes, most of them have been designed for relatively homogeneous audiences (e.g. all government officials, all environmental scientists, all librarians). Although there are advantages to homogeneous group work such as shared values, interests, reward systems and vocabularies, important benefits including new perspectives, new ways of collaboration, and new ways of using information, will ensue only from heterogeneous group work. Joint training experiences can translate into joint professional work with creative outcomes.

The organizers of regional TRT/IM workshops should make every effort to reach information professionals with different agendas and other professionals with different backgrounds. Information professionals may include:

Practitioners (information managers, data manager, librarians, archivists, records managers)
Policy analysts and negotiators
Educators and trainers
Researchers
Information disseminators and communicators

Other specialists who may fruitfully interact with information professionals are:

Accountants
Agricultural extension agents
Agricultural scientists
Business managers
Community leaders
Computer scientists
Educators
Engineers
Entrepreneurs
Environmental scientists
Government officials
Health care administrators
Journalists
Rural and urban planners
Social service personnel

Principles of TRT/IM Workshops

Because participants in the regional workshops are recruited from different fields and national backgrounds, they will be encouraged to identify principles in order to create an underlying philosophy for each workshop. Examples of principles include:

- Social transformations in developing countries caused by new communication and information technologies will benefit people as long as these technologies are coordinated with local values and approaches.
- The development process is guided by different strategies in each country; these strategies form the environment of information management, and techniques should be adjusted accordingly.
- Information systems and services do not operate in a vacuum but in the framework of economic and social interests that drive activities in each sector.
- The relationship between information management and productivity is poorly understood. Organizers should identify research in this problem area and make readings available to the workshop. Conversely, participants are to make recommendations for future research.
- Interpersonal communications, professional ethics and technological skills are the essential elements to undergird effective information management training.
- Discussions during the workshop sessions should be unbiased, with respect to the different views of the participants.

Goals and Objectives of TRT/IM Workshops

There are certain needs for information management training that apply to all regions and countries. There are also techniques and skills that should be adapted to local circumstances. With respect to long-range goals, the TRT/IM program is to be conceptualized and structured to assist trainers in developing countries in:

- Perceiving the overall process of sustainable development as the motivation and basis of all information-related work
- Obtaining information about their countries' national development plans and about regional trade strategies to assure that the training they will offer in the home country is relevant
- Understanding the ethical and cultural implications of information

management and the role of information managers and consultants as policy negotiators, intercultural communicators and trainers
- Forming partnerships with professionals in various economic sectors, creating specialized networks, and organizing joint training programs.

Following the regional TRT/IM workshops, the new trainers return to their countries where their skills may be tested and sometimes challenged by local circumstances. They will have to depend on their own competence and creativity in finding constructive ways to apply their new skills. In terms of immediate specific objectives, the workshops should provide the trainers with the capability to handle all or some of the following:

- Coping with changeable conditions and frustrations in their home countries
- Assessing local training needs and adjusting training models; writing training objectives
- Securing funding, support by the government and industries, managing finances, and sustaining training opportunities over periods of time
- Developing up-to-date, relevant and comprehensive programs together with continuous performance assessment and review
- Integrating concepts and policy models of development and information infrastructures
- Assessing, selecting and implementing demonstrations of technology for information management; encouraging locally produced information systems, software, and other products
- Promoting cultural understanding in interpersonal and intergroup communications
- Building a commitment to development ethics and information ethics to new trainers.

Methods of TRT/IM Workshops

Training methods have taken on many forms in recent years, from computer-assisted instruction to satellite-transmitted video sessions. The United Nations Educational, Scientific and Cultural Organization (1984, pp. 39–40) identified the importation of educational technology to developing countries, the growing role of the private sector in the education system, changes in formal education programs, and the influence of international organizations as the main factors leading to the diversification of nonformal education. One of the most interesting methodological developments is the convergence of education dissemination and mass communication which are reaching formerly neglected rural areas (Hanson and Narula 1990).

Within a workshop, the following methods may be considered:

Demonstrations
Field trips
Group discussions
Group projects
Guest lectures
Practice work
Presentations
Problem solving exercises
Role playing
Simulation
Study tours.

We may encounter these activities in any training program. What makes the TRT/IM model unique is the role of its networked preparation phase and follow-up phase which are integrated into a unity with the workshop.

In the PREPARATION PHASE, participants are sent readings and a questionnaire probing into their preferences and expectations, and are asked to select an information management project relevant to their home country. In addition to indigenous guest lectures and hands-on skills with multimedia learning systems, the workshop provides time for participants to work on their own projects and to propose management and policy solutions for group discussions. The goal is to support rather than criticize each other.

In the FOLLOW-UP PHASE, the near-finished projects are taken back to the home countries for relevancy-check and completion.

The electronic network (or, in the case of technological scarcity, nonelectronic interaction) is used for discussions during both the pre- and the post-phases. The highlights of the workshop process are the participants' choice of a project, determination of the learning approach, independent judgment exercised throughout the program, and tolerance of each other's political and ideological views. Informal discussions and sharing of personal memories are characteristic features. At its best, a workshop audience acts like a team (Dyer 1987); and evolving a team spirit is more important than any formal arrangement.

Evaluation of TRT/IM Workshops

For purposes of selecting and adapting training models, the evaluation of these methods is problematic because the outcome of each communication and teaching approach is assessed as much by the culturally-based responses of the participants as by technical criteria. Numerous evaluation methodologies may be found in the literatures of development science and education, including assessment models based on (a) development indicators, (b) the concept of social learning, and (c) economic theories. The paramount assumption is that evaluation is worthwhile only if it identifies information useful for future workshops.

Decisions must be made during the Preparation Phase as to

- Who will evaluate?
- What is to be evaluated?
- When to evaluate?
- By what standards?
- With what methodology?
- What will happen to the data?

Other questions for evaluation research might include the following points which may yield interesting insights:

- Where will trainees work?
- What will be their mission?
- What factors are expected to influence their future work?
- What will be the context of the training?
- Who will employ the trainees?
- How will the learned material be used?
- What criteria had been set for evaluation?
- What limitations exist?
- What adjustments are necessary?

Evaluation methodology that originated in industrialized regions cannot be readily used for a workshop designed for a developing region (Chapman and Boothroyd 1988, Hofstede 1980). However, the project assessment models that we have derived from development science research can be adapted for the purposes of evaluating TRT/IM workshops (Coombs and Hallak 1987; Deren, D'Silva and Ward 1991). We also note speculations resulting from research (some empirical, others descriptive) concerning computer and telecommunication applications in developing countries. This growing literature yields new perspectives on the relationship of information technology and development (Agha and Akhtar 1992, Ayres 1990, Matta and Boutros 1989, Mowlana and Wilson 1990). We see a combination of qualitative and quantitative assessment techniques applied, with emphasis placed on gathering information about people's direct experiences with development projects.

Expected Benefits of TRT/IM Workshops

A cooperative program to prepare information management trainers in developing countries represents an important contribution toward development goals for several reasons.

- By launching the proposed program, the international informatics community expresses its conviction that information is part of the development process, and increases public awareness of information policies.
- The systematic investigation of trends in the information workforce has already received international attention (United Nations Educational . . . 1991); the proposed program provides continuity as well as future direction for training efforts.
- The program leads to research on the relationship between information management and the innovation process.
- Active cooperation with professionals in various sectors establishes new ties between information management and key economic activities.
- The use of electronic networks for the preparation and follow-up of the workshops, personalizing each participant's learning, creates a new prototype TRT/IM program that can be adjusted to the needs of different countries.

Conclusion

An overview of the international trend toward training the trainers as a dimension of development tasks was followed by a proposal for a prototype TRT program to build information management capability in various economic sectors. Participants in face-to-face workshops use electronic networks, or alternative means of communication, to plan, direct and evaluate their own learning experiences.

The literature review identified a consistent pattern of nonformal education, including training and information dissemination, in the service of sustainable development. Both education and communication science produced useful organizational and evaluation models.

The United Nations Educational, Scientific and Cultural Organization (1984, p. 33) suggested four major research themes on education for the future:

1. How does the training system adjust to social needs?

2. What is the relationship between government policy and the importation of technology?
3. What are the functions of educational planning?
4. What are the optimal means of technology development in low-
   technology countries?

Little is known about the characteristics of information management
training in developing countries, and about the factors that affect its outcome. The proposed regional training program can form the basis of a
research agenda to fill several gaps in our knowledge. Research themes
may include: (a) team training and teamwork in information management, (b) comparison of information management (IM) and information
resources management (IRM) in development projects, and (c) cooperative approaches to evaluating crosscultural training.

Based on the experience that "few policies promote development as
powerfully as effective investment in human resources" (The World
Bank, 1991, p. 153), the proposed program moves toward the integration
of education, communications, and the new management of information.

References

Agha, S.S. & Akhtar, S. (1992). The Responsibility and the response:
    Sustaining information systems in developing countries. *Journal of
    Information Science,* 18(4), 286–292.

Altbach, P.G. (1987). *The Knowledge Context.* Albany: State University
    of New York Press.

Ayres, R. & Zuscovitch, E. (1990). Technology and information: Chain
    reactions and sustainable economic growth. *Technovation,* 10(3),
    163–183.

Brown, O. & Hendrick, H. eds. (1986). *Human Factors in Organiza-
    tional Design and Management, II. Proceedings of the Second Sym-
    posium . . . Vancouver, 1986.* Amsterdam, Netherlands: North-
    Holland.

Bunge, M. (1981). Development indicators. *Social Indicators Research,*
    9, 369–388.

Chapman, D.W. & Boothroyd, R.A. (1988). Evaluation dilemmas: Con-
    ducting evaluation studies in developing countries. *Evaluation and
    Program Planning,* 11, 37–42.

Coombs, P.H. & Hallak, J. (1987). *Cost Analysis in Education: A Tool
    for Policy and Planning.* Baltimore, MD: The Johns Hopkins Univer-
    sity Press for the World Bank.

Deren, B.J., D'Silva, E.H. & Ward, W.A. (1991). *The Economics of*

Project Analysis, A Practitioner's Guide. Washington, DC: The World Bank.

Dyer, W.G. (1987). *Team Building: Issues and Alternatives.* 2nd ed. Reading, MA: Addison-Wesley.

Hanson, J. & Narula, U. (1990). *New Communication Technologies in Developing Countries.* Hillsdale, NJ: Lawrence Erlbaum Associates.

Hofstede, G. (1980). Motivation, leadership, and organization: Do American theories apply abroad? *Organizational Dynamics,* 9(1), 42–63.

Holland, D. & Quinn, N. eds. (1987). *Cultural Models in Language and Thought.* Cambridge, UK: Cambridge University Press.

Kaye, T. (1987). Introducing computer-mediated communication into a distance education system. *Canadian Journal of Educational Communication,* 16(2), 153–166.

Korten, D.C. (1980). Community organization and rural development: A learning process approach. *Public Administration Review,* 40(5), 480–511.

Lynton, R.R. & Pareek, U. (1978). *Training for Development.* West Hartford, CT: Kumarian Press.

Matta, K.F. & Boutros, N.E. (1989). Barriers to electronic mail systems in developing countries. *The Information Society,* 6, 59–68.

Mingat, A. & Tan, J-P. (1988). *Analytical Tools for Sector Work in Education.* Baltimore, MD: The Johns Hopkins University Press for the World Bank.

Moravcsik, M.J. (1982). "Assessment of science in developing countries." In Srinivasan, M. ed. *Technology Assessment and Development.* New York, NY: Praeger.

Mowlana, H. & Wilson, L.J. (1990). *The Passing of Modernity: Communication and the Transformation of Society.* White Plains, NY: Longman.

Schein, E.H. (1987). *Process Consultation, Lessons for Managers and Consultants.* Vol. 2. Reading, MA: Addison-Wesley.

Servaes, J. & Arnst, R. (1992). Participatory communication for social change: Reasons for optimism in the year 2000. *Development Communication Report,* 79, 18–20.

Shields, P. & Servaes, J. (1989). The Impact of the transfer of information technology on development. *The Information Society,* 6, 47–57.

Simpson, D. & Sissons, C. (1989). *Entrepreneurs in Education: Canada's Response to the International Human Resource Development Challenge.* Ottawa, Canada: International Development Research Centre (IDRC).

Summers, L.H. (1990). "Knowledge for Effective Action." In *Proceedings of the World Bank Annual Conference on Development Economics, 1989,* 7–14. Washington, DC: The World Bank.

United Nations. (1985). *Teaching, Education, Culture and Information as Means of Eliminating Racial Discrimination.* New York, NY: UN.

United Nations. (1987). *Popular Participation Policies as Methods for Advancing Social Integration.* New York, NY: UN.

United Nations Educational, Scientific and Cultural Organization (1984). *Educational Planning in the Context of Current Development Problems.* Paris, France: UNESCO. 2 vols.

United Nations Educational, Scientific and Cultural Organization (1991). Information Manpower Forecasting. Papers Presented at the FID/ET Seminar, Espoo, Finland, 24–27 August 1988. Ed. by M. Dosa, T. Froehlich and H. King. Paris, France: UNESCO.

Van Arkadie, B. (1990). "The Role of Institutions in Development." In *Proceedings of the World Bank Annual Conference on Development Economics, 1989,* 153–175. Washington, DC: The World Bank.

The World Bank. (1991). *The Challenge of Development, World Development Report 1991.* Washington, DC: The World Bank.

The World Bank. Development Committee. (1992). *Development Issues.* Washington, DC: The World Bank.

Wright, F.L. (1953). *The Future of Architecture.* New York, NY: New American Library of World Literature, Inc.

Zeisel, J. (1981). *Inquiry by Design, Tools for Environment-Behavior Research.* Cambridge, UK: Cambridge University Press.

Part VI

The American Transnational Corporation and Information

21

The American Transnational Corporation in Developing Countries

Introduction

This paper describes a study supported by a Visiting Scholarship from AT&T Bell Laboratories and conducted between March 1992 and March 1993. Background, objectives, methodology and results will be summarized from the full study report.

The large-scale political and economic transformations we are witnessing today, together with the spread of communication and information technologies, may lead either to more scientific and professional co-operation or to more international tensions. The dependence of most countries of the South on the technological capabilities and knowledge resources of the North has been aggravated by the inability of most developing economies to join the international trade in data products and services.

Economically developing countries (EDCs), except the newly industrializing countries (NICs) of Southeast Asia, are considered neither competition nor threat by most Americans. Popular media attention focuses on the political and social crises, the relentless poverty, and the low technological capacity of the Third World. The superficial impression is that most developing societies form a homogeneous mass characterized by instability, and surviving mainly through international aid. However, each society is a unique entity with complex political, social and cultural attributes. To ignore the potential of economically developing countries (EDCs)—vastly diverse and continually changing—for business partnerships, joint research and professional cooperation would be a grave mistake. Sustainable development policies call for the strengthening of human resources, entrepreneurship, R&D, and training and management skills. Development scientists with a long-range view argue that now is the time for American corporations, educational institutions and research programs to lay the foundations of cooperation with the professional and entrepreneurial sectors and scientific communities of developing economies.

What is the current outlook for laying such foundations? There is evidence in the policy research literature of a growing school of thought suggesting that international assistance and lending to EDCs provide only a temporary Band-Aid rather than a lasting cure. We do not know how to relieve international tensions and ills. However, trends described in this paper seem to suggest that international scientific and professional cooperation can contribute more effectively to the capacity of EDCs to absorb and integrate technology transfers, improve institutional infrastructures, and develop sound relations with the North than continuing dependence on foreign technology.

Assumptions and Objectives

This study is built on the conviction that constructive relationships between American transnational corporations (TNCs) and economically developing countries (EDCs) is in the interest of the United States as well as of the developing nations.

The objectives of the study were to

- investigate the social and cultural factors that affect the relationship, information access and use, and intercultural communications between American TNCs and economically developing countries (EDCs)
- study the perceptions of the role of technology transfer, international information flows and communications in corporate cultures, specifically in AT&T
- review approaches to the improvement of information flows and communications between TNCs and EDCs
- create a framework for thinking about TNC-EDC relationships, international information and communications, and identify implications for AT&T.

Audiences and Approaches

The work of the study proceeded in three stages: (1) Review and synthesis of evidence of TNC-EDC relationships in research papers and policy documents, (2) interviews with executives in different AT&T departments, and focus group meetings with information professionals at AT&T, and (3) report on conclusions, implications for AT&T, and recommendations.

Research and policy resources used in the review sometimes represented the EDC's point of view and at other times those of TNC's. In each case, the review aimed at objectivity. Interviews and focus groups then explored the views within AT&T.

The research and policy review addressed three broad audiences:

- Corporate decision makers, researchers and professional staff in AT&T who want to better understand international information and communication patterns
- Information managers and information professionals in American companies who seek insights into the social, cultural and business environment of international information transfer
- Information users and suppliers anywhere who are concerned about the barriers and facilitators of information flows to and from the economically developing countries.

Research and Policy Review

It has been noted that the effectiveness of an organization relative to its customers or clients depends on environmental and human factors as well as on the social framework of decision making, marketing and business transactions (Bose 1992, Keen 1991). The purpose of this review was to capture trends in the international environment in which information moves between the American TNC and developing countries. Research papers, case studies and policy documents which touch upon characteristic themes were selected from a number of disciplines and international organizations. The intent was to detect the factors which influence the relationship of TNCs and EDCs, including conflicting perceptions of technology transfer, domestic technological capabilities in EDCs, the restructuring of domestic telecommunication industries, and communication/information movements.

Research on TNCs

Keen (1991) distinguishes between multinational enterprises (MNEs) and transnational corporations (TNCs), describing the transition from the former to the latter. The multinationals' operational base is "composed of relatively independent national and regional units . . . Management of IT [information technology] is usually local (except shared international telecommunication networks) . . . [and it] avoids global planning that might be construed by national business units as an intrusion on their autonomy" (Keen 1991, p. 71). Multinationals will eventually have to adjust to the requirements of international business by bringing more coordinated planning to their overseas branches and subsidiaries.

In the transnational corporation's culture, "corporate management is tightly coupled in many areas of the business, including global

manufacturing, product development, coordination of R&D and marketing. Such a firm will treat IT as a resource to be coordinated worldwide,
necessitating a common technical platform for telecommunications, information management, and many aspects of other IT services and operations" (Keen 1991, p. 73). According to the United Nations Economic
and Social Council, the term "transnational corporation" refers to "all
enterprises which control assets—factories, mines, sales offices and the
like—in two or more countries" (Jenkins 1987, pp. 1–2).

For several decades, the role of TNCs has given rise to many controversies. Firms based in the United States are looking for expansion, joint
ventures and new contracts. In considering the selection of new projects
in EDCs, firms weigh economic rather than cultural issues: bargaining
power, competition by European and Japanese firms, and the strength of
local companies as potential joint investors (Dobkin 1988, Vernon and
Wells 1981). On the other hand, developing countries see the TNC not
only as a source of technological growth, but also as a form of economic
oppression (Lall 1982).

Jenkins (1987) pointed out that research on TNCs has been producing
two kinds of studies. Quantitative investigations focus on finances, direct foreign investment, structure of companies, and management issues.
Qualitative research probes the characteristics of firms and factors affecting their growth. The first kind of research can assist the TNC in corporate decisions on foreign expansion; the second type contributes to a
better understanding of how decisions can be implemented without conflicts with host countries.

Comparisons with non-American TNCs from the perspective of developing countries show that Japanese firms "in contrast to the giant,
high-technology, high-marketing investors from the U.S., tend to be relatively small, low-technology firms making standardized products and
investing abroad mainly to exploit lower costs of labor or access to raw
materials" (Lall et al. 1983, p. 3). Comparisons with local firms in EDCs
demonstrate that these firms often have a competitive advantage over
much larger overseas investors because they are able to use localized
technical knowledge, adapt the technology, and provide products and
services that meet indigenous needs (Lall et al. 1983, p. 5).

Research on TNCs by development experts sheds light also on the historical experience that has shaped cultural attitudes toward foreign investors in EDCs. Industrialization, first embraced as a panacea to all
Third World woes and a solution to access to markets, gradually became
suspect in the 1970s and 1980s. National development policies blindly
supporting foreign direct investment were criticized as barriers to much
needed social transformation (Singh 1989). By the early 1980s, foreign
TNCs were regarded "with a mixture of cautious welcome and pragmatic
hard-headedness by many developing countries" (Lall 1985, p. 66).

Whenever foreign ownership exerted overly strong control, host governments began to look for companies which were willing to bring technology and skills into the country with minimum control. About the same time, a growing number of local regulations were introduced in EDCs to curb foreign investment dominance (United Nations Centre . . . 1988).

Relationship of TNCs to Development

Based on evidence brought forth by empirical research, several consolidating trends and policy issues may be summarized (Bereznoi 1990, Covello and Frey 1990, Ghosh 1984, Goodman 1987, Robinson 1991, Roth 1987, Sauvant 1986). The same trends and issues surface in the reports and policy statements of intergovernmental organizations (Organization for Economic . . . 1992b, 1992c; United Nations 1988; United Nations Centre . . . 1986). What follows is a summary of the main recurring themes.

- TNCs are sources of innovation, R&D, and new skills for EDCs, and may facilitate the development of technology for local use.
- Export of TNC products and services to international markets may lead to business contacts for EDCs and eventually to the export of their own domestic products.
- In spite of the benefits of TNC presence, more and more host governments are intervening in TNC activities through the introduction of domestic regulations.
- In EDCs local involvement in the planning of trade relations is on the rise, with cultural preferences influencing the choice of products and services TNCs are offering.
- Local private entrepreneurship has been expanding as services, especially telecommunications, are being privatized and smaller, diversified firms enter markets.
- Recently, environmental and health issues have become vital to EDCs, and concern over the TNC's handling of environmental and occupational health and safety matters is growing.
- Data resources and services are seen in many EDCs as essential national resources that, together with the restructuring of the telecommunications sector, can lead to the emerging "information society."

There are two areas where the impact of TNCs on the host country's development is seen as especially ominous. First, with respect to the electronic transmission by TNCs of firm-related data to the home office for processing and analysis, host governments fear that their own fledgling data processing industries and analytic skills are being thwarted (Sauvant 1986). Second, the impact of TNC's hiring practices, wage policies and their marketing of products and services which cannot be integrated into local societies is deemed deleterious. Indeed, "The growing power of the TNCs may not augur well for the poor unless governments show a better understanding of the development process" (Lall 1985, p. 65).

Factors Affecting the Relationship of TNCs and EDCs

Rapport between an American TNC's organization abroad and the host country, or the lack of it, can drastically affect potential benefits for both. In this area, where intelligence gathering by the TNC is vital, the obstacles to obtaining unbiased information are the worst. In addition to the dearth of credible and timely information channels, social and cultural factors impede information exchange needed to support positive relations between TNC managers and locals. Only more understanding of all factors may lead to improvements.

Generally, the relationship of developing countries and transnational corporations is perceived in the international literature as advantageous only for the TNCs. However, several benefits, such as foreign direct investment, technology development, and new skills can accrue to developing nations. The United Nations Environment Programme estimates that in the last decade 60 percent of industrial investment in developing countries originated from external sources, especially transnational corporations (Covello and Frey 1990). In the case of Mexico's Border Industrialization Program (BIP), fueled almost exclusively by U.S.-based TNC's investment, the estimated $3 billion in foreign exchange earnings the program pumps into the Mexican economy each year now exceeds revenues from tourism, and is second only to Mexico's oil and gas exports. Virtually all new manufacturing jobs created in Mexico in the past decade and a fifth of the country's manufacturing jobs overall have resulted from the rapid growth of the BIP (LaDou 1991). EDCs also obtain large amounts of technical information, assistance, and expertise from TNCs (Covello and Frey 1990).

Though developing countries extract many benefits from TNCs, there is a price to pay for any gains. The overriding question is: how high a price is considered exorbitant? The export of hazardous technologies and products from industrialized countries to the Third World receives some attention in the American press, though most of these stories are sensational rather than investigative. Dependence by EDCs on foreign technology and knowledge often reduces the number of technological choices available to EDCs and places them in a weak bargaining position. As Covello and Frey (1990, p. 166) maintain, "Given the special vulnerability of developing countries to technology-related health risks, and given the limited ability of developing nations to assess and manage environmental health risks, these exports contribute significantly to environmental health problems in developing countries."

In some EDCs, industrial taxation policy can affect the health of the population in an indirect way. "Countries that spend little on things like sewage systems, water treatment plants, and environmental and occupational safety can offer tax rates dramatically lower than those in the industrialized world. Foreign-based manufacturers take the bait and move in, polluting waterways and endangering workers. Yet the host government can't afford remedies because of the low tax rate" (LaDou 1991, p. 48).

Increased international awareness of positive and negative aspects of the relationship between American TNCs and host governments, local firms and urban and rural populations, may bring about substantial improvements. The perceived image of a TNC in the host country is a strong determinant of the firm's success. Sometimes cultural elements have as much weight in business negotiation and conflict resolution as have economic or political factors. Relevant themes in the literature include personnel policies, industrialization and poverty, the privatization of public services, the proliferation of private entrepreneurship, environmental issues, technology transfer, the improvement of telecommunication infrastructures, and trade in data services.

The Information Asset in TNCs

Competition from the Asia Pacific region and the European Community is driving the globalization of American business. Developing countries have become economic magnets attracting acquisitions, mergers, and joint ventures. "In 1970, foreign direct investment accounted for more than half of all private capital flows to the Third World; by 1985 that proportion had fallen to less than 20%. Recent data show that in 1986, foreign direct investment in the amount of $12.5 billion again represented nearly one-half of private capital flows to Third World countries" (Pollio and Riemenschneider 1991). The International Finance Corporation's survey of private investment in EDCs between 1970 and 1991 confirms the overall trend (Pfefferman and Madarassy 1993).

The American TNC's information system is facing the challenge of intercultural business activities at the macropolicy level, the national level, and the firm level. In the past, international policies exerted a direct impact on the American firm only as they affected business with foreign partners or were integrated into the American legal framework. A change is apparent in the expanding area of information use and the protection of confidentiality and secrecy from the points of view of both consumers and firm management. The reasons seem to be that (1) consumer rights movements have alerted people to the existence of personal information in databases and ways it is passed along by electronic networks, and (2) corporate leadership have come to recognize that information is key to competitive advantage.

A vast literature on corporate management, decision making, and information disclosure and control has grown out of these realizations. However, when the information consumer is a foreign citizen or an American working at a great distance from a TNC's home office, corporate information policies seldom address the attendant problems beyond the well-treated issues of trade secrets and proprietary information. As a member of the Organization for Economic Cooperation and Development (OECD), the United States has played a vital role in consolidating recommendations for TNCs to deal with today's volatile global business environment (Organization for Economic . . . 1986, 1992a, 1992b). But these expressions of macropolicy seldom reach the firm-level where individuals deal with everyday decisions about international contacts.

Information at the Firm Level

New trends have created new information requirements for the TNC in intelligence gathering, management, and the manipulation of information technology. The definition of intelligence as "the organizational capability . . . to acquire and use information in a creative way for action" (Radosevic 1991, p. 55) requires that firms distinguish between the acquisition of information (traditional role) and its use/application (new role). As the emerging primary areas of corporate intelligence, Toffler (1990) identifies economics, technology and ecology. Markets penetrated with more speed than in the past, longer time spans needed for research, and more resources required for new products are among the factors that contribute to the centrality of intelligence gathering to the firm's success (Toffler 1990).

In the management and shaping of organizational cultures, two ideology-based directions are dominating, each determining a different way of information use/application. As is widely known, "total quality" means "knowing what needs to be done, having the tools to do it right, and doing it right the first time" (Total Quality . . . 1991, p. 3). The "learning organization" is based on the principle that "in a continual cycle of learning, unlearning, and relearning, workers need to master new techniques, adapt to new organizational forms, and come up with new ideas" (Toffler 1990, p. 211). "Managers . . . are now faced with the task of optimizing efficiency, responsiveness, and learning simultaneously in their worldwide operations" (Bartlett and Ghoshal 1987, pt. 1, p. 7).

The company dedicated to total quality brings together people in groups to commit themselves to corporate goals and to discuss error-free work. The learning organization promotes the open group discussion of errors and failures in order to learn from the experience. The total quality approach uses information to prevent problems, monitor progress, and measure the cost of quality; the learning paradigm creates evidence of human failures as well as successes, building organizational memory. Both kinds of organizational culture emphasize communication, group dynamics, and problem solving skills (Applying . . . 1991, Cernea 1991, Hanson and Narula 1990, Zierden 1984).

Total quality management is well established, prominently known, and deeply imbedded in the operations of TNCs. Less well known, but in the process of rapid ascent, the concept of the learning organization holds great promise. The two directions are converging, and their merger as a powerful corporate management mechanism holds tremendous potential. The balance between striving for error-free performance and simultaneously learning from the way problems were analyzed, treated, resolved, unsolved, unattended or unnoticed in the past, would create a very constructive management culture, eminently applicable to international information activities.

More than a decade ago Porter and Millar (1979) urged that information must be conceived as both the information content created and used by business, as well as the technologies that process and access that information. New opportunities, created by the skillful merging of the information content and related technologies, become especially intriguing with respect to American business with developing countries:

- Can the exporting American company bundle more information with the product?
- What information generated (or potentially generated) in the business could the company sell [or barter]?
- Does information technology make it feasible to produce new items related to the company's product? (Porter and Millar 1979, p. 43).

When TNCs begin to explore the information technology environment in the Third World, American concepts and assumptions cease to apply. In the North, networks are expected to communicate data, images, video, sound, and more; in the South, we encounter vast rural areas using radio and satellite in the absence of a telecommunication infrastructure. Therefore, at the firm level, thinking about information from and for EDCs must adjust to technological options ranging from the advanced to the rudimentary. Such flexibility is essential because, as Radosevic (1991, p. 68) warns: " . . . intelligence failures, caused by an exclusive technological orientation" are not rare. On the other hand, information channels appropriate to participating EDCs may realize the optimistic forecast made a decade ago:

> . . . in the past, there were gross inefficiencies—some purposeful, some not—in the flow of information around the world. New technologies are eliminating those inefficiencies, and, with them, the opportunity for a kind of top-down information arbitrage . . . (Ohmae 1983, p. 4).

Management's Response to the Challenge

Keen (1991, p. 10) conducted interviews with members of top management teams in more than two dozen large firms, all industry leaders in North America and Europe. Few of the executives felt that they had the opportunity to exert a strong influence on the shaping of information technologies (IT) within their companies. The study found no apparent differences in attitudes toward IT across either country or industry, a finding not at all surprising in the light of the relative homogeneity of company cultures in the North. Replication of the study in developing countries probably would detect substantial differences both across countries and industries.

All the international operations of companies studied by Bartlett and Ghoshal (1987) were in a state of transition. More than 250 managers in nine of the world's largest TNCs were interviewed to discover perceptions of transnational opportunities and constraints. Findings led to the recognition that "the ability of a company to survive and succeed in today's turbulent international environment . . . depends on its organizational behavior and capabilities to adapt to new conditions." Managing the interdependence of a TNC's overseas organizations and the center, and responding to "the need to manage the flow of intelligence, ideas and knowledge," were found to be complex tasks that required proactive strategies. Why did some companies fall behind, while others adapted to changing demands? Constraints in organizational capability rather than lack of insight were found to create problems.

Among the manufacturers of telecommunication switching equipment, "the ability to learn and to appropriate the benefits of learning in multiple markets differentiated the winners from the losers" (Bartlett and

Ghoshal 1987, p. 10). Innovations created jointly by a TNC's headquarters and national organizations were found to be successful. Avoiding such dichotomies as domestic/global businesses and centralized/decentralized organizations, many companies are delegating influence to groups which perform particular tasks. Teamwork, coordination, and cooperation are deemed indispensable. Various socialization processes, especially the fostering of personal contacts, informal communication networks, and forums are facilitating the transfer of vast amounts of information. In another study, Bartlett and Ghoshal (1986, p. 94) examine factors contributing to the ups and downs of EMI, the U.K.-based TNC that had developed the CAT scanner, and find that "national companies [located overseas] must not be regarded as just pipelines but recognized as sources of information and expertise that can build competitive advantage."

White (1988) describes the experience of a manufacturing firm to exploit international market opportunities. From the perspective of company policies rather than research, he concludes that the acquisition, filtering, and use of external information proceed in four major phases of internationalization:

- Search for overseas markets ("we believed then, and do today, that the newly industrializing countries [NICs] are the best long-term bet for engine market growth")
- Search for high-quality, low-cost sources of supply ("important entry points . . . in this effort have been our own operations and international affiliate relationships with . . . Brazil, Mexico, India and China")
- "Rationalizing" in the industry ("taking out excess and obsolete capacity")
- Responding to foreign competition by setting higher standards in management and product quality ("there was real learning, and a lot of it").

Kim (1987) speaks of the American TNC's political crisis during the growth of economic nationalism in developing countries. To meet successfully a host government's intervention in the operations of a TNC requires prior awareness, familiarity with the political situation, and the ability to obtain up-to-date local information on the part of the company. The managers of TNC subsidiaries and organizations must be recognized as active sources of expertise on their host countries (Bartlett and Ghoshal 1986). New information requirements at the firm level include knowledge of new contractual forms, such as debt-for-equity swaps between TNCs and developing countries. Pollio and Riemenschneider (1991) observe that aggressive interventions or threats by host governments are on the decline. While in the 1970s the international rhetoric charged large-scale exploitation of EDCs by TNCs, today both have economic incentives to work together.

Information Ethics

Ethical conduct as a pragmatic issue rather than a conceptual proposition is claiming attention in both the public and private sectors in the United States. The federal Ethics in Government Act of 1978, as amended, put Designated Agency Ethics Officials (DAEOs) into federal agencies, and resulted in several studies, reviews and hearings (U.S. General Accounting Office 1988). Since the passage of the Ethics Reform Act of 1989, the scrutiny of ambiguities and transgressions in ethics has become a major political and public issue. The private sector lacks any similar mechanism. In spite of legislation on information disclosure to the government and the public, guidance on most of the open-ended information issues is left to institutional efforts such as legal codes, arbitration, professional codes of conduct, the statements of associations and public interest groups, and the resolutions of intergovernmental organizations. Within firms, many international information-related decisions are up to the individual.

The field of ethics is poorly defined and variously interpreted in terms of moral, behavioral, corporate-cultural and managerial issues. Gellerman (1986) refers to questions of human judgment in everyday situations. Through the analysis of three cases (suppressed evidence of asbestos risk by a corporation, overzealous following of corporate interests by a bank, and mail and wire fraud in a large brokerage house), he shows how managers rationalize their decisions and fail to observe the fine line between acceptable and unacceptable decisions. Edmonstone (1985) asks whether we should be concerned with the ethics of organizational ends or the means to achieve them. The author notes that organizational development (OD) must choose between a normative approach and a vaguely defined, value-free direction that leaves decisions to practitioners.

Several articles address information ethics. From an attorney's perspective, Toth (1989) recommends heightened sensitivity toward corporate use of electronic monitoring of personnel and telemarketing. To "substitute insight for judgment" is Schein's (1988) recommendation. In firms where diversity and innovation are critical, conformity is to be minimized and the freedom of individual decision making is to be encouraged. Obviously, asserts Schein, the culture of diversity needs a richer information base than does that of conformity. Gross (1988, p. 34) warns that "digital media are quietly eroding the foundations of our society's system of knowledge." Gross suggests that current cultural assumptions about information ought to change, and the prevailing belief that units of knowledge (news items, books, electronic data, etc.) are interchangeable ought to be defeated.

The protection of privacy in corporate databases is provoking much thought. Speaking of the changing role of the information systems manager, Owen (1986, p. 60) observes two universal pressures: technological advances and increased demands by management. The rapid transformation of the data processing environment led to "semiordered, technologically induced chaos." Westin (1991, pp. 34–36) suggests ten activities each company should introduce:

1. A Privacy Task Force endorsed by top management
2. An audit of all types of information collected by the company about customers
3. A detailed privacy analysis, taking as a starting point the Fair Information Practice Principles (used by American businesses for two decades), and collecting the Privacy Codes or Policy Guidelines of various companies. Privacy analysis examines the following:
    a) The need for collecting each piece of personal information
    b) Legal and regulatory rules governing the collection of personal information about the consumer, and legal actions
    c) New and emerging issues of privacy as expressed by advocacy groups, the media, and public and group opinion
    d) Existing rules and procedures for assuring the confidentiality of consumer personal information (both electronic and paper-based)
    e) Rules and procedures for providing individuals with notice of what is being done with their personal data, and eliciting consent
    f) Experience with customer complaints and litigation (if any) . . . and other indicators of problems
4. A technology analysis of existing and proposed products, including a data security study
5. Identification of customer opinions about the company's practices
6. Results of all previous steps reviewed by staff experts and operating executives, and a Consumer Privacy Code drawn up
7. Approval of top management
8. Training and implementation plan
9. A public communication program
10. Continuing reviews of the Code.

A description of the Data Protection Commissioner's responsibilities at the Volkswagen Company and other large firms in Germany is also useful as a point of reference. Weise (1992) reports that "the internal data protection commissioner together with the supervisory authority guarantees a most favorable data protection, both for the individual and for the company." The commissioner's "first duty is to safeguard personal data, but his knowledge of the company organization also enables him to achieve this in harmony with the legitimate interests of the company." Weise comments on the *Guidelines on the Protection of Privacy and Transborder Flows of Personal Data* [1981], issued by OECD and adopted by some TNCs, that "it would be impossible to ensure effective data protection primarily by control measures."

From Hungary comes an article by Szekely (1991) outlining the principles which underlie the abolishment of the personal identification number (PIN) by the Hungarian Constitutional Court on April 9, 1991. The decision is expected to have broad financial and organizational consequences. Szekely (1991, p. 26) indicates that many of the big users in the public and private sectors (population registry, the military, the tax office, banks, hospitals, service providers, and businesses) "have not even realized their tasks from the technical point of view, not to mention the new concept itself."

A number of researchers have used survey data for a better understanding of the role of information ethics in firms (Cohen and Czepiec 1988, Garrett et al. 1989, Vitell and Davis 1990). The impact of electronic surveillance in organizations is a form of potentially dangerous information gathering according to Parker (1988, who recommends ten steps firms may use to avoid escalation of this threat. Several ethics-enhancing social devices are described in the literature, including corporate credos, training workshops, ethics audits, and codes structured for a specific area of activity.

Glastonbury and LaMandola (1992, p. 3) represent the voice of the international advocates of information ethics: "If we are to have a technology with integrity, . . . a moral framework must be worked out, and established quickly, before the charge of scientific progress leaves the world's communities too far behind." The authors propose a Bill of Rights for the information age, and numerous other pragmatic approaches.

The Information Asset in EDCs

Involvement with markets, joint ventures, and government contracts in developing countries greatly increases the need of the American TNC for international information. National organizations are embedded in foreign cultures; laws and regulations of the United States become enmeshed with foreign legal systems; and information practices of the TNC's home office come face-to-face with foreign information patterns. It has been suggested that "acceptance of diversity and an organizational memory strengthen global competitiveness . . . . In an ideal system, people in the field would regularly feed information of all kinds to a central point, such as a headquarters strategic-planning or 'intelligence' unit. Even informal information is useful . . . "(Bose 1992, p. 28). Gathering information within EDCs presupposes an understanding of the foreign information environment. At the same time, information transactions with partners and local contacts in the host country have to be reciprocal to create a mutually supportive climate.

How do levels of access to local information change from country to country? How reliable are data gathering efforts? Who controls local information sources? This section attempts to point to main trends, problems and resources in EDCs. Coverage is limited to selected themes: information for innovation, information for research, national information infrastructures, and information trends affecting both EDCs and TNCs.

Information for Innovation

Every nation is searching for information assets in order to identify opportunities for innovation. Development specialists have been looking for clues as to the factors that support or hinder innovations. Is there a set of incentives typical for EDCs? Is it possible to identify and strengthen these factors? Has innovation itself become a different concept in the cultural environment of EDCs? Future research on information use for innovation may lead to some answers to these questions.

For decision makers in EDCs who perceive innovation for national technological self-reliance as a goal, the availability of information systems responsive to their needs is a major step toward the achievement of that goal (Bardini 1992, Friend and Rapport 1991). Common characteristics of emerging and proposed systems include system design based on indigenous needs, and databases constructed from indigenous knowledge. Thus a significant shift in the relationship between information and development is occurring: information is becoming an integral part of, rather than a mere support to, national development.

Examples of national policies and institutions in support of indigenous innovative capability include Thailand and Malaysia. The Thailand Development Research Institute defines a country's innovative capability as the ability to carry out R&D; radical product modification; radical process modification; major changes achieved by producing firms; and new inventions (Swierczek and Nourie 1992). Malaysia's science and technology policy, the main instrument for innovation strategies, is grounded in the country's cultural and religious orientation (Malaysia . . . 1986):

The National Science and Technology Policy is to promote the utilisation of Science and Technology as a tool for economic development, the improvement of human physical and spiritual well-being and for the protection of national sovereignty being an integral part of the socioeconomic development of the nation.

Innovation in enterprises is spurred by economic competitiveness and the availability of technology. Due to its role as a predictive signal of accelerating development, the innovative capability of a country is closely watched by investors. Partnership with an innovative local firm is one of the vehicles to success for foreign businesses. Innovation is the result of an intricate process that organizations strive to discover and incorporate into their very existence. Political skills, managerial intuition, creativity, learning, risk-taking, and the absorption of information are tightly interwoven with the process. However, without supportive public policies, organization-level innovation is a rarity.

An analysis by Dana (1987) compares public policies toward small enterprises in Malaysia and Singapore. The Small Enterprise Bureau of Singapore assists business operators not only by loans, grants, and tax incentives, but also by establishing networks of enterprises for experience and information exchange. Malaysia offers similar loan and tax incentives, but pays less attention to the diverse individual needs of borrowers. The study uses interesting data, but fails to explore the link between industrial policy and the cultural traits of each country. This link may be an essential element in the nation's innovative capability. The example of Korea suggests that a country wishing to upgrade its technologically-based competitiveness needs local institutional mechanisms for supporting industrial innovation through science, small business start-ups, and government incentives (Crow and Nath 1992).

Empirical research on the innovative activities of firms in EDCs by Western researchers was originally based on wrong assumptions, and took wrong directions. The dominating assumption had been that Third World firms were perennially low-technology, low-skill and small-scale operations. Researchers were interested only in major breakthroughs rather than small innovations that eventually led these firms to success (Lall 1982, p. 59).

Wells (1983, p. 19) observes that most research on TNCs in industrialized countries emphasizes the competitive technological advantages of firms. Multinational operations of the Third World are developing a different kind of technological advantage that supports not only the companies, but also the economic and social development of their countries. To a great extent, their innovation consists of the adaptation of technology acquired elsewhere. But the special skills, information, and knowledge these firms have accumulated are quite extensive. As Lall (1982, pp. 5–7) stated, "even very poor countries may develop a comparative advantage in the sales of skills and know-how . . . for the technologies in which . . . [they] have asserted their advantage, we may well see an increasing flow of exports . . . "

Gerstenfeld and Wortzel (1977) investigated three characteristics of innovation in developing countries: (1) Changes in product's life-cycle phase, (2) incentives for introducing the change, and (3) information sources used in the process. Data were collected by structured interviews on 47 innovations in 33 companies in Taiwan. A domestic market proved to be a fundamental condition for innovation. Products did not have to reach a mature state before they could be innovated. Similarly to researchers studying innovation in industrialized countries, Gerstenfeld and Wortzel found that the major information source for innovation was personal contact. U.S.-trained scientists and engineers in Taiwan "form somewhat of an information network," because external information sources play an important role.

Swierczek and Nourie (1992) studied barriers to innovation at the macro-level in Thailand and found numerous deterrents (in the following order):

- Shortage of skilled people
- Inadequate information services
- Inadequate government funding for R&D
- Lack of specialized technology research centers
- Weak government policies
- Few supportive industries
- Lack of intellectual property protection
- Ineffective infrastructures
- Lack of R&D facilities
- Poor managerial attitudes
- Limited private financial support
- Limited raw materials.

More subtle institutional difficulties were identified by the Technology Atlas Team (1987, pt. 1):

- Nature and complexity of technology
- Underlying preferences, perceptions, misconceptions and assumptions
- Organizational infrastructure and management practices:
  Ineffective public sector R&D
  "Knowing science" (knowledge) being given preference over "doing science" (applications)

Absence of institutionalized attempts at monitoring, forecasting, and assessing technology
- Level of commitment to technology-related considerations and leadership behavior:
    Technologists and scientists not being exposed to management and socioeconomic development concepts
- The climate represented by the attitudes and preoccupations of the people:
    Scarcity of time, as intellectual priorities are clogged with trivia and ceremonial duties.

The second phase of the project addressed the various components of technology that act as catalysts ("transformers") of resources (Technology Atlas Team 1987, pt. 2):

- Technoware (object-embodied technology)
- Humanware (person-embodied technology)
- Infoware (document-embodied technology)
- Orgaware (institution-embodied technology).

A shortcoming of this set of definitions is the narrow perspective on one type of information resource, the "document," instead of a vision of the broad integrative nature of "information." More inquiry into the innovation process in Third World countries will be needed to learn about the links between development, technology, and information.

Perspectives in AT&T

This study was designed to produce descriptive information from three sources: (1) analysis of the research and policy literature, (2) exploration of perspectives within AT&T as expressed by individuals who participated in unstructured interviews, focus groups, and responses to a structured questionnaire, and (3) AT&T publications and documents.

The second part of this paper discusses the perspectives and views of AT&T executives and information professionals who are involved in international activities. This case-study approach will seek to supplement the broadly based information gained from the literature review that examined the intercultural environment in which different kinds of transnational corporations operate.

Research Approach

The questions explored by the study addressed the relationship of one American transnational corporation, AT&T, with developing countries in regard to (1) business partnerships, (2) intercultural communications, (3) the transfer of information, and (4) potential ways to improve such relationships through innovation in information acquisition and delivery. Interactions between the company and EDCs may take place face-to-face within a host country, in another foreign country, within the United States, or they may be transactions using communication and information media.

The population queried consisted of two groups within AT&T: executives in charge of international planning and decision making, and information professionals experienced in international information transfer. The small sample forestalls any generalization. The case-study approach of multiple strategies, comprising mainly qualitative and, to a smaller extent, quantitative methods, included in-depth personal interviews and focus groups using unstructured interview guides, followed by a structured questionnaire on information resource use and by an examination of representative AT&T publications.

The process of the analysis of responses was threefold. Using the interview guide as a starting point, remarks from the *interviews with executives* were matched with the question most similar in context and content. New response categories were created for themes spontaneously introduced during the interviews. Remarks then were summarized for each question and thematic links (contrast and comparison) were established, relating responses to one question to comments pertinent to one or more other questions.

In the case of *focus groups with information professionals,* key points of topical responses were listed in bulletin format, using the interview guide as a framework. Especially illustrative examples offered by respondents were quoted verbatim or paraphrased. Responses to the International Information Survey (designed by Ronnye Schreiber in AT&T) were tabulated for each selection, for each question. Percentages, calculated for each selection, were used to rank selections for each forced-choice question. Answers to open-ended questions were grouped with like responses, then tabulated.

Study Conclusions

Conclusions of this study rest upon (a) the synthesis of the relevant research and policy literatures, (b) information gathered from personal interviews and focus groups, and (c) information from AT&T documents.

- All three types of resources emphasize the rapidly growing strategic relevance of INTERNATIONAL COMMUNICATIONS AND INFORMATION to corporate goals.
- DEVELOPING COUNTRIES are viable sources of new opportunities

for American business; changes in their technological and social pattern, the process of privatization, and emerging consumer needs of their societies have the capacity to affect international commercial relationships. This and the presence of persistent poverty in most developing countries are not contradictions but the phenomena of new inequalities.

- To a great extent, constructive business relationships depend on INTERNATIONAL COMMUNICATIONS, while the effectiveness of communications most often depends on RELEVANT INFORMATION about infrastructures, cultures, situations, expectations, the social environment, and the legal framework.
- GLOBAL INFORMATION FLOWS are determined by the changing nature of scientific cooperation; new technologies; the role of TNCs; telecommunication developments; intercultural technology transfer; transborder data flow; and intellectual property rights.
- NATIONAL INFORMATION FLOWS in developing countries are affected by political, economic and social factors; local governments; elites; new private enterprises; indigenous cultural developments, and ethnic relationships.
- International communications and information transfer to and from THE AMERICAN TNC are becoming increasingly complex, moving in a growing number of formal and uncharted informal channels.
- Advanced technology and multimedia support but do not guarantee communication/information success. NEW THINKING ABOUT INFORMATION INFRASTRUCTURES, HUMAN LINKS AND INFORMATION ETHICS IS ESSENTIAL.
- WITHIN THE AMERICAN TNC, CLOSE INTERACTION among information users, providers, and managers can greatly improve access to high quality international information, thus enhancing the total quality management of U.S.-based and overseas operations.
- There is a danger that economic pressures will be allowed to slow INNOVATIONS in information management, research, and dissemination. However, INNOVATIVE SPIRIT AND MOMENTUM are guarantees against stagnation and the only promise of sustained and sound progress.

Persuasive Changes in the Role of Information

"International information" is a concept poorly defined and used with multiple interpretations in the R&D and policy processes. Each transnational corporation (TNC) must formulate its own definitions, goals, principles and strategies for international information.

The first step is to identify and manage the corporate interdependence of international business intelligence, information/communication flows and information/communication technology. The next step is to identify and manage the interdependence of the quality, integrity and effectiveness of corporate information and communication processes. These two steps are prerequisites of formulating corporation-wide strategies for international information generation and use and represent a major challenge for research.

Four principles relevant to the role of information are emerging. The successful utilization of international information is determined by

- the analytical understanding of problems and the synthesis of information into knowledge units applicable to tasks and problems
- the quality of information
- the integrity of the information/communication process
- the integrated flow of knowledge, created of information, permeating corporate R&D, organization development, and marketing.

Closing Note

Research evidence and international policy documents identified a number of factors that have caused revolutionary changes in the information environment of the American transnational corporation (TNC) and its relationship with economically developing countries (EDCs). Changes and trends that are creating new information and knowledge demands for the TNC are taking place in the

- relationships of TNCs and EDCs
- factors affecting these relationships
- environmental issues in EDCs
- the EDCs' drive for technological capability
- technology transfer to EDCs
- restructuring of telecommunications in EDCs
- international information utilization in TNCs
- information infrastructures and resources in EDCs
- crosscultural communications.

Perceptions and experiences of AT&T executives and information professionals, and observations in selected AT&T publications, confirmed some of the effects of economic and social transformations in developing countries described in the literature. As expected, the links

between international changes and new corporate information requirements are not clear. People refer to such links abundantly, but always in
vague and undefined terms.

Information/communication issues AT&T executives and information professionals are concerned with include:

- dynamics of business relations between AT&T and EDCs
- market potential of EDCs
- quality and effects of intercultural communications
- credibility and validity of international information and data
- legal and ethical issues, especially intellectual property rights
- information flows to and from EDCs
- the cost of international information
- international information requirements and resources with AT&T
- access to business intelligence about EDCs.

Recommendations

Based on the evidence of research and international policy, as well as on
the perceptions within AT&T, the study concluded with the following
recommendations:

- Increased PROACTIVE ATTITUDES AND VISIBILITY, without losing the capability for systematic and well-grounded processes and activities
- Application of the PRINCIPLES OF STRATEGIC DYNAMICS
  to international information services, without overlooking the need
  for solid, research-based, HIGH-INTEGRITY KNOWLEDGE that
  has always been valued by information users
- Close COOPERATION of all existing international information
  sources (centers, networks, databases, information products) in
  AT&T organizations
- Introduction and testing of innovative approaches such as INFOR-
  MATION COUNSELING (IC) by synthesizing and formalizing
  the numerous information counseling-related activities already
  present in the organization
- Construction of a DATABASE of international information agencies, resources, experts, and technology transfer cases, with emphasis on developing countries
- Development of NETWORKS OF INDIGENOUS EXPERTS in
  each developing country to advise AT&T of culturally specific factors which may affect the accuracy and completeness of business
  information

- A program to exchange DOCUMENTS with developing countries as a means of increasing the volume of electronically searchable material and make documents available.

A valid goal for future research is to identify why and how innovations in external and internal international information practices contribute to the achievement of corporate goals in the intercultural business climate.

References

Applying the Principles Seminar. (1991). Corning, NY: Corning, Inc. Rev.

Bardini, T. (1992). Linking indigenous knowledge systems and development: The Potential uses of microcomputers. *Knowledge and Policy: The International Journal of Knowledge Transfer and Utilization,* 5(1), 29–41.

Bartlett, C.A. & Ghoshal, S. (1987). Managing across borders: New strategic requirements, Pt. 1. *Sloan Management Review,* 28(4), 7–17. Managing across borders: New organizational responses, Pt. 2. *Sloan Management Review,* 29(1), 43–53.

Bartlett, C.A. & Ghoshal, S. (1986). Tap your subsidiaries for global reach. *Harvard Business Review,* 64(6), 87–94.

Bereznoi, A.V. (1990). *Third World Newcomers in International Business.* New Delhi, India: Ajanta Publications.

Bose, R.K. (1992). *Asia: Strategic Blunders and Tactical Errors: Lessons for Western Business.* London Borough of Croydon, UK: SRI International.

Cernea, M. (1991). *Using Knowledge from Social Science in Development Projects.* Washington, DC: The World Bank.

Cohen, W. & Czepiec, H. (1988). The Role of ethics in gathering corporate intelligence. *Journal of Business Ethics,* 7(3), 199–203.

Covello, V.T. & Frey, R.S. (1990). Technology-based environmental health risks in developing nations. *Technological Forecasting and Social Change,* 37(2), 159–179.

Crow, M.M. & Nath, S.A. (March 1992). Technology strategy development in Korean industry: An assessment of market and government influence. *Technovation,* 12(2), 119–136.

Dana, L.P. (1987). Industrial development efforts in Malaysia and Singapore. *Journal of Small Business Management,* 25, 74–76.

Dobkin, J.A. ed. (1988). *International Technology Joint Venture in the Countries of the Pacific Rim.* Singapore: Butterworth (Asia).

Edmonstone, J. (1985). The Values problem in OD. *Leadership and Organization Development Journal,* 6(2), 7–10.

Friend, A.M. & Rapport, D.J. (1991). Evolution of macro-information systems for sustainable development. *Ecological Economics,* 3, 59–76.

Garrett, D.E. et al. (1989). Issues management and organizational accounts: An analysis of corporate responses to accusations of unethical business practices. *Journal of Business Ethics,* 8(7), 507–520.

Gellerman, S.W. (1986). Why 'good' managers make bad ethical choices. *Harvard Business Review,* 64(4), 85–90.

Gerstenfeld, A. & Wortzel, L.H. (1977). Strategies for innovation in developing countries. *Sloan Management Review,* 19(1), 57–68.

Ghosh, P.K. ed. (1984). *Technology Policy and Development, a Third World Perspective.* Westport, CT: Greenwood Press.

Glastonbury, B. & LaMandola, W. (1992). *The Integrity of Intelligence.* New York, NY: St. Martin's Press.

Goodman, L.W. (1987). *Small Nations, Giant Firms.* New York, NY: Holmes and Meier.

Gross, D. (1988). The Need for knowledge integrity. *Information Today,* 5(3), 9, 34.

Hanson, J. & Narula, U. (1990). *New Communication Technologies in Developing Countries.* Hillsdale, NJ: Lawrence Erlbaum Associates.

Jenkins, R. (1987). *Transnational Corporations and Uneven Development: The Internationalization of Capital and the Third World.* London: Methuen.

Keen, P.G.W. (1991). *Shaping the Future: Business Design Through Information Technology.* Cambridge, MA: Harvard Business School Press.

Kim, W.C. (1987). Competition and the management of host government intervention. *Sloan Management Review,* 28(3), 33–37.

LaDou, J. (1991). Deadly migration. *Technology Review,* 94(5), 46–57.

Lall, S. (1982). *Developing Countries as Exporters of Technology, a First Look at the Indian Experience.* London: The Macmillan Press.

Lall, S. (1985). *Multinationals, Technology and Exports, Selected Papers.* New York, NY: St. Martin's Press.

Lall, S. et al. (1983). *The New Multinationals: The Spread of Third World Enterprises.* New York, NY: Wiley.

Malaysia. Ministry of Science, Technology and the Environment. (1986). *Science and Technology Policy.* Kuala Lumpur (Unpublished).

Ohmae, K. (1983). "Managing in a Borderless World." In *Going Global: Succeeding in World Markets,* 3–12. Boston, MA: Harvard Business School Publishing.

Organization for Economic Cooperation and Development (OECD). (1992a). *Information Networks and New Technologies: Opportunities and Policy Implications for the 1990s.* Paris, France: OECD.

Organization for Economic Cooperation and Development (OECD). (1992b). *Integration of Developing Countries into the International Trading System.* Paris, France: OECD.

Organization for Economic Cooperation and Development (OECD). (1992c). *The OECD Declaration and Decisions on International Investment and Multinational Enterprises, 1991 Review.* Paris, France: OECD.

Organization for Economic Cooperation and Development (OECD). (1986). *The OECD Guidelines for Multinational Enterprises.* Paris, France: OECD.

Owen, D.E. (1986). SMR Forum: Information systems organizations — keeping pace with the pressures. *Sloan Management Review,* 28(1), 59–68.

Parker, D.B. (1988). Ethics for information systems personnel. *Journal of Information Systems Management,* 5(3), 44–48.

Pfefferman, G.P. & Madarassy, A. (1993). *Trends in Private Investment in Developing Countries 1993.* Washington, DC: The World Bank (IFC Discussion Paper 16).

Pollio, G. & Riemenschneider, C.H. (1991). "The Coming Third World investment revival." In *Going Global: Succeeding in World Markets,* 129–134. Boston, MA: Harvard Business School Publishing.

Porter, M.E. & Millar, V.E. (1979). "How information gives you competitive advantage." In Michael E. Porter, *On Competition and Strategy,* 33–44. Boston, MA: Harvard Business School Publishing.

Radosevic, S. (1991). Techno-economic intelligence in the 1990s: A development policy perspective. *Social Intelligence,* 1(1), 55–71.

Robinson, P. (1991). The International dimension of telecommunications policy issue. *Telecommunications Policy,* 15(2), 95–100.

Roth, G. (1987). *The Private Provision of Public Services in Developing Countries.* New York, NY: Oxford University Press.

Sauvant, K.P. (1986). *Transaction in Services, the Politics of Transborder Data Flows.* Boulder, CO: Westview Press, (Atwater Series on the World Information Economy, 1).

Schein, E.H. (1988). Organizational socialization and the profession of management. *Sloan Management Review,* 30(1), 53–65.

Singh, M. (1989). "Development Policy Research: The Task Ahead." In *Proceedings of the World Bank Annual Conference on Development Economics 1989,* 11–20. Washington, DC: The World Bank.

Swierczek, F.W. & Nourie, C. (1992). Technology development in Thailand: A private sector view. *Technovation,* 12(3), 145–161.

Szekely, I. (1991). Hungary outlaws personal number. *Transnational Data and Communications Report,* 14(5), 25–27.

Technology Atlas Team. (1987). A Framework for technology-based national planning. *Technological Forecasting and Social Change (Pt. 1),* 32(1), 5–18.

Technology Atlas Team. (1987). Components of technology for re-
    sources transformation. *Technological Forecasting and Social Change
    (Pt. 2)*, 32(1), 19–35.
Toffler, A. (1990). *Powershift*. New York, NY: Bantam Books.
Total Quality Orientation Seminar. (1991). Corning, NY: Corning Inc.,
    Rev.
Toth, V.J. (1989). Update on telecom privacy and free speech. *Business
    Communications Review*, 19(9), 80–87.
United Nations. (1988). *Transnational Corporations in World Develop-
    ment: Trends and Prospects*. New York, NY: UN.
United Nations Centre on Transnational Corporations. (1988). *National
    Legislation and Regulations Relating to Transnational Corporation*.
    Vol. 6, New York, NY: UNCTC.
United Nations Centre on Transnational Corporations. (1986). *Transna-
    tional Corporations and Technology Transfer: Effects and Policy Is-
    sues*. New York, NY: UNCTC.
United States General Accounting Office. (1988). *Ethics: Office of Gov-
    ernment Ethics' Policy Development Role*. Washington, DC: GAO.
Vernon, R. & Wells, Jr., L.T. (1981). *Economic Environment of Inter-
    national Business*. 3d ed. Englewood Cliffs, NY: Prentice-Hall.
Vitell, S.J. & Davis, D.L. (1990). Ethical beliefs of MIS professionals:
    The Frequency and opportunity for unethical behavior. *Journal of
    Business Ethics*, 9(1), 63–70.
Weise, K.T. (1992). The Company data protection commissioner. *Trans-
    national Data and Communications Report*, 15(2), 30.
Wells, L.T. Jr. (1983). *Third World Multinationals, the Rise of Foreign
    Investment from Developing Countries*. Cambridge, MA: The MIT
    Press.
Westin, A.F. (1991). Managing consumer privacy issues—A checklist.
    Transnational Data and Communications Report, 14(1), 34–36.
White, B.J. (1988). The Internationalization of business: One company's
    response. *The Academy of Management Executive*, 1(1), 29–32.
Zierden, W.E. (1984). *Pursuing Excellence Through Quality*. Char-
    lottesville, VA: University of Virginia, The Colgate Darden School of
    Business Administration.

Further Readings

Economic, Social and Cultural Issues in Development

International Studies

Amirahmadi, H. & Wu, W. (1994). Foreign direct investment in developing countries. *The Journal of Developing Areas,* 28(2), 167–189.

Beaumont, J.R. (1993). A new world order and managing the environment. *Futures,* 25(2), 196–202.

Brugmann, J. (1994). Who can deliver sustainability? Municipal reform and the sustainable development mandate. *Third World Planning Review,* 16(2), 129–146.

Chambers, R. (1994). The origins and practice of participatory rural appraisal. *World Development,* 22(7), 953–969.

Chiang, J-T. (1993). From industry targeting to technology targeting: A policy paradigm shift in the 1980s. *Technology in Society,* 15(4), 341–358.

Coveney, P. & Highland, R. (1995). *Frontiers of Complexity: The Search for Order in a Chaotic World.* New York, NY: Fawcett Columbine.

Dia, M. (1996). *Africa's Management in the 1990s and Beyond: Reconciling Indigenous and Transplanted Institutions.* Washington, DC: The World Bank.

Dorraj, M., ed. (1995). *The Changing Political Economy of the Third World.* Boulder, CO: Lynne Rienner Publications.

Edwards, S. (1993). Openness, trade liberalization and growth in developing countries. *Journal of Economic Literature,* 31(3), 1358–1393.

Fellizar, F.P. (1994). Achieving sustainable development through community-based resource management. *Regional Development Dialogue,* 15(1), 201–217.

Gibson, H.D. & Tsakalotos, E. (1994). The scope and limits of financial liberalization in developing countries: A critical survey. *The Journal of Development Studies,* 30(3), 578–628.

Golembiewski, R. T. (1993). Organizational development in the Third World: Values, closeness of fit and culture-boundedness. *International Journal of Public Administration,* 16(11), 1667–1691.

Grabowski, R. (1994). The successful development state: Where does it come from? *World development,* 22(3), 413–422.

James, J. (1993). New technologies, employment and labor markets in developing countries. *Development and Change,* 24(3), 405–437.

Jones, M.L. & Blunt, P. (1993). Organizational development and change in Africa. *International Journal of Public Administration,* 16(11), 1735–1765.

Kaplinsky, R. (1994). From mass production to flexible specialization: A case study of microeconomic change in a semi-industrialized economy. *World Development,* 22(3), 337–353.

Kumara, U.A. (1993). Investment, industrialization and transnational corporations in selected Asian countries. *Regional Development Dialogue,* 14(4), 3–22.

Lall, S. (1993). Understanding technology development. *Development and Change,* 24(4), 719–753.

Nussbaum, M.C. (1995). *Poetic Justice: The literary imagination and public life.* Boston, MA: Beacon Press.

Okoroafo, S. & Russow, L.C. (1993). Impact of marketing strategy on performance: Empirical evidence from a liberalized developing country. *International Marketing Review,* 10(1), 4–18.

Page, J. M. (1994). The East Asian miracle: An introduction. *World Development,* 22(4), 615–625.

Perkins, D.H. (1994). There are at least three models of East Asian development. *World Development,* 22(4), 655–661.

Schweigert, T. (1994). Penny capitalism: Efficient but poor or inefficient and (less than) second best? *World Development,* 22(5), 721–735.

Sengupta, J.K. (1993). Growth in the NICs in Asia: Some tests of new growth theory. *The Journal of development Studies,* 29(2), 342–357.

White, R.R. (1994). Strategic decisions for sustainable urban development in the Third World. *Third World Planning Review,* 16(2), 103–116.

Wong, S.Y. (1994). Globalization and regionalization: The shaping of new economic regions in Asia and the Pacific. *Regional development Dialogue,* 15(10, 3–17.

Yaron, J. (1994). What makes rural finance institution successful? *World Bank Research Observer,* 9(1), 49–70.

Country Studies

Aina, T.A., Etta, F.E. & Obi, C.I. (1994). The search for sustainable urban development in metropolitan Lagos, Nigeria: Prospects and problems. *Third World Planning Review,* 16(2), 201–219.

Amanor, K.S. (1994). Ecological knowledge and the regional economy: Environmental management in the Asesewa District of Ghana. *Development and Change,* 25(1), 41–67.

Apibunyopas, P. (1993). Transnational corporations and impact on industrialization in Thailand. *Regional Development Dialogue,* 14(4), 94–117.

Atkinson, A. & Vorratnchaiphan, C.P. (1994). Urban environmental management in a changing development context: The case of Thailand. *Third World Planning Review,* 16(2), 147–169.

Balisacan, A.M. (1993). Agricultural growth, landlessness, off-farm employment, and rural poverty in the Philippines. *Economic Development and Cultural Change,* 41(3), 533–562.

Bomfin, A. & Shah, A. (1994). Macroeconomic management and the division of powers in Brazil: Perspective for the 1990s. *World Development,* 22(4), 535–542.

Bos, A. & Cole, W.E. (1994). Management systems as technology: Japanese, U.S. and national firms in the Brazilian electronic sector. *World Development,* 22(2), 225–236.

Burns, J.P. (1993). Administrative reform in China: Issues and prospects. *International Journal of Public Administration,* 16(9), 1345–1369.

Cantarero, R. & Gaber, J. (1994). Introducing political considerations into technical plans: A case study of Nicaragua's economic reorganization in a post-Sandinista administration. *International Journal of Public Administration,* 17(9), 1583–1629.

Chang, K.S. (1994). Chinese urbanization and development before and after economic reform: A comparative reappraisal. *World Development,* 22(4), 601–613.

Chia, L.S. (1993). Megainfrastructure system linking cities and regions to the global economy: The experience of Changi Airport, Singapore. *Regional Development Dialogue,* 14(2), 1–24.

Chow, C.K. (1993). The role of megainfrastructure systems in the urban development of Hong Kong. *Regional Development Dailogue,* 14(2), 73–91.

Cohen, B. & House, W.J. (1993). Women's urban labor market status in developing countries: How well do they fare in Khartoum, Sudan? *The Journal of Development Studies,* 29(3), 461–483.

Evers, H. D. & Mehmet, O. (1994). The management of risk: Informal trade in Indonesia. *World Development,* 22(1), 1–9.

Gershenberg, I. (1994). Gender, training, and the creation of a managerial elite: Multi-nationals and other firms in Jamaica. *The Journal of Developing Areas,* 28(3), 313–324.

Gonzalez, A. (1993). The Philippines in the near future. *International Social Science Review,* 68(2), 51–59.

Gu, S. (1996). The emergence of new technology enterprises in China: A study of endogenous capability building via restructuring. *The Journal of Development Studies,* 32(4), 475–505.

Haddad, M. & Harrison, A. (1993). Are there positive spillovers from direct foreign investment? Evidence from panel data for Morocco. *Journal of Development Economics,* 42(1), 51–74.

Himbara, D. (1994). The failed Africanization of commerce and industry in Kenya. *World Development,* 22(3), 469–482.

Hobday, M. (1994). Technical learning in Singapore: A test case of leapfrogging. *The Journal of Development Studies,* 30(4), 831–858.

Huang, D., Tang, D. & Chow, K.W. (1993). Public administration in Hong Kong: Crisis and prospects. *International Journal of Public Administration,* 16(9), 1397–1430.

Illori, M. O. (1994). The role of local government in technical and industrial development in Nigeria. *Technovation,* 14(3), 172–179.

Laquian, A.A. (1996). China and Vietnam: Urban strategies in societies in transition. *Third World Planning Review,* 18(1), iii-xi.

Liou, K.T. (1994). The performance of state-owned enterprises in Taiwan. *International Journal of Public Administration,* 17(8), 1459–1484.

Manuel, P. (1993). *Cassette culture: Popular music and technology in North India.* Chicago, IL: University of Chicago Press.

Perkins, F.C. (1996). Productivity performance and priorities for the reform of China's state-owned enterprises. *The Journal of Development Studies,* 32(3), 414–444.

Prabatmodjo, H. & Kusbiantoro, B.S. (1993). Indonesia: Case study of transnational corporations. *Regional Development Dialogue,* 14(4), 25–37.

Pragtong, K. (1993). Social forestry in Thailand: Policy evolution and institutional arrangements. *Regional Development Dialogue,* 14(1), 59–69.

Rodriguez, A.G. (1994). Comparison of determinants of urban, rural and farm poverty in Costa Rica. *World Development,* 22(3), 381–397.

Sivalingam, G. & Yong, S.P. (1993). Transnational corporations and industrialization in Malaysia: Organizational behavior and local and regional impacts. *Regional Development Dialogue,* 14(4), 40–64.

Staal, P.V.D. (1994). Communication media in Japan: economic and regional aspects. *Telecommunications Policy,* 18(1), 32–50.

Thornton, W.H. (1994). The Korean road to postmodernization and development. *Asian Pacific Quarterly,* 26(1), 1–11.

Timmer, C.P. (1993). Rural bias in the East and South-East Asian economy: Indonesia in comparative perspective. *The Journal of Development Studies,* 29(4), 146–176.

Xie, Q.K. (1993). Chinese public administration: Misunderstanding and implications. *International Journal of Public Administration,* 16(9), 1431–1458.

Special Issues

Alcorta, L. (1994). The impact of new technologies on scale in manufacturing industries: Issues and evidence. *World Development,* 22(5), 755–769.

Brauer, G.W. (1994). The future of information technologies for health care in developing countries: An examination of some problems. *IFIP Transactions A [Computer Science and Technology],* A-52, 509–516.

Broad, R. (1994). The poor and the environment: Friends or foes? *World Development,* 22(6), 811–822.

Chatterjee, P. (1994). Slush funds, corrupt consultants and bidding for bank business. *Multinational Monitor,* 15(7), 17–20.

Chia, A. (1994). Convergence: Impact and issues for the media. *Media Asia,* 21(3), 126–129.

Choguill, C.L. (1994). Implementing urban development projects: A search for criteria for success. *Third World Planning Review,* 16(1), 26–39.

Colchester, M. (1994). Sustaining the forests: The community-based approach in South and South East Asia. *Development and Change,* 25(1), 69–100.

Eashwer, L. (1994). Impact of new communication technology on women as users and producers of the means of communication. *Media Asia,* 21(1), 32–38.

Freeman, C. & Hagedoorn, J. (1994). Catching up or falling behind: Patterns in international interfirm technology partnering. *World Development,* 22(5), 771–780.

Goldman, K.A. (1994). Compensation for use of biological resources under the Convention on Biological Diversity: Compatability of conservation measures and competitiveness of the biotechnology industry. *Law and Policy in International Business,* 25(2), 695–726.

Jamias, J.F. (1993). The impact of new communication technologies on cultural identity in rural Asia. *Media Asia,* 20(4), 205–207.

Lin, C.S. (1994). Changing theoretical perspectives on urbanization in Asian developing countries. *Third World Planning Review,* 16(1), 1–23.

Montgomery, J.D. (1993). A program for enhancing environmental technology choices in Asia and the Pacific. *The Journal of Development Studies,* 28(1), 31–38.

Moore, M. (1993). Economic structure and the politics of sectoral bias: East Asian and other cases. *The Journal of Development Studies,* 29(4), 79–128.

Noam, E., Komatsuzaki, S. & Conn, D.A. eds. (1994). *Telecommunications in the Pacific Basin: an Evolutionary Approach.* Oxford, UK: Oxford University Press.

Singer, S.F. (1992). Sustainable development vs. global environment: Resolving the conflict. *Columbia Journal of World Business,* 27(3/4), 154–162.

Singh, J.B. & Caraso, E.F. (1996). Business ethics, economic development and protection of the environment in the New World Order. *Journal of Business Ethics,* 15(3), 297–307.

Takano, T., Nakamura, K. & Akao, C. (1995). Assessment of the value of videophones in home health care. *Telecommunications Policy,* 19(3), 241–248.

Tan, K. Y. (1993). Participatory land-use planning as a sociological methodology for natural resource management. *Regional Development Dialogue,* 14(1), 70–83.

Thahane, T.T. & Amin, H. (1994). Technological and communications revolutions: A critical dimension of development. *IFIP Transaction A [Computer Science and Technology],* A-52, 205–212.

Information and Development

International Studies

Abid, A & Pelliser, D. (1994). CD-ROM in developing countries: A UNESCO perspective. *INSPEL,* 28(3), 366–376.

Association of Research Libraries. (1993). *Gateway to the Pacific Rim: Information Resources for the 21st Century. Minutes of the 122nd Meeting, Honolulu, Hawaii, 1993.* Washington, DC: Association of Research Libraries.

Avgerou, C. (1993). Information systems for development planning. *International Journal of Information Management,* 13(4), 260–273.

Bourne, J. et al. (1994). Implementing the information highway. *Telesid,* 98, 4–25.

Bowonder, B., Miyake, T. & Monish Singh, T. (1993). Emerging trends in information technology: Impications for developing countries. *International Journal of Information Management,* 13(3), 183–204.

Burn, J.M. (1995). Confucian culture or cultural confusion? The impact of information technology in Asia. *Information Infrastructure and Policy,* 4(3), 193–209.

Chang, A.M., Holsappe, C.W. & Whinston, A.B. (1994). A hyper-knowledge framework of decision support systems. *Information Processing & Management,* 30(4), 473–498.

Deschatelets, G. & Legault, M. (1994). An inventory of CD-ROM in developing countries and East European countries. *Quarterly Bulletin of the International Association of Agricultural Information Specialists,* 39(1–2), 36–42.

Duff, A.S., Craig, D. & McNeill, D.A. (1996). A note on the origins of the "information society." *Journal of Information Science,* 22(2), 117–122.

Gardner, B.R. (1994). Ensuring successful IT utilisation in developing countries. *South African Computer Journal,* 11, 63–67.

Garfield, E. (1995). The internationalization of the information industry. *Information Services & Use,* 15(1), 49–52.

Grover, V., Segar, H. & Durand, D. (1994). Organizational practice, information resource deployment and systems success: A cross-cultural survey. *Journal of Strategic Information Systems,* 3(2), 85–106.

Heitzman, J (1992). Information systems and urbanization in South Asia. *Contemporary South Asia,* 1(3), 363–380.

Hoft, N.L. (1995). *International Technical Communication: How to Export Information about High Technology.* New York, NY: Wiley.

Hudson, H. (1994). Universal service in the Information Age. *Telecommunications Policy,* 188, 658–667.

International Federation For Information and Documentation (1996). *Copernicus & Cyberspace: The Electronic Superhighway: A New View of the World.* The Hague, Netherlands: FID. (FID News Bulletin, vol 46, no. 1/2).

Kahen, G. (1995). Assessment of information technology for developing countries: Appropriateness, local constraints, IT characteristics and impacts. *International Journal of Computer Applications in Technology,* 8(5/6), 325–332.

Lu, H-P & Gustafson, D.H. (1994). An empirical study of perceived usefulness and perceived ease of use on computerized support system user over time. *International Journal of Information Management,* 14(5), 317–329.

Martin, M.S. (1995). Problems in information transfer in the age of the computer. *Information Technology and Libraries,* 14(4), 243–246.

McConnell, P. ed. (1995). *Making a Difference: Measuring the Impact of Information on Development, Proceedings of a Workshop, Ottawa, Canada, 1995.* Ottawa, Canada: International Development Research Centre.

Menou, M. ed. (1993). *Measuring the impact of information on development.* Ottowa, Canada: International Development Research Centre.

Osigwe, C.C. (1993). Sustainable information management and services: An overview. *Quarterly Bulletin of the International Association of Agricultural Information Specialists,* 38(4), 205–210.

Stokes, R. (1994). New information technology: acquiring, processing and accessing resources in Asian languages. *Australian Library Review,* 11(3), 337–343.

Stone, M. B. (1993). Assessment indicators and the impact of information on development. *Canadian Journal of Information & Library Science,* 18, 50–64.

Stuart, T.H. (1994). Participation for empowerment and sustainability: How development support communication makes a difference. *Media Asia,* 21(4), 213–220.

Talero, E. & Gaudette, P. (1996). *Harnessing Information for Development: A Proposal for a World Bank Group Strategy.* Washington, DC: The World Bank. (WB discussion paper 313).

Tung, L-L & Turban, E. (1996). Information technology as an enabler of telecommuting. *International Journal of Information Management,* 16(2), 103–117.

Wright, D. (1995). Reaching out to remote and rural areas: Mobile satellite services and the role of Immarsat. *Telecommunications Policy,* 19(2), 105–116.

Country Studies

Al-Shammari, M. & Al-Shaikh, F.N. (1993). Computer utilization in Jordanian industrial companies. *International Journal of Information Management,* 13(6), 413–423.

Chisenga, J. (1993). Meeting information needs of researchers in Zambia. *Third World Libraries,* 4, 65–66.

Correia, A.M.R. (1993). Scientific and technical information towards technical and industrial development: The case of Portugal. *Journal of Information Science,* 19(1), 25–35.

Dedrick, J. & Kraemer, K.L. (1993). Information technology in India — the quest for self-reliance. *Asian Survey,* 33(5), 463–492.

Ehikhamenor, F.A. (1993). Information technology and scientific and technical information in Nigeria: Revolution or evolution. *African Journal of Library, Archives & Information Science, 3*, 113–123.

Fransman, M. (1996). The future of Japanese telecommunications. *Telecommunications Policy, 20*(2), 83–88.

Hashim, Y. (1994). "From educational technology to information technology: Malaysian experience". In Proceedings of the Third International Conference on Systems Integration, Sao Paolo, Brazil, 1994. Los Alamitos, CA: *IEEE Computer Society Press*, vol. 1, 134–140.

Hassan, S.Z. (1994). Environmental constraints in utilizing information technologies in Pakistan. *Journal of Global Information Management, 2*(4), 30–39.

Hayashi, E. (1994). Regional network in Japan. *Joho-shori, 35*(8), 699–707.

Iwe, J.I. (1994). Responding to information needs of Nigeria's university communities in the 1990s. *African Journal of Library, Archives & Information Science, 4*, 63–67.

Kanamugire, A. B. (1994). Developing a CD-ROM service in Saudi Arabia: Some lessons for developing countries. *Journal of Information Science, 20*(2), 9–107.

Kaniki, A.M. (1994). Community resource centres and resource centre forums in the transformation era in South Africa. *African Journal of Library, Archives & Information Science, 4*, 47–54.

Kim, M-J. (1996). A comparative analysis of the information sectors of South Korea, Singapore, and Taiwan. *Information Processing & Management, 32*(3), 357–371.

Majid, S. (1993). Strengthening agricultural libraries in Pakistan (Management of Agricultural Research and Technology Project). *International Information & Library Review, 25*, 233–245.

Nidumolu, S.R. & Goodman, S.E. (1993). Computing in India: An Asian elephant learning to dance. *Communications of the ACM, 36*(4), 15–22.

Odi, A. (1994). Library and information dissemination in a traditional society: The Ogbo of Eastern Nigeria. *International Information & Library Review, 26*, 1–9.

Odini, C. (1993). An overview of information systems in Kenya. *Library Review, 42*(5), 44–49.

Pavri, F. & Ang, J. (1995). A study of the strategic planning practices in Singapore. *Information & Management, 28*(1), 33–47.

Phiri, P.N.C. (1993). Why CD-ROM is better than online database systems for developing countries: A critical review of these technologies with reference to libraries in Zambia. *Libri, 43*, 343–353.

Stoss, F.W. (1995). Managing global change information. *Oak Ridge National Laboratory Review,* 28(2/3), 30–37.

Tiamiyu, M.A. (1993). The realities of developing modern information resources management systems in government organization in developing countries with particular reference to Nigeria. *Journal of Information Science,* 19(3), 189–197.

Wanasundra, L. (1994). Information Network on Rural Development (INRD), Bangladesh. *Third World Review,* 5(1), 11–16.

Wang, P. & Turban, E. (1994). Management information systems issues of the 1990s in the Republic of China: An industry analysis. *International Journal of Information Management,* 14(1), 25–38.

Westerveld, R. & Prasad, R. (1994). Rural communications in India using fixed cellular radio systems. *IEEE Communications Magazine,* 32(10), 70–77.

Wong, C. (1993). The important role of international exchange in the development of medical informatics in developing countries: A report from China. *Medical Informatics,* 18(1), 1–10.

Zorpette, G. (1994). Technology in India—overview. *IEEE Spectrum,* 31(3), 24–32.

Research, Innovation and Development

International Studies

Albala, A. & Rubenstein, A.H. (1994). Significant issues for the future of product innovation: The coming revolution in Latin America; the urgent need for explicit technology policies/strategies in the firm. *Journal of Product Innovation Management,* 11(2), 156–161.

Bamane, B.D. (1994). Impact of technical change. *Technovation,* 14(1), 3–5.

Bardhan, P. (1996). "Research on poverty and development twenty years after Redistribution with Growth." *Annual World Bank Conference on Development Economics, 1995.* Washington, DC: The World Bank, 59–82.

Behringer, J.W. (1994). Foreign patents: Timing is everything. *Management Review,* 83(4), 58–59.

Chatman, E.A. (1996). The impoverished life-world of outsiders. *Journal of the American Society for Information Science,* 47(3), 193–206.

Crowe, T.M. & Siegfried, W.R. (1993). Conserving Africa's biodiversity-stagnation versus innovation. *South African Journal of Science,* 89(5), 208–210.

Doryan, E.A. (1993). An institutional perspective of competitiveness and industrial restructuring policies in developing countries. *Journal of Economic Issues,* 27(2), 451–458.

The European Commission (1995). *Green Paper on Innovation.* Luxembourg, Luxembourg: The European Commission: Directorate Xlll/D.

Felipe, J. & Resende, M. (1996). A multivariate approach to the measurement of development: Asia and Latin America. *The Journal of Developing Areas,* 30(2), 183–210

Gryskiewicz, S.S. (1992). Discovering creativity. *Proceedings of the 6th International Creativity & Innovation Networking Conference, Greensboro, NC, 1992.* Greensboro, NC: Center for Creative Leadership.

Herbig, P.A. & Kramer, H. (1992). The phenomenon of innovation overload. *Technology in Society,* 14(4), 441–462.

Hobday, M. (1995). Innovation in East Asia: Diversity and development. *Technovation,* 15(2), 55–63.

James, J. & Bhalla, A. (1993). Flexible specialization, new technologies and future industrialization in developing countries. *Futures,* 25(6), 713–732.

Kendon, G. et al. (1995). Supporting customized reasoning in the agroforestry domain. *New Review of Applied Expert Systems,* 1, 179–192.

King, J.L. et al. (1994). Institutional factors in information technology innovation. *Information Systems Research,* 5(2), 139–169.

Lee, M. & Om, K (1994). A conceptual framework of technological innovation management. *Technovation,* 14(1), 7–16.

Makovetskaya, D. & Bernadsky, V (1994). Scientometric indicators for identification of technology system life cycle phase. *Scientometrics,* 30(1), 105–116.

Massimo, L., Caraca, J.M.G. & Silva, C.M. da. (1993). Research and development indicators and socio-economic cohesion. *Scientometrics,* 26(2), 293–309.

Miyamoto, K. (1995). A pilot system for evaluating integrated policy measures of metropolitan land use, transport, and the environment. *Regional Development Dialogue,* 16(1), 73–86.

Mytelka, L.K. (1993). Rethinking development: A role for innovation networking in the other two-thirds. *Futures,* 25(6), 694–712.

Narayan, D. (1996). *Toward Participatory Research.* Washington, DC: The World Bank.

Odedra, M. et al. (1993). Sub-Saharan Africa: A technical desert. *Communications of the ACM,* 36(2), 25–29.

Puris, A. (1993). Economic sanctions and research and development. *Scientometrics,* 25(3), 415–424.

Tolentino, P.E.E. (1993). *Technological innovation and Third World Multinationals.* London, UK: Routledge.

Wincesmith, D. (1993). New approaches to innovation. *Issues in Science and Technology,* 9(2), 11–12.

Country Studies

Baba, Y., Kikuchi, J. & Mori, S. (1995). Japan's R & D strategy reconsidered: Departure from the manageable risks. *Technovation,* 15(2), 65–78.

Bhaduri, S. (1994). Science and technology in India—an evaluation. *Current Science,* 66(1), 14–15.

Boon, S.N. (1994). IT—enabled business re-engineering: A study of Singapore's trade clearance process. *IFIP Transactions A [Computer Science and Technology],* A-54, 433–442.

Bowonder, B. & Miyake, T. (1993). *Technology forecasting in Japan. Futures,* 25(7), 757–777.

Bozeman, B. & Pandey, S. (1994). Cooperative R & D in government laboratories: Comparing the US and Japan. *Technovation,* 14(3), 145–159.

Cabral, R. (1993). The financing of biotechnology in developing countries: A Brazilian case in point. *Telecommunication Journal,* 15(3), 311–326.

Cutcliffe, S.H. (1993). Some impressions of science, technology and society studies in China. *Technology in Society,* 15(2), 243–252.

Igbaria, M. & Zviran, M. (1996). Comparison of end-user computing characteristics in the U.S., Israel and Taiwan. *Information & Management,* 30(1), 1–13.

Lee, J., Bae, Z.T. & Lee, J. (1994). Strategic management of a large-scale technology development: The case of the Korean telecommunications industry. *Journal of Engineering and Technology Management,* 11(2), 149–170.

Lee, J. & Lee, J. (1994). Competitive structure and strategic types in the Korean software industry. *Technovation,* 14(5), 295–309.

Menon, M.G.K. (1994). "Excellence and accountability in Indian science." In *P.N. Srivasta, ed. Science in India—Excellence vs Accountability.* New Delhi, India: Angkor Publishers, 232–240.

Murrell, K.L. (1993). Evaluation as action research: The case of the Management Development Institute in Gambia, West Africa. *International Journal of Public Administration,* 16(3), 341–356.

Okamoto, T. (1994). The current situations and future directions of intelligent CAI research/development. *IEICE Transactions on Information and Systems,* E77-D(1), 9–18.

Prahladachar, M. (1994). Innovations in the use and management of groundwater in hardrock regions in India. *Ecological Economics,* 9(3), 267–272.

Raut, L.K. (1995). R & D spillover and productivity growth: evidence from Indian private firms. *Journal of Development Economics,* 48(1), 1–23.

Sikka, P. (1991). Strategies for technology development in India. *Technovation*, 11(7), 445–451.

Swierczek, F.W. (1992). Strategies for business innovation: Evaluating the prospects of incubation in Thailand. *Technovation*, 12(8), 521–533.

Thomas, A.S. & Philip, A. (1994). India: Management in an ancient and modern civilization. *International Studies of Management and Organization*, 24(1/2), 91–115.

Technology Transfer

International Studies

Bromby, R. (1993). Digital switching markets in developing countries: Report. *Telecommunications [International Edition]*, 27(1), 16–18.

Cunningham, R.B. & Sarayrah, Y.K. (1994). The human factor in technology transfer. *International Journal of Public Administration*, 17(8), 1419–1436.

Debou, C., Fuchs, N. & Saria, H. (1993). Selling believable technology. *IEEE Software*, 10(6), 22–27.

Izawa, K. (1992). The role of plant exports in the North-South equation. *Japan 21st*, 37(7), 42–44.

Larson, B.A. & Anderson, M. (1994). Technology transfer, licensing contracts, and incentives for further innovation. *American Journal of Agricultural Economics*, 76(3), 547–556.

Lepkowski, W. (1994). Export outlook modest for green technologies. *Chemical and Engineering News*, 72(14), 23.

Lien, L. (1994). Transferring technologies from developed to developing industrial and commercial environments. *IFIP Transactions A [Computer Science and Technology]*, A-45, 87–98.

Martinsons, M.G. (1994). Benchmarking human resource information systems in Canada and Hong Kong. *Information & Management*, 26(6), 305–316.

Miyagiwa, K. (1993). Large is beautiful: The welfare effect of technology transfer reconsidered. *Journal of Development Economics*, 41(1), 179–190.

Mwinyimbegu, R.M. (1993). Obstacles to information technology transfer to the Third World. *Library Review*, 42(5), 28–37.

Oka, H. (1994). Energy and environment technologies and NEDO's (New Energy and Industrial Technology Development Organization) international cooperation. *Japan 21st.*, 39(2), 7.

Robinson, C.W. (1994). International Trade Administration promotes exports of technology products and services. *Business America*, 115(8), 16–19.

Wesley-Tanaskovic, I. (1994). The United Nations University and information development. *Information Development,* 10(1), 35–37.

Country Studies

Barrett, T.H. (1995). Ignorance and the technology of information: Some comments on China's knowledge of the West on the eve of the "Western Invasion." *Asian Affairs,* 26(pt. 1), 20–31.

Chang, P.L., Chintay, S. & Hsu, C.W. (1994). The formation process of Taiwan's integrated circuit industry: Method of technology transfer. *Technovation,* 14(3), 161–171.

Gozlu, S. (1994). Transfer of information technology to a developing environment: The Turkish case. *IFIP Transactions A [Computer Science and Technology],* A-53, 465–470.

Kudo, A. (1994). I.G. Farben in Japan: The transfer of technology and managerial skills. *Business History,* 36(1), 159–183.

Liu, C.Y. (1993). Government's role in developing high-tech industry: The case of Taiwan's semiconductor industry, *Technovation,* 13(5), 299–309.

Marcinkiewicz, H.R. (1995). Educational technology transcends the Saudi desert and cultural mores. *Tech Trends,* 40(2), 19–22.

Nakamura, M. (1994). *Technology Change and Female Labour in Japan.* Tokyo, Japan: United Nations University Press.

Sahu, S. K. (1994). Technology transfer as the Indian experience. *Asian Profile,* 22(3), 239–255.

Schmoch, U. & Schnoring, T. (1994). Technological strategies of telecommunications equipment manufacturers: A patent analysis. *Telecommunications Policy,* 18(5), 397–413.

Sikka, P. (1996). Indigenous development and acquisition of technology: An Indian perspective. *Technovation,* 16(2), 85–90.

Straub, D.W. (1994). The effect of culture on IT diffusion: E-mail and fax in Japan and the US. *Information Systems Research,* 5(1), 23–47.

Yahya, A.H. (1994). Towards a viable computer industry in developing nations: The West Bank case. *IFIP Transactions A [computer Science and Technology]* A-53, 65–70.

Yuan, J-D (1996). United States technology transfer policy toward China: Post-Cold War objectives and strategies. *International Journal,* 51(20), 314–338.

Human Resource Networking

International Studies

Bennet, V.M. & Palmer, E.M. (1994). Electronic document delivery using Internet. *Bulletin of the Medical Library Association,* 82(2), 163–167.

Bidet, J.C. (1993). The PANGIS network. *Bulletin of the American Society for Information Science,* 19(3), 26–27.

Bosco, M.F. (1994). Initiatives towards science and technology cooperation with developing countries in the field of information technologies. *IFIP Transactions A [Computer Science and Technology],* A-52, 349–354.

Brown, J.M. (1994). The global computer network: Indications of its use worldwide. *International Information and Library Review,* 26(1), 51.

Burleigh, M. & Weeg, P. (1993). KIDLINK: A challenging and safe place for children across the world. *Information Development,* 9(3), 147–157.

Bush, R. (1993). FidoNet: Technology, tools and history. *Communications of the ACM,* 36(8), 31–35.

Chadwick, T.B. (1993). Using the Internet (and other Computer Mediated Communications Systems) for practical business research and development. In *Proceedings of the Fourteenth National Online Meeting, New York, NY, 1993.* Medford, NJ: Learned Information, 67–76.

Chai, T.H. (1994). Collaborative learning—a new direction in educational computing. *Media Asia,* 21(3), 155–156.

Goodman, S.E. et al. (1994). The global diffusion of the Internet: Patterns and problems. *Communications of the ACM,* 37(8), 27–31.

Kaku, M. (1994). *Hyperspace: A Scientific Odyssey Through Parallel Universes, Time Warps, and the Tenth Dimension.* New York, NY: Oxford University Press.

Kaufman, S. (1995). *At Home in the Universe: The Search for Laws of Self-Organization and Complexity.* New York, NY: Oxford University Press.

Morris, M. & Ogan, C. (1996). The Internet as a mass medium. *Journal of Communication,* 46(1), 39–50.

Parks, M.R. & Floyd, K. (1996). Making friends in cyberspace. *Journal of Communication,* 46(1), 80–97.

Qureshi, S. (1994). COMNET-IT: The Commonwealth Network of Information Technology for Development. *Bulletin of the American Society for Information Science,* 20(3), 27–28.

Ruth, S.R. & Gouet, R. (1993). Must invisible colleges be invisible? An approach to examining large communities of network users. *Internet Research,* 3(1), 36–53.

Sadowsky, G. (1993). Network connectivity for developing countries. *Communications of the ACM,* 36(8), 42–47.

Schwartz, M.F. & Quarterman, J.S. (1993). The changing global Internet service infrastructure. *Internet Research,* 3(1), 8–25.

Vatikiotis, M. (1994). Networking strategy. *Far Eastern Economic Review,* 157(21), 76.

White, W.D. & Barad, B. (1993). FidoNet technology applications [simple, inexpensive electronic network for African countries]. *Bulletin of the American Society for Information Science,* 19(4), 20–21.

Country Studies

Al-Khulaifi, M. (1995). Gulfnet in Saudi Arabia: An overview. *Information Services & Use,* 15(1), 53–56.

Bagga, R.K. & Bagga, V. (1994). Human resource generation in information technology: Indian effort. *IFIP Transactions A [Computer Science and Technology],* A-53, 109–114.

Do Rosario, L. (1993). China: Network capitalism. *Far Eastern Economic Review,* 156(48), 17.

Douglass, M. & Zoghlin, M. (1994). Sustaining cities at the grassroots: Livelihood, environment and social networks in Suan Phlu, Bangkok. *Third World Planning Review,* 16(2), 171–200.

McChesney, R.W. (1996). The Internet and U.S. communication policy-making in historical and critical perspective. *Journal of Communication,* 46(1), 98–124.

Ramachandran, K. & Ramnarayan, S. (1993). Entrepreneurial orientation and networking: Some Indian evidence. *Journal of Business Venturing,* 8(6), 513–524.

Riedinger, E.A. (1993). The electronic library network frontier in Brazil [beginnings of an online national union catalog]. *College & Research Libraries News,* 54(5), 255–256.

Tseng, S.S. & Lo, K.K. (1993). Access to a Taiwan OPAC on the Internet: Accessing the Academia Sinica's Chinese/English library catalog. *[Academia Sinica], Committee on East Asian Libraries Bulletin,* 101, 51–55.

Van Brakel, P.A. (1993). Implications of networking CD-ROM databases in a research environment. *South African Journal of Library & Information Science,* 61(1), 28–34.

Zheng, C. (1994). Opening the digital door: Computer networking in China. *Telecommunications Policy,* 18(3), 236–242.

Information Policies

International Studies

Blau, A. (1993). Bringing the promise home: Policy options and strategies to promote medical information networking. *Journal of Medical Systems.* 17(6), 339–348.

Comer, E.A. ed. (1994). *The global political economy of communication.* New York, NY: St. Martin's Press.

Dedrick, J. & Kraemer, K.L. (1995). National technology policy and computer production in Asia-Pacific countries. *The Information Society,* 11(1), 29–58.

Desirable basic policy directions for realizing the advanced information infrastructure society. *JIPDEC Information Quarterly,* 98, 25–26.

Hunter, R.D. (1993). Standards: The keys to domestic and international competitiveness. *Document Image Automation,* 13(2), 4–8.

Lopez, X. R. (1995). "Impact of law and information policy on access and commercialization of spatial data." In *GIS/LIS '95 Annual Conference and Exposition, Nashville, TN. Bethesda, MD: American Society of Photometry and Remote Sensing.* vol. 2, 669–678.

Luger, M.I. (1994). Science and technology in regional economic development: The role of policy in Europe, Japan and the United States. *Technology in Society,* 16(1), 9–34.

Moore, N.C. (1993). Information policy and strategic development: A framework for the analysis of policy objectives. *ASLIB Proceedings,* 45(11–12), 281–285.

Morah, E.U. (1996). Obstacles to optimal policy implementation in developing countries. *Third World Planning Review,* 18(1), 79–106.

Roche, E.M. & Blaine, M. (1994). Public policy and information technology in the developing world: Difficult financial options. *IFIP Transactions A [Computer Science and Technology],* A-53, 483–488.

Rowlands, I. (1996). Understanding information policy: Concepts, frameworks and research tools. *Journal of Information Science,* 22(1), 13–25.

Supapol, A. B. & Swierczek, F.W. (1994). The role of intellectual property rights in stimulating commercialization in ASEAN: Lessons from Canada. *Technovation,* 14(3), 181–195.

Talero, E. (1994). A demand-driven approach to national informatics policy. *IFIP Transactions A [Computer Science and Technology],* A-53, 17–25.

Zulu, S.F.C. (1994). Africa's survival plan for meeting the challenges of information technology in the 1990s and beyond. *Libri,* 44, 77–94.

Country Studies

Arif, M. & Meadows, A.J. (1994). The provision of information to industry: A comparative study of Saudi Arabia and the UK. *Journal of Librarianship & Information Science,* 26, 29–33.

Athreya, M.B. (1996). India's telecommunications policy: A paradigm shift. *Telecommunications Policy,* 20(1), 11–22.

Bastos, M.I. (1994). How international sanctions worked: Domestic and foreign political constraints on the Brazilian Informatics Policy. *The Journal of Development Studies,* 30(2), 380–404.

Boon, J.A. et al. (1993). size of the information sector in South Africa. *South African Journal of Library and Information Science,* 61, 109–123.

Carosella, M.P. (1994). Documentation and information in Italy. *Information Development,* 10(3), 189–195.

Chaudhry, A.S. (1993). Information policies in Saudi Arabia and Malaysia. *Information Development,* 9(4), 228–234.

Dedrick, J. & Kraemer, K.L. (1993). Caught in the middle: Information technology policy in Australia. *Information Society,* 9(4), 333–364.

Dedrick, J. & Kraemer, K.L. (1995). National technology policy and computer production in Asia-Pacific countries. *Information Society,* 11(11), 29–58.

Goonasekera, A. (1993). Media technology and social imperatives: An examination of communication policies in selected Asian countries. *Media Asia,* 20(4), 194–201.

Hong, J. (1995). The evolution of China's satellite policy. *Telecommunications Policy,* 19(2), 117–133.

Karki, M.M.S., Krishnam, K.S. & Gary, K.C. (1993). Patenting activity in the Third World: A case study of biotechnology patents filed in India. *World Patent Information,* 15(3), 165–170.

Kraemer, K.L. & Dedrick, J. (1993). Turning loose the invisible hand: New Zealand's information technology policy. *Information Society,* 9(4), 365–390.

Kraemer, K.L., Dedrick, J. & Jarman, S. (1994). Supporting the free market: Information technology policy in Hong Kong. *Information Society,* 10(4), 223–246.

Le Coadic, Y.F. & Chambaud, S. (1993). Politics and policies in the scientific and technical information sector in France. *Journal of Information Science,* 19(6), 473–479.

Liu, Z. (1994). Considerations on the development of China's information industry. *ASLIB Proceedings,* 45, 49–54.

Mokhtarian, P.L. & Sato, K. (1994). A comparison of the policy, social and cultural contexts for telecommunicating in Japan and the United States. *Social Science Computer Review,* 12(4), 641–658.

Nissimbeni, M. (1994). Constructing national library and information policy options for South-Africa within the framework of educational transformation. *Journal of Librarianship and Information Science,* 26(3), 149–156.

Ogwang-Ameny, R. (1993). Information technology manpower and the national information system in Uganda. *Information Development,* 9, 235–239.

Orna, E. (1993). Full, cooperative and profitable use of China's information resources: Foundations for a policy. *ASLIB Proceedings,* 45(10), 257–259.

Petrazzini, B.A. (1996). Telecommunications policy in India: The political underpinnings of reform. *Telecommunications Policy,* 20(1), 39–51.

Qi, Yanli, (1994). Chinese patent law and patent information service. *International Information and Library Review,* 26, 11–18.

Sillince, J.A.A. (1994). Coherence of issues and coordination of instruments in European information policy. *Journal of Information Science,* 20(4), 219–236.

Sillince, J.A.A. (1994). Information policy in the European Community: Balancing protection and competition. *Journal of Government Information,* 21(3), 215–230.

Steidlmeier, P. (1993). The moral legitimacy of intellectual property claims: American business and developing country perspectives. *Journal of Business Ethics,* 12(2), 157–164.

Subbaram, N.R. (1994). Intellectual property protection in the Council of Scientific and Industrial Research (CSIR), India. *World Patent Information,* 16(2), 101–103.

Ure, J., ed. (1995). *Telecommunications in Asia: Policy, Planning and Development.* Hong Kong: Hong Kong University Press.

Education and Training in the Information Professions

International Studies

Cheney, P.H. (1994). Globalizing the information systems curriculum. *Journal of Global Information Management,* 2(3), 3–4.

Cronin, B., Stiffler, M. & Day, D. (1993). The emergent market for information professionals: Educational opportunities and implications. *Library Trends,* 42(2), 257–276.

Johansson, E. (1992). Program for the advancement of librarianship in the Third World. *Bulletin of the American Society for Information Science,* 19(1), 25–26.

Lancaster, F.W. (1994). The curriculum of information science in developed and developing countries. *Libri,* 44(3), 201–205.

McCook, K. & Gonsalves, T.O. (1993). The research university and education for librarianship: considerations for user-centered professionals in libraries. *Journal of Library Administration,* 19(3/4), 193–207.

Peterson, L. (1994). Teaching the practitioners: One professor's attempt at library education and sensitivity to multicultural diversity. *Reference Librarian,* 45–46, 23–38.

Pettinger, G. & Bawden, D. (1994). Information support for the training function. *Journal of Information Science,* 20(4), 288–294.

Rahman, S. (1993). Manpower preparation for developing and implementing information policies. *Library Review,* 42(6), 23–37.

Ramaiah, C.K. & Meadows, A.J. (1993). A study of hypertext teaching to undergraduate students in library and information studies. *Information Processing and Management,* 29(2), 257–262.

Weingand, D.E. (Ed.) (1994). The Second World Conference on Continuing Education for the Library and Information Science Professions. *Journal of Education for Library and Information Science,* 35(1), 56–58.

Yoon, G-S. (1994). The effects of instructional control, cognitive style, and prior knowledge on learning of computer-assisted instruction. *Journal of Educational Technology Systems,* 22(4), 357–370.

Country Studies

Aina, L.O. (1994). The characteristics of Anglophone Library and information science educators in Africa. *Journal of Education for Library and Information Science,* 35(2), 98–108.

Aina, L.O. (1993). Education and training for information technology in Africa. *INSPEL,* 27(4), 242–250.

Aiyepeku, W.O. (1991). The challenge of implementing an African programme in information science: TRARECON (Training/Retraining, Research and Consultancy). *Journal of Information Science Principles & Practice,* 17(5), 315–320.

Aman, M.M. (1993). Education for library and information science in the Soviet autonomous republics. *Journal of Information Science Principles & Practice,* 19(2), 155–160.

Aman, M.M. (1994). Education, training and employment of library and information professionals in South Africa. *Journal of Education for Library & Information Science,* 35(1), 61–63.

Antonio, I. & Balby, C.N. (1994). The state of computer training in Brazilian library schools. *Journal of Education for Library & Information Science,* 35(2), 109–123.

Bertrand-Gastaldy, S., Bernhard, P. & Cyr, J. (1993). Reconstructing a master's degree program in library and information studies: The Université de Montréal experience. *Journal of Education for Library & Information Science,* 34(3), 228–243.

Correia, A.M.R. & Wilson, T.D. (1992). The Msc. in Information Management of the University of Sheffield taught in Portugal: An example of knowledge transfer in education. *Journal of Information Science Principles & Practice,* 18(1), 77–82.

Gupta, J.N.D., Wang, P. & Ravichandran, R. (1994). An assessment of information systems education needs in Taiwan. *International Journal of Information Management,* 14(5), 369–384.

Ingwersen, P. (1994). The human approach to information science and management: The framework and prospects underlying the new Danish MSc. programme. *Journal of Information Science,* 20(3), 194–208.

Johnson, I.M. (1994). Education and training in the Arab states. *Journal of Education for Library & Information Science,* 35(1), 59–61.

Kirk, J. (1993). Computer-assisted learning and teaching in library and information studies in Australia. *Information Processing & Management,* 29(2). 249–256.

Kisiedu, C.O. (1993). A survey of past post-graduate diploma students of the Department of Library and Archival Studies of the University of Ghana: 1970/71–1980/81. *Journal of Information Science,* 19(6), 481–487.

Liu, K.J. (1994). On the teaching model of education for library and information science in China. *Journal of Education for Library & Information Science,* 35(3), 249–258.

Loh, L., Sankar, C.S. & Wee, Y.Y. (1995). Job orientation, perceptions and satisfaction: A study of information technology professionals in Singapore. *Information & Management,* 29(5), 239–250.

Mokhtari, M. (1994). Library and information science education in Morocco: Curriculum development and adaptation to change. *Journal of Education for Library & Information Science,* 35(2), 159–166.

Morris, A. (1993). The teaching of IT in departments of information and library studies in the United Kingdom. *Journal of Information Science,* 19(3), 211–224.

Patrinos, D. (1993). Documentation practices: The national scene in Greece. *Journal of Information Science Principles & Practice,* 19(1), 41–49.

Payne, W. & Yoshizawa, K. (1995). Kansai University's Faculty of Informatics. *Technological Horizons in Education Journal,* 22(6), 58–61.

Scibberas, L. (1994). Library and information studies in Malta. *Information Development,* 10(3), 196–199.

Van der Starre, J.H.E. (1993). Library schools and information technology: A European overview. *Information Processing & Management,* 29(2), 241–247.

Wang, P. & Khan, M.B. (1994). MIS skills of IS graduates in the Republic of China. *Journal of Global Information Management,* 2(3), 3–4.

Zaman, H.B. (1993). Information technology and education (in Malaysia). *Information Development,* 9, 142–146.

Name Index

Aboyade, O.: 1976, 13, 21
Adamolekun, L.: 1990, 125, 131, 249
Adelman, I., et al.: (1979), 32–33, 37
Agha, S.S.: and S. Akhtar (1992), 338, 340
Agnew, J.A.: ed. (1980), 298, 306
Ahmed, A.G.M.: 1974, 105, 118
Aiken, M.: Bachruch and Aiken (1977), 193, 217
Aiyepeku, W.O.: 1982, 189, 217
Ajuogu, M.O.: 1981, 44, 68, 196–97, 217, 286, 289
Akhtar, S.: Agha and Akhtar (1992), 338, 340
Aldrich, H.: and D. Herker (1977), 193, 217
Alexander, A.: Swinth and Alexander (1990), 245, 251
Alkhafaji, A.: 1986, 213, 217
Allen, T.J.: J.S. Piepmeier, and S. Cooney (1971), 144–45, 155, 189–90, 217; and S. Cooney (1973), 190, 196, 217
Altbach, P.G.: 1987, 122, 131, 197, 217, 313, 322, 330, 340
Alter, S.L.: 1976, 189, 217
American Library Association: 1989, 317, 322
American Society for Information Science: *Proceedings . . .* (1975), 219; *Proceedings . . .* (1980), 184; *Proceedings . . .* (1984), 184
Amoh, K.O.: 1987, 317, 322–23
Anand, R.P.: and P.V. Quisumbing (1981), 64, 68
Andreasen, A.R.: Kotler and Andreasen (1987), 314, 324
Annis, S.: and P. Hakim, eds. (1988), 262, 265
Ansari, J.A.: Singer and Ansari (1988), 202, 223, 241, 251
Aráoz, A.: ed. (1981), 171, 173

Arief, S.: 1982, 27, 37
Arnst, R.: Servaes and Arnst (1992), 327, 341
Arora, J.: S.P. Kaur, H. Chandra, and R.K. Bhatt (1992), 74
Arora, J., et al.: (1992), 74
Ascroft, J.: 1978, 161, 173
Athanassiades, J.C.: 1973, 191, 217
Atherton (Cochrane), P.: ed. (1972), 220
Ayres, R.: and E. Zuscovitch (1990), 338, 340
Ayub, M.A.: and S.O. Hegstad (1987), 209, 217

Baark, E.: 1985, 297, 302, 306
Bachruch, S.: and M. Aiken (1977), 193, 217
Baker, D.B.: 1970, 144, 150
Baker, H.K.: 1981, 189, 217
Baker, N.R.: and J.R. Freeland (1972), 190, 218
Bamberger, M.: 1988, 126, 131, 203, 218
Bande, A.B.: 1985, 201, 218
Bandhu, D.: and R.K. Garg, eds. (1986), 64, 68
Baney, L.: McDowell and Baney (1983), 216, 221
Bannon, L.: U. Barry, and O. Hoist, eds. (1982), 44, 68
Baranson, J.: 1981, 162, 173; 1984, 19, 21
Bardini, T.: 1992, 72–73, 78, 81, 84, 359, 367
Barry, S.G.: 1976, 196, 218
Barry, U.: Bannon, Barry, and Hoist, eds. (1982), 44, 68
Bartee, E.M.: 1973, 99, 102, 177, 184, 283, 289
Bartlett, C.A.: and S. Ghoshal (1986), 355, 367; and S. Ghoshal

Subject Index

About the Author

MARTA DOSA is Professor Emerita in the School of Information Studies at Syracuse University. Her teaching and research span four areas: information policies; technology transfer to developing countries; environmental information; and gerontology/health care information. The common element in these fields is the interdisciplinary approach. She is adjunct professor at the State University of New York, College of Environmental Science and Forestry, where she advises doctoral students. In 1992–93 she was a visiting scholar with AT&T Bell Laboratories conducting a study on "Transnational Corporations and Developing Countries," and a consultant to the International Clearinghouse on Gerontology.

Dr. Dosa was principal investigator of a six-year research project on networks of health professionals under National Library of Medicine sponsorship and of a five-year research project on information in support of gerontological service delivery funded by the Administration on Aging. She conducted studies for the World Bank, the U.S. Agency for International Development, the Environmental Protection Agency, and the Center for Environmental Information, Inc. She consulted for products of the Institute for Scientific Information, Inc. In cooperation with the Syracuse University School of Education's Kellogg Project, she investigated the potential of information counseling in developing countries. In 1989 she was co-investigator of a UNESCO pilot study of "Innovation and Human Resource Networking."

International work by Dr. Dosa concentrated on emerging information science curricula and policies in Australia, Brazil, Ghana, Hungary, India, Kenya, Malaysia, Mexico, and Nigeria, where she has served as consultant to governments and universities. In 1986, she assisted in the development of national information policies in the People's Republic of China. In 1989, she presented a seminar on "The New Information Gatekeeper" in Tokyo, Japan. Her papers on the role of information in development appeared in numerous journals and book chapters. She was chair of the Education and Training Committee of the International Federation for Information and Documentation 1983–1988. She has been responsible for developing and testing a prototype International Clearinghouse and for organizing network-based seminars in Hong Kong (1982), Vienna (1983), The Hague (1984), Montreal (1986), Helsinki (1988), and Madrid (1992). Her lectures and consultation abroad have been sponsored by the International Development Research Centre, UNESCO, the U.N. International Atomic Energy Agency, and the U.S. State Department's International Scholars program.

In 1986, Dr. Dosa was recipient of the Outstanding Information Science Teacher Award of the American Society for Information Science. In 1990 she was honored with the Distinguished Alumni Award of the University of Michigan where she had received her Ph.D. Earlier, she received fellowships from the Carnegie Endowment and the U.S. Office of Education. Her book, *Libraries in the Political Scene* (Greenwood Press), analyzed the role of libraries in Germany under National Socialism. She is an honorary fellow of the International Federation for Information and Documentation.